Personal Information Management

Personal Information Management

Edited by

William Jones and Jaime Teevan

University of Washington Press
Seattle and London

We dedicate this book to our mothers,
Lorna L. Buckingham-Jones and Connie M. Teevan

© 2007 by the University of Washington Press
Printed in the United States of America
Designed by Ted Cotrotsos
12 11 10 09 08 07   5 4 3 2 1

University of Washington Press
P.O. Box 50096, Seattle, WA 98145 U.S.A.
www.washington.edu/uwpress

Library of Congress Cataloging-in-Publication Data
Personal Information Management / edited by William Jones and Jaime Teevan.
p. cm.
Includes bibliographical references and index.
ISBN-13: 978-0-295-98755-2 (hc : alk. paper)
ISBN-13: 978-0-295-98737-8 (pbk. : alk. paper)
ISBN-10: 0-295-98755-3 (hc : alk. paper)
ISBN-10: 0-295-98737-5 (pbk. : alk. paper)
1. Personal Information Management. I. Jones, William P., 1952 – II. Teevan, Jaime.
HD30.2.P472   2007
650.1—dc22   2007010636

This book is printed on New Leaf Ecobook 50, which is 100 percent recycled, containing 50 percent post-consumer waste, and is processed chlorine free. Ecobook 50 is acid free and meets the minimum requirements of ANSI/NISO Z39~V48~W1992 (R1997) (Permanence of Paper).

Contents

Part III. PIM and the Individual

Part IV. PIM and Other People

Personal Information Management

1 Introduction

William Jones and Jaime Teevan

In his autobiography (1790), Benjamin Franklin describes thirteen virtues. The third, Order, was the one that gave him the most trouble: "*Order* . . . with regard to places for things, papers, etc., I found extreamly [*sic*] difficult to acquire." Over two hundred years later, order continues to be an elusive goal—especially as this relates to the information that impacts us in our daily lives.

Personal information management or PIM is both the practice and the study of the activities people perform to acquire, organize, maintain, retrieve, use, and control the distribution of information items such as documents (paper-based and digital), Web pages, and email messages for everyday use to complete tasks (work-related and not) and to fulfill a person's various roles (as parent, employee, friend, member of community, etc.).

Concerns about PIM have probably been with the human race since our ancestors first began to make drawings on the walls of caves. However, the modern dialog on PIM is generally thought to have begun in 1945 with Vannevar Bush's description of a "memex" as a "device in which an individual stores all his books, records, and communications, and which is mechanized so that it may be consulted with exceeding speed and flexibility" (Bush 1945).

The phrase "Personal Information Management" was first used in the 1980s (Lansdale 1988a, b) in the midst of general excitement over the potential of the personal computer to greatly enhance the human ability to process and manage information. The 1980s also saw the advent of so-called PIM tools, with basic support for the management of appointments, to-do lists, and contact information.

Interest in PIM has increased in recent years; it is now not only a hot topic but also a serious area of inquiry focusing the best work from a diverse set of disciplines including cognitive psychology, human-computer interaction, database management, information retrieval, and library and information science.

Renewed interest in PIM is double-edged. On one side, the pace of improvements in various PIM-relevant technologies gives us reason to believe that some visions of PIM may soon be realized. Digital storage is cheap and plentiful. Better search support can make it easy to pinpoint the information we need. The ubiquity of computing and the miniaturization of computing devices make it possible for us to take much of our information with us wherever we go.

But renewed interest in PIM also comes from an awareness of the problems that new technologies can create. The information that Benjamin Franklin struggled to order in paper form is now scattered in multiple versions between paper and digital copies and isolated in separate applications and devices. Even a seemingly simple action like responding to an email request can cascade into a time-consuming, error-prone chore that requires bringing together information from various collections of paper and electronic documents, emails, Web pages, and other sources.

The purpose of this book is to provide readers with a deeper understanding of what PIM is and what it includes as a field of inquiry. Here we set the stage for this discussion, beginning with a consideration of PIM-related concepts. We then explore a conceptual framework that helps to connect many of the key concepts of PIM that are used throughout the book. We provide a comparison of PIM to other fields of inquiry such as cognitive science and human-computer interaction, and conclude with a preview of the chapters to come.

1.1 A Scenario and a Cast of Characters

Throughout this book, the chapters track the personal information management behaviors of the Monroe family members and family friends as they plan a 75th surprise birthday party for the family matriarch, Edna. As you read, you will get to know family members better and you will come to understand their different approaches to PIM. You may identify with some behaviors even as you are surprised and dismayed by other behaviors.

Here is the cast of characters:

Alex Monroe, male, 27, 6' 3" tall, of large build, and used to be in shape, but doesn't work out very much anymore. He's getting a little paunchy. Alex works as a securities analyst at a large firm. Alex is very well organized, especially with respect to work-related information. He has to be. In his position, losing information could be catastrophic. Whenever Alex receives a new information item—be it a new email message or a proffered business card—he tries to take some immediate action even if this is to sort the information item in to a "check this out later" pile. Alex's clothing is also very well organized, with separate walk-in closets for summer and winter clothing and categories within each closet ranging from "black-tie formal" to "nice, informal" to "day off." Alex immediately sorts and puts away his clean laundry. Matching socks are carefully paired. Alex considers this time well spent; he hates it when he can't find things immediately, whether it's an item of information or a pair of matching socks.

Brooke Monroe, female, 23, 5'8" tall and of slender build (like her mother, Connie). Brooke is Alex's sister. She works as a software developer at a hot start-up. In her choice of job, friends, and fun-time activities, Brooke embraces a lifestyle that is spontaneous, dynamic, and somewhat chaotic. Brooke lets incoming information, in all its various forms, pile up. Her cubicle at work is overflowing with piles of paper. Her email inbox has over 2000 messages. She also communicates frequently via instant messaging. Her virtual desktop is jammed with hundreds of icons representing files, applications, and Web references. Brooke maintains that her job is too unpredictable and fast changing for there to be much point to filing information. Similarly, Brooke's clothing is scattered in various piles around her apartment. She doesn't even bother to pair matching socks. Brooke often follows a "grab and go" approach to dressing— even when she is going to work.

Connie Monroe, female, 58, 5'6" tall and of slender build. Connie is mother to Alex and Brooke. Connie has always prided herself on being organized with respect to both her information (mostly still paper-based) and other things in her life including her clothing. But about a year ago, as she was showing a long-lost high school friend around her house, Connie experienced a moment of crisis. Her conception of herself did not match a reality—there was clutter in several piles throughout the house. Connie (and her visitor) saw piles of paper documents in her home office and even on the dining-room table. There were also piles of clothing in her bedroom. Connie's information management challenge is complicated by the extra information (still mostly paper-based) and increased stress, lost time, and low energy associated with her recent battle with breast cancer. Now clearly on the road to recovery, Connie has returned to her work as a middle manager in a large nonprofit organization.

Derek Williams, male, 23, 5'10" tall, of average build and clean cut. He lives with and is engaged to Brooke. Derek relies heavily on his tablet PC, which he takes with him nearly everywhere—to take notes in class, to do homework in the library (where he goes for the quiet, not the books), and even when he and Brooke go out for dinner. He would like to "banish paper" from his life but finds that paper still keeps coming his way even so.

Edna Salazar, female, 74, 5'2" tall, of somewhat stocky build. Edna is retired and owns a considerable amount of real estate as part of her nest egg. (She used to work as an independent real-estate broker). Her information world is almost totally paper-based (and was even when she was a real-estate agent). Edna has a desktop computer that no longer works properly and she has not bothered to repair it. Edna does not use email, preferring, instead, to call people on the phone or write letters. Edna dated Connie's now deceased father for over ten years prior to his death three years ago. Connie maintains a very close relationship with Edna and has lunch with her several times a week and checks in on her regularly. Because of her closeness with Alex and Brooke's grandfather, Edna views Alex and Brooke as extended grandchildren although she never had children herself.

Felicia Williams, female, 20, 5'5" tall. Felicia is Derek's younger sister. She is still living with their parents while she attends the local state college. Felicia is interested in music and art, especially photography. She has been taking pictures since she was a little girl, first with the little automatic film camera her dad gave her when she was seven, and now with her first digital camera, a gift from Derek two birthdays ago. Felicia uses a laptop to keep up with her friends through instant messaging (IM) and email, for her schoolwork, and also to edit and organize her digital photographs. Many of her photographs are not on her laptop though—she has lots of old developed photos, and lots of photo CDs from a mail-order photo developer as well. Since Felicia is not actively involved in the planning of Edna's birthday party (described below) she is only occasionally mentioned in the remainder of this book.

The project that brings everyone together

Alex, Brooke, Connie, and Derek are planning a surprise birthday party for Edna (who is turning 75). One of Edna's favorite restaurants is an Argentinean restaurant attached to a big hotel, so they are making arrangements to reserve the party room at the restaurant for the evening. They're expecting to invite around 40 people, many of whom will be coming from out of town for the weekend of the party, so they'll reserve rooms at the same hotel for them. After dinner, they will give Edna a special "this is your life" presentation that includes photographs, humorous "roast" style talks by her friends, and assembled memorabilia from her past (perhaps giving Edna a scrapbook—they are not sure yet).

In the remaining chapters of this book, as Alex, Brooke, Connie, Derek, Edna, and Felicia practice PIM, each in their own life, each in their own way, they will illustrate a range of PIM challenges as well as approaches to meeting these challenges. Even in these brief descriptions, we see distinctly different approaches to the PIM activities of keeping, finding, and organizing personal information.

■ **Keeping.** Alex spends time up front to put items in their proper place—both items of clothing and items of information. Brooke considers this effort to be a waste of time.

■ **Finding.** Alex hates not knowing where things are. The costs of not having an item when it is needed—whether a document or a tie—are very high in Alex's world. In Brooke's world, the costs of losing items are low. And Brooke doesn't mind searching. She delights in the serendipitous discoveries she frequently makes along the way to a sought-for item.

■ **Organizing.** Connie meant to be organized but, over time, her organizational scheme stopped working for her. For a long period of time Connie didn't notice, and piles (of clothing or paper documents) receded into a background of things to do "someday." Connie was moved to "get organized"—including the update of her schemes of organization—only as prompted by the arrival of an old friend.

This introduction to PIM presents a framework that interrelates keeping, finding, organizing, and other kinds of PIM activity. But first we introduce some basic terms that will help to describe the framework.

1.2 The Information Item and Its Form

Discussions of PIM often center on the management of information items:

An **information item** is a packaging of information in a persistent form that can be acquired, created, viewed, stored, grouped (with other items), moved, given a name and other properties, copied, distributed, moved, deleted, and otherwise manipulated. Examples of information items include: (1) paper documents, (2) electronic documents and other files, (3) email messages, (4) Web pages, or (5) references (e.g.,"shortcuts" or "aliases") to any of the above.

An information item has an associated information form:

The **information form** or **information type** of an information item is determined by the constellation of tools and applications that make it possible to manipulate (acquire, create, view, store, etc.) the item. Common forms of information include paper documents, e-documents and other files, email messages, and Web bookmarks.

Paper documents as an information form, for example, have supporting tools that include paper clips, staplers, filing cabinets, and the flat surfaces of a desk or table. In interactions with digital information items, we depend upon the support of various computer-based tools and applications such as email applications, file managers, Web browsers, and so on. The "size" of current information items is partly determined by these applications. There are certainly situations in which we might like an information item to come in smaller or larger units. A writer, for example, might like to treat paragraphs or even individual sentences as information items to be re-accessed and combined in new ways (e.g., Johnson 2005).

Consider how much of our interaction with the world around us is now mediated by information items. We consult the newspaper or, increasingly, a Web page to read the day's headlines and to find out what the weather will be like (perhaps before we even bother to look outside). We learn of meetings via email messages. We receive the documents we are supposed to read for this meeting via email as well.

On the sending side, we fill out Web-based forms. We send email messages. We create and send out reports in paper and digital form. We create personal and professional Web sites. These and other information items serve, in a real sense, as a proxy for us. We project ourselves and our desires across time and space in ways that would never have occurred to our ancestors.

The information item establishes a manageable level of abstraction for the consideration of PIM. Certainly, a person's interactions with an information item vary greatly depending upon its form. Interactions with incoming email messages, for example, are often driven by the expectation of a timely response and perhaps also by the awareness that, when an email message scrolls out of view without some processing, it is apt to be quickly forgotten. A person may make a paper printout of the same email message, to be folded, carried in a briefcase, marked up, and ultimately discarded when its information has been consumed.

But there are many essential similarities in the way people interact with information items, regardless of their form. Whether people are looking at a new email message in their inbox, a newly discovered Web site, or the business card they have just been handed at a conference, many of the same basic decisions must be made: "Is this relevant (to me)? To what does it relate? Do I need to act now or can I wait? If I wait, can I get back to this item later? Where should I put it? Will I remember to look?"

At the same time, an information item does not blur to include all things informational. A hallway conversation between two people, for example, conveys information but is not itself a packaging of information. A conversation is not an information item. A cassette recording of this same conversation is an information item. The recording can be stored away, sent, copied, and so on. A person's memory of an impending doctor's appointment is not an information item. The scrap of paper of paper containing a written reminder of this appointment is an information item.

Another point concerning information items—in contrast, for example, to what we hear or see in our physical world—is that we can often defer processing until later. We can, and do, accumulate large numbers of information items for a "rainy day." This is quite unlike, for example, the scenarios of situation awareness such as those faced by the driver of an automobile or the pilot of an airplane. In these situations, acceptable delays in processing information are short (Durso & Gronlund 1999) and there is no option to "look at this later when I have time."

1.3 What Is Personal Information?

Personal information can be used in any of several senses, including:

- The *information a person keeps,* directly or indirectly (e.g., via software applications), for personal use. This information is, at least nominally, under the person's control. Nevertheless, the rights of ownership for portions of this information are frequently in dispute. In the context of a person's work inside a company or in collaboration with others, for example, it is often unclear who owns what information.
- *Information about a person but kept by and under the control of others.* Personal information in this category includes the information about a person kept by doctors and health organizations, for example, or the information kept by tax agencies and credit bureaus.
- *Information experienced by a person but not necessarily in the person's control.* The book a person browses (but puts back) in a traditional library or the pages a person views on the Web are examples of this kind of personal (or personally experienced) information. This category can be further enlarged to include other personally relevant information "out there" that the person might like to encounter.
- *Information directed to a person.* Included in this category is the email that arrives in the inbox and also the pop-up notifications that this new email has arrived. Alerts raised by a person's computer, the "push" of advertisements on a visited Web page or the television or the radio, the ringing telephone are all examples of information directed toward a person. The information itself may or may not be personally relevant. But the intended impacts of directed information certainly are personal.

For better or worse, information directed to a person can distract the person from a current task, consume a person's attention, and convince the person to spend time, spend money, change an opinion, or take an action.

All senses of personal information are relevant to discussions of PIM. Much of this book's discussion relates to the first sense of personal information—information a person keeps for later use and repeated reuse. The book also considers the second sense of personal information—information about the person kept by others—especially in chapter 15's discussion of privacy, distribution, and the flow of information. Information a person has experienced or might like to experience is also considered, especially in chapter 9's coverage of efforts to provide personalized views of the Web.

Chapters throughout the book address issues pertaining to another sense of personal information—information directed to a person from elsewhere. In managing this kind of information the challenge is less to protect the information itself than to protect ourselves and our precious time and attention from its incursions. As human beings, we are wired to attend to the ring of a phone, the appearance of a new email alert, or the drop-by visit of a colleague at work. We can't easily change our nature. What we can do is to adjust the flows of information in our environment in order to create spaces and times in which we are relatively protected from these informational intrusions. We can close our door at work. We can turn off email or at least the alert for arrival of new email. We can turn off the phone during the dinner hour.

It should be acknowledged that distinctions between the different senses of personal information can quickly blur. For example, a session of Web browsing can be recorded by a history facility in the person's Web browser so that this record becomes a part of the information kept by (for) the person. The person may also, knowingly or unknowingly, provide identifying information to a visited Web site, which can then go into a record about the person (his or her Web site visits) that is maintained by others (e.g., the Webmaster of the Web site). Or consider the newspaper delivered to a person's doorstep. The delivered newspaper is owned by and under the person's control. But others walking by on the street can see the newspaper. If newspapers pile up while the person is on vacation, others can see this too.

1.4 A Personal Space of Information?

Personal information, in each of its senses, combines to form a *single personal space of information* (PSI) for each individual.[1] A person has only one PSI. At its center, a person's PSI includes all the information items that are, at least nominally, under that person's control. The PSI contains a person's books and paper documents, email messages (on various accounts), and e-documents and other files (on various computers). The PSI contains Web bookmarks that reference Web pages. The PSI also includes applications, tools (such as a desktop search facility) and constructs (e.g., associated properties, folders, piles in various forms) that a person has acquired or created to help in the management of this information.

At its periphery, the PSI includes information that the person might like to know about and control but that is under the control of others. Included is information about the person that others keep. Also included is information in public spaces, such as a local library or the Web, that is or might be relevant to the person.

The PSI might be visualized as a vast sea of personal information. If the "home waters" represent information under the person's control, then, at the periphery of a PSI, are waters of information that are shared, disputed, or under exploration. The periphery includes information about the person, the use of which the person might like to control (or at least monitor) but which is currently under the control of others (credit agencies, tax authorities, insurance companies, etc.). At the periphery of a person's PSI are also oceans of available information (on the Web, corporate intranets, public libraries, etc.) only the tiniest fractions of which the person explores in order to complete various tasks and projects and in order to fulfill various roles in the person's life.

Even in the home waters of the PSI, a person's sense of control over information is partly illusory. For example, an email message can be deleted and no longer appear. However, the message is very likely still in existence (as some figures in the public eye have learned to their chagrin). We're adrift in a sea of information. Our own personal spaces of information are large and mostly unexplored, with uncertain boundaries and an extensive overlap (with the PSIs of other people, organizations, etc.).

1.5 Personal Information Collections

Several researchers have discussed the importance of collections in managing personal information. Boardman (2004, p. 15) defines a collection of personal information to be "a self-contained set of items. Typically the members of a collection share a particular technological format and are accessed through a particular application."

It useful to consider personal information collections (PICs) not as defined by technical format or application, but rather as defined by activities of people in relation to their PSIs. PICs are personally managed subsets of a PSI. PICs are "islands" in a PSI where people have made some conscious effort to control both the information that goes in and also, usually but not necessarily, how this information is organized. PICs can vary greatly with respect to the number, form, and content coherence of their items. Examples of a PIC include:

- The papers in a well-ordered office and their organization, including the layout of piles on a desktop and the folders inside filing cabinets.
- The papers in a specific filing cabinet and their organizing folder (when perhaps the office as a whole is a mess).
- Project-related information items that are initially dumped into a folder on our notebook computer and then organized over time.
- A carefully maintained collection of bookmarks to useful reference sites on the Web.
- An Endnote database of article references.[2]

In a sea of personal information, PICs are islands of relative structure and coherence. A PIC includes not only a set of information items but also their organizing representations, including spatial layout, properties, and containing folders. A PIC may, or may not, be strongly associated with a specific application (such as an application to manage digital photographs or digital music). The items in a PIC will often be of the same form—all email messages, for example, or all files. But this is not a necessary feature of a PIC. People might like to place several forms of information in a PIC even if doing so is often difficult or impossible with current software applications. Information relating to a personal project, for example, may be in the form of Web pages and references, electronic documents, paper documents, and email messages. Later, this book reviews research efforts aimed at supporting an integrative organization of information, regardless of form. Put another way, these efforts aim at building a form-neutral layer of support for the management of information items.

Just as the information item is self-contained as a unit for the storage and transmission of information, the PIC is self-contained with respect to the maintenance and organization of personal information. People typically refer to a PIC when they complete a sentence such as "I've got to get my ____ organized!" The organization of "everything" in a PSI is a daunting, perhaps impossible, task. But people can imagine organizing a collection of Web bookmarks, their email inbox, their laptop filing system (but probably only selected areas), and so on. Likewise, in the study of PIM, PICs are a tractable unit of analysis whereas consideration of a person's entire PSI is not. Why do people go to the trouble of creating and organizing PICs and how are these then used? The answers have implications for the larger study of PIM.

1.6 Definitions of Personal Information Management

PIM is easy to describe and discuss. We all do it. We all have firsthand experiences with the challenges of PIM. But PIM is much harder to define. PIM is especially hard to define in ways that preserve focus on the essential challenges of PIM.

Lansdale (1988a, p. 55) refers to PIM as "the methods and procedures by which we handle, categorize and retrieve information on a day-to-day basis." Bellotti et al. (2002, p. 182) describes PIM as "the ordering of information through categorization, placement, or embellishment in a manner that makes it easier to retrieve when it is needed." Barreau (1995, p. 327) describes PIM as a "system developed by or created for an individual for personal use in a work environment." Such a system includes "a person's methods and rules for acquiring the information, . . . the mechanisms for organizing and storing the information, the rules and procedures for maintaining the system, the mechanisms for retrieval and procedures for producing various outputs."

Boardman (2004, p. 13) notes that "Many definitions of PIM draw from a traditional information management perspective—that information is stored so that it can be retrieved at a later date." In keeping with this observation, and as exemplified by Barreau's definition, PIM can be analyzed with respect to a person's interactions with a large and amorphous personal space of information or PSI. From the perspective of such a space, the essential operations are input, storage (including organization), and output.

In rough equivalence to the input-storage-output breakdown of actions associated with a PSI, essential PIM activities can then be grouped as follows:

■ **Finding/re-finding activities**[3] move from need to information. These activities affect the output of information from a PSI.

■ **Keeping activities** move from information to need. These activities affect the input of information into a PSI.

■ **Meta-level activities** focus on the PSI itself and on the management and organization of the PICs within. Efforts to "get organized" in a physical office, for example, are one kind of meta-level activity.

PIM activities can then be interrelated with reference to the diagram shown in Figure 1.6, and according to the following statement:

PIM activities establish, use, and maintain a mapping between information and need.

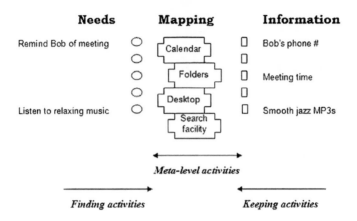

Figure 1.6 – PIM activities viewed as an effort to establish,
use, and maintain a mapping between needs and information

Needs, as depicted in the leftmost column of Figure 1.6, can be expressed in several different ways. Consider a situation where Brooke, while driving, remembers that she needs to make restaurant reservations for Edna's surprise birthday party. The need may have been triggered by Brooke's reference to the information item in her to-do list, calendar, or the proverbial string on a finger. Or it may come via the question from her brother Alex (such as "Have you made the reservations yet?"). Or the need may have come to Brooke out of the blue (though still often triggered indirectly by something informational such as the sight of a billboard advertising Edna's favorite restaurant). A need triggers finding/re-finding activities. Chapter 2 will review research relating to the ways people go about finding information to meet their needs and the problems they encounter as they do so.

Information, as depicted in the rightmost column, is also expressed in various ways. Alex gets information from his mother, Connie, via aural comments ("You seem to be putting on a lot of weight"), email messages, photographs (on paper), and paper printouts. Information triggers keeping activities. Chapter 3 will review research relating to the decisions, actions, and problems of keeping.

Connecting between need and information is a *mapping*. Only small portions of the mapping have an observable external representation. Much of the mapping has only a hypothesized existence in the memories of an individual. Large portions of the mapping are potential and not realized in any form, external or internal. A sort function or a search facility, for example, has the potential to act as a guide from a need to desired information.

But parts of the mapping can be observed and manipulated. The folders of a filing system (whether for paper documents, electronic documents, email messages, or Web references), the layout of a desktop (physical or virtual), and the choice of names, keywords and other properties for information items all form parts of an observable fabric helping to knit need to information. Several distinct kinds of PIM activity relate to the meta-level and the maintenance of a mapping between need and information. These activities are briefly discussed in the next section.

1.7 The Meta-Level and the Mapping Between Needs and Information

A large and diverse set of PIM activities operate broadly upon collections of information within the PSI and on the mapping that connects need to information for these collections. At the level of keeping and finding, "managing" often equates with "getting by" (as in, "I finally managed to find the information"). The meta-level puts a more proactive "big M" spin on Management. How can people take charge of their PIM practice? How should the information be structured? According to what schemes of organization? Following which strategies? How can tools help, either to structure or to obviate structuring? How is the effectiveness of a current practice measured? Issues of privacy and security are also addressed at the meta-level. Who has access to what information under what circumstances? How does information get distributed (medical information, airplane seating preferences, a resume, etc.) for best effect?

Several kinds of meta-level activity are described in greater detail here:

▓ **Maintaining and organizing**. We implement our meta-level scheme of organization through the actual creation of folders and a folder hierarchy (or through the creation of properties). Periodically, this structure needs to be updated. Some folders, for example, may no longer be needed. Some folders have grown too large and may need to be divided into subfolders. Folders may need to be moved or renamed. Similarly, information items themselves may need to be deleted or moved. And information must be backed up. As increasing amounts of personal information are digitized, it is imperative that we deal with issues of long-term archival storage, relating, for example, to the durability of storage media and the continued support of digital formats. Chapter 3 explores some of the issues that surround the organization of personal information for current and repeated use. Chapter 4 explores issues pertaining to the long-term maintenance of personal information.

▓ **Managing privacy, security, and the distribution of information**. A discussion of privacy and security brings us back again to a consideration not only of "our information" but also of information "about us" and the large overlap between these two kinds of personal information. If our first reaction is to say "personal information is personal and no one else can see it," we are likely to have a later realization that some distribution of our personal information can be very useful. We want the travel agent to know about our seating preferences. We want colleagues and friends to know about our schedule. We may want close friends and family to know about our current condition if we are battling a serious illness. The increasing use of personal Web sites as a means to publish (and project) information naturally brings a desire for technology that can support a personal policy on privacy that allows for finer distinctions than "everyone can access" or "no one can access." Given this greater control, however, there is a need for user interfaces that can guide us in our choices and make clear their implications. Chapter 15 explores issues relating to the privacy and security of personal information, and relating to establishing a basis for trust to support the exchange of information.

▓ **Measuring and evaluating**. These activities involve the way we assess and evaluate the effectiveness of a mapping, as well as the structures, strategies, and supporting tools associated with its creation, use, and upkeep. We must periodically ask ourselves, Is it working? Are the structures we've selected maintainable? Are the strategies we try to follow sustainable? Is this tool really helping or is it more trouble than it's worth? For paper documents, the signs that things aren't working are sometimes all too clear. For example, if paper documents continue to pile up in a "to be filed" stack and we never have time to actually file these documents away, this may be a sign that our great new organizational scheme, for all its promise, is simply not sustainable.

As we look for efficient, accurate, objective ways to evaluate our own practice of PIM we run into many of the same problems, at an individual level, that are also in evidence for the field of PIM. We return to this topic in chapters 5 and 11.

▓ **Making sense of and using information**. We try to understand our information and its implications for our lives. What does the information mean? How should it inform our decisions? Making sense of our information often means that we try to arrange the information in various ways so that it is literally in view. Information in our field of vision offers a powerful extension of our limited ability to keep things in mind and at the forefront of attention. For information in paper form, one time-honored method is to arrange paper documents on a desktop or other flat surfaces that surround the desk (perhaps even on the floor). Although the virtual desktop of a computer may be inspired by the desktop metaphor, its own support for viewing and manipulation of information is much more limited. On the other hand, the computer supports new kinds of manipulation for digital information. For example, sorting through digital documents can take place in seconds versus the minutes, hours, or days required to do a comparable sort of paper documents. Actions such as copy and paste or drag and drop are a much more effective means of doing a paste-up of a digital document than the old-fashioned scissors, glue, and pasteboard are for doing comparable actions with paper documents. Chapter 8 explores unifications of personal information that may support a person's efforts to make sense of this information. Chapter 3 presents research concerning the efforts people make today to structure their information and what this may suggest for better tool support.

"Meta-" is commonly used to refer to a higher level, as in "beyond" (everyday PIM activities) or "about" (the mapping or a PIM practice overall).[4] But a more original sense of "meta-" may be equally relevant—"meta" as in "after."[5] For many people, meta-level activities such as maintenance and organization occur only after other, more pressing, PIM activities of keeping and finding are done. This frequently means not at all. Activities of keeping and finding are triggered by many events in a typical day. Information is encountered and keeping decisions are made (if only the decision to do nothing). The information needed for a variety of routine activities (calling someone, planning the day's schedule, preparing for a meeting, etc.) triggers various finding activities. Few daily events speak out for meta-level activities, and these are easy to postpone and to avoid altogether.

1.8 PIM in Relation to Other Fields of Inquiry

As a final background task to complete before moving to PIM-related research, connections should be made and distinctions drawn between PIM and the following areas of inquiry:

Human-computer interaction. Much of the work reviewed here originates from practitioners in the field of *human-computer interaction* (HCI). However, a considerable amount of research in HCI remains focused on specific genres of application and associated forms of information, specific devices to aid the interaction, and, increasingly, on group and organizational issues of HCI.

In the study of PIM, the focus remains primarily on the individual, but it also broadens to include key interactions with information over time. PIM includes a consideration of our personal use of information in all of its various forms—including paper. Although it is difficult these days to imagine a practice of PIM that doesn't involve computers, nevertheless, computers are not a primary focus; information is.

Human-information interaction. In recent years, there has been discussion of human-information interaction (HII) in contrast to HCI (Fidel & Pejtersen 2004; Gershon 1995; Jones, Pirolli, Card et al. 2006; Lucas 2000; Pirolli 2006). Interest in HII in the HCI community is driven partly by a growing realization that our interactions with information are much more central to our lives than are our interactions with computers. This realization is reinforced by trends toward ubiquitous computing. Success in computing and, perhaps paradoxically, in HCI may mean that the computer "disappears" (Streitz & Nixon 2005) into the backdrop of our lives much as electricity does. If we move toward "transparent interfaces," then we are left with our information. However, a recognition of the importance of the human-information interaction is neither new nor recent. Fidel and Pejtersen assert that the terms human-information interaction and human information behavior represent essentially the same concept and can be used interchangeably. As such, HII-relevant discussions have been a longtime mainstay of the library and information science field (see, for example, Belkin 1993).

Personal knowledge management. Finally, there is sometimes discussion of personal knowledge management (PKM).[6] Given the usual ordering of data < information < knowledge, one is tempted to think that PKM is more important than PIM and, ultimately, this may be so. One major challenge of PKM, however, just as with knowledge management more generally, is in the articulation of rules and "lessons of a lifetime" in a form that we (and possibly others) can understand. Knowledge expressed and written down becomes one or more items of information—to be managed like other information items.

1.9 An Overview of the Book's Content

The chapters in this book are divided into four parts:

Part I, Understanding Personal Information Management, includes chapters that review what is currently known about how people perform PIM—specifically how they find, keep, organize, and maintain their personal information. Understanding people's PIM behaviors is important if we're to build tools and use technologies to best advantage. The last chapter in Part I, chapter 5, gives insight into how this understanding is extended through fieldwork study.

Part II, Solutions for Personal Information Management, gives special focus to noteworthy approaches in the development of new tools and the application of new technologies. Approaches reviewed include efforts to create digital memories for a life's worth of experiences (chapter 6) and efforts to apply technologies of database management and artificial intelligence in order to structure personal information for multiple, repeated use (chapter 7). Chapter 8 reviews various efforts toward a greater unification of personal information. Chapters 9 and 10 review developments in search technology and in email support of special relevance to PIM. Finally, chapter 11 addresses some of the challenges associated with the evaluation of PIM solutions. What really works?

Part III, PIM and the Individual, provides an exploration into some of the many variations among people and in practical situations of PIM. Chapter 12 reviews individual differences in the way people do PIM. Chapter 13 considers the special challenges faced by people who must also manage information relating to a serious medical condition along with the information for other aspects of their lives.

Part IV, PIM and Other People, looks at the challenges associated with managing personal information in a larger world. Chapter 14 explores the issues that arise when people must exchange and share information as part of their membership in a larger group. Chapter 15 looks at issues of privacy, security, and trust—especially as these relate to information about us that others keep (e.g., medical providers, credit card companies, etc.). Finally, chapter 16 provides an afterword of sorts concerning the special problems that arise when information about us is made easily, anonymously available as a matter of public record through Web databases.

Information is a means to an end. Not always, not for everyone, but mostly. We manage information to be sure we have it when we need it—to complete a task, for example, or to get an uplifting glimpse at a picture representing a trip we hope to take. Information is generally not even a very precious resource. We usually have far too much of it. Even a document we have spent days or weeks writing is typically available in multiple locations (and, sometimes confusingly, in multiple versions). We manage information because information is the most visible, tangible way to manage other resources that are precious—most especially our time. In a vision of better and better PIM, we spend less time with the burdensome and error-prone activities of managing information and more time making creative, intelligent use of the information at hand to get things done. And as Benjamin Franklin said, "Do not squander time; for that's the stuff life is made of."

NOTES

1. Why "PSI"? A simple answer is that "personal information space" does not produce an attractive acronym. Some readers will also note that PSI is frequently used as the Roman alphabet spelling of the Greek letter 'Ψ' which, in turn, is frequently associated with psychology. The Merriam-Webster Online Dictionary defines "psychology" as the "science of mind and behavior" (http://www.m-w.com/dictionary/psychology). "Psych" has its origins in the ancient Greek word for breath, essence of life, or soul. One thread to be explored in PIM research is the extent to which a personal space of information can be said to reflect the mind and life of its owner. Research might also explore the ways in which elements in a PSI—a calendar or a to-do list, or a even a set of touchstone words of wisdom placed on the bathroom mirror—can provide not only a passive reflection of a person's mind but can also serve, more actively, to complement and facilitate the development of mind and soul—in the same way that a person's space of things reflects, complements, and facilitates the development of the body.
2. In personal communication, one researcher told us that she uses 12 separate custom properties and "lives by" her EndNote database.
3. Instead of "information finding" (or simply "finding") we could just as easily speak of "information seeking" activites. The interchangeable relationship between the terms "information finding" and "information seeking" is discussed in greater detail in chapter 2.
4. See, for example, the entry for "meta-" in the online Wikipedia (http://en.wikipedia.org/wiki/Meta-).
5. See, for example, the entry for "meta-" in the Merriam-Webster Online Dictionary (http://www.m-w.com/dictionary/Meta-).
6. See, for example, this Web site: http://www.global-insight.com/pkm/.

PART I

Understanding
Personal Information
Management

2 How People Find Personal Information

Jaime Teevan, Robert Capra, and Manuel Pérez Quiñones

2.1 Introduction

As mentioned in the previous chapter, finding information is a basic task of personal information management. Consider the following example:

> Alex has a note in his calendar to make reservations at his grandmother Edna's favorite restaurant to celebrate her 75th birthday and thus needs to find the restaurant's phone number. He knows the name of the restaurant, types it into his favorite search engine, follows the first link that comes up to a review of the restaurant, and scans the review to find the phone number listed at the end.

Sometimes finding personal information can be simple, as in the above scenario, but at times it can be a complex multistep process. People often encounter problems even with a task as seemingly simple as finding a phone number. Consider a scenario similar to the one above, except that Alex has forgotten the restaurant's name:

> Without the name of the restaurant, Alex cannot easily run an online search for the phone number. He remembers briefly visiting the restaurant's Web page, so the information may still be in his browser history. He also remembers that his sister, Brooke, sent him an email a while back with the name of the restaurant. However, as well organized as Alex is, he is not sure exactly where he filed the email—in a folder relating to its topic (the restaurant not being the main topic) or in a folder of emails from family members. Eventually he finds the email, and the restaurant name, in his inbox where he left the email since he still needs to reply to his sister.

Even with the restaurant's name, finding the phone number can be difficult. Imagine that the restaurant name ("Jaguar") is not unique enough, considering the many mentions of cars and big cats on the Web, to identify the particular restaurant Alex is interested in. In this case, Alex may need to further specify his search by, for example, searching only his browser history or searching within an online listing of local businesses, to eventually find what he is looking for.

This scenario reflects the complexity of the seemingly simple finding tasks that we perform every day as part of our personal information management. Finding is a mainstream activity, both on the Web and on desktops. A recent Pew Internet and American Life report showed that Internet searches are a top Internet activity, second only to email (Rainie & Shermak 2005). Nonetheless, according to one study searchers are unable to find what they are looking for over 50 percent of the time, and knowledge workers are estimated to waste 15 percent of their time because they cannot find information that already exists (Feldman 2004). Finding within one's personal space of information is particularly challenging since the tools are only in their infancy and tend not to take into account the particular characteristics of personal information finding (Miller 2005).

The purpose of this chapter is to provide an understanding of the factors that influence the finding of personal information so that we can build better tools to support it. We discuss how the individual (Alex or Brooke), the information target (Jaguar's phone number or any restaurant Edna might like), and the task (to make a reservation or to plan a birthday party) all affect finding behavior. Because finding behavior in personal information management commonly involves the re-finding of previously viewed information (e.g., Alex needed to re-find the name of the restaurant even though he had seen it before), we present a discussion of what makes re-finding different from the finding of new information. We highlight important factors such as how the information was originally encountered and kept, and whether the information environment in which it exists has changed. We conclude the chapter with a discussion of the future of information finding and suggest ways tools can best support natural finding behavior.

2.1.1 Definitions

Finding as it relates to personal information management is part of a large and active area of study on information seeking.

> **Information seeking** (or just **seeking**). The purposive seeking of information as a consequence of a need to satisfy some goal. In the course of finding, the individual may interact with manual information systems (such as a newspaper or a library), or with computer-based systems (such as the World Wide Web) (Wilson 2000).

Information seeking includes all activities directed toward accessing information to meet an information need. The need can be very specific, like the phone number of Edna's favorite restaurant in the example above, or broader and less defined, like a birthday gift for Edna. Associated actions can include the specification of a focused query to a search service (e.g., typing "Jaguar" into a search engine's query box) as well as less directed browsing through a list of results, through a Web site, or even a list of emails in an inbox.

The definition of information seeking applies equally well to personal information finding, and in fact the terms are often used interchangeably. In the context of personal information management, *finding* is used in this chapter (and throughout this book) in preference to *seeking* because, as outlined by Jones (in press) finding tends to involve more limited, closed actions (the finding of a phone number), as opposed to the more open-ended activity of seeking (the seeking of a good birthday gift). Such directed tasks fall within a narrow slice of most existing information seeking and searching models. Further, the searcher's relationship with what is being sought is often more intimate for finding than is typical for information seeking.

The target and the corpus being searched through often consist of information that has been created or received by the searcher. Consequently, we often speak of *re-finding* information. Even when finding is directed toward new information in a public store, the motivating need is often triggered by personal information, such as Alex's search for the restaurant phone number that was triggered by a note in his calendar.

Because the finding of previously viewed information is such an important piece of personal information finding, we define it here, and talk about it further in this chapter:

Re-finding. The process of finding information that has been seen before.

The finding of new information and the re-finding of previously viewed information are often interleaved as part of a larger information-seeking task. In the scenario above, Alex needed to re-find his sister's email message in order to conduct a search to find a new piece of information (the phone number of the restaurant).

Re-finding is a complementary action to *keeping*, which is discussed in the next chapter. When people encounter valuable information, they decide how to keep it based in part on their expected future information needs. There is often a tradeoff between investing more time during the initial encounter to keep the information or more time later to re-find it. For example, when Alex located Jaguar's Web site he could have invested the time to bookmark it. Instead, he chose to invest more time later to re-find details about the restaurant when and if they became necessary.

Note that the focus of re-finding is not on repetition of a previous finding activity but, rather, on the retrieval of information previously experienced. The process of re-finding may actually be very different from the process of finding new information. This is because as people remember experiencing the information before, they may think of different ways to find the information again. For example, Alex re-found the name of Edna's favorite restaurant by returning to an email in his inbox, which is similar to the way he originally encountered the name, but he might have chosen to re-find the restaurant's name on the Web, using information he remembered about it from his original encounter to guide his search. And if Alex didn't remember ever learning about Jaguar, the process of re-finding it would look like an entirely new search for Edna's favorite restaurant. Re-finding differs from finding when the seeker takes advantage of knowledge remembered from the initial encounter, and we will highlight how this difference affects re-finding later in the chapter.

2.2 Research Overview

Information science (IS) research has identified factors that influence people's information seeking and searching behaviors, and modeled such behavior to help guide the design of information seeking and information retrieval systems (Wilson 1999). As mentioned earlier, finding personal information is typically a specialized form of information seeking, with characteristics that are not yet fully understood. Here we show that, like information seeking, personal information finding is a multi-stepped process, and discuss a variety of factors that affect finding, including the person doing the finding, the information being sought, and the greater task context of the search.

2.2.1 Finding Is a Multi-Stepped Process

Information seeking is well understood to be a multi-stepped process. For example, Marchionini (1995) detailed the importance of browsing in information seeking, and O'Day and Jeffries (1993) characterized the seeking process by outlining common triggers and stop conditions that guide people's search behaviors as their information needs change. Bates (1989) and Belkin, Marchetti, and Cool (1993) proposed search interfaces that allow users to modify and refine their queries as their information need evolves, thus modeling search as an information-gathering activity rather than a single, static search.

Although personal information finding typically involves simple searches for information that is known in advance, the search behavior follows a similar pattern. Several studies of finding behaviors (Barreau & Nardi 1995; Ravasio, Schar & Krueger 2004; Teevan, Alvarado, Ackerman & Karger 2004) have reported that users prefer to find their personal information by *orienteering* via small, local steps using their contextual knowledge as a guide, rather than by *teleporting*, or jumping directly to it using a keyword-search utility. For example, Alex, in looking for the email with the restaurant name, could have teleported by typing in several keywords into his email client that he thought would bring him the appropriate email. Instead he orienteered by first clicking on the folder he thought contained the email, then sorting the folder by sender so he could find all of Brooke's emails, and then browsing her emails until he saw the one that looked right—even though such a process took more steps and possibly more time. (See Teevan et al. 2004 for a description of PIM orienteering behaviors.)

Researchers have identified several reasons why people often choose orienteering over teleporting. One is that tools that support teleporting, and in particular tools for searching one's personal space of information (PSI), don't always work (Ravasio et al. 2004). For example, Alex's email client may not have had good support for searching the body text of messages if they are stored on the email server. Another reason orienteering may be preferred is that it can provide both an overview of the information space being searched (for Alex, he better understands his email organization after searching for his sister's email) as well as context about where the desired information is located in that space. Alex may find it easier to search by *recognizing* the information he is searching (e.g., "This looks like the right folder where I stored the email") rather than *recalling* it (e.g., "This is a keyword I recall that is associated with the email") (Teevan et al. 2004). While orienteering is common when finding information—both in external sources such as the Web and "internal" sources such as one's own PSI—people are particularly likely to orienteer when searching within their personal space because these advantages are particularly prevalent there (Ravasio et al. 2004).

2.2.2 Individual Factors

Although it is true that people in general tend to find information by orienteering, aspects of the individual performing a search have an impact on the resulting behavior. Different people have different ways of approaching problems, and these different approaches carry over to how they find information. For example, if a person approaches learning in a holistic manner, starting with a big picture and then diving in to understanding the details, they are likely to be more exploratory in their information finding behavior (Ford, Wilson, Foster, et al. 2002). People also have different backgrounds, and both their knowledge of the Web and searching techniques (Hölscher & Strube 2000) have been shown to influence search behavior. On the other hand, the searcher's familiarity with the search task or domain has commonly been investigated as an influencing factor (Bhavnani & Bates 2002; Kelly & Cool 2002; McDonald & Stevenson 1998; Shiri & Revie 2003; Wildemuth 2003), but the effect on the search process remains unclear (Wildemuth 2004). The importance of individual differences in PIM behavior is discussed further in chapter 12.

2.2.3 *Information Target*

Factors related to the information being sought can also play a role in information seeking behaviors. For example, the corpus of information being searched (e.g., the entire Web, a folder of personal email messages, or a digital library of documents), the location of the target, the type of information being sought (e.g., a "nugget" of semi-structured information or a summary of information collected from a variety of sources) (Lieberman, Nardi & Wright 1999), and the addressability of the target (e.g., how many different ways are there to locate the target and how easy is the location to describe?) (Ramakrishnan 2005) are important factors to consider when trying to understand how people find information. They influence the way people express what they're looking for, the strategies they employ to find it, and how easy it is to recognize when found.

One important aspect of the target is whether it is digital or physical. Most of this chapter and much of this book focuses on the finding of digital information. But people also find and re-find within their personal physical spaces. There are both similarities and differences between these two domains. Malone (1983) noted that spatial location helps support the finding of physical information. Similarly, the location of a piece of digital information is a particularly important type of context used when orienteering for personal information (Teevan et al. 2004). This may be because robust search by keyword has not been available until recently and folder navigation is the primary access method afforded by a file system (Fertig, Freeman & Gelernter 1996a). Desktop search tools are starting to be more widely available (e.g., Google Desktop) and future research should examine if and in what way they have an effect on users' finding behaviors.

Malone (1983) observed the use of files and piles to organize physical documents, and noted that some people ("filers") are more comfortable organizing and finding within rigid organizational structures, while others ("pilers") are more comfortable with loose structures. Visible items on a physical desktop help support re-finding by supporting reminding. Barreau and Nardi (1995) noted a similar reminding function of electronic files on a computer desktop. Whittaker and Sidner (1996) describe a related issue for email—users are often reluctant to file email messages because once a message is out of their inbox, it may be forgotten and difficult to re-find.

2.2.4 Information Task

While the individual searching and the information target are both important, task is perhaps the single most important factor influencing finding and re-finding strategies. The importance of task has long been understood by the human-computer interaction and information science communities and is essential to understanding PIM strategies and behaviors. Many models of information seeking incorporate characterizations of task and stage of task (Belkin et al. 1995; Kuhlthau 1991; Vakkari 1999). Researchers studying Web information seeking behaviors have also created taxonomies of task types including dimensions such as the purpose (why?), method (how?), and content (what?) of the search (Morrison, Pirolli & Card 2001).

The stage of a task is of special interest for PIM. Kuhlthau (1991) discusses stages of initiation, selection, exploration, formulation, collection, and presentation in information seeking. For example, if at some point in the past Alex spent time in the initiation and selection stages of looking at restaurants for his grandmother's birthday (e.g., by browsing the Web sites of local restaurants on the Web), this invested effort could influence his behavior during the collection and presentation stages shown in the scenario in the introduction. With PIM, there are also stages to consider associated with re-finding, reusing, and managing the information—recall, for example, that Alex thought the Web page for Jaguar might still be in his browser cache.

2.3 Diving In: A Focus on Re-finding

Re-finding is a particularly important aspect of finding for personal information management. Even though we have seen most of our personal information before, we still have problems getting back to it. Earlier in the example we saw that Alex had seen the name of Edna's favorite restaurant earlier, and needed to re-find that information in order to make the reservation. One of the primary reasons that people invest time in organizing information is to make it easy to re-find and reuse it. If we can improve our understanding of information re-finding, not only can we develop better tools to support it (saving time and money), but we may also be able to help reduce the difficulty and effort required to archive and organize information in the first place.

In this section, we begin with a description of how re-finding differs from the finding of new information. We then look at several factors that have particular influence over re-finding, and show that the way a person keeps and organizes their personal information can influence the way they re-find it. Because changes to the information space can cause problems in re-finding, we also look briefly at re-finding in dynamic environments.

2.3.1 *Re-finding is Different from Finding New Information*

There exists a continuum from finding tasks where little is known about the information target to well-known, frequent re-finding tasks. As a result, searches for information that have been seen before can be similar to searches for new information, or they can differ greatly.

One distinguishing feature of re-finding is that the searcher may know a lot of meta-information about the target, such as its author, title, date created, URL, color, or style of text. For example, Alex knew that Brooke had emailed him the name of the restaurant, and had a good idea as to the subject of her email. Several types of meta-information seem particularly important for re-finding: the people associated with the target (Dumais, Cutrell, Cadiz, et al. 2003), the path taken to find the information (Capra & Pérez-Quiñones 2005a; Teevan 2007b), and temporal aspects of the information (Lansdale & Edmonds 1992; Ringel, Cutrell, Dumais & Horvitz 2003). Lansdale and Edmonds (1992) argue that time is so important that the default ranking for information retrieval should be chronological, and chronology does indeed turn out to be a dominant ranking factor for the Stuff I've Seen search engine (Dumais et al. 2003). Some of the meta-information used in re-finding is self-generated, and thus may be easier to remember. Alex, for example, had a good idea as to where he might have filed the email with the restaurant name. Search failure during re-finding appears to be particularly frustrating in part because the information sought has been seen before and is known to exist (Teevan 2007a).

2.3.2 *Factors That Affect Re-finding*

Because people develop knowledge about a piece of information during their original encounter with that information, there are influencing factors that are important to consider for re-finding in addition to the factors we saw that influenced general finding. These factors include the amount of time that has elapsed since the information was initially found, the perceived versus actual future value of information when found, the similarity of the initial finding and re-finding tasks, whether the location or context of the information changed, and the fungibility of the information source needed (i.e., is the exact same source necessary?).

Capra (2006) conducted a controlled laboratory study to examine many of the factors that affect re-finding behavior, including information type, task type, and task familiarity. In the study, 17 individual participants completed two experimental sessions held approximately one week apart. In the first session, participants found information on the Web for a set of 18 tasks. The tasks were primarily well-defined, directed information-seeking tasks (e.g., "Find the phone number of the Kroger grocery store on Main Street," or "Find a Web page that describes how to solve the Rubik's Cube"), but included several less defined tasks as well (e.g., "Find two sweatshirts that you would like to buy for a friend"). In the second session, participants were asked to perform tasks that involved re-finding the same or similar information that was found in the initial session (e.g., "Find the phone number of the Kroger grocery store on University Boulevard," or "Find a Web page that describes how to solve the Rubik's Cube").

Results indicated that users have strong patterns for information access and that they are likely to use these patterns when re-finding (Capra 2006; Capra & Pérez-Quiñones 2005b). This result is supported by a separate study by Capra and Pérez-Quiñones (2005a). For example, users often approached re-finding tasks using the same starting Web page that they used to originally find the information. The frequency with which a user previously performed similar tasks had significant effects: high-frequency tasks were completed more quickly, involved fewer URLs, and involved less use of Web search engines. However, search engine use did not differ significantly between the two sessions, suggesting that the use of search engines may be strongly linked to specific tasks and may not be influenced by whether the searcher is finding or re-finding. The results also suggest that, as for information finding, keyword search is not a universal solution for re-finding. Instead, participants used a variety of methods to re-find information, including the use of waypoints and path retracing.

2.3.3 *How Information Is Kept and Organized Affects Re-finding*

Another particularly important influencing factor in re-finding is how information is kept and organized. In a study where participants were cued to return to selected Web sites after a delay of three to six months, both Bruce and Jones (Bruce et al. 2004; Jones et al. 2003) report a strong preference for methods of returning to Web sites that require no overt prior keeping action. These methods include searching again, following hyperlinks from another Web site, or accepting the Web browser's suggested completion to a partially entered Web address. Nevertheless, for Web sites and for other many other forms of information, people often expend considerable effort in making their information available for future use, and have different strategies for doing so. These strategies can affect people's search strategies. For example, Teevan et al. (2004) showed that pilers prefer to orienteer with small steps, while filers are more likely to teleport or orienteer with large steps by using keyword search.

Organizing information for re-finding is hard because the future value of the information is hard to predict, and people regularly misjudge the difficulty they'll have returning to information. Often, the value of encountered information is not realized until well after it is originally encountered—a phenomenon referred to as *post-valued recall* (Wen 2003). For example, Alex could have made re-finding the name of Edna's favorite restaurant easy by flagging the email from his sister as important, but he did not consider it to be of high value at the time he received the email. Some tools have been developed to help bring potentially relevant personal information to the user's attention (Dumais, Cutrell, Sarin & Horvitz 2004), but additional study is necessary to understand what happens when people forget important information and when and how they want to be reminded of it.

We saw earlier in this chapter that people often structure their personal information stores to support reminding and recognition. A fear of forgetting what they believe to be important information can even lead people to behaviors such as emailing information to themselves (Jones, Bruce & Dumais 2001) as a way to support re-finding it later. However, just as it is hard to decide what information is important to keep, it can be difficult to organize and classify information believed to be important because the future value and role of the information is not fully understood. People's difficulty classifying can cause problems retrieving. Lansdale (1988b) noted that people had difficulty retrieving information when they were forced to group their information into categories that were not necessarily relevant for retrieval.

Difficulties in organizing information also often lead to information fragmentation. Personal information can become fragmented among different devices, applications, and computers. For example, Alex may have a particularly hard time finding Brooke's email because some of his emails are stored on his home computer, some on his work computer, and some on a free online mail account he maintains. Fragmentation can cause problems re-finding for many reasons. The desired information may be inaccessible from the user's current location, or it may be stored in different forms. Consider the difficulties Alex might encounter trying to locate the final version of a slide show he and his sister are putting together for Edna's birthday. He may find a copy in his file system labeled "version 7," but not know if it is the final version. A more recent version may, for example, be saved in an email Brooke sent him. Boardman and Sasse (2004) investigated issues that occur with cross-tool PIM and found considerable variation in the strategies that people used for PIM across different tools.

2.3.4 Re-finding in Dynamic Environments

Confounding many of the factors that affect re-finding is the fact that a person's electronic information often changes. The search results for a search of files on one's computer change as new files are stored. The online news stories an individual has read change when new stories are written, and the list of emails in a person's inbox changes as new emails arrive. Even traditionally static information like a directory listing on a personal computer has begun to become dynamic; Apple, for example, has introduced *smart folders*, folders based on queries that change their content as new information becomes available.

Changes are often useful—people want to see new email, better search results, and new news stories—but they can disrupt the user's ability to re-find information. As an example, dynamic menus were developed to help people access menu items faster by bubbling common items to the top of the menu. Rather than decreasing access time, research revealed dynamic menus actually slow their users down because commonly sought items no longer appear where expected (Mitchell & Shneiderman 1989). As another example, White, Ruthven, and Jose (2002) tried to help people search better by giving them lists of relevant sentences that were dynamically reranked based on implicit feedback gathered during the search process. To the authors' surprise, people did not enjoy the search experience as much or perform as well as they did when the sentence list was static. Similarly, a large-scale analysis of Yahoo's query logs by Teevan, Jones, Adar, and Potts (2007) revealed that when people repeat queries they are significantly less likely to click on a result they've clicked before if the result's rank has changed, and significantly slower to click when they do.

To help people deal with changes while re-finding, Teevan (2007a) has proposed it is important to understand which aspects of previously viewed information are memorable. This understanding can then be used to highlight important changes (by having changes occur to memorable aspects), or to hide unimportant changes (by only allowing changes to occur to unmemorable aspects). For example, if a person only paid attention to results 3 and 5 during an initial keyword search, changes to results 3 or 5 would appear obvious, but changes to other search results (e.g., result 4) would not. Teevan (2007a) has shown that sneaking new information into a search result list enables people to find new information as quickly as if the new information were presented without regard to past context, while not interfering with their ability to re-find.

2.4 Looking Forward

The importance of being able to successfully find personal information is stressed again and again throughout this book. It affects the way people keep the information they encounter, how much information they can store and understand, how they organize their information, and how they use the tools available to them. In this chapter, we have shown that, for a variety of reasons, the finding of personal information is typically a complex, multi-stepped process, even when the information target is well known. Finding behavior is affected by many factors, including the information form, the seeker, and the task. Re-finding has many similarities to the finding of new information, but can also be very different because of the additional knowledge the seeker has about their target. Re-finding is further influenced by factors such as the way the information was originally encountered, people's organizational structure, and whether the information environment has changed since the information was last encountered.

People currently have a hard time finding their personal information, and as the size of the personal information store grows, successful finding will likely become more elusive and more important. In this section we briefly describe implications of the research described here on tool development and discuss important directions for future research. Tools that support personal information finding are presented in greater detail in chapter 9.

Keyword search is an important tool used for finding personal information, but is not likely to be the end solution (Teevan et al. 2004). We have seen that people generally prefer to orienteer to their information target over using tools like keyword search to teleport directly to it. Reasons for this included the need to see information within the context of related cues, a desire to be reminded of the documents and structure of the personal information space, and a lack of robust keyword search tools. Finding tools should support these benefits of orienteering by going beyond typical keyword search to find ways to incorporate context, and in particular location. Re-finding tools may do well to integrate the organization of information (or creation of context) with search. For example, Google's Gmail does not include folders per se—instead, folders are simply queries that filter a user's email messages based on metadata such as the email's sender field.

In this chapter, we have also seen that multiple devices and multiple information forms lead to fragmentation of data, forcing people to remember where the correct information is located in order to find it. Until recently, search tools for file systems and email were typically restricted in the content they indexed (e.g., only filenames or only email subjects) and had limited user interfaces. In the last year, more sophisticated tools such as Google Desktop, Microsoft Desktop Search, and Apple Spotlight have been released. These index the full text of documents, email, and saved Web pages stored on a user's hard disk and allow users to issue keyword queries over their personal collection of documents in a way that is similar to their use of Web search engines (in fact Google Desktop presents results in a format similar to Google's main Web search engine). The deployment and adaptation of these tools will provide users keyword-search capabilities for their personal store of information that rival those for Web pages.

Although finding new information and re-finding previously viewed information may require different strategies, tools will need to support both activities. As discussed earlier, information organization has a value in reminding the user where documents or information are stored, and going forward it will be interesting to consider how search tools can provide reminding functionality without organizational overhead. In an example of the task-artifact cycle (Carroll & Rosson 1992), PIM activities are often heavily influenced by the available tools (Fertig et al. 1996a). Search tools (Amento, Terveen, Hill, et al. 2003; Robertson, Czerwinski, Larson, et al. 1998; Woodruff, Rosenholtz, Morrison, et al. 2002), and result organization (Amento et al. 2003; Dumais et al. 2003; Robertson et al. 1998) influence finding behavior. Thus as new tools are deployed and used, researchers will need to explore how they affect information finding behavior.

3 How People Keep and Organize Personal Information

William Jones

3.1 Introduction

Many events of daily life are roughly the converse of finding events: People encounter information and try to determine what they should do with this information; that is, people must match the information to anticipated needs. Decisions and actions that attempt to map from information currently under consideration to anticipated needs are collectively referred to in this chapter as *keeping activities*.

People keep information that they have actively sought, but don't have time now to process. A search on the Web, for example, often produces much more information than can be consumed in the current session. Both the decision to keep this information for later use and the actions to do so are keeping activities.

People also keep information they encounter by happenstance. Examples include an announcement for an upcoming event in the morning newspaper, or an FYI email that arrives with a pointer to a Web site. The ability to effectively handle information that is encountered unexpectedly may be key to a person's ability to discover new material and make new connections (Erdelez & Rioux 2000).

As information accumulates in a collection, people may decide to organize or reorganize this information. Organizing may take the form of a periodic "spring cleaning" (Whittaker & Sidner 1996) in which older items such as email messages or files or Web bookmarks are deleted or moved to less visible, less accessible storage. People also organize so that items all still share the same kind of storage but are more effectively ordered and grouped according to their content and their anticipated uses. For example, people may decide to order the items scattered across the virtual desktop of their computer so that these are grouped according to their various roles and enduring areas of interest. Or people may decide upon a scheme of nested folders in which information is organized according to projects, subprojects, and component tasks. Decisions and actions relating to the selection and implementation of a scheme of information organization are collectively referred to as *organizing activities*.

This chapter reviews research relating to the ways people keep and organize their information. The initial focus here is more on keeping, because, along with finding, that's where the action is in a person's daily practice of personal information management (PIM). In a typical day, people are more or less constantly encountering information for which the response is some kind of keeping activity. The keeping activity may be to make a mental note, write down a reminder or to-do on paper, make an entry in calendar—paper-based or electronic—send oneself an email with short note, and so on. Even if the decision is "no, I won't need this information later" or "no, I can get to this information later with no need to do anything special"—these too are keeping decisions. By contrast, efforts to organize or reorganize a collection of personal information, such as the email messages in an email account or the paper piles in an office, occur much less frequently.

But, as many of us may know from personal experience, a good organization already in place makes keeping new things—food, tools, clothing, and also information items—much easier. In concluding sections, the chapter explores research relating to the thesis that some challenges of keeping are best handled by a step back to consider the overall organization for a personal information collection.

3.1.1 *Scenarios*

We return to Alex, Brooke, Connie, and Derek as they make plans for Edna's surprise birthday party.

Connie is taking the lead in organizing the surprise birthday party for Edna. She has given special attention to Edna's "this is your life" all-in-good-fun roast. Connie still uses paper as her primary means for saving information and for sending information to other people. When she meets with Alex, Brooke, and Derek to plan the surprise party, for example, she distributes her script for the roast via paper printouts.

Alex's work-related information is well organized but his nonwork information is less so (Alex jokes that he *has* no life outside of work these days). When Alex receives paper printouts from Connie containing plans for Edna's party and a script for her roast, he's not sure what to do with the information. He lets it build up in his briefcase where it gets intermingled with work-related paper documents.

Brooke lets things pile up in both physical and virtual space and doesn't much care if she can't get back to a particular item of information. Instead she makes heavy use both of her excellent memory and of the friends and colleagues around her. When unsure about details of the party she simply asks Alex, Connie, or Derek.

Derek has made a deliberate attempt to put nearly everything onto his tablet PC. He wishes Connie would distribute party planning information via email rather than by paper printouts. However, his approach is to take digital notes immediately and then discard the paper printout. Derek once tried putting most information, including appointment and contact information, into a PDA. But he then noticed that he was spending significant amounts of time maintaining and synchronizing his PDA, his PC (then a laptop), and his cell phone. These days, Derek is down to two primary devices—his tablet PC and his cell phone.

Edna, as she freely admits, is something of a packrat. Her house is filled with knickknacks and memorabilia. If the past is any indication, Edna will likely want to save one or two of the paper party napkins from the party along with the paper invitation. Edna saves things, including information items, with no clear purpose in mind other than to be reminded of a pleasant time she had with friends and family.

3.1.2 Key Points about Keeping and Organizing

These stories about Alex, Brooke, Connie, Derek, and Edna illustrate several key points concerning the keeping and organizing of personal information:

- People vary greatly in their approaches to keeping and organizing information. Members of the same family may represent opposite extremes.[1] The same person may move from one extreme of orderliness to the other depending upon the information form. A person may have organized collections of digital documents or email messages, for example, while being disorganized with respect to bank statements, bills, and other material that comes in paper form. Or the opposite may be true.
- Keeping and organizing are related but distinct activities. For example, as Alex continues to keep party-related paper printouts in his briefcase, he may reach a "time to get organized" saturation point that prompts him to devise a better way of organizing this information. Or maybe not . . .
- Challenges of keeping and organizing are greater when several devices and applications are involved. Derek, for example, must manage information on both his cell phone and in the several organizations of his tablet PC. He is nevertheless happy that he now has one less device to

deal with (his PDA). Derek would like to simplify further by getting rid of paper, but paper still has a way of coming into Derek's life (e.g., through handouts from Connie and also, it turns out, from his boss at work).

■ People don't always keep information with a specific purpose in mind. Sometimes people keep information to evoke memories (Marshall & Bly 2005), to represent something about themselves (Kaye, Vertesi, Avery, et al. 2006), or "just because" (see chapter 13).

3.1.3 *Why Keeping and Organizing Are Important*

With reference to chapter 1 and its conceptual framework for PIM, keeping can be seen as an essential part of an informational handoff to later acts of re-finding and use. An act of keeping might be likened to throwing a ball into the air toward a place where we expect to be at some future point in time and space. The attempt to re-find and reuse information often depends on earlier efforts to keep this information—even if the keeping act is only to make a mental note to use the information later on.

People's decisions concerning whether and how to keep information are naturally influenced by an assessment of anticipated uses of the information (Kwasnik 1989). However, anticipating future uses or needs for an information item is a fundamentally difficult process that is prone to error (Bruce 2005; Jones 2004, 2006; Jones & Ross 2006). The ongoing proliferation of information forms and supporting tools and gadgets makes keeping even harder. The information people need may be at home when they're at work or vice versa. It may be on the wrong computer, PDA, smart phone, or other device. Information may be "here" but locked away in an application or in the wrong format so that the hassles associated with its extraction outweigh the benefits of its use.

Keeping, more broadly considered, applies not only to information but also to channels of information. Subscribing to a magazine or setting the car radio to a particular station is a keeping decision. Even the cultivation of friends and colleagues can be seen as acts of keeping (and certainly friends and colleagues often represent important channels of information).

Keeping activities are triggered when people are interrupted in the midst of a current task and look for ways of preserving a current state so that work can be quickly resumed later (Czerwinski, Horvitz & Wilhite 2004). People keep appointments by entering reminders into a calendar. People keep good ideas or lists of things to pick up at the grocery store by writing down a few cryptic lines on a loose piece of paper.

Organizing activities, with their focus on an information collection, occur less frequently. Their importance seems to vary considerably depending upon the person, the job, the situation, and other factors. (See chapter 12 for a more in-depth discussion of individual differences in PIM.) For people like Alex, organizations of work-related information are critical and well worth an investment of time and effort. For other people, like Brooke, organizing information is not so important. The chapter returns to the role(s) and value of organizing information after first considering research relating to keeping.

3.1.4 *Definitions*

Although the terms *keeping* and *organizing* often co-occur in sentences throughout this chapter, the terms refer to two distinct kinds of activity:

Information keeping (or just **keeping**). Decision-making and actions relating to the information item currently under consideration that impact the likelihood that the item will be found again later. Decisions can range from: (1) "ignore, this has no relevance to me"; (2) "ignore, I can get back to this later" (by asking a friend, searching the Web, or some other act of finding) to purposive seeking of information as a consequence of a need to satisfy some goal; and/or (3) "keep this in a special place or way so that I can be sure to use this information later."

Information organizing (or just **organizing**). Decision-making and actions relating to the selection and implementation of a scheme of organization and representation for a collection of information items. Decisions can include: (1) How should items in this collection be named? (2) What set of properties make sense for and help to distinguish the items in this collection? (3) How should items within this collection be grouped? Into piles or folders?

Keeping and organizing activities are triggered by different events and operate at different levels. The focus of keeping activities is on a single information item. The focus of organizing activities is on a personal information collection. Keeping activities are triggered or "spoken for" by a constant flow of events in a typical day. Organizing activities are seldom triggered by the events of a typical day. Organizing activities can be triggered seasonally, or sporadically—as when people make a New Year's resolution to "get organized" or need to get prepared for a move.

The words "organizing" and "maintaining" also occur together frequently and sometimes interchangeably. In this chapter, a distinction is made between the two terms as follows:

Information maintaining (or just **maintaining**). All decisions and actions relating to the composition and preservation of a personal information collection. Decisions involve what kind of new items go into a collection, how information in the collection is stored (Where? In what formats? In what kind of storage? Backed up how?), and when do older items leave the collection (e.g., When are they deleted or archived?).

The object of maintaining, like organizing, is a collection of information. Maintaining personal information, especially for the long run, is discussed in chapter 4 and is not discussed further in this chapter.

3.2 Research Overview

In contrast to the considerable research relating to how people find and re-find information (see chapter 2 for a review) there is much less research relating to how people keep information, and perhaps even less information relating to how people organize collections of information.

3.2.1 *What Has Been Learned So Far?*

Research indicates that:

■ Decisions relating to keeping are multifaceted and error-prone.
■ Across different forms of information people have a general choice between *filing* and *piling* the information they wish to keep. Each approach has its limitations.
■ The keeping challenge is harder due to the proliferation of information forms introduced by new applications and new devices.

Each of these points is now considered in greater detail.

Decisions Relating to Keeping Are Multifaceted and Error-Prone

An act of keeping involves not one but several decisions, each involving several considerations, each a potential misstep. Kwasnik (1989, 1991) identified a large number of dimensions that might potentially influence the placement and organization of paper-based mail and documents in an office. In addition to attributes of the document itself (e.g., title, author), keeping behavior was influenced by disposition (e.g., discard, keep, postpone), order/scheme (e.g., group, separate, arrange), time (e.g., duration, currency), value (e.g., importance, interest, and confidentiality), and cognitive state (e.g., "don't know" and "want to remember"). Overall, a document's classification was heavily influenced by the document's intended (anticipated) use or purpose—a finding subsequently reproduced by Barreau (1995).

Jones, Bruce, and Dumais (2001) and Jones, Dumais, and Bruce (2002) observed that the choice of method for keeping Web information for later use was influenced by a range of considerations or functions. Marshall and Bly (2005) also note that the reasons for keeping information vary and are not necessarily task-related or even consciously purposeful. Some participants appeared to keep some information (e.g., newspaper clippings) for the pleasure of expanding their collection of like items (e.g., recipes) and a few participants used the word "packrat" to describe their keeping behavior. Kaye et al. (2006) postulate that some people acquire information in order to build a "legacy" collection of information that stands for a person's lifework and that can be bequeathed to others.

Consider Alex, Connie's son, who works as a securities analyst. In the course of a typical day he gets lots of email, encounters lots of Web pages of potential value, and sees lots of documents, both as attachments in email and in paper form. Alex also gets handed lots of business cards. In a typical day at work, Alex will encounter several hundred different information items, in various forms, and must make roughly the same decisions for each. The business card someone has just handed Alex at the end of a meeting will illustrate the process.

Is the information potentially useful? Alex gets business cards from people he has no intention of contacting again later. He has acquired a habit he first observed in Japan of respectfully studying the card for a moment before placing it in his right front pocket. Cards in this pocket are later discarded.

Do special steps need to be taken to keep it for later use? Assuming that the item represents useful information, does anything need to be done to be sure the item can be accessed again later? Again, Alex may decide "no" in the case of the business card for any of several reasons. Perhaps he knows the person already and has his or her contact information, or perhaps he is confident that he can easily locate this information from the Web or from a colleague.

How should the item be kept? Where? On what device? In what form? To be accessed again when? If Alex decides to keep the business card, he has many choices. Alex generally places cards representing near-term to-dos in a special place in his briefcase. He has another spot in his briefcase for "rainy day" cards that he'll sort through and possibly use as he has free time (e.g., while waiting in airports). Alex also tries to write a note on business cards he keeps in order to remind himself of things to discuss with or reasons to contact the person who gave him the card. This too is an act of keeping.

For some cards, Alex will want to transcribe contact information into a contact-management database so that people can be added to mailing lists, holiday card distribution lists, and so on. In these instances, information is transformed to appear in a new information item: the record of the contact-management database. Alex will also sometimes enter the phone number from the card and an abbreviated name into his cell phone—another transformation.

However, neither transformation, to database or to cell phone, necessarily eliminates the need for the original business card. The card, for example, acts as a visible reminder of actions to be taken. Alex experiences both the contact database and his cell phone as "black holes" into which information disappears to be forgotten. Out of sight; out of mind. But if Alex needs to be sure to contact someone, he may keep the business card information in still other ways—by sending himself an email message with card information, for example, or by entering a name and phone number from the card into his electronic calendar.

Here we see that even a routine event—receipt of a business card—can prompt a sequence of keeping decisions none of which is straightforward. Moreover, acts of keeping can be separated from reciprocal acts of finding by days, months, or even years. Alex, for example, learned of one failure of keeping two years after its occurrence. He met someone at a banquet and then remembered meeting the same person two years earlier. Business cards had been exchanged and Alex had made a promise to call the next day. But the card was misplaced and now, two years later, this potential client was working with another firm.

Keeping decisions often occur in a gray area where determination of costs, reciprocal benefits and outcome likelihoods is not straightforward (Jones 2004). In the logic of signal detection, this middle area presents people with a "damned if you do; damned if you don't" choice. If Alex keeps a card, he may never use it but he still pays a small cost in time to put the card in one of his piles, and he pays a small extra cost to sort through the cards with each new card added. If Alex doesn't keep the card, he may find that he really needs its information later. Alex may pay double for finer-grained failures of keeping. If he places a document in the wrong folder, for example, he may not find the document later when he needs it. Worse, the document in the wrong folder may hinder later access to other documents in the folder.

File or Pile? Each Approach to Keeping Has Its Limitations

One essential decision people face, across forms of information, is between filing and piling the information at hand. The outcome of the decision is most apparent with paper documents, which can either be placed in physical piles or filed away in a filing cabinet (Malone 1983). Piling is relatively fast and easy to do. Items left in piles are also accessible and visible—providing, of course, that the number of piles does not begin to overwhelm. Similar pile-like advantages are realized by leaving email in the inbox, accepting the default location (e.g., "Documents" or "My Documents") for a newly created document, or placing a newly created Web bookmark in the top level of a Web bookmark collection. In each case, people can choose to file items into folders instead.

Both options—filing and piling—have their advantages and disadvantages. Filing information items—whether paper documents, e-documents, or email messages—correctly into the right folders is a cognitively difficult and error-prone activity (Bälter 2000; Kidd 1994; Lansdale 1988a, 1991; Malone 1983; Whittaker & Sidner 1996). Difficulty arises in part because the definition or purpose of a folder is often unclear from the label (e.g., "stuff"), and then may change in significant ways over time (Kidd 1994; Whittaker & Hirschberg 2001; Whittaker & Sidner 1996). Determining a folder's definition may be at least as problematic as determining a category's definition (e.g., Rosch 1978; Rosch, Mervis, Gray, et al. 1976; Wittgenstein 1953; Zadeh 1965). Worse, people may not even recall the folders they have created and so create new folders to meet the same or similar purposes (Whittaker & Sidner 1996).

Placing or leaving information items in piles, as an alternative to filing, has its own problems. In Malone's study (1983), participants indicated that they had increasing difficulty keeping track of the contents of different piles as the number of them increased. Experiments by Jones and Dumais (1986) suggest that the ability to track information by location alone is quite limited. Moreover, the extent to which piles are supported for different forms of information is variable, limited, and poorly understood (Mander, Salomon & Wong 1992). The computer desktop may serve as a place to pile items for fast access or high visibility (Barreau 1995; Barreau & Nardi 1995). But if the desktop is often obscured by various open windows, the accessibility and visibility of its items are much reduced (Kaptelinin 1996). The email inbox provides pile-like functions of accessibility and visibility, but these functions are clearly reduced as the number of items in the inbox increases and especially for older messages that scroll out of view.

People may file in reaction to the pileup of information just to get things out of the way. Or people may file as a way of closing the books on a project either canceled or completed. Kaye et al. (2006) note that sometimes "archives were meant for storage, but not necessarily for retrieval: putting things away and into the right place was much more important in this type of archive than ever retrieving items again" (p. 277).

A Proliferation of Information Forms Increases the Keeping Challenge

The information world described by Malone (1983) was largely paper-based. Today paper documents and books are still an important part of the information space for most people (Sellen & Harper 2002; Whittaker & Hirschberg 2001). In addition, people must contend with the organization of e-documents, email messages, Web pages (or references to these), and possibly also a number of additional forms of digital information (each with its own special-purpose tool support), including phone messages, and digitized photographs, music, and videos. The number of keeping considerations further increases if a person has multiple email accounts, uses separate computers for home and work, uses a PDA, smart phone, or special-purpose PIM tools.

As the example for Alex illustrates, people freely convert from one form of information to another (Jones et al. 2002) and may keep information in several different ways to be sure of having it later (Jones et al. 2002). But doing so can increase the later challenges of updating and synchronization (e.g., when the phone number changes). And still not all needs are met. Neither the calendar nor contact entry will help, for example, if the person needs to contact the client on his cell phone while stuck in traffic.

3.2.2 *What Now?*

As the business card example illustrates, technology has increased some of the challenges associated with keeping and organizing information. Alex has to decide not only whether to keep a business card but also where and in what form he should keep it. In his cell phone? In his contract-management database? Transcribed and sent in email as a reminder? And if he keeps the card's information in several forms he has to manage issues of synchronization and updating. But Alex would never go back to an earlier simpler time with no computing applications and no hand-held devices. Neither would most of us.

Just as technology complicates, it can also assist and simplify. Technologies of search and storage have dramatically reduced or even nullified some costs associated with mistakes in keeping, for example. These reductions invite a consideration of two decision-free extremes in keeping strategy (Jones 2004): keep everything (storage is cheap) or keep nothing at all (and search for the information again later).

System support can also automate keeping in ways that combine local storage and a reliance on the Web. The history and the auto-complete facilities in most Web browsers, for example, keep references locally to information that remains on the Web.

Approaches that automate keeping, or that free people from a need to decide what is kept, point to a problem identified by Lansdale (1988a). If people do not take specific actions to keep encountered information, they may be less likely to remember to look for this information later in the right situations. Jones and Ross (2006) review basic research from cognitive psychology that supports this possibility.

Some alternatives to the "keep everything," "keep nothing" and "keep automatically" approaches are those that help people to "keep smarter" by making better decisions concerning future needs for current information (Jones 2004). Assisted support, for example, may involve using information-filtering technology (e.g., Foltz & Dumais 1992) but in ways that preserve user involvement (e.g., Segal & Kephart 1999).

Another approach to smarter keeping is to have a better organization in place from the outset. Jones and Ross (2006) review research suggesting that an organization of information can have a large impact on the way new information is perceived and categorized. The value of information organizations and of organizing as a kind of PIM activity is considered in greater depth in the next section.

3.3 Diving In: A Closer Look at How People Organize

This section looks at research relating to the ways people organize information and then considers implications of this research for tool support.

3.3.1 *Introduction: Research on Organizing*

Differences between people are especially apparent in their approaches to the organization of their information. Malone (1983) distinguished between "neat" and "messy" organizations of paper documents. "Messy" people had more piles in their offices and appeared to invest less effort than "neat" people in filing information. Comparable differences have been observed in the ways people approach email (Bälter 1997; Gwizdka 2002; Mackay 1988; Whittaker & Sidner 1996), e-documents (Boardman & Sasse 2004; Bruce, Jones & Dumais 2004), and Web bookmarks (Abrams, Baecker & Chignell 1998; Boardman & Sasse 2004). (See chapter 12 for a more in-depth review of research relating to individual differences in PIM.)

Across information forms, differences in approaches to organization correlate with differences in keeping strategy. For example, people who have a more elaborate folder organization—whether for paper documents, e-documents, email messages, or Web bookmarks—tend to file sooner and more often. However, people are often selective in their maintenance of different organizations. Boardman and Sasse (2004), for example, classified 14 of 31 participants in their study as "pro-organizing" with respect to email and e-documents but not with respect to bookmarks; 7 of 31 participants only took the trouble to organize their e-documents. (The study did not include a look at organization of paper documents.)

The fragmentation of information by forms (paper, e-documents, email, etc.) poses special challenges for organizing of information. Folders with similar names and purposes may be created in different information organizations, especially for email messages and e-documents (Boardman & Sasse 2004). Maintaining consistency is difficult and organizations can easily get out of synch. For example, people may have a "trips" email folder and a "travel" e-document folder.

The fragmentation of information across forms also poses problems in the study of PIM. There is a natural tendency to focus on one form of information in order to manage the scope of inquiry—to study only email, for example, or the use of Web bookmarks, or the organization of paper documents. But a focus by information form can have the effect of endorsing current application-centric partitions of information and the information fragmentation that results from these partitions—certainly one of the most vexing problems of PIM today.

From the small number of studies that have looked at how the same person manages across different forms of information (Boardman & Sasse 2004; Jones, Phuwanartnurak, Gill & Bruce 2005; Ravasio, Schär & Krueger 2004) the following composite emerges:

- People do not generally take time out of a busy day to assess their organizations or their PIM practice in general.
- People complain about the need to maintain many separate organizations of information and about the fragmentation of information that results.
- Even within the same folder organization, competing organizational schemes may suffer an uneasy coexistence with each other. People may apply one scheme on one day and another scheme the day after. Lack of consistency in how information is kept may not be a problem in the near term when memories for filing an item are fresh. But weeks or months later people may not remember where to look. Is the expense report for the trip to Denver in the "expense reports" folder or in the "Denver trip" folder?[2]
- People sometimes make extraordinary efforts to consolidate

organizations. One participant in the Jones et al. (2002) study, for example, reported saving all "keeper" Web references and email messages into a file folder organization. Another participant sent e-documents and Web references in email messages.[3]

3.3.2 *The Importance of Organizing*

Connie would tell us that keeping things in their place is a lot easier if there is a place to put things to begin with. Connie has an elaborate paper-based filing system in her home office that includes filing cabinets for financial information (including taxes and bills), medical information for herself and her children (mostly from when they were younger), and also for items relating to her various volunteer activities. Connie experiences her biggest keeping problems when some new document doesn't fit neatly into her existing filing system. These documents start to pile up and may eventually prompt Connie to make space for new folders or even to rethink her organizational scheme altogether.

But Connie's information is still mostly paper-based. Her space for storage is limited by the number of flat surfaces, shelves, and filing cabinets she has available. She can't use search facilities to help locate her information.

Does organization really matter for digital information? Some suggest that, given the ongoing dramatic increases in the power of desktop search facilities and the capacities of digital storage, organizing information is no longer necessary—certainly not necessary to insure its accessibility, maybe not necessary at all (Cutrell, Dumais & Teevan 2006). Folders in particular, as an organizing construct, are targeted for obsolescence. Sentiment against folders is reflected even in popular press articles (Death to folders! 2005).

The next subsection describes research in support of an alternate position. The organization of personal information is important for reasons that go beyond merely promoting its accessibility.

3.3.3 *Toward Better Support for Organizing and Making Sense of Things*

People often structure and organize information as part of a process to make sense of the information and to make sense of the situations where it will be used (Dervin 1992). Russell, Stefik, Pirolli, and Card (1993) provide an excellent analysis in which structures (representations) are acquired and discarded depending upon a perception of costs—the costs to stay with a current structure versus the costs to switch to a new structure. As a human activity, sense-making and the search for structures involves both internal representations (IRs) and external representations (ERs), which combine to form an integrated cognitive system (Hutchins 1995; Kirsh 2000).

On the Keeping Found Things Found or KFTF project

On the University of Washington Information School's Web site, Web address http://kftf.ischool.washington.edu, we have begun to explore the ways in which common organizing constructs, such as the folder, can support people in their efforts to make sense of their information (Jones, Munat, Foxley, et al. 2005a; Jones et al. 2005b). We often ask study participants, for example, to give us guided tours of their various folder organizations for paper documents, e-documents, email messages, and Web references. Sometimes the focus of the tour is on information relating to a particular project (e.g., "plan our summer vacation"); sometimes the focus is on overall organization, as revealed in the top two or three levels of each organization that a participant maintains. Folder structures, as described by their owners, often point to uses of features either not supported or even impeded by current tools supporting information organization.

Figure 3.3.3a – A participant's folder hierarchy for planning a wedding.[4]

Folders in Support of Project Planning

Consider Figure 3.3.3a, with its representation of one participant's organization of information relating to her wedding after six months of planning and preparation.

The participant's comments made it clear that the folder structure shown in Figure 3.3.3a functioned as more than simply a way of getting back to files. The folder hierarchy represented important information in its own right. In one view, albeit intermingled, the participant could see a record of tasks completed, decisions made, and a reminder of tasks and decisions still to be addressed. The folder hierarchy, then, was a partial external representation (ER) of a project plan for the wedding and appeared to realize some of the benefits observed elsewhere for ERs of a problem or project (Hutchins 1995; Larkin & Simon 1987; Russell et al. 1993). For example, subfolders of the wedding folder represented not only the information kept within but also the information that was still needed or might be relevant.

If a folder organization helps in project planning, it may support a person not only to "keep faster," by providing a ready location for incoming information, but also to "keep smarter," that is, to see more readily the relevance of encountered information to a given project, even if the project is not the current focus of attention (Seifert & Patalano 2001).

Nevertheless, the participant's file manager[4] was never designed to support the use of a folder hierarchy as an ER. Here are but a few of the many features that are not adequately supported but that might be useful:

- *A manual ordering of folders.* Many participants in our studies force an ordering of folders through the selection of leading characters in folder names (e.g., "1," "2," "_," "zz").
- *An ability to set reminders, due dates, and other tasklike properties.* Many subfolders seem to correspond to tasks that need to be done (e.g., "decide on wedding dress").
- *An ability to add notes.* Some of the subfolders contain short documents explaining their contents.
- *The ability to use and reuse structures.* Many of life's activities share similar structures. One business trip is much like another, for example, with a need to complete many of the same kinds of tasks (make plane reservations, make hotel reservations). There is currently little system support for the location and reuse of structure.

Plan the Project and Let the Information Follow

Fieldwork observations such as those mentioned above are guiding the development of a prototype in support of PIM activities, called the *universal labeler* (UL) (Jones, Bruce & Foxley 2006; Jones, Bruce, Foxley & Munat 2006; Jones, Munat & Bruce 2005). The UL is motivated by the following assertions:

  ▓ People use their information organizations to get back to the information organized but in many other ways as well.

  ▓ People are hampered in their efforts to organize information by a lack of adequate system support for basic features (such as ordering or the reuse of structure) and by a lack of support for the integrative use of a single organization for different forms of information (e.g., e-documents, email, Web references, informal notes).

  ▓ Organizing information is often separated from other activities a person must do, such as planning a project and the acquisition of information needed to complete the project. But this needn't be so. *An effective organization of information can emerge as a by-product of efforts to plan a project for which the information is acquired.*

In efforts to develop the UL, there is no presumption that there is a better or right way to organize information. Instead, the approach is to make it easier (less costly) for people to organize their information as (much as) they wish and also to allow people to get more out of an organization (more benefit) once it is expressed. The UL is a constellation of features designed to work with and extend existing applications such as the user's file manager, Web browser, word processor, and email application.

For example, the UL includes a *Label With* feature. It allows people, in a simple variation on the Save As dialog, to use their file folder structures as a more general classification scheme for the organization not only of e-documents and other files but also of email messages and Web pages.

KFTF research suggests that folders often include information relating to a task and its outcome. The UL includes a *Task Reminder* feature that can be used to set "Remind by" and "Due by" properties for any selected folder. Properties are represented as special appointments in the Microsoft Outlook calendar. In this way, Task Reminder supports a rudimentary integration of information and task/time management.

Organizations such as depicted in Figure 3.3.3a invite a simple question: Why not combine support for task and project management with support for organizing information? The UL includes a *Project Planner* module inspired by the thought that an integrative organization of information can emerge as an outgrowth of efforts to plan a project and manage its tasks.

Users can begin their work on a project top-down by building a project outline with high-level components, or bottom-up by typing in notes and gathering bits and pieces of information from Web pages, emails, and e-documents. By simply dragging text sections or entire documents into the project, the text is linked back to its source, but is displayed in its project context.

Over time, an entire project plan emerges such as that depicted in Figure 3.3.3b. The plan is essentially another view of the user's file folder hierarchy, where headings are folders, subheadings are subfolders, and links are shortcuts. In addition to linking text and typing formatted notes, users can order headings and subheadings in ways that help them make sense of a plan or to see things in order of importance—just as they might like to do in a word processor.

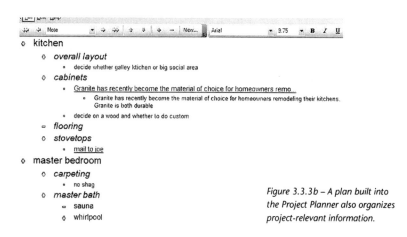

Figure 3.3.3b – A plan built into the Project Planner also organizes project-relevant information.

In-Context Creation of Information Items

What is especially important is that users can send new email messages and create new documents in the context of a project plan. Documents so created reside in the nearest containing heading/folder. For email messages, links are placed in the nearest containing heading/folder and the email messages themselves are still managed by the email application (Microsoft Outlook).

Consider the benefits of in-context creation with respect to an email message. After an email message is sent, a common question arises later: "Did I get a reply? If so, what?" When scores of email messages arrive in a day, it is easy to lose track of responses to a particular email message. One way to check is to locate the sent email message, either in the sent mail folder or possibly in the inbox if the message was copied to the sender. A query can then be issued for all responses to the email message. But locating the original email message can take time, especially if this is done several times per day.

A project plan such as that in Figure 3.3.3b provides an alternate way to locate a sent email message and, through this message, responses. One task in the home remodel plan, for example, is to "find out what the budget allows" for countertops. Underneath is a link to an email message from the homeowner to the contractor with the subject line "quick question about budget for counter-tops." If the homeowner later wants to locate the contractor's response to this message, she can do so with reference to the project plan. Since the email message is still managed by the email application, the homeowner can still choose to locate the message via searches and sorts in the folder for sent mail.

Planner Architecture

Behind the scenes, the Planner is able to support its more document-like outline view by distributing XML fragments as hidden files, one per file folder; these contain information concerning notes, links, and ordering for the folder. The Planner assembles fragments on demand to present a coherent project plan view, including notes, excerpts, links, and an ordering of subfolders.

The distribution of XML fragments in association with file folders has more general application as a way to support a variety of views into a collection of personal information. Other potentially useful views include workflow views, decision tree views, and tabular views.

3.4 Looking Forward

Research into how people organize their information collections points to several directions for improved support and also to new directions in fieldwork investigation:

Reusing a Perfectly Good Structure

People attempt to reuse organizing structures now even though tool support is minimal. In the Jones et al. (2005b) study of project-related folder structures, 5 of 14 participants indicated some effort to reuse folder structure. One student, for example, made an empty course-folder structure (with the top folder named "xx-xxx-Course Name" and subfolders such as "assignments" and "readings"), which was then copied for repeated use as an organizing structure for actual courses. A good organizing structure deserves to be reused.

Consider, for example, a simple *Paste Structure* feature as a small step toward better support for the reuse of structure. For a folder selected by the Copy command, Paste Structure might copy the folder and its subfolder descendants but leave behind individual files. This could be used, for example, to copy the folder structure from one business trip to reuse it for another business trip.

Automated, In-place Archival

People may work for weeks or months in a cluttered space before making any effort to reduce its clutter—and then perhaps only as prompted by an external event like the visit of an earnest researcher or an especially troubling failure to find information that "is right there in front of me." After all, who has time to delete or move old information? Also, moving information within the hierarchical structures that still predominate in today's information organizations means leaving behind some of the organizing context—the connection to containing folders in the hierarchy. There is then a situation aptly described by one of the Boardman and Sasse (2004, p. 585) participants: "Stuff goes in but doesn't come back out—it just builds up."

Boardman and Sasse reported that 12 of 31 participants in their study performed "ad hoc tidying" of their information during the interview itself. In the Jones, Phuwanartnurak, et al. (2005b) study, all 14 participants made comments during the interview such as "I really should clean this up." Four participants actually insisted on interrupting the interview while they moved or deleted files and whole folders as "old stuff that really shouldn't be there anymore."

Old information items don't just take up storage space on a computer; they can also take up visible space, and are a potential distraction of a person's precious attention.

Suppose that the visibility of an item is itself as a property that changes over time according to use? Old items could fade gradually from view, perhaps stepping through shades of gray from a state of normal visibility to a state of "invisibility." Invisible items remain searchable and can easily be returned to a state of visibility. Other properties of an item, including its position in an organizing hierarchy, need not change at all. More generally, as Malone (1983) noted so long ago, visible, attention-directing properties might ideally change dynamically as due dates near, projects are completed, or simply with use and disuse. A person can't be expected to manually tinker with attention-directing property values for items. Why can't the system help?

Reflecting Mental Representations in the Visible Structures
of a Personal Information Collection

Folders are used by some people in some situations for project planning—not merely as holding bins for project-related information but also to represent key components of a project. More generally, folders represent a rudimentary decomposition of the project. This understanding opens the door to many interesting questions and possibilities. For what kinds of people is this true? On what kinds of projects? With what key variations? Would people be more inclined to give external expression to their emerging understanding of a project if supporting tools were better? But the challenge is to provide the right kind of support and then not too much support and enforcing too much structure (Shipman & Marshall 1999).

More generally, it is important to understand the roles that manually imposed structure plays in the management of personal information collections. Efforts to structure personal information find expression not only in folder hierarchies but also in physical piles and analogous groupings of items on a computer desktop (e.g., Mander et al. 1992), user-assigned property and value combinations, annotations, file and folder names including leading characters, and so on.

Certainly we would expect that techniques of information visualization (see, for example, Bederson & Shneiderman 2003; Card, Mackinlay & Shneiderman 1999) will provide increasing support for people as they try to make sense of their information. However, there is also abundant evidence to indicate that the ability to directly manipulate the items in an information collection plays a critical role in facilitating a person's understanding of this collection (Russell, Slaney, Qu & Houston 2006). Enhancing our understanding of the ways people structure collections of personal information and the role this plays in sense-making is important if we are to provide better support for PIM.

3.4.1 *Outstanding Challenges*

How should a person's information be organized? Or can people effectively keep information for later use and repeated reuse without bothering much about information organization? For some people in some situations, the answer may be that organization is not that important.

But for other people, in other situations, their own intelligent efforts to structure and organize information are critical to the creation of supporting external representations of a project or problem. Results from the field of cognitive science are intriguing even if the connection is by no means direct. For example, the right diagram can allow one to make inferences more quickly (Larkin & Simon 1987). The way information is externally represented can produce huge differences in a person's ability to use this information in short-duration, problem-solving exercises (Kotovsky, Hayes & Simon 1985). Different kinds of representations, like matrices and hierarchies, are useful in different types of problems (Cheng 2002; Novick 1990; Novick, Hurley & Francis 1999).

There is also a large body of research from the field of library and information science (LIS) addressing questions concerning the organization of information in a library (e.g., Chan 1994; Taylor 2004). What about the organization of *personal* libraries (music, photographs, articles)? Again, although the mapping is not direct, we might still hope for some transfer of knowledge.

For example, in KFTF studies, participants' folder structures often reveal a tension that is certainly familiar to researchers in LIS between organizing in a project-centric way for current use versus organizing information into collections of similar items (images, articles, recipes, photos) for repeated reuse. Organization for current use is often hierarchical according to the structure of the current project, whereas organization for reuse is often more property-based.

Figure 3.4.1 depicts a situation in which a college professor has several "Images" and "Readings" subfolders scattered under containing folders representing courses that he teaches. The professor also has "Images" and "Articles" folders that stand by themselves separate from current courses. File names in these larger folders seem to follow a naming scheme that encodes distinguishing property information. Article files, for example, are named by concatenating the first author, year of publication, and title (or a key phrase from the title).

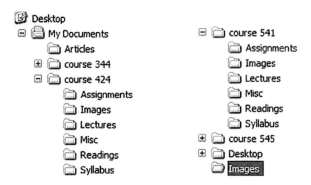

Figure 3.4.1 – Images are organized both for current use (as subfolders under course project folders) and for repeated re-use (in a single larger folder).

Research in fields such as the cognitive sciences and LIS may guide not only the development of supporting tools but also the development of teachable techniques and strategies of PIM. How do we manage for current use and repeated reuse? How do we manage for multiple versions or key variations of the same document (presentation, spreadsheet, etc.)?

More generally, a quest continues to better understand how people manage their information and to discover how they might manage better. Better support for organizing information may help some people to bring the pieces together—in their information and also in their lives.

NOTES

1. The subject of individual differences and PIM is considered in greater depth in chapter 13.
2. When memories for filing an item fade, full-text search can provide an alternate way of getting back to an item. But not always. A search for "expense report" AND "Denver" for example, may return no matches (perhaps because "expense report" is not actually in the item) or may return too many matches (if trips to Denver are common).
3. These particpants made it clear in their comments that these transformations—from e-documents to email, for example, or from email to file—were done in order to consolidate so that only one or a smaller number of organizations needed to be maintained. Other participants sometimes transformed items as needed in order to bridge gaps between different information organizations or to realize features present in one form of information not present in another. Many particpants reported, for example, sending documents in email to bridge between home and work computers.
4. The participant used the Microsoft Windows XP operating system.

4 How People Manage Personal Information Over a Lifetime

Catherine C. Marshall

4.1 Introduction

How will we manage our heterogeneous collections of digital information over a lifetime? How will we look through many decades worth of digital belongings? What will our digital legacy be? We can think of long-term PIM issues from three equally important perspectives: (1) storing the digital belongings we have amassed over the years (long-term storage); (2) maintaining these belongings in a form that allows them to be viewed, used, or possibly even changed (preservation); and (3) providing individual and collaborative mechanisms for reclaiming these belongings from long-term digital storage (access).

4.1.1 *Scenarios Characterizing Important Long-Term PIM Issues*

Many PIM scenarios are focused on immediate information needs and uses; for example, browsing through vacation photos to find one to send to a favorite aunt, or gathering the right documents to prepare for a meeting. The following vignettes couple the characters created for this book with interview data collected during recent studies to highlight longer-term issues.

Predicting value and metaphors for long-term access. Brooke tapes two tickets to her dressing-table mirror to remind herself that she's going to a concert Wednesday night with Derek and some other friends. After the concert, she tacks one of the ticket stubs to the wall of her cube at work as a memento of a wild evening. After the start-up goes under and she brings her personal items home, the ticket stub goes into her "treasure box," an old footlocker she keeps in the guest room closet. Originally this personal information is kept in sight to remind Brooke when the concert is and to give her an emotional lift as she anticipates the event. After the concert, the ticket stub changes roles—it becomes a reminder of a fun evening in the recent past. Finally, Brooke puts her ticket stub in a place she expects that she'll encounter it again—possibly many years later—and that this small ragged piece of printed cardboard will evoke a number of associated memories. She'd never think to go looking for a ticket stub, but she knows that when she sees it again it will not only remind her of the concert, but also of her friends, her musical tastes, and a whole period of her life. The value of the ticket changes as time passes: Brooke could have tossed the stub after the concert or when she took down the things pinned to her cube wall, but instead she has elected to keep it "forever."

Digital context. Alex has performed research on an esoteric topic intermittently since he was in college; it's his secret—not even his family knows he's interested in Rongorongo. He has even published several papers about the Easter Island script and saved numerous resources he has discovered on the Internet. He has cited some of the articles in his publications, but others he has not. In fact, he hasn't even read all of them, but he keeps the whole collection with the idea that he'll refer to the articles when he needs to and read them carefully—when he has time. Some are from the gray literature and, as such, have not been published through normal commercial channels (Wood 1984), but others are retrieved from digital libraries and special collections. Although he acknowledges that it would be easy to recover the resources, he feels that if he lost them he would never be able to remember them all. He has even considered making an index for his collection, so that if anything happened to his computer he would know which articles he'd lost.

Distributed storage and format opacity. Felicia is Derek's younger sister. Like many people, Felicia's most important personal information management concern is maintaining her photos so she'll have them when she's older. She's in college now, but she already has collected a substantial number of photos. She cares for some of them herself—particularly those she has taken using her digital camera—but her mother still takes care of those she considers "family photos." Felicia's own photos are by no means stored in one place: she has printed some to organize in traditional albums and to tape to her bedroom door; others are digital-only, stored on the hard drive of her laptop and on photo CDs in a cabinet. Still other photo CDs are scattered around her room; sometimes they get mixed in with her music CDs and software. She lost several batches of photos in a recent crash that she attributes to a virus she got from sharing music on Limewire. Felicia does not consider herself to be a computer expert and usually enlists Derek's help when she has computer troubles like this virus. She knows her camera can produce several different resolutions and formats—and that some of the applications she uses to manipulate the photos produce files that her friends can't display—but she's never confident about which format to use and just uses the default settings.

Curatorial effort and predicting value. Derek has kept his email for as long as he can remember; he keeps both school-related email, especially for the attachments, and personal correspondence. Both are important to him: his school email serves as a means for maintaining a record of his work—he knows he'll dip back into it when he's studying for the bar—and his personal email acts as a journal and an index into his rich store of memories. It is also storage of the last resort: if he can't find a file in his primary computer's file system, he looks for it in his email. He has even sent attachments and other important bits of information to himself to ensure he has copies available at all times. In spite of the varied and important roles that email plays in his life, Derek maintains that he wouldn't be overly upset if he lost his current email file—all 11,000 messages—in part because it is such a troublesome accumulation of content. He never feels like it has been properly culled and he doesn't know how to back it up.

4.1.2 *The Importance of Long-Term Personal Information Management*

From these vignettes, and from growing attention in the digital library community (Beagrie 2005) and the news media (Hafner 2004), it should be evident that storing and maintaining personal information over the long haul is an important topic that raises particularly challenging issues in a digital environment. These issues cover significant technical, social, and legal territory. Technically, we must address the storage, preservation, and long-term access of digital materials. Socially, we need to consider the roles of various emerging genres (such as blogs and personal Web sites) in our culture and over the course of our lives, including how and when we want others to have access to them and how we can make these things we have saved intelligible to others. Legally, we must consider how personal digital materials interact with the holdings of other online services (such as personal financial records that are held by a bank), as well as how material protected by Digital Rights Management (DRM) (Stefik 1999) may be preserved, and how a personal archive can contain materials that are drawn from digital libraries and other stores of copyrighted material.

Despite the acknowledged importance of digital personal information, it is difficult to convince many people of the urgency of this problem. On one hand, we have been trained to approach technological progress with an air of optimism: by the time we want to open the 50-year-old photos of our children, a viewer will have been implemented to decode whatever obsolete format they were stored in and will render the photos with perfect fidelity on the display of the moment. This perspective goes hand in hand with the strategy of benign neglect that most people apply to keeping their physical personal materials. Photos, letters, legal and financial records, and other important keepsakes are tossed into boxes (or, at best, filed carefully) and put somewhere safe, in an attic, under the bed, in a safety deposit box, or in a closet, and left undisturbed for many years. Thus, many of us believe we are accumulating our valuable digital stuff in a small number of circumscribed places, and when the time comes, we expect to be able to simply pull out the files and look at them in much the same way as we would look at our second-grade class picture in the box on the closet shelf.

On the other hand, digital information invites an attitude of radical ephemeralism. We have all lost digital materials, and by now many people tend to view disk crashes, computer viruses, and media obsolescence with a certain sense of inevitability. They commonly use the metaphor of a house fire and assert that one must simply move on. From this perspective, we cannot expect to have any of our personal digital information in 50 years; it will be long gone and we might as well get used to it.

In practice, most people inhabit a space somewhere in between these two caricatures and recognize themselves in both extremes. They know they should make copies of valuable files; they know they should worry about the life span of various digital storage media; they believe they should cull the valuable files lest they get lost amid an accumulation of indifferent digital dross; they believe that digital formats can be converted without loss to newer formats; and they suspect that anything they have found rather than created can be found again through clever searching (Marshall, Bly & Brun-Cottan 2006). But everyday human actions belie these good intentions: files are not copied; storage media are not refreshed; and digital files accumulate at a frightening rate. Simply put, benign neglect will not be sufficient to keep our digital things safe for a lifetime.

4.2 Research Overview: PIM Archiving Issue

Libraries and cultural heritage institutions—along with records management organizations—have long grappled with archiving problems and were among the first to address digital archiving issues. These institutions have been joined by other disciplines on the forefront of the production and use of digital information, the digital arts and sciences, as well as folk historians and Internet guardians. But are they all talking about the same thing when they talk about digital archiving? Not really, but there is considerable overlap in their missions and shared concern with literally preserving the bits that represent heterogeneous digital materials, ensuring that we will have access to them and be able to view or use them in the future. At the very least, digital preservation efforts must address issues associated with storage media (such as reliability, durability, and media format), hardware and software environments (operating systems, drivers, and shared libraries), application-specific formats and functionality (file formats and codecs), and display capabilities (resolution, fonts, and color). Figure 4.2 illustrates some of the additional concerns that different disciplinary practices and institutions bring to the table.

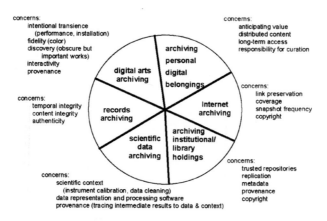

Figure 4.2 – Digital archiving concerns arising from different disciplinary practices and institutions

This diversity of interests may make the problem seem hopelessly complex; but instead we can view each discipline as providing traction on a slightly different set of issues. For example, e-science archiving efforts are establishing best practices for managing distributed datasets. Digital arts archiving is addressing tricky questions associated with preserving the interactivity or visual fidelity of a handcrafted work. Records archivists are developing techniques that may be used to maintain the integrity of our personal records. Libraries are driving the development of institutional repositories (Tansley, Bass, Stuve, et al. 2003), canonicalization and migration procedures (Lynch 1999), and replication techniques (Cooper & Garcia-Molina 2002). Finally, the Internet Archive is implementing policies and methods for preserving large-scale hyperlinked structures (Lyman & Kahle 1998). In short, although the problems are far from solved, substantial efforts and programs are underway (Arms 2000).

But what of the requirements that are unique to personal digital archiving? Naturally, personal archiving revolves around the same basic technological issues as other types of digital archiving—how materials are stored; how they may be preserved, and how long-term access may be supported—but if we reexamine these issues from a PIM perspective, there is still much work to do.

In this chapter, we consider seven key attributes of personal digital belongings that should shape our development of archiving technologies:

1. Digital material accumulates quickly, obscuring those items that have long-term value;
2. Digital material is distributed over many different off- and online stores, making it difficult to keep track of individual items;
3. Digital material derives a substantial amount of meaning from context that may not be preserved with an item (for example, references to email attachments, links to Web pages, and application-specific metadata);
4. Digital material is easily passed around and replicated, introducing a tension between protection (of privacy, copyright, and security) and future access;
5. Digital formats are not only opaque to many users, but may also be incompatible with available applications or may become obsolete;
6. Curating personal digital archives is time-consuming and requires specialized skills; and
7. Our current computing environments have yet to incorporate mechanisms and metaphors that support long-term access.

Predicting value. Most personal information in the digital world is not collected intentionally as part of a coherent collection; instead heterogeneous materials accumulate invisibly over time. Because it is inherently difficult to anticipate future value even among professionals trained to evaluate and discard (Baker 2001; Levy 1998), personal digital belongings often accumulate very quickly. This trend has been exacerbated by drastic reductions in storage cost; it seems much cheaper to keep everything than it does to assume the overhead of up-front evaluation of individual items (Beagrie 2005; Gray & Shenoy 2000). Furthermore, personal digital belongings have varying lifecycles; some of the accumulated items are valuable for a decade, some for a lifetime, and some beyond, and few of us can tell the difference. The complexity of the digital lifecycle lends further credence to the argument that we should keep everything and worry about decoding or evaluating it later (Cutrell, Robbins, Dumais & Sarin 2006; Gemmell, Bell, Lueder, et al. 2002).

However, there have been serious critiques of the "keep everything" approach because of its eventual consequences, chiefly the effect that having too much has on human attention (Jones 2004). There is also a profound question about the emotional or economic viability of keeping everything, even if it isn't visible, as suggested in Czerwinski, Gage, Gemmell, et al. (2006); discarding unwanted or unpleasant material is often a valuable exercise and it may even be legally mandated in some situations (for example, personal information that belongs to an employer).

Distributed storage. Personal information is often stored in a distributed way—on the hard drives of different home and work computers, on removable storage media, on remote servers, on personal devices, and printed as hard copy. Not only does this distribution cause people to lose track of where specific digital belongings are and which version of a file is the most recent, but digital storage media are also vulnerable to failure, obsolescence, and loss, and may be unreliable from the outset.

One way digital belongings become distributed is through replication, often for safety's sake. For example, a person might save and share favorite pictures in multiple places: on a local hard drive, on external media such as CDs, on photo-sharing services such as Flickr, on personal Web sites (often provided through hosting services), on camera memory cards, and on friends' and family members' computers (possibly in their email). While this replication provides a simple and effective safety net, it also introduces curatorial complications such as identifying the preferred version for a particular use (e.g., choosing among photos stored at different resolutions) or retaining appropriate metadata (e.g., the real creation date).

Digital context. Archival best practices require careful attention to preserving the material's original *context*. Thus when we wrestle with the problem of the long-term maintenance of personal digital belongings, we can't simply attend to each digital object as a stand-alone item, but rather we need to capture the characteristics that make it part of a whole. For example, a digital photo is more than just the image content: it is also the metadata the camera records, the metadata the photographer adds (for example, tags to identify the subject of the photo), and its membership in a set of photos the photographer has taken at the same event. It may be attached to an email message, included in a blog posting, or shared on a Web site. One of the most powerful aspects of maintaining digital materials in their original form (rather than, for example, saving them in print) is that it provides a context in which these materials may be kept alive over time. However, preserving a large, distributed, linked structure and its metadata is a daunting problem (Lyman & Kahle 1998). Furthermore, context may be lost when digital belongings are moved to new computers or accessed by different applications. For example, a file creation date is often lost when the file is copied or moved. From our vignette describing Derek's personal digital library, it is easy to see how the metadata may be as important (or more important) than the item itself.

Conflicting interests of protection and long-term maintenance. Individuals, institutions, and organizations all have an interest in protecting their digital belongings from unwanted access, unauthorized use, or digital piracy. They gravitate toward strong solutions such as encryption or DRM in addition to minimal protection such as passwords. While these solutions provide attractive short-term protection, over the long term they may inhibit the ability to preserve and access the data they are protecting (Lavoie & Dempsey 2004). For example, passwords and encryption help us keep personal information private; however, they may also render it inaccessible as passwords are forgotten or encryption keys are lost. Copyright protection such as DRM may make publishers more comfortable with the safety of their intellectual property; however, DRM can prevent individuals from taking appropriate preservation measures (such as creating extra copies or migrating content to newer formats).

Format opacity, incompatibility, and obsolescence. Most straightforward strategies for the long-term management of personal information are complicated by *format opacity* and a growing number of standard formats, many of them incompatible, and some already obsolete. Format opacity mainly arises from the desire to keep complexity hidden from the user. For example, instead of asking a user whether she wants to encode her video in MPEG-1 or MPEG-2, an interface might ask whether the video will be saved on a CD or a DVD. The user may not be aware of the consequences of using one format over another; for example, codecs may be unavailable for certain platforms.

Curatorial effort. Institutional archiving is time-consuming and costly. Often solutions that require user action (for example, converting files to canonical formats like PDF, or assigning metadata values) also mandate that institutions introduce incentives (or punishments) to ensure participation (Beagrie 2003). This problem is exacerbated for PIM. Many individuals keep their computing environments running by enlisting ad hoc IT support—relatives, friends, or colleagues who perform common system administration tasks on their behalf, such as installing new applications, setting up new peripheral devices, or coping with malware infections (Marshall et al. 2006). These ad hoc IT people have varying degrees of knowledge and sometimes come into conflict with one another. Any sort of long-term personal archiving technology will need to consider the demands it places on this variable support environment; the success of a solution may depend on its ability to run without significant intervention.

Long-term access challenges. One of the most provocative problems that arises from personal archiving is one of access. Clearly you can't deliberately look for something that you don't remember you have, so even the most functional desktop search is no panacea (Marshall & Jones 2006). In fact, field studies often reveal that not only do people forget particular items that they've saved; they also forget entire categories of saved material or places that they've stored treasured items (Bruce, Jones & Dumais 2004; Marshall & Bly 2005; Whittaker & Sidner 1996). They believe they have kept things that they haven't and they are surprised by what they do find in their long-term stores. This experience of keeping valuable material (or what is conceived of as valuable material at storage time) in a specific well-known place—such as the box under the bed—leads us away from the desktop metaphor and into a realm of place and value. While these storage places for valued material may share some of the properties of the desktop—they may be well organized and highly structured, or they may be informal catchalls, or some of both—the desktop is aimed at short-term information management strategies, not for keeping a lifetime's worth of belongings.

4.3 Case Study: A Long-Term Collection of Email Correspondence

In this section we describe an effort to assemble a single archive from six years' worth of email between two correspondents, M and Q; this description captures some archiving issues and allows us to introduce technologies to address them. Over the six-year period, close to 1,400 unique messages—800 pages of text—were exchanged. Both correspondents value and save their email, much as other people value and exchange photos.[1] Unifying separate email streams into a single archive for storage is important both for preservation (canonicalizing the formats) and for access (mostly done through selective browsing, not through targeted search).

In the past, benign neglect was sufficient to ensure that old letters would survive into the future; people would bundle them together with a ribbon, put them in the box under the bed, then be able to read them 60 years later. Putting only six years' worth of email into a coherent archive entailed a significant amount of effort and was at times a test of IT skills. In principal, it would have required far less effort with automated support for "real" archiving.[2] We will explore each of the issues we discussed in the last section as they apply to this email archive.

Predicting the value of email. Even though both correspondents thought of the entire archive as valuable chronicle of their lives during the six-year period, the individual exchanges varied greatly in their archival worth. This value discrepancy mainly stemmed from the fact that the email spanned the normal range of message types (Boardman & Sasse 2004). Messages used to coordinate face-to-face meetings ("See you at Bridgepointe at 1:30") or just to keep in touch may be less valuable later on than messages that were more substantive[3]. Even the substantive messages varied greatly in tone and worth. Some contained everyday news; others were ruminative; and still others were accounts of crises and remarkable circumstances.

This unpredictable variety of content ensures that there is no easy way to filter it for the most interesting messages; nor would a search capability stand alone as a mode of access to the collection. Much like other material saved over a long period of time, some crucial elements have been forgotten, and others have changed in function. In the next section, we will discuss the implications of value on heuristics for visualizing and accessing a long-term accumulation of digital belongings.

Distributed storage of email. Many people manage multiple email accounts. They may have a variety of motivations for doing so: to separate personal and work correspondence; to address various limitations of their various computing environments (for example, some email accounts are better suited to receive or send attachments and some have size limits); or to maintain a multiplicity of identities coupled with divergent interests (for example, people who participate in online dating or auctions often have separate identities for these specialized activities). Yet the exigencies of real-world situations dictate that this separation may not be strictly maintained. People receive personal email at work; their separate identities blend; and they violate their own policies for using one account over another. To make matters more complicated, some email storage is server-based; some is client- or device-based; and some allows people to maintain distributed collections. Thus, the trend is toward distributed materials.

Our illustrative case is no exception. Over the six years covered by the archive, Q and M each used six different email accounts, some personal and some professional, to support their correspondence. While the email in question formed a single conceptual collection, the de facto archive was fragmented and difficult to reintegrate. Figure 4.3 illustrates this fragmentation; each email account is shown according to the duration it was active. The gray bars represent local storage, white corresponds to device-based storage, and black indicates client-side storage. For example, from this visualization, we can see that during the second quarter of 2000, Q's mail might have been sent or received using any of four different accounts and M's might have been sent or received from any of three accounts.

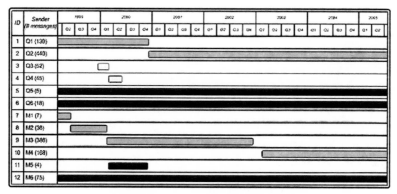

Figure 4.3 – Long-term use creates a distributed collection,
with multiple email accounts active at any given time.

The flip side of distribution and replication is redundancy. A coherent browsable archive must anticipate redundancy to support future access. Some redundancy is planned as risk-reducing replication (for example, an entire personal email file may be copied to a server). Other redundancy stems from common practices such as including the whole of the thread in the current message or cc'ing oneself to make the email accessible from another account. Over time, redundancy is both a safety net and an annoyance. For example, an included thread may contain the only copy of a message; on the other hand, messages sent to two or three accounts means that there will be multiple copies of these messages in a merged archive.

Digital context as attachments and URLs. Increasingly, personal email is not a stand-alone collection of messages that refer only to one another (Whittaker, Bellotti & Gwizdka 2006). Two distinct phenomena add complexity to the long-term sustainability of email: (1) references to external material using URLs or links to Web pages, and (2) attached material such as formatted documents, photos, and other email (which paradoxically may be in a format unintelligible to the individual's own email application). Some of these references and attachments are transient and do not contribute substantially to the value of the exchange, such as jokes and newspaper clippings sent as "thinking of you" gestures (Marshall & Bly 2005). But others, such as personal photos, are valuable additions to the archive; in fact, email is an important mechanism for keeping this kind of material (Bruce et al. 2004). Furthermore, some of these references, while not significant in and of themselves, may be vital to understanding an elliptical discussion. Yet it is relatively common to lose both Web references and attachments over the life of an email archive, in spite of existing functionality that makes it easy to save them at the time of receipt.

Let's look at a few of the attachments and references to identify some common problems. Most simply, attachments may be missing: they may have been downloaded and deleted at the time of receipt. Similarly, references may point to missing Web pages or sites, which is unsurprising since the average Web page is only active 44 days (Lyman 2002). Sometimes the Web pages themselves have been attached to messages; unless the sender has been careful, this may result in incomplete content (e.g., images or component frames may be missing). Furthermore Web pages are at best fluid; when accessed later, the content may be changed so as to render the reference nonsensical.

Thus, retrieving and preserving the content at the time of original access seems like a sensible strategy for ensuring that the intelligibility of the exchange is maintained. But this not only creates technical problems—it is yet another window onto the general problem of preservation—it also requires attention to the fair use provisions of copyright law. How much external content may be kept without further permission? What about attachments like newspaper clippings that are free when they are current, but must be retrieved for a fee later on? It is easy to see that any solution is not without attendant complications.

Conflicting interests of protection and maintenance: the case of the missing password. Personal email is usually private; thus in the case study we might expect problems arising from the correspondents' efforts to ensure privacy. Fortunately this did not involve tackling the problem of missing encryption keys; instead passwords were used to protect email stored locally.

Unsurprisingly, all of Q's email is password-protected. Server-side passwords are usually easy to recover by contacting a system administrator or issuing an automated password request. In fact, these email stores will not become problematic until the account owner is no longer capable of accessing them. At that point, the tide will turn, since no provision has been made for changes in who may see the email (Czerwinski et al. 2006). This seemingly remote possibility has proven to be a very real obstacle in military situations in which soldiers' email cannot be accessed by relatives after the soldiers' deaths.

The inactive Microsoft Outlook file (Q1 in Figure 4.3) is the stream we will focus on. It was stored locally on a household computer, one shared by other family members and houseguests; thus password protection seemed prudent. Over time the password was forgotten and could not be reconstructed by normal means such as trial and error or consulting likely-looking scraps of paper. The email was adjudged to be sufficiently valuable to justify the cost of attempting a break-in. Efforts to locate instructions and a utility to remove a local password were successful, but opened the door to malware (the software could not be obtained from a trusted source) and damaged message headers, including dates.

From this simple example, it is apparent how security interests may render older personal information inaccessible. Security may be too effective to be so easily thwarted, even by the originating parties; issues of trust may make it difficult to choose an acceptable solution if it involves running a strange executable; or the problem may be too longstanding to be addressed by solutions currently available.

Format incompatibility of merged email. Streams Q1 through Q6 are stored in four different email formats, reflecting the different applications used to manage the email. If these streams are stored without the application used to manage them (a common archiving scenario), they may be indecipherable later; they will require canonicalization either at merge time or when they are displayed. Not only must the formats be renderable, but also they must be made *readable*. An important consequence of format differences, genre shifts, and mail application conventions, defaults, and options is that a merged stream may be difficult to read. For example, forwarding, replying, and device characteristics all result in odd line-breaks. Although on the face of it this seems like a relatively minor problem, it detracts from the experience of reading emotionally valuable old email.

Although it can be argued that email presents special formatting issues, there are more profound challenges in other media, especially as it accumulates over time. In some cases, such as digital video, shifting standards and ever-improving resolution and capabilities represent a rendering quagmire—just preserving the ability to view the digital object is the central aim of many standardization efforts and much research. To achieve some kinds of stability, such as stabilizing a document's appearance, special archival formats such as PDF/A have been proposed (LeFurgy 2003). To maintain the editability of a document, others have speculated that fully emulative solutions are necessary (Rothenberg 1998), although such emulation solutions must be justified by use, since full emulative fidelity may be more expensive than it looks at the outset (Reichherzer & Brown 2006). Still other digital belongings may require attention to interactivity (Marshall & Golovchinsky 2004; Wardrip-Fruin 1999). This aspect of preservation is perhaps the most thoroughly investigated in a variety of domains; it is wise not to become too embroiled in this single issue at the expense of the others.

Curatorial effort in assembling and maintaining an email archive. Our observations about the time-consuming and often difficult nature of digital curation are borne out by the case study. Not only was the construction of the unified archive labor intensive, but even maintaining the separate streams of email over long periods presented challenges. As we have already noted, it is not uncommon for an individual to manage multiple email streams involving different applications, devices, and stores.

First, let's consider the personal/professional separation (the Outlook email files in our case study); these are tied to work email accounts on Exchange servers. Curation usually starts to be an issue when the individual leaves a job; personal email must be culled from the work email that must be left behind. Moving Outlook .pst files is not straightforward; they are not located in a place in the file system that consumers are apt to be familiar with, nor can they be moved using a straightforward copy. For those people who consider email as a fundamental PIM record, the files may also be very large. Furthermore, attachments require separate attention if they are to be moved and tracked with the email stream; they are often stored in temporary directories that are ignored by utilities. Maintaining the Outlook .pst files thus requires specialized knowledge and cannot be left to benign neglect.

Next, let's consider the ubiquitous free server-side email accounts. Often they seem to require little or no maintenance; in fact, consumers are increasingly relying on the archival properties of these email accounts (Marshall et al. 2006). However, there is no assurance in the end user license agreements that this email will be stored permanently. Without curatorial attention, these accounts represent a paradoxically chimerical form of archiving: most consumers have no idea how they would reclaim the content of this type of email stream if they decided to abandon the account or the provider stopped offering this service. The demonstrated consumer impulse is to go through the messages, copying them one by one if the email is perceived to be at risk. Surely this is not a viable curatorial strategy.

Long-term access of email in the case study. It is easy to defer the problem of long-term access to the powers of search: desktop search and techniques like Implicit Query (Cutrell et al. 2006) have improved greatly in recent years. But is search going to be the only mode of access to many years' worth of personal digital belongings? Certainly it will address information-needs scenarios: a lost piece of financial information, a dimly remembered photo from one's childhood, or the name of a friend of a friend. However, in our case study, much of the reason for keeping the correspondence is far less tangible; it will be used to remember times, people, and places not documented anywhere else.

That said, it is a considerable volume of text. How might interesting or valuable content be highlighted? It is tempting to think that we can organize an archive according to the information in a personal gazetteer. Analogous to a geographical gazetteer, a personal gazetteer might draw on records from an individual's calendar, contacts, and maps to create a database of important people, places, and events. This technique would combine the work on gazetteer-based digital reference services (Buckland 2004) with automated personal media organizers such as those described by Graham, Garcia-Molina, Paepcke, and Winograd (2002).

However, such heuristics should be approached with caution. If we look at the material gathered in the case study, important events (birthdays, holidays, and the like) are acknowledged, but they are more often the occasion for platitudes and brief greetings ("As the Subject line says, Happy Birthday! ... We'll have to do something to celebrate.") On the other hand, remarkable events—uncomfortable Match.com coffee dates, alarming nightmares, and unexpected conversations—are more likely to spur the kind of documentation that is evocative and worth rereading. Breakups are not on the calendar, nor in a hypothetical personal gazetteer:

> Unfortunately, things didn't turn out better than expected this time.
> D. broke up with me yesterday evening. (Actually, I had to practically
> play 20 questions to get him to actually do it.) He wants to be friends.
> Gross. I had to tell him twice I thought he should leave before he
> actually got up and left.

It is the unexpected nature of these events, and the details told in accounts of them, that make the email interesting to browse.

Message characteristics such as length, structure, threadedness, and temporal proximity are apt to be better predictors of value than content semantics; these intrinsic properties are readily available from the header (if it is intact) or from straightforward analysis. Unsurprisingly, in our example corpus, longer messages were more interesting than shorter ones. Messages with many short paragraphs signified newsiness. Longer messages sent after a long period of silence often flagged an important event. On the other hand, the tail of a longish thread—often consisting of short messages sent close together—usually proved to be of less long-term interest. As past studies have shown, the subject field is often uninformative in predicting the value of a message (Whittaker & Sidner 1996). In this case, many subjects were simply openings (e.g., "wassup?" or "you're probably in Portland") and had little to do with the extended content of the message. As Whittaker and Sidner noted, message replies are a convenient way of reinitiating contact, so a message with a subject line, "Re: Amused about the slammer," probably has strayed from the original subject. In practice, even though both correspondents were familiar with the other's email address and used autocomplete, about two-thirds of the messages were written using the "Reply to" feature, often with little concern for whether they were actually replies.

How can we visualize a collection like this as a whole? Work on visualizing email archives has focused on the ebb and flow of relationships among correspondents or social ties (Donath 2004; Perer, Shneiderman & Oard 2005) and is more oriented toward characterizing academic collaboration, rather than on this more ruminative or emotive kind of correspondence between two friends. In the concluding section, long-term access techniques for other types of material will be discussed in greater depth.

Despite the fact that email might be considered a very different kind of PIM content than, say, a digital photo collection or an accumulation of personal documents in a file system, the case study demonstrates that email raises many of the same long-term issues related to storage, preservation, and access as these other types of personal digital content.

4.4 Looking Forward

Given the seriousness and ubiquity of the issues, several questions come to mind. Is personal digital archiving an insoluble problem? Should we give up and simply regard our digital belongings as transient? Or should we be digital Pollyannas and keep buying more and more storage with the hopes that both storage media and the bitstreams written on them will still be viable and decodable when we want to see them again?

It is clearly more productive to focus on the most important and tractable of the issues now, while we can still implement up-front strategies and before too much has been lost. Problems directly related to storage, preservation, and access require technology development. Other issues—for example, the balance between content protection using various security mechanisms and the ease of reclaiming the content in individual and collaborative settings—must be worked out socially and legally as well as technologically. Still other issues, such as curation, rely on pragmatic attention to the dovetail between technology and practice. Even if in principle people are happy to take curatorial responsibility for their digital belongings, we have observed that in practice, people don't apply even the simplest of digital safekeeping strategies and their beliefs about digital media, technologies, and the networked information environment are often contradictory and riddled with misconceptions (Marshall et al. 2006).

In the storage arena, tools for managing distributed content and techniques for stabilizing digital references are two areas for future work that emerge readily from this discussion. The management of distributed content can take advantage of a federated index (Jantz 2005) rather than fully merging streams into a single database. It is unrealistic to conceive of one's digital belongings as being held in a single store, especially in the intermediate term; we can expect personal information to continue to be distributed among multiple stores, including server-based email, digital libraries and archives, trusted personal records repositories held by institutions like banks and the government, and storage-based media-sharing services like Flickr.

Similarly, sophisticated preservation techniques—such as format registries (Arms & Fleischhauer 2005), universal virtual machines (Lorie 2002), format migration services (Hunter & Choudhury 2004), or emulation and decoding services (Heminger & Robertson 1998)—and digital archiving practices (Hodge 2000; Smith 2005) are under development in academic and institutional settings. There is ample reason to believe that these techniques and practices will be applicable to personal digital materials, especially if digital belongings are preserved according to the best practices of specific genres. Records may best be preserved with the specialized techniques developed by records archivists; the consumer imaging industry has developed its own techniques and standards for archiving image collections (for example, see http://www.everplay-spec.org/); and Web-based material may benefit from lazy preservation (Smith, McCown & Nelson 2006).

However, it is important to acknowledge that the cost structure of these preservation activities will be different for individuals than they are for institutions; cost/benefit trade-offs must be evaluated. Before we jump into a costly emulation strategy, for example, it would be wise to consider use. Are we emulating a complicated digital application that runs in a particular computing environment so we can render a modified photograph? The emulation will be far more important if we want to further modify the photograph than it will be if we simply want to view it. Many promising preservation strategies involve encapsulating multiple representations of a single digital object (Jantz & Giarlo 2005). These preservation strategies allow the original version to be retained for reasons of provenance. Furthermore, if any canonicalization or migration steps are loss-y, they can be redone later. Finally, this approach supports emulation if it is required but does not mandate it if it is not.

Access technologies provide us with the most wiggle room in the immediate future. They can safely be developed over time on top of the other technological solutions as accumulations of personal digital belongings expand and our understanding of long-term use continues to develop. Promising personal information access directions include:

1. Automatically generated visualizations that provide us with an overall gestalt of what we have (see chapter 7);

2. Manually defined and circumscribed digital places and geographies that give us the digital equivalent of "the box under the bed" (for the most valued stuff) and "remote storage lockers" (for the things we aren't sure we'll continue to want);

3. Heuristics for detecting the relative value of individual items, because people demonstrate the worth of their belongings much more reliably than they declare it; and

4. Methods and tools for examining individual items that reveal an item's provenance and help increase its intelligibility (to oneself and possibly to others)—for example by allowing a user to distinguish among related copies of an item (Marshall 2006).

Table 4.4 summarizes long-term PIM technologies; it is not intended to be a comprehensive set of technologies, but rather it is representative of promising directions.

Issue	Item-level technologies	Repository-level technologies	Accumulation-level technologies
Predicting value	Heuristics for assessing item value as a function of demonstrated worth, emotional impact, creative effort, and reconstitutability.	Services that maintain records of value and context; access methods that rank items by value.	Inter-repository services, e.g., tools that help users distinguish among multiple copies of an item.
Distributed storage	Automated replication methods; digital object surrogates that represent content held elsewhere.	Repositories that combine surrogates for distributed objects with local content.	Federated indices; inter-repository communication.
Digital context	Up-front techniques for gathering and storing context for objects and collections.		
Protection vs. maintenance	Mechanisms to track protection schemes and help consumers recover protected items and collections.		
Format	Digital object models that encapsulate multiple representations.	Repository-based automated canonicalization and migration.	Format migration services; emulation and decoding services; format registries.
Curatorial effort	Services similar to Symantec's Genesis and Microsoft's OneCare, where much of the curatorial effort is performed remotely on the consumer's behalf.		
Long-term access	Retrieval time tools for inspecting an item's provenance and context	Circumscribed digital places coupled with collection visualization techniques	Exploratory visualization and knowledge discovery to discover patterns

Table 4.4 – Examples of Promising Technological Approaches

Understanding individuals' needs and the characteristics of the global information environment will help us develop a viable approach to personal archiving. A strong use perspective can prevent us from taking on the most general—and often the most costly and most difficult—problems. For example, suppose we agree that to preserve email context we need to save external Web references. Understanding anticipated use will tell us whether we need to preserve a single destination page or crawl the destination site and preserve multiple pages and their interconnections (Lyman & Kahle 1998). It will also tell us whether the page can be preserved as a static view, where the emphasis is on content and visual appearance, or whether the destination's full interactivity needs to be maintained (Marshall & Golovchinsky 2004; Wardrip-Fruin 1999). Understanding the global information environment will tell us whether we need to cache the page or pages up front or whether we can rely on lazy preservation methods to reconstruct it later (Smith, McCown & Nelson 2006).

In 1998, Terry Kuny suggested that we may be entering a digital dark age due to our lack of a coherent socially based strategy for addressing the long-term issues raised by the transition from physical documents to digital (Kuny 1998). Not only are our cultural assets at risk; so too are our personal digital belongings. Personal information management must be approached not only with an eye toward the information overload and task-management problems of here and now, but also with attention to how our digital belongings will survive into the future.

NOTES

1. It should be noted that the literary letter is considered an imperiled form due to the shift to electronic communication (Donadio 2004); we expect email archiving to become part of managing special collections.
2. Many email systems allow one to archive messages, but it is not archiving in the sense that the word is used here. It is archiving relative to that particular email application and it is primarily designed to sort inactive mail from active mail.
3. Although, much like the ticket stub in our introductory vignettes, a brief coordination message may change its role over time, after the event has taken place.

5 Naturalistic Approaches for Understanding PIM

Charles M. Naumer and Karen E. Fisher

5.1 Introduction

In this chapter we discuss how personal information management (PIM) behavior may be studied using naturalistic approaches. For our purposes, personal information management behavior is defined very broadly to include information communicated and stored in multiple formats, including verbally, in print, and in digital format. In later chapters, research methods used to evaluate PIM tools will be discussed.

As the term implies, personal information management entails the way individuals manage their personal information over the course of a day, a month, a year or, a lifetime. The process of managing information may span several different personal contexts at once (Kelly 2006). A person may have many different roles, such as that of a professional, a parent, and a community member. The process of managing personal information crosses these invisible boundaries. PIM cannot be relegated to one category at a time since personal information and methods for managing it may move between these contextual boundaries.

Naturalistic inquiry is holistic and contextual, concerning itself with the natural setting of the actors—or people of concern—and the context(s) in which they are immersed. In this way, naturalistic inquiry may lend itself to understanding human behavior in terms broader than the workplace or interactions with a specific technology. Naturalistic inquiry may be used to study PIM in terms of everyday life behavior, thus broadening the scope of inquiry beyond workplace boundaries and toward understanding people's PIM behavior in the context of the entirety of their lives.

As Boardman and Sasse (2004) point out, much of PIM research has taken the form of empirical studies and prototype investigation. This research has often been limited to one context—such as the workplace over a relatively short period of time. They also note that PIM research has commonly focused on a single tool and has not explored the way multiple types of information are managed using multiple tools. As a result, PIM researchers can benefit from using a methodological toolkit that comprises a wider array of approaches, one that includes qualitative or naturalistic approaches in addition to the more commonly used quantitative means. Considering the different contexts, methods, and tools associated with PIM, mixed-method approaches may be particularly well suited to the study of PIM behavior. In this chapter, we will focus on naturalistic approaches as complimentary methods to commonly used quantitative research methods.

According to Patton (2002), researchers such as Guba (1978) have described naturalistic inquiry as a discovery-oriented approach that minimizes investigator manipulation of the study setting and places no prior constraints on what the outcomes of the research will be. In this way, naturalistic inquiry may be used to enable PIM researchers to gain a holistic view of the process of managing personal information, decoupling research from a specific tool, technology, or setting such as a workplace. As we will discuss, this approach expands the boundaries of past research to encompass a broader picture of a person's experience.

5.1.1 Scenario

If we were to study the PIM behavior of Connie Monroe, for example, using a naturalistic approach, we might begin by identifying the holistic nature of Connie's information behavior. We would need to consider that there are many facets to Connie's life. She works as a middle manager for a nonprofit, she is a cancer patient, and she is active socially. In managing her personal information Connie may have a foot in the world of paper-based information and also technology-centered information. Considering Connie's age, 58, she is likely to have a considerable amount of information stored in paper formats, and as a computer user with two email accounts she is also likely to store information in electronic formats. Additionally, Connie may receive quite a bit of her information verbally, requiring her either to commit it to memory or to store it in some way. Thus, Connie provides us with a complex, multifaceted case of PIM. These contextual factors are longitudinal, and broadly reflect varied roles.

Naturalistic inquiry techniques can be a powerful means for better understanding the contextual factors that affect an individual's PIM style. For Connie, the following methods could be used to study aspects of her PIM:

Unobtrusive observation. Observing Connie's routines and methods for managing her personal information may reveal important information about her PIM.

- **Interviews.** Interviewing Connie may provide insights into how she manages personal information, and how these ways have evolved, and learning about why they have evolved may provide important insights into her behavior.

- **Diaries.** Through the process of keeping a diary, Connie can record details about the information she acquires, how she manages it, and why it is or isn't important to her. This information may be used as a means for generating discussion points during subsequent interviews.

- **Text analysis.** Connie's notes, email, correspondence, and other written material can be analyzed to gain insight into the types of information acquired and the methods used to manage that information.

- **Pictures and video.** Connie's behavior could be recorded using video technology. Digital cameras could also be used to capture visual data regarding her practices.

5.1.2 Research Overview: Situating Naturalistic Approaches to Studying PIM

An area cognate to PIM is information behavior, broadly defined as the study of how people need, seek, give, manage, and use information in different contexts (Pettigrew, Fidel & Bruce 2001), or as Wilson (2000) describes it, "the totality of human behavior in relation to sources and channels of information, including both active and passive information-seeking, and information use" (p. 49). According to Dervin and Nilan's landmark review (1986), the 1980s bore witness to a paradigm shift in how information behavior researchers approached phenomena, as they turned away from the system-centered approach to developing user-centered ones. This new paradigm values a holistic view of experience that focuses on users as constructive and active participants in their daily activities. In a subsequent review article, Hewins (1990) remarked how the user-centered approach to studying information behavior was under-scoring the design and management of information systems. This shift in focus resulted in increased interest in qualitative methods to explore the hows and whys of information behavior. Relatedly and in the larger context of disciplinary studies, Denzin and Lincoln (2005), claim that over the past quarter century a methodological revolution has occurred, one blurring the disciplinary boundaries between the social sciences and humanities and moving toward a congruence of focus on interpretive, qualitative approaches to research and theory.

As part of this shift several new theories supported by naturalistic inquiry emerged. These information theories include Belkin's "anomalous state of knowledge" (1980), Kulthau's "information search process" (1991), Dervin and colleagues' "sense-making" (2003), and Bates's "berrypicking" (1989). These researchers, among others, used qualitative methods to better understand information behavior in a social context. Their studies resulted in important new insights and inspired a new generation of scholars to explore human-information phenomena using naturalistic approaches.

During the same time period, Grudin (1990) asserted that human-computer interaction (HCI) research was moving into a new stage that focused more on the work setting and the context in which a user was embedded. In an effort to better understand the work setting, researchers turned to disciplines such as sociology and anthropology for research methods to support their investigations into work settings. An important method employed by these disciplines is ethnography, a field that is primarily concerned with the activities of humans in a social and cultural context, and focuses on understanding people's values, standards, practices, methods, relationships, and ways of categorizing or identifying aspects of an environment. Ethnographic methods were particularly important to the development of new methods in the fields of HCI and computer-supported collaborative work (CSCW). Ethnomethodology and situated action are two important developments resulting from this shift in focus. Ethnomethodology, an ethnographic/fieldwork approach that focuses on explaining the methods by which people make sense of their world, emerged as an important means for exploring people's interactions in a work context. Ethnomethodology is based on the premise that practical reasoning about action is an important aspect of studies in human behavior within a social context (Suchman 1987).

Also of considerable importance was Suchman's critical examination of the planning view of action as a way of understanding human behavior. An anthropologist, Suchman argued that the cognitivist approach did not adequately explain action and that action is situated in a social context. Taking the view that "every course of action depends in essential ways upon its material and social circumstances" (Suchman 1987, p. 50), she defined situated action as "an emergent property of moment-to-moment interactions between actors, and between actors and the environments of their action" (p. 179). In order to study behavior in this context, Suchman turned to audiovisual technology to provide a record of the action and its circumstances. She explained that this approach reduces the pitfalls associated with reliance on written descriptions of action, which are dependent on the observer's perspective.

This tradition has been followed by many PIM researchers. Recent PIM studies demonstrate a commitment to naturalistic methods of inquiry in addition to traditional quantitative methods from the fields of HCI and information retrieval (Cutrell, Robbins, Dumais & Sarin 2006; Czerwinski, Horvitz & Wilhite 2004; Dumais, Cutrell, Cadiz, et al. 2003; Jones, Bruce & Dumais 2001, 2003). An analysis of this research reveals a commitment to a mixed-method approach for studying PIM. This approach may not only improve the validity of results but also facilitate new insights into PIM.

5.2 The Nauralistic Approach

There are many terms for describing the expanding area of naturalistic research. While a number of them, such as qualitative methods, ethnography, and case-study research, are used interchangeably, as explained by Patton (2002) and Schwandt (2001), there are distinct differences. For the purpose of this chapter, however, we use the term naturalistic approach to broadly encompass those methods from the social sciences that "emphasize understanding and portraying social action (i.e., the meaning, character, and nature of social life) from the point of view of social actors" (Schwandt 2001, p. 173), and thus draw heavily on the approaches described by Lincoln and Guba (1985). The *naturalistic approach* to conducting empirical research in information science has been on the increase since the 1980s when it was first advocated by Chatman (1984), and later by Mellon (1990), Fidel (1993), Sutton (1993), Westbrook (1994), and Sandstrom and Sandstrom (1995), among others. Borrowed from the social sciences, particularly anthropology, sociology, nursing, and education, naturalistic approaches represented powerful new ways of gaining understanding about information-related phenomena that had eluded the traditional quantitative, positivist approaches associated with information retrieval and library use research, namely experimental design and large-scale surveys. In essence, the naturalistic approach has the following characteristics:

 ▪ Studies whole systems, in real-life or field settings, inductively with emphasis on broad context;
 ▪ Seeks to understand the individual and specific phenomena from the perspective of varied stakeholders, and thus asks "How do the participants define the concepts?"
 ▪ May not use theory at the study's outset, but theory building is an expected outcome;
 ▪ Views the researcher as an insider and as the primary data collection instrument;
 ▪ Employs emergent design where field methods are added or changed as needed;

▓ Triangulates methods (to enrich data collection and counter weaknesses/limitations with a single method), and may also triangulate investigators and theory;

▓ Examines study parts for how well they fit together and how well they agree with the overall data;

▓ Produces deep, rich, valid data;

▓ May involve intensive interpersonal interaction with participants, which may involve the risk of ethical concerns;

▓ Allows for adjustment of initial working expectations or hypotheses, which often change during the research hermeneutic process;

▓ Uses a process in which data collection and analysis occur iteratively;

▓ Bases data analysis codebooks on the data collected, so that codes and themes emerge from the data;

▓ Uses saturation to signify when to cease data collection (i.e., when no new themes are emerging);

▓ Judges the quality of the research using criteria of trustworthiness.

▓ Employs technique to identify and control researcher bias.

As a result of using naturalistic approaches in information behavior research, strong advances have occurred in the development of existing frameworks and in the proposal of new ones. The 2005 monograph *Theories of Information Behavior* comprises descriptions of 74 frameworks, most of which emerged through using naturalistic approaches (Fisher, Erdelez & McKechnie 2005). The techniques of ethnography have emerged as an important means of research to support knowledge of PIM.

5.3 Data Collection Techniques

The collection and analysis of qualitative data enables the researcher to develop an understanding of human experience. It is an ideographic approach that is concerned with discovering the particulars of a relatively narrow area of study. The ideographic method of inquiry seeks understanding through the study of the anomalies that define a narrower element of inquiry than quantitative approaches. As will be discussed in chapter 13, research indicates that there are many anomalies in how, and how well, people manage their personal information. The naturalistic approach seeks to uncover the themes and patterns that are representative of a specific area of inquiry. As shown in Table 5.3a and Table 5.3b, standard naturalistic techniques for collecting data include interviews, focus groups, observation, diary keeping, surveys, think-aloud, and text analysis; each approach has many variations. Interviews, for example, may be short or long in duration, and may be characterized as one-offs or as repeated over time, and in terms of structure (high to low), degree of open questioning, probing, and so on. The in-depth interview, a special technique according to Taylor and Bogdan (1984), consists of "repeated face-to-face encounters between the researcher and informants directed toward understanding informants' perspectives on their lives, experiences, or situations as expressed in their own words . . . [in which] the interviewer, not an interview schedule or protocol, is the research tool" (p. 77). Interviews thus enable the researcher to gain an understanding of another person's perspective and to discover things that cannot be directly observed such as thoughts, feelings, and motivations.

Observation similarly has ranges, and may be chosen for its degree of researcher participation (nonparticipant versus complete participant) and overtness versus covertness (the latter is particularly difficult to obtain institutional human subjects approval for because it requires deceit). It may entail "going into the field" and having direct contact with the people being studied; such observation requires direct contact with participants and enables the researcher to develop an understanding of the intricacies of their lives. Observing participants in their natural setting thus enables researchers to discover interworkings of the

Table 5.3a – Data Collection Methods

Method	Description
Observation	Observations may include individual behavior or group behavior. The observer may be unobtrusive or obtrusive. Resources: recording devices such as video camera, video recorders.
Interview	Subjects may be interviewed using a range of styles, from conversational to closed fixed response.
Diaries	Subjects are asked to keep diaries documenting behavior, thoughts, or feelings related to a phenomenon to be studied. Other subject-initiated documentary techniques include picture-taking or video recordings of daily life.
Surveys	Closed fixed-answer format surveys are often associated with quantitative research methods. Surveys may also include open-ended questions that allow the responders to elaborate on their answers, yielding qualitative data.
Think aloud	This approach asks subjects to verbalize their thought processes as they undertake a task or series of tasks.
Focus groups	Small groups of people who are asked a series of questions to promote discussion regarding phenomena of interest.
Text analysis	Personal documents such as email, journals, calendars, to-do lists, or activity logs.
Case study	Entails an investigation and rich description of a phenomenon such as a setting, subject, event or series of events.

environment directly (Erlandson, Harris, Skipper & Allen 1993). Observations may allow a more complete understanding of the complexities of certain situations than other approaches utilizing verbal exchanges.

When planning a study researchers will need to consider resources required for each method employed. All the methods listed above require access to subjects or material generated by the subjects. Certain methods, such as observations and interviews, may require the use of recording devices such as tape recorders and video recorders. Additionally, researchers may need to compensate subjects for their involvement in the study with monetary compensation or gifts.

There are advantages and disadvantages of each of these methods. Table 5.3b describes a few of the pros and cons of each of these methods.

Table 5.3b – Data Collection Methods - Advantages and Disadvantages

Method	Advantages	Disadvantages
Observation	• Allows for a variety of perspectives • May be unobtrusive, reducing observer effect • Actions may be observed instead of observer having to rely on description • Allows for studying behavior that might not lend itself to description • Permits for the study of people who may not be willing to participate otherwise	• Subjects may change behavior when they know they are being observed (observer effect) • Requires access to observe spontaneous event or behavior • Not all types of activity lend themselves to observation • Can be very time-consuming • Is dependent on and subject to the observer's interpretation of events
Interview	• Immediacy – data may be quickly collected • May allow for mutual exploration of ideas between interviewer and subject • May allow for the investigation of causation • Provides an opportunity for personal contact with subjects and increased awareness of phenomena being studied	• May be time-consuming • When subjects are being compensated could be costly • May not be critical and hence prone to interviewer bias
Diaries	• Lends itself to studying behavior over time rather than at a point in time • Allows participants to be active in data collection • Allows participants to determine what is important	• May result in unstructured data • May be costly if participants are paid • Diaries may be inconsistent • Requires participants to be self-disciplined • May be prone to participant bias. Subjects may change behavior or report different aspects of their behavior in their diaries
Surveys	• Allows for a relatively large sampling • May allow data to be collected for hard-to-access populations using mail or Internet • May be a fast way to collect data • Provides for structured data	• Ability to explore open-ended questions may be limited by survey instrument length and subjects' ability to articulate responses in writing • May be prone to bias by subjects inaccurately reporting their actions or behavior • May be costly when participants are paid or response rates could be low when participants not adequately compensated • Could be subject to sampling error according to which subjects respond to the survey
Think-aloud	• May provide a unique opportunity to better understand cognitive tasks that are difficult to uncover using other approaches • May provide an opportunity to more deeply explore though processes for certain behaviors • May provide a unique way to understand the context of actions	• May be time consuming • May be costly when participants are paid • Requires participants to adequately describe behavior • May be prone to observer effect, or process of thinking out loud may artificially alter actions and behaviors
Focus Groups	• Allows for open exploration of ideas • Group dynamic may provide for the development of questions not considered by researcher • May result in rich detail and explanation of an issue or behavior as a result of multiple perspectives being offered	• May be subject to bias toward a dominant participant or participants • Subjects may not express themselves as freely in a group as they would individually • Data may be unstructured and may not be focused on phenomena being studied
Text Analysis	• May be unobtrusive, which may reduce observer effect • Allows for a variety of perspectives in examining data • Actions may be observed instead of observer having to rely on description • Allows for studying behavior that might not lend itself to description • Permits for the study of people who may not be willing to participate otherwise	• Subjects may change behavior when they know they are being observed (observer effect) • Not all types of activity lend themselves to observation using personal documents • Can be very time-consuming • May result in a lot of extraneous data • Is subject to the observer's interpretation of text • May lack context that lends itself to interpreting the artifact (such as a conversation preceding the sending of an email)
Case Study	• Provides for the identification of themes, characteristics, and conditions • Allows for a broad holistic examination of a situation • May help to identify what works and what does not work • May provide a contextual understanding that could inform additional research methods	• Subject to bias from case study writer • Requires access to phenomena being described and often dependent on third parties for descriptions of events or actions • Limited to one particular moment in time or one situation

In any qualitative study, the primary data collection instrument is the researcher. Reliance on the researcher as the primary data collection instrument introduces the potential risk of bias. Therefore, it is standard practice to use multiple methods of data collection (triangulation) to increase the trustworthiness of the data. Triangulation entails using multiple and different data sources, methods, investigators, and theories in a single study. By drawing on other types and sources of data, observers gain a deeper and clearer understanding of the setting and people being studied. In this way, greater insights may be gained into the phenomena being investigated and the potential for bias is reduced.

To support the researcher's role as primary data collection instrument, Chatman (1992), the foremost ethnographer in information science, advocates that researchers maintain three types of notebooks: (1) a field diary for recording observational notes, the "simple reporting of phenomena," which is used, as part of triangulation, for testing criterion validity; (2) method notes, which consists of "strategies employed or that might be employed to obtain data" and thus record observations and ideas about the usefulness of certain methodologies, their effects, and how they may be changed for future research; and (3) a theory notebook for "testing construct validity and the generation of propositional statements to explain phenomena," which is used as part of theory building (p. 15).

5.4 Analyzing Qualitative Data

Qualitative data emerging from the methods described in section 5.3 may consist of quotations, excerpts from documents, activity logs, journals, rich descriptions, observations, video recordings, and images or excerpts from documents. Within naturalistic approaches, data collection and data analysis occur iteratively where data are analyzed as they are collected. Thus each round of analysis guides the purposive collection of more data and each return from the field leads closer to an understanding of the phenomena under study. While texts on different ways of analyzing qualitative data abound, classic approaches include those recommended by Lofland and Lofland (1995) and Miles and Huberman (1994), which consist of coding, memoing, and diagramming.

Glaser and Strauss's (1967) constant comparative method remains a standard theoretical approach in which the coding of data is combined with the generation of theoretical ideas, and is consistent with Strauss's (1987) "coding from the data" method. Using these methods, codebooks—which include rules of application—are iteratively derived from the qualitative data and used to assign final terms to all data segments that reflect particular concepts, especially the primary units of analyses.[1] To prepare data for analysis, pseudonyms and codes should be established for all participants and any other agencies or persons named in the ethnographic records, while taped interviews should be transcribed (either verbatim or loosely, depending on one's needs) according to standard procedures. During the later analytic stages, the collapsing of data into large families of codes is based on theoretically derived categories and findings from the research literature and is always considered in terms of how the participants perceive the phenomena.

The analytic technique of "memoing"[2] begins at the outset of data collection through recording certain observations and ideas in the theory notebook. Later, as data analysis progresses, these theory notes are rewritten in the form of extensive memos that connect the researcher's thoughts on different phenomena and are later used as part of theory building, for which emphasis is placed on identifying negative cases or anomalies that refute any theoretical framework established for the investigation. Miles and Huberman (1994, p. 72) cite Glaser and Strauss's (1967) definition of memoing, which is a classic: "the theorizing write-up of ideas about codes and their relationships as they strike the analyst while coding . . . it can be a sentence, a paragraph or a few pages . . . it exhausts the analyst's momentary ideation based on data with perhaps a little conceptual elaboration."

The technique of diagramming is also a key element of the analytic process; it consists of typologizing, matrix making, concept charting, and flow charting (Lofland & Lofland 1995). These strategies enable the researcher to "visually represent relationships between concepts" (Strauss & Corbin 1990, p. 197) and are part of theory building.

An important element of data analysis involves intercoder reliability testing, which takes place when sample transcripts and the near-final codebook are given to other researchers for testing. In some cases these testers may be domain experts uninvolved with the study or simply other members of the research team. In brief, the coding results from the testers are compared against those of the researcher for levels of agreement. The researcher and testers then meet to discuss the areas of disagreement, the researcher revises the codebook accordingly, the transcripts are recoded, and the agreement rates recalculated. The codebook modifications and retesting typically result in final intercoder reliability rates that exceed the 70 percent and 90 percent agreement levels recommended by Krippendorff (1980, p. 147) and Miles and Huberman (1996, p. 64)[3] respectively, and such results suggest that the coding schemes are valid as applied.

5.4.1 *Trustworthiness*

A common criticism of naturalistic or qualitative approaches is that they lack rigor. In particular they are cited for weaknesses regarding availability bias (i.e., participants or cases are chosen based on convenience as opposed to the random approach associated with quantitative research), overreliance on initial data, overreliance on vivid instances (e.g., with interviews), too much protection of an initial theory against discontinuing evidence, the researchers' failure to recognize and question their own background assumptions (biases), and too much reliance on analogy and the associated failure to recognize disanalogies. While qualitative researchers take efforts to avoid these pitfalls, Lincoln and Guba (1985, p. 290) specifically use the term "trustworthiness" to address such questions as "How can an inquirer persuade his/her audiences (including self) that the findings of an inquiry are worth paying attention to, worth taking account of? What arguments can be mounted, what criteria invoked, what questions asked, that would be persuasive on this issue?" As they further explain (p. 301), different paradigms make different knowledge claims; therefore, the criteria for what counts as significant knowledge will vary from paradigm to paradigm. In particular, the standards for judging quantitative research are inapplicable to the naturalist approach, although the following rough equivalents can be made: credibility (internal validity), transferability (external validity), dependability (reliability), and conformability (objectivity).

The primary techniques for ensuring trustworthiness are summarized in Table 5.4.1. One aspect of particular note that is not overly emphasized in qualitative research texts is the notion of *observer effect*, as when "the methodology used in a study affects its results."[4] Though observational methods are said to "embody the least potential for generating observer effects" because the "naturalness of the observer role, coupled with its nondirection, makes it the least noticeable instrument of all research techniques," the likelihood of avoiding observer effect on all participants is an "idealistic improbability" (Adler & Adler 1994, p. 382). Therefore when collecting observational data researchers employ multiple field strategies to reduce the incidence of observer effect on the participants. In addition, learning and adopting participants' "language" greatly improves the efficiency of any naturalistic study and increases the trustworthiness of the data. By employing interview, observational, and other methods, researchers listen for and adopt the participants' languages, thus allowing for subsequent interpretation from the participants' perspectives.

Table 5.4.1 – Summary of Techniques for Establishing Trustworthiness.
Source: Adapted from Lincoln & Guba 1985 and Erlandson et al. 1993.

Criterion	Naturalistic Technique
Credibility (internal validity)	Activities in the field that increase the probability of high credibility
	• Prolonged engagement in the research setting • Persistent observation • Triangulation (sources, methods, investigators, and theories)
	Peer debriefing (with one's professional colleagues)
	Negative case analysis (considering alternative interpretations of data)
	Referential adequacy (provide background meaning, context)
	Member checks (in process and terminal with stakeholder groups)
Transferability (external validity)	Thick description (low-level abstractions from database)
Dependability (reliability)	Dependability audit, including the audit trail (means for an external check on processes by which study conducted). According to Chatman (1992), also increased through (1) consistent note-taking, (2) exposure to multiple and different situations when studying participants, (3) comparing themes as they emerged from the data with findings from previous studies on related phenomena, (4) audio-recording interviews and observations, (5) using intracoder and intercoder checks, and (6) analyzing data for incidents of observer effect.
Confirmability (objectivity)	Confirmability audit, including the audit trail (means for ensuring if the researcher's conclusions and other processes are supported by the study).
All of the above	Reflexive journal (daily schedule, personal dairy, methodological log; in Chatman (1992) terms: field, theory, and method notes.

5.5 Looking Forward

As discussed in this chapter, naturalistic inquiry is a discovery-oriented approach that examines behavior holistically and considers a person's entire life experience. This approach may be particularly useful to studying PIM given that PIM encompasses a wide range of behavior not restricted to a certain technology or workplace setting. PIM is a complex activity that needs to be viewed in the context of a person's entire life. Naturalistic inquiry provides us with a research methodology that allows us to explore information in this context.

Naturalistic inquiry or qualitative research approaches have been increasingly employed during the past two decades to develop new understandings of human behavior. Technology has allowed researchers to capture information in new ways through the use of digital imaging and recording technologies.

As a result of this increased interest and technical capability, a rich set of tools, techniques and methods has evolved to support this type of research. By utilizing this research methodology for PIM research we may gain valuable new insights into PIM behavior.

Looking forward, researchers are expected to continue to innovate in the use of technology to collect rich sets of qualitative data and to further develop methods, tools, and techniques for studying personal information management behavior. Furthermore, the trend of PIM research to employ mixed methods in which qualitative and quantitative research approaches are used to compliment each other will continue to evolve. The coming years present many challenges as well as opportunities to gain greater understanding of PIM behavior.

NOTES

1. For large data sets especially, it is common to use software to assist with analysis. CAQDAS (Lewins, Silver, Lee, et al. 2006) is a comprehensive resource for understanding the strengths of different programs: http://caqdas.soc.surrey.ac.uk/
2. Miles and Huberman (1994, p. 72) cite the following definition of memoing by Glaser as classic: "the theorizing write-up of ideas about codes and their relationships as they strike the analyst while coding. . . . it can be a sentence, a paragraph, or a few pages . . . it exhausts the analyst's momentary ideation based on data with perhaps a little conceptual elaboration."
3. According to Miles and Huberman, initial reliability rates tend to be no higher than 70 percent while final rates "should be up in the 90 percent range, depending on the size and range of the coding scheme" (1994, p. 64).
4. Discussing another response similar to observer effect, Singleton et al. (1988, p. 112) defined reactive measurement effect as when a "respondent's sensitivity or responsiveness to a measure is affected by the process of observation or measurement."

PART II

Solutions for Personal Information Management

6 Save Everything: Supporting Human Memory with a Personal Digital Lifetime Store

*Desney Tan, Emma Berry, Mary Czerwinski, Gordon Bell,
Jim Gemmell, Steve Hodges, Narinder Kapur, Brian Meyers,
Nuria Oliver, George Robertson, and Ken Wood*

6.1 Introduction

One of the things that distinguishes human beings from other species is the magnitude to which we manipulate our (largely synthetically created) environments and our technologies in order to augment ourselves physically and mentally. Supporting our individual as well as collective memory has been a particularly important endeavor as we have continued to build upon past experiences and improve our way of life. We are now at a time when each of us is generating and handling more information than ever before. Fortunately, we are now also equipped with technologies that can begin to record, store, summarize, and retrieve all this content. Various governments have recognized the potential of realizing these augmentations and created programs to fund work in the area, as for example in Memories for Life Grand Challenge in the UK, Fitzgibbon and Reiter (2003), and the LifeLog program in the United States (DARPA, n.d.), the work of which has now been distributed into multiple other programs.

In chapter 3 of this book, Jones describes the distinction between information keeping, whereby a user decides what to store, and information organizing, the creation of the structures within which information is stored and retrieved. He reviews strategies and tools that make decisions about keeping information easier for users by having better organization in place from the outset. In this chapter, we build on this work and attempt to completely remove information-keeping decisions by employing what Jones calls a "keep everything" strategy. We explore how we could build personal digital stores that save every bit of information we have touched or record every event we have experienced through our entire lifetime. We believe that this strategy has the potential to support users ranging from the most organized to the least organized (e.g., Alex, Connie, and Brooke). We examine the implications this has on how we organize and retrieve this information.

6.2 Research Overview

The idea of supporting human memory with an all-encompassing personal digital store is not new. In 1945, Vannevar Bush proposed, in his now-iconic article "As We May Think," that "instruments are at hand which, if properly developed, will give man access to and command over the inherited knowledge of the ages" (Bush 1945, p. 101). He described an all-inclusive personal information management (PIM) system he called Memex (from memory extender), which would store all his books, records, communications, and experiences. The user would of course be able to consult the system with exceeding speed and flexibility, and "with one item in its grasp, it snaps instantly to the next that is suggested by the association of thought" (p. 106).

Various aspects of Bush's Memex vision have already been realized. While we do not have the space to review all of this work, we briefly discuss a few important examples. Recording devices that increasingly capture more data, and more *kinds* of data, have been implemented by various wearable computing researchers like Steve Mann, who has also considered some of the related social, artistic, and legal issues (Mann & Niedzviecki 2001). Similarly, the University of Tokyo has developed a system that continuously captures video, along with other sensor data, including GPS, gyroscope, accelerometer, and a brain wave sensor (Hori & Aizawa 2003). Wearable A/V capture systems have even been augmented by interaction with a robot in an exhibition setting (Sumi, Ito, Matsuguchi & Fels 2004).

Extending the use of such recording devices, researchers at Rank Xerox used Active Badges and automatic video recording to automatically generate user diaries (Lamming & Newman 1992) and researchers at AT&T used Active Bats and audio recording for similar purposes (Harter, Hopper, Steggles, et al. 2002). Other researchers have built wearable memory-augmentation devices. For example, the Remembrance Agent provides users with a heads-up display, one-handed chording keyboard, and location awareness, and runs note-taking software that selects old notes to show based on current location, people nearby, and the text of notes being written (Rhodes 2003).

Many storage and implicit query ideas were realized as digital technology as early as the 1960s by Douglas Engelbart, whose hypermedia groupware system supported bookmarks, hyperlinks, recording of email, and a journal (Engelbart, Watson & Norton 1973). Similarly, hypertext visionary Ted Nelson advocated keeping personal recordings of everything and suggested novel computational infrastructure (Nelson 1999). More recently, storage for large personal archives of digital data has been explored by projects such as MIT's Haystack (Adar,

Karger & Stein 1999) and Microsoft's Stuff I've Seen (Dumais, Cutrell, Cadiz, et al. 2003). To tie these efforts together, Bell (2001) describes the CyberAll project, aimed at creating a system that records, stores, and allows easy retrieval of a person's entire information for personal and professional use. This project could be considered a predecessor to the efforts to build MyLifeBits, which we describe in the next section.

Since our memories are critical to nearly every activity we perform, we assert that an appropriately designed personal digital store could significantly empower us in our daily lives. For example, in the simplest scenario, the store could be used to *remind* us of things we need to do, or provide information we need to have in various contexts. It could also allow us to quickly *retrieve* digital artifacts such as minutes from a specific meeting or an email message received, perhaps years ago. Since the store records life events as well, it could help us *recall* specific memories such as the names and faces of people we have met, or where we last left our keys. In most current systems, retrieving a document requires remembering its name, deducing keywords that are likely to be in it, or thinking about other properties of the document. Designed correctly, the user would also be able to *recollect* some aspect of the past and use it as a cue for searching. For example, a person may retrieve meeting minutes by remembering something about the event, such as where it was held and who was present.

More complex queries and associations could enable us to *remember* much richer aspects of otherwise forgotten experiences, or to view the experiences from a radically different perspective. For example, a user might look at the amount of time spent on various tasks within the day in order to *reflect* upon and improve their time management skills. Alternatively, they could examine behavioral patterns to monitor medical conditions and improve personal health.

A personal digital store should also promote *reminiscing*, or *reexperiencing* the past for purely social reasons. Reminiscing can be a rewarding experience and an end in itself, supporting the feeling of *reliving* a shared experience as well as providing a basis for storytelling. Sometimes a user might even prefer to let the system choose the memories to be viewed, either because they do not have a specific experience in mind, or because serendipitous reminiscence is often quite pleasurable. When done with others, such activities could allow people to *relate* their memories to others and could help to socially and emotionally connect people.

Our approach to exploring the space of personal digital lifetime stores has been to interactively design and build systems that we can deploy and observe as people use them. We begin this chapter with a broad view of the technologies we have been working on. We first describe our efforts in creating our MyLifeBits infrastructure, as well as SenseCam, a specific recording device that we believe is important for logging life events. We then describe a specific case study in which we examine the effectiveness of these technologies for the therapeutic support of a woman with severe memory loss. This support encompasses many of the activities we have described and provides encouraging evidence for the usefulness of a personal digital store. Finally, we again take a broad view and discuss some of the interesting development and deployment challenges we have experienced. We also consider some of the broader research questions that systems like MyLifeBits inevitably raise with respect to the technical, personal, social, and legal issues associated with storing vast quantities of data about one's life.

6.3   Diving In

6.3.1 *MyLifeBits: Infrastructure for a Personal Digital Store*

MyLifeBits is the infrastructure upon which we base most of our work. MyLifeBits provides a pluggable architecture that allows us to encode, store, access, and manipulate vast arrays of personal information (Gemmell, Bell, Lueder, et al. 2002; Gemmell, Williams, Wood, et al. 2004). This system was initially built to understand how we could digitize a lifetime of legacy content and eliminate paper as a storage medium. As we worked more on MyLifeBits, the original goal of storing files of scanned papers quickly evolved into an exploration of future computing possibilities.

Two of our goals in building this infrastructure were aimed at addressing problems raised in multiple chapters within this book. First, we hoped to unify the various data "islands" created by current application and data-storage boundaries. We believe that partitioning information the way our systems currently do creates artificial restrictions on how flexibly we can interact with information. Second, we wanted to substantially improve the ability to organize, annotate, search, and utilize the vast quantities of content with which we were working. Faced with folders full of digital media with rich metadata tags, we needed a framework to hold and link all of these objects in the arbitrary, Web-like fashion that Bush described.

With these goals in mind, MyLifeBits was built on a SQL Server database that stores content and metadata for a variety of item types. Currently, the MyLifeBits database supports 25 item types, such as contacts, documents, email, events, photographs, music, and video—but arbitrarily many could be added. Each item is stored in a database table containing both shared and type-specific attributes. Items can be linked either implicitly with attributes such as time, or explicitly with typed links such as a "person in photograph" link between a contact and a picture. While many of these links are still manually created, we hope to continue to automate more and more of this process. In this scheme, the traditional directory tree is replaced by more general "collections" in which objects (including a collection) can be filed in more than one parent collection.

Rather than trying to capture and convert small amounts of data from many people, we have focused most of our efforts on creating a single large store containing records of Gordon Bell's life experiences, including a document and activity archive. We now use this store as a vehicle for our research. In addition to continuing conversion of paper documents and physical artifacts, we also populate the database with data from legacy applications such as NTFS files and Outlook email stores. These sources are monitored, and their metadata are integrated along with the full text of each item to enable optimal search. The system also captures items such as Web pages visited, Instant Message chat sessions, telephone conversations, office and meeting audio and video, as well as radio and television program usage. Furthermore, an interface logger records all mouse and keyboard activity. This log can reveal the significance of an item based on frequency or recency of use, or can provide insight into how one spends time with the computer.

To facilitate retrieval and interaction with the data, the core MyLifeBits user interface allows users to query the data and visualize results as a list, variable sized thumbnails, or on a timeline. Users can explore the data by pivoting according to metadata and links. Users can also annotate content with text and voice comments, or assign them to collections. Various plug-ins provide additional functionality to the core system. These currently include a screensaver that displays random photos and video segments and gives the user an opportunity to comment and rate items, simple authoring tools that create side-by-side timelines and HTML-based slide shows with audio, as well as FacetMap, a visual approach that exposes more of the metadata to support more effective data browsing (Smith, McCown & Nelson 2006).

As we gain experience building the infrastructure and utilities, and as we observe more and more people using MyLifeBits with their own data, we continue to iterate on its design and evolve our ideas. In the next section, we describe SenseCam, a wearable system we developed to extend data-capture facilities and allow people to easily record rich life experiences into MyLifeBits.

6.3.2 SenseCam: Capturing Life

A personal digital store is only as useful as the information it has available to it, and while capturing artifacts that are created as a result of computer use is a good start, we believe that our everyday experiences are also an extremely rich source of data. Hence we have designed SenseCam, a wearable digital camera that takes photographs passively, without user intervention, while it is being worn (Hodges, Williams, Berry, et al. 2006).

Unlike a regular digital camera or a cameraphone, SenseCam does not have a viewfinder or a display that can be used to frame photos. Instead, it is fitted with a wide-angle (fish-eye) lens that maximizes its field of view. This ensures that nearly everything in view of the wearer is captured by the camera. This is important because a regular wearable camera would likely produce many uninteresting images. SenseCam also contains a number of different electronic sensors. These include light-intensity and light-color sensors, a passive infrared (body heat) detector, a temperature sensor, a multiple-axis accelerometer, and audio level detection. We are also currently working on integrating audio recording and GPS location sensing into SenseCam. These sensors are monitored by the camera's microprocessor, and certain changes in sensor readings can be used to automatically trigger a photograph to be taken. For example, a significant change in light level, or the detection of body heat in front of the camera can cause the camera to take a picture. Alternatively, the user may elect to set SenseCam to operate on a timer, for example taking a picture every thirty seconds.

In our current design, users typically wear the camera on a cord around their neck, although it would also be possible to clip it to pockets or on belts, or to attach it directly to clothing (see Figure 6.3.2). One advantage of using a neck-cord to wear the camera is that it is reasonably stable when being worn—it tends not to move around from left to right when the wearer is walking or sitting—but at the same time it is relatively comfortable to wear and it is easy to put on and take off. Also, when worn around the neck, SenseCam is reasonably close to the wearer's line of sight, and so generates images taken from the wearer's point of

Figure 6.3.2 – The SenseCam v2.3 prototype is shown as a stand-alone and as typically worn by a user. The model pictured here has a clear plastic case that reveals some of the internal components.

view—that is, it creates a "first person" view. Informal observations suggest that this results in images that are more compelling when subsequently replayed.

SenseCam currently takes pictures at VGA resolution (640 x 480 pixels) and stores them as compressed .jpg files on internal flash memory. Surprisingly, most users seem happy with the relatively low-resolution images, suggesting that the time-lapse, first-person viewpoint sequences represent a useful media type that exists somewhere between still images and video. It also points to the fact that these are used as memory supports rather than rich media. Along with the images, SenseCam also stores a log file, which records other sensor data along with their timestamps. Once imported to a PC, files can be stored and manipulated in MyLifeBits, or any other such application.

6.3.3 *Case Study: SenseCam in Support of Severe Memory Loss*

In this section, we describe a specific case study in which we explore the potential of SenseCam and a personal digital store to support a patient with severe memory loss due to brain injury. While this is a single case study, and more work is needed to understand how users adopt such technology in their lives, we believe that the findings from this study are interesting and expose many issues surrounding the development, deployment, and adoption of such technologies.

This work is based on the assertion that psychological intervention and rehabilitation can alleviate some of the debilitating memory and cognitive problems encountered by people with brain injury. It is also based on the assertion that one of the most valuable and effective ways to aid rehabilitation is to use external memory aids to help people to compensate for their memory deficits (Kapur, Glisky & Wilson 2002). Most research on external memory aids aim to improve prospective memory functioning, or memory for future events, such as remembering to keep appointments (Wilson, Evans, Emslie & Malinek 1997). However, people with memory problems following brain damage often exper-ience difficulties with their autobiographical memory, or memory for both remote and recent events from their own personal past. In this case study, we evaluated the use of a personal digital store as an aid to improving autobiographical memory for past events in a patient with amnesia following brain inflammation. We hoped that the patient could use SenseCam images as a pictorial diary to trigger and consolidate her memories. We compared this to a condition in which the same patient used a written diary to aid recall of recent events.

Method

Mrs. B. is a well-educated, 63-year-old woman, and her husband, Mr. B., is a retired businessman. In March 2002 Mrs. B. was admitted to the hospital and diagnosed with limbic encephalitis (inflammation of deep structures of the brain). MRI scans revealed bilateral cell loss in the hippocampus. Mrs. B. would only have partial recall of events that happened in her life after a couple of days, and would typically have no recall at all after about a week. This was true even of significant events. Because of her memory problems, Mrs. B. said she "lacked confidence" in company and was generally anxious in everyday life.

We designed this study to have two conditions: a SenseCam condition and a written diary (control) condition. Medical evidence suggested that Mrs. B. was making a good recovery and that her cognitive functioning would improve over time. Hence, to avoid favoring the SenseCam condition, we decided that it should take place first over a period of three months. The written diary control condition replicated the SenseCam condition as far as possible and took place later over a period of one month. During these time periods, we had Mr. and Mrs. B. use either the SenseCam or a written diary to record events that they particularly wanted Mrs. B. to remember (i.e., beyond everyday, routine events).

In the SenseCam condition, Mr. and Mrs. B. would upload the relevant SenseCam images from an event they wanted to remember to a laptop computer at their earliest convenience. In the written diary condition, Mrs. B. did not wear a SenseCam. Instead, Mr. B. wrote a diary of the events. In both cases, Mr. and Mrs. B. did not look at the images or view the diary together that day. The next day, Mr. B. would ask his wife if she recalled the previous day's events, and noted what she said. Mr. B. would then immediately show Mrs. B. the SenseCam images or written diary of the previous day's events. They viewed and talked about the images or diary entries up to three times that day. Two days later, Mr. B. would again ask his wife what she remembered of the event. Again, he recorded her responses and then showed her the SenseCam images or written diary as before. They repeated the procedure six times, once every two days.

In this way, Mr. B. was able to keep a log of how many times Mrs. B. had viewed the images or diary of a recent event, and her corresponding recall of that event. Mrs. B.'s responses were then graded on a scale of 0 to 100 percent. For each event, Mr. B. documented a number of key points that he felt were important or memorable. For example, if Mr. B. recorded 10 key events, and Mrs. B. remembered 7 of them, she scored 70 percent.

In addition to this short-term testing of recall, we also carried out a longer-term assessment of these autobiographical memories. In the SenseCam condition, Mr. B. showed Mrs. B. all nine of the SenseCam movies that had been created at the end of the three-month period during which the device was used. She then did not view the images for one month, and at the end of that month, Mr. B. tested his wife on her recall of all nine events. He graded her responses in the same way he did before. Two months after this test, Mrs. B. was again presented with images from all nine events, but this time was asked not to view them for a period of two months. She was then tested at the end of these two months. Immediately after this trial, Mrs. B. was again presented with images from all nine events, but this time was asked not to view them for a period of three months. Note that this means that the time interval between the original occurrence of some of the earlier events and eventual testing was as much as 11 months.

In the diary condition, after a month using the diary, Mr. B. showed Mrs. B. the three written diary events that had been created. She then did not view the diary entries for a month, and at the end of this month, Mr. B. tested Mrs. B. on her recall of all three events. He again graded her responses.

Results

Mr. and Mrs. B. recorded nine key events in the SenseCam condition and three key events in the written diary condition. Mrs. B.'s average recall across the events with successive SenseCam/written diary viewings is illustrated in Figure 6.3.3. The results show that there is a significant effect across SenseCam presentations ($x2$ (1) = 62.59, p<0.001). In other words, the more SenseCam images were seen, the greater the percentage of key points about an event were recalled. No such effect was found across the written diary viewings ($x2$ (1) = 0.29, p > 0.6). The results also show that there was an overall difference in average percentage of recall, with SenseCam giving rise to a higher rate of recall than the written diary ($x2$ (1) = 13.10, p < 0.001).

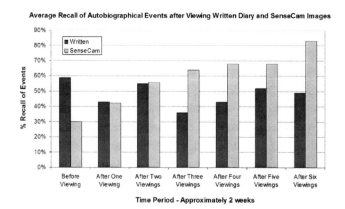

Figure 6.3.3 – The graph represents Mrs. B's average percentage recall of events with successive SenseCam and written diary viewings. The time between viewings was typically two days.

With regard to longer-term effects, Mrs. B.'s recall of events in the SenseCam condition was 80 percent, 67 percent, and 76 percent for one-, two-, and three-month lags respectively. In the written diary condition, she could not recall anything (0 percent) even after one month. No subsequent testing with this technique took place after the one-month interval. This shows that recall with SenseCam remained quite high even after relatively long intervals despite the fact that no additional viewing of the images took place within that interval. This can be contrasted with the written diary, which failed to trigger any recall for Mrs. B. even after a one-month interval.

Discussion

These results show that Mrs. B. demonstrated a consistent improvement in her recent autobiographical memory of events after viewing SenseCam images, which can be contrasted to her results with a written diary. This beneficial effect was maintained in the longer term, many months after the event, and without looking at the SenseCam images for up to three months.

An important point here is that Mrs. B.'s descriptions demonstrated that she remembered the event itself, rather than remembering the SenseCam pictures alone. This was indicated by the fact that Mrs. B. could recall details of the events not captured in the images. In addition, Mr. B. was always quick to point out when his wife was having a true recollective experience as opposed to retelling facts or a narrative that she had learned. Thus, while we would like to collect more evidence, we are encouraged that SenseCam was able to help consolidate memories and re-evoke experiences using the images as triggers. We are also very encouraged by Mrs. B.'s reports that SenseCam reduced her levels of anxiety and increased her confidence, and Mr. B.'s expression of "sheer pleasure" at being able to share experiences with his wife again.

We believe that the positive results seen with SenseCam can be partially attributed to the support it provides for rich visual imagery, which is commonly considered to be associated with autobiographical memory (Brewer 1986, 1988). In fact, brain regions underlying visual memory are an important part of the network that subserves autobiographical memory (Conway 2005; Greenberg & Rubin 2003). SenseCam is different from standard photographic diaries in that it produces a "movie" taken from the point of view of the wearer. When the images are played back, the user is able to see a concise time-lapse movie of their day, similar to the way they experienced it, and these images may be providing a powerful set of stimuli or triggers that cue recall of previously stored memories. Of course, this is a single case study and further research is needed to evaluate the usefulness of SenseCam and personal digital stores in aiding memory and rehabilitation for people with different forms of memory loss.

6.4 Looking Forward

Our attempts to build important components of a Memex-like system in the MyLifeBits platform, and our testing of the SenseCam part of this system with a brain-injured person, raise a number of research challenges both in the short and the long term, and in terms of technical and social issues. In this final section, we discuss some of these challenges as well as potential solutions we have considered. Many of these challenges have also been discussed in varying levels of detail in other chapters. We break the discussion down into subsections dealing with (1) data capture (chapters 4, 5, 9); (2) storage (chapters 4, 5, 8, 9); (3) retrieval, sense-making, and presentation (chapters 4, 8, 10, 14); (4) security, privacy, and access control (chapters 14 through 17); and finally (5) legal and societal issues (chapters 16 and 17).

6.4.1 *Data Capture*

One of the central assumptions of the Memex vision is that the more data one captures, and the more *kinds* of data one captures, the better the system will be. While it may seem tempting to label many artifacts of everyday life as disposable, it is often impossible to predict exactly which items in our lives we might value or need in the future. Hence, the easiest and safest thing is to record as much of it as possible, especially if this requires no effort on the part of the user. The more the system logs, the better the chance of having the memory hook that will help users find what they seek.

In line with the philosophy to record as much as we can, it is essential that we treat anything accessible outside a person's control as transient, and hence create a copy of it in the person's own Memex. For example, while Web-page capture initially struck us as somewhat trivial, we now see this as an essential feature that has changed our everyday behavior. The Internet is constantly morphing, and having a cached personal copy of the particular version viewed is essential. In fact, this is true of much of the information we deal with, even locally.

In practice, of course, some kinds of data are currently more difficult to capture than others. For example, scanning every book that we read is not something we have incorporated into MyLifeBits. The benefits of having this data do not yet outweigh the cost for acquiring appropriate copyright permissions and digitizing content. The reality is that there are many kinds of data that cannot yet be effortlessly and automatically captured.

Hence, we believe that we need to carefully consider the reasons for capturing data and to prioritize various sources and media. For example, we saw in the study with Mrs. B. that the use of SenseCam images provided powerful triggers for recollection. Following this, psychologists have begun to speculate whether there is something special about images, and in particular the kinds of images that SenseCam captures, that may support recollective memory. Studies such as these can help direct and decide where we might best expend our resources with regard to capture. It also points to the fact that there are many unanswered questions as to the data that is the most potent in triggering the kinds of memory we wish to support.

Fortunately, more and more traditional content is being "born digital," reducing the need for expensive conversion. We expect that this will eventually be true of all information, including bills, correspondence, financial statements, news, scholarly articles, music, health data, photos, and more. An added benefit of creating digital content is the opportunity for metadata to be included with little overhead. For example, rather than requiring artificial intelligence to determine the metadata for your dental bills, the software that generates the e-bill could embed the metadata when the content is generated (including that it is a dental bill, whom it is from, for what service, the total due, etc.). Attaching metadata to everything, however, presents a challenge for software to process content and convert it among competing schema. We will discuss the need for a more comprehensive ontology in more detail when we discuss retrieval, sense-making, and presentation.

6.4.2 *Storage*

For decades, storage was a scarce and expensive resource. Today, it is plentiful and affordable. In fact, the storage density a dollar can buy has doubled every 12 months and shows little signs of slowing. If this trend continues, we should see desktop PCs with terabyte storage devices by 2008. When we started this project, we calculated that without audio and video a terabyte would be more than adequate for a lifetime storage of information that a user touches, as it provides more than 1 GByte/month for the duration of an 80-year life. However, changing usage patterns are quickly invalidating this assumption.

While we started thinking we could record things speculatively, storing only digital content we might want to see later, our recent efforts to capture everything have pushed us far beyond what could be stored in a terabyte. Additionally, we have moved beyond storing legacy content—such as paper, photos, and video—into a second phase that includes real-time capture of conversations, meetings, sensor readings, health monitors, and computer activity. In short, while a terabyte might hold a lifetime at 20th-century resolutions and quantities, we speculate that 21st-century users may expect to record their lives more extensively and in higher fidelity—and will drive the market for much greater storage. Even with current trends our ability to generate data will far outpace our ability to store it, and we will necessarily have to consider solutions that employ servers or distributed systems to store our lifetimes of data. Along with this distribution, it is crucial that Memex-like systems be adequately backed up. The failure of one author's hard drive resulted in losing months worth of captured data. Even now, he searches for information expected to be in the archive, only to realize that there is a fairly sizable gap in his personal digital store. Much future work remains on the architecture and reliability of such systems if they are to scale appropriately.

Similarly, as the hardware requirements grow with much more data, we will have to consider scaling the software infrastructure as well. The original instantiation of MyLifeBits utilized only a generic file system with careful naming of files and judicious use of folders and shortcuts. However, as the collection grew the use of files in folders went from unwieldy to overwhelming. Current desktop search tools still work for searching repositories of files and folders. As the amount and types of information grew, we quickly needed more powerful capabilities, such as access by metadata—including written and spoken comments about items and the ability to organize and classify items in multiple ways. The current MyLifeBits uses an SQL-database as the underlying data store for the information, and we imagine that this will continue to evolve as demands get larger and more complex.

6.4.3 *Retrieval, Sense-making, and Presentation*

With recent advances in technology, we are making it easier and easier to create, receive, record, store, and accumulate digital materials. However, it is still extremely difficult to manage and use them in a sensible way, especially as time passes and their immediacy has faded. While some of the issues faced in this research are not new, many of the larger research challenges revolve around coping with the sheer quantity of material that we are now able to record and store.

For example, the strategy of recording and keeping everything often raises concern that clutter may obscure valuable content and add to an individual's personal information management burden, creating distracted attention, information overload, and less-effective searching and browsing (Marshall & Jones 2006). We believe that well-designed technology must hide details and deletions, thus eliminating clutter and the oppressive task of managing it, while still retaining these records for future use. Furthermore, information must be abstracted and displayed in useful and attractive visualizations if people are to be able to interpret and use it appropriately. This must ultimately be linked to an understanding of the particular kinds of tasks people want to carry out with these systems, and the goals they have in mind as they use the data.

When the MyLifeBits project began, there were about 30,000 named items placed in about 1,500 folders. Retrieval was principally by folder location and file name. This quickly turned out to be unwieldy. One possible alternative to this might be to store everything in one large folder and retrieve items using a search engine with knowledge of the folders' content, and with no attention to location. However, full text search is not always enough. Many items require other attributes in order to be found. Unfortunately, with the quantities of information we are dealing with, users are not just unwilling to classify, but are also unable to do it.

We are currently exploring a middle ground that lies between the intricately hand-crafted, and arguably brittle, foldering scheme and no organization. To avoid having to become professional curators constructing our own personal classifications, we have become interested in classification sharing. We are experimenting with hierarchical classifications that will be developed by others to be downloaded by the user, and which contain extra information such as synonyms and descriptions to ease their use. These hierarchical classifications should allow scoping searches in a meaningful way and should lead to systems that scale more gracefully.

But even with convenient classifications and labels ready to apply, we are still asking the user to become a filing clerk—manually annotating every document, email, photo, or conversation. More must be done automatically. The first, easy step is to stop throwing out any potentially useful metadata. Time is probably the most important attribute in our database, yet some photo-editing programs erase the value for date taken. Even capture itself must be more automatic on this scale, so that the user is not forced to interrupt their normal life in order to become their own biographer.

While these are some of the general issues we are tackling, focusing on particular domains and applications is helping us to understand some of the specific technical and design issues. Two examples are (1) visualization to support personal reflection, and (2) monitoring and managing personal health information.

Visualization to Support Personal Reflection

Reporting tools with appropriate visualization form a class of very useful applications supporting reflection. A simple query-based tool can be remarkably insightful and useful—whether it is "how I spend my time" or "count the space used" by different items. In the simplest case, the amount of work on a document, spreadsheet, or Web page can be logged and displayed. Alternatively, reports can track what the user is working on or perhaps even thinking about—for example, by plotting the "budget" or "nominating committee" tasks against time.

Programs that can assist in the creation and visualization of trip diaries and key lifetime event stories will considerably increase use, especially for future viewers who have no familiarity with the content. For example, a fishing trip diary with a timeline, animated maps, and annotations is substantially more valuable to us and our progeny than a collection of unlabelled photos in a labeled folder. Visual autobiographies that summarize a person's life could also be envisioned.

Monitoring and Managing Personal Health Information

Another possible application of these personal lifetime stores is in the area of monitoring and managing one's health (Oliver & Flores-Mangas 2006). This would imply that our system should hold all of a person's health records, associated health financial transactions, and wellness information in order to assist users, caregivers, and health-care providers. Wearable physiological and environmental monitoring is becoming increasingly pervasive, allowing for the continuous, noninvasive collection of many of these signals, such as heart rate, body temperature, and other vital signs. These records could be maintained by an individual and form a baseline indicator of his/her health. Deviations from the average pattern in these metrics could flag potential changes in health.

Important components of such a monitoring system are machine learning and data mining algorithms for finding correlations, trends, and deviations from these trends. These trends would be useful not only in keeping a centralized repository of one's health information, but could also allow the system to provide reminders or actions that would promote better health for the user. The explosion of multisource, heterogeneous, and continuous data in general poses interesting challenges for sense-making utilities.

6.4.4 *Security, Privacy, and Access Control*

As we evolve to record everything for all time, we find significantly more opportunities for research around security, privacy, and access control, as well as ownership and the control of what bits get stored and which get thrown away. If the system is built as a stand-alone computer that stores and retrieves digital records, security is of little concern. Locking a hard drive is not difficult. However, ease of access makes it desirable to connect personal digital memories to a broader virtual network, even the Internet. The network will inevitably connect nearly all of the digital and physical information sources one would like to capture with the digital store. This makes things very convenient, but also very vulnerable, and more work needs to be done in protecting digital stores from malicious attackers.

Security concerns aside, when a user decides to share information with other users, specifying who should have access to the information and in what form imposes a non-trivial burden on the user. Additionally, a particular user may have several different personas within their store. For example, meeting recordings in a workplace setting may be owned by the company and should be partitioned from the rest of the user's social store. When the user moves to a different company, part of their digital memory store might have to be destroyed. Given the volume of data and the diversity of data sources, the choice between private and public could become an onerous one, not just on a daily basis, but also over longer periods of time. We believe that the eventual solution must leverage the nuanced ideas of groups of people and specific contexts within which information should be shared.

Once shared, there are many concerns with the amount of private information that can be inferred from other data. Taken over a long enough period, we expect that everyone will have something recorded that they would prefer to keep private. While there has been a great deal of research in this area (e.g., Ackerman 2000a; Bellotti & Sellen 1993; Cheng, Golubchik & Kay 2004), another chapter in this book concerns itself with these issues specifically, so we will defer to the more thorough treatment of this important subject there.

6.4.5 *Legal and Social Issues*

Many of the issues relating to control, ownership, privacy, security, and modification rights of digital memories are being defined and redefined with new laws in various countries.

It is illegal in some countries to make a copy of anything, including an owner's personal items such as articles, books, and CDs that are protected by copyrights. Similarly, photos of people or objects are protected by copyright such that it is necessary to have permissions for the use of these images. Some of these issues may already be clear from camera, video camera, and phone conversation capture—for example, in many states in the U.S. phone capture is only permitted as long as the party being recorded is informed. Hence, all MyLifeBits dialed or received calls open with a statement that the call is being recorded. Phone calls are really jointly owned, independent of permissions. Hence the ability to share jointly owned content makes the problem even more complex.

Conversion of all information forms to accessible digital forms will create continuing opportunities resulting in needs to access everything, everywhere. In trying to capture more and more data, we may even see a progression from archives on personal computer systems to archives on organizational systems whereby every event is captured throughout a company, government agency, or professional meeting. In this case, privacy and ownership rights will be key impediments and yet safeguards for this vast content.

Organizational relationships are important in our work. While links allow items to be related to one another, we require tools that support doing this across multiple personal stores. In this fashion, one can create family trees, organization charts, or broader social networks. This is especially useful for "contacts," as used by Outlook and other mail systems. Given the incredible mobility of individuals in our personal and professional contact list, it is essential to have a contact for just a company and position, independent of the name of any person who currently holds the position. For example, bankers, brokers, doctors, and other professionals that we maintain relationships with are much more transient than any of us would like. Updating this content is a continual hassle that a store would ideally handle.

6.5 Conclusion

This chapter has introduced the notion of a personal digital lifetime store that could be used for retrieving, recollecting, reminiscing, and reflecting on one's life experiences and information. We described our work on building such a system, including the MyLifeBits platform and the SenseCam data-recording device. We also discussed a specific case study and presented encouraging results for such a SenseCam–based system for supporting a patient with memory deficits. Our goal in writing this chapter was to describe our own personal usage of these technologies to aid and support human memory capabilities, as well as to point toward potential benefits if the technologies are further developed with particular user, corporate, and societal needs in mind. There is much future work that needs to be carried out, both in terms of understanding how useful a personal store of this kind can be, as well as how better to summarize, make sense of, visualize, and share this kind of information. Furthermore, much needs to be done to ensure that the store is of high fidelity, in addition to being safe and secure. Despite the large amount of work that remains, we feel that our early work has begun to demonstrate the real value behind personal digital lifetime stores.

6.6 Acknowledgments

We would like to thank Abigail Sellen for inspiring discussions and insightful feedback on this work; Roger Lueder, Greg Smith, and the rest of the MyLifeBits Development Team; Jim Gray for advice on database aspects of our work; Kentaro Toyama and the World Wide Media Exchange for their assistance with mapping photos; Aleks Aris for making the GPS trails useful as logs resulting in stories; Ed Cutrell and Daniel Robbins for assistance with the graphical user interface for the logger and visualizations; Lyndsay Williams for her instrumental role in CARPE (Continuous Archiving and Retrieval of Personal Experience) and her work with the SenseCam; and everyone else at Microsoft Research who has contributed their ideas, work, and encouragement.

⧆ Structure Everything

Tiziana Catarci, Luna Dong, Alon Halevy, and Antonella Poggi

7.1 Introduction

The availability of vast amounts of information on the Internet and the sharp decrease in the cost of digital storage has enabled today's desktops to become personal information archives. Desktops contain collections of work- and hobby-related data as well as rich collections of personal multimedia files. However, the typical lack of structure of one's desktop data makes it difficult for the user to easily search and benefit from the information it contains.

Consider an example, a scenario where Alex's laptop contains a huge amount of information that is stored in several different formats, including emails, pictures, text documents, media files, address books, and more. In particular, Alex uses email extensively to communicate with many friends, his mother, Connie, and his sister, Brooke. When he receives a voicemail from Connie asking him to help plan a surprise birthday party for Edna, who is turning 75, he needs to find the name of her favorite restaurant and its phone number so that he can make reservations. Alex immediately starts searching his laptop for the name of the restaurant. He remembers that it was an Argentinean restaurant inside a hotel and that he took a picture of it once when he was going for a Sunday walk with Edna and Connie. Luckily, just last week he installed Google Desktop on his laptop. He therefore launches the tool and enters the keywords "Edna restaurant." However, instead of getting the name of the restaurant he is looking for, he sees a list of Edna's pictures and a list of messages that he exchanged last Christmas with Brooke when they were planning to go out for dinner with Connie and Edna.

The above scenario illustrates the weakness of keyword-based search. Keyword search engines, in the context of personal information management (PIM)—or in the context of the Web—are limited in that they only return documents that contain the keywords mentioned in the query, instead of returning other possibly relevant information. Hence, unless Alex had explicitly labeled a document with the appropriate keywords he would not find the information he's looking for.

Finally, suppose that later in the planning stages, after discovering that the name of the restaurant is "Jaguar," creating the invitations for Edna's friends with all the details of the restaurant, preparing a funny "This is your life" presentation, and making up dinner place cards for each guest, Alex were to discover that the restaurant had overbooked for that evening. Then he would probably easily find another good Argentinean restaurant. However, he would also have to update all the references to the Jaguar restaurant contained in the material he had prepared for the party.

The scenario above shows how frustrating it may be to fulfill even a simple task with the scant support provided by our desktop search and management tools, even when all the information we need is already stored on our desktop.

7.1.1 *Why Structure Is Important*

The aforementioned scenario is quite a realistic one and happens on a daily basis. It illustrates how far we actually are from leveraging the potential of personal computers and the information stored on them. As described in the chapter on MyLifeBits, the entirety of a user's life may easily fit on a computer disk. However, desktops have evolved into information archives in an ad hoc fashion, and we are now suffering from the lack of organization of this data, aside from that provided by the underlying file system.

On the other hand, many years of database research have shown how structure is fundamental in letting the user organize and subsequently find data of interest. This has led, for example, to efficient database management systems (DBMS), that let the user store structured data according to a schema, and to access them very efficiently by means of expressive query languages. Typically, this kind of system offers the access to a single specific data source, such as a single set of data; whereas, in the last decade, research in the field has partially migrated toward data integration systems, which provide the user with an access to several distributed autonomous and heterogeneous data sources via an integrated schema. Such systems deal with a very difficult problem—the problem of how to integrate and reconcile data.

The main focus of this chapter is therefore to show how, by structuring data, it is possible to offer better personal information management systems services.

7.1.2 *Definitions*

Note that when discussing database issues we will distinguish between the (database) *schema*, which specifies the structure of the database and can be seen as a virtual view over data, and the (database) *source(s)* containing the actual data. Let us now introduce few terms that are crucial for the rest of the chapter.

Data integration. The problem of providing users a uniform interface to a collection of heterogeneous and autonomous data sources. (Lenzerini 2002; Levy 2000).

Digital Library (DL). A set of electronic resources and associated technical capabilities for creating, searching, and using information contained in them (Borgman 1999).

Ontology. Attempt to formulate an exhaustive and rigorous conceptual schema within a given domain. Often an ontology is a hierarchical data structure containing all the relevant entities and their relationships and rules (theorems, regulations) within that domain (Wikipedia 2006).

Taxonomies. Hierarchical structures for classifying a set of objects. They are less expressive than ontologies as a means for expressing structure on objects in the world. They only allow subclass relationships, and cannot represent relationships between concepts.

Thesaurus. A data structure designed for indexing, where we associate with every important term in the domain a set of terms related to it.

Personal ontology. User's personal conceptualization of her/his domains of interest.

Instance. Object in the real world that belongs to the set of objects represented by a concept of the ontology.

Reference. Actual representation of an instance, contained in the user's desktop data (typically a string or a tuple of strings).

Reference reconciliation. The problem of recognizing when different references represent the same instance, that is, the same real-world object.

7.1.3 Basic Issues, Problems, and Challenges

Several basic issues that have been actually solved in the general database research field are becoming critical challenges in the context of PIM and require solutions that are unique to the PIM context. In particular, whereas querying data that has been structured can be achieved by adapting well-established database techniques, issues relating to updating, reconciling, and cleaning information still require additional research.

To illustrate, consider our introductory scenario. In order for Alex to reflect the change of restaurant, he would need to change the name and the address of the restaurant across several different files that were obtained by using independent software applications, such as the email client, the editor for the invitations and place cards, and the editor used for the presentation. The point here is that in addition to managing data PIM also deals with the problem of managing actual files that are somehow related to the data. Therefore, whenever the user needs to perform an update, it may be reflected in several files that are managed via independent software applications.

Since data in a PIM context typically come from multiple sources, and are therefore in multiple formats, reference reconciliation is critical. For example, a contact in Alex's address book may correspond to the subject of a picture, as in the case of Edna's favorite restaurant. Similarly, his coworker's name, Patricia Lober, may occur in one email message she sent to Alex as *Pat*, occur in another message as *Ms. Lober,* and occur in a report authored by the two of them as *Patricia A. Lober.* In order to combine multiple sources and to support effective browsing and querying across different data sources, a PIM system needs to solve the reference reconciliation problem; that is, to decide when two references represent the same object in the world. Unlike previous work, the reconciliation problem is exacerbated in a PIM context because each of the references typically contains only a little information, such as a name or even an abbreviated first name.

Finally, among classical data-quality issues, some become critical and very specific to PIM, namely:

■ **Standardization** (or normalization) is the modification of data with new data according to defined standard or reference formats, such as the change of Channel Str. with Channel Street, or a change of Bob with Robert. The user may want to perform such a normalization, but in PIM he may also want to keep the old information as in the case of the latter change example, where he may want to use Robert or Bob depending on whether he is writing an official email or not.

■ **Quality-driven query processing** is the task of providing query results on the basis of a quality characterization of data at sources. In PIM the quality characterization of the sources may result from subjective criteria that depend from the user's profile.

■ **Schema cleaning** provides rules for transforming the conceptual schema in order to achieve or optimize a given set of goals (e.g., readability, normalization), while preserving other properties (e.g., equivalence of content). Given the fact that PIM is personal, that is, it should fit individual requirements, this activity should crucially depend on the user.

7.2 Research Overview

7.2.1 *What Is Being Done*

As soon as we need to access information that is scattered across different autonomous and heterogeneous sources, such as databases stored in different database management systems, documents created by different applications, or, more generally, files with different extensions, we face the problem of overcoming heterogeneity, structuring the information to be accessed, and reconciling it according to data semantics. This is of course the case with PIM, but it has for a long time also been the case for database integration and digital libraries. Depending on the application, many ad-hoc solutions have been proposed. The data integration and digital library communities have pursued two different approaches to this general problem, but have recently begun to converge toward a "semantic-based" information solution. Indeed, database researchers started from the problem of querying alphanumeric data stored in very structured repositories, and subsequently extended such an approach to cover different kinds of data, in particular text and images, richer relationships among data, and various data structures, while also coming up with the need to integrate different data sources. Digital library researchers, on the other hand, initially had the problem of finding text containing certain natural language terms using keyword-based searches, and then moved to accessing diverse data collections containing not only text but also semistructured data, images, and videos, using more powerful and semantic-based access mechanisms. The two approaches thus slowly converged to integrating and accessing structured, heterogeneous collections of multimedia data through semantic languages. In this section we will present what is being done in these two areas of research. For instance, we will see in the following how Connie has to search and integrate data coming from a variety of databases and disparate information environments accessed via the Internet.

Data Integration Approach

Data integration is a huge area of research, involving different aspects including design time as well as run-time aspects (Halevy 2004). PIM poses a special kind of data integration challenge since personal information—for example, the information a person needs to complete a current project—is often drawn from several sources represented in several different formats. Consider the scenario given in the introduction, where Alex needs information that comes from his email, his address book, and his pictures. Such different information needs to be integrated and reconciled in order to be efficiently accessed by Alex.

In what follows, we will first briefly present some important issues of data integration with special relevance to PIM:

▪ **Personal information structuring.** In setting up a logical framework for data integration, the process begins by specifying the mediated schema to be accessed by users and the data sources. The relationships between the sources and the mediated schema are called *mappings*. The mappings are needed for query processing when the query execution engine will reformulate a query posed over the mediated schema into appropriate queries over the data sources.

For example, in our scenario an appropriate logical framework may specify a relational mediated schema, such as a set of relations, among which the relations *People, AreFriends, Restaurants,* and *LikesFood,* containing respectively (1) all the people that Alex knows; (2) all the pairs of people that are known to be friends; (3) all the restaurants, their addresses, and characteristics; and (4) all the people for which Alex knows the preferences in terms of restaurants. The data sources are, as already mentioned, the set of Alex's pictures, documents, emails, and his address book. Finally, the mapping between the schema relations and the data sources establishes, for example, how to map data from Alex's address book to information about restaurants. Note that other mappings may be suggested by the system. In particular, one possibility may be the following: by highlighting two names contained in a document, Alex may be asked by the system to choose among possible relationship that may exist among different people. This would be a different kind of mapping, since it establishes a relationship between a particular pair of instances in the data (the ones being highlighted).

▪ **Data extraction.** The process continues with the construction of *wrappers,* which are responsible for transforming the data at the sources into a form that makes them suitable for use in the data integration system (see, for instance, Baumgartner, Flesca & Gotlob 2001). In particular, it is common practice to require that wrappers produce data that all conform to the same data model, such as the relational data model, thereby enabling all further processing on the data to be performed in a single data model. For example, given a picture, a wrapper may extract from it a set of metadata, such as the subject of the picture and the author. This metadata would then appear as a tuple of a relation that characterizes each picture. Another example may be a wrapper that extracts from the emails the sender, the receiver, and the subject.

113

■ **Schema matching** (Rahm & Bernstein 2001). The goal of this element is to provide tools that take two schemas as input and produce a semantic mapping between elements of the two schemas. In our scenario, this would correspond to developing a module in a PIM system which, given an address book, is able to compute the appropriate mapping between the relation *Restaurants* and the address book.

■ **Quality.** The problem also involves incorporating in the data integration setting notions of *data quality, quality of answers* (Mecella, Scannapieco, Virgillito et al. 2002) and *data cleaning* (Bouzeghoub & Lenzerini 2001). Of course, since personal information may come from an unreliable source, or may be obsolete, it is important to associate with data a notion of quality. For example, the address book may be considered very reliable, whereas information extracted from emails coming from unknown contacts should be considered much less reliable. Then, it may be useful to clean data that do not conform to some criterion. For example, imagine that Brooke was hired last year. She was assigned a new email address for work, but she gave Alex the wrong spelling of the email address. Then, after a certain number of emails that Alex received from Brooke's new email address, the PIM system should detect the wrong spelling and perform a cleaning of the corresponding data. Note, however, that in the PIM context, the data-cleaning procedure should be very cautious, since some times we may want to keep track of data, even if we know that it is not valid anymore. Suppose for example that Brooke has a private Gmail account that she may want to keep for some reason. Of course in this case the data-cleaning procedure should not behave as before, even if it turns out that Brooke doesn't use that private address anymore.

All the above aspects need to be considered when designing a general data-integration system, and in particular when attempting to support the integration of personal information. Indeed, by considering the personal ontology as the mediated schema of a data integration system, a PIM can be seen as an enriched data-integration system whose sources are the files contained in the desktop. Note, however, the focus of this chapter is on the first challenge, structuring personal information. Suppose that Alex's laptop provides an ontology that he can access when looking for the name of Edna's favorite restaurant. Then, the ontology would be such that:

■ It contains the concepts *Restaurant, Person,* and *Friends,* and there is a "IS-A" relation between *Friends* and *Person;*

▓ It includes the relation *LikesFood* relating the concept Person to the concept *Restaurant,* whose semantics is that a pair **(a,b)** of objects belongs to the relation *Likes Food* if and only if the person **a** likes the food of the restaurant **b**;

▓ It contains a relation *IS-friend* relating the concept Person to itself, such that the pair **(c,d)** belongs to the role *IS-friend* if and only if **c** is a friend of **d**.

Clearly, by accessing the ontology, Alex is now able to find all the information he needs to help plan the surprise party, provided that when he saved the data about Edna on his laptop he defined the appropriate mappings—that is, he established the right relationship between the data sources and the ontology. Of course, this point is critical in that the user must be supported in order to let him define the mappings easily and in most of the cases guessing them correctly for him.

Let us now consider the issue of querying a data integration system. Queries over a data integration system are expressed in terms of the personal ontology. The system accesses the sources and reassembles the results in order to answer the query appropriately. For example, in our scenario the personal ontology may be the one proposed above. Then, in order to obtain the name and the address of Edna's favorite restaurant, Alex may query the system for all restaurants that Edna likes, and then among these Alex may look for ones inside a hotel, and of which he took a picture. Indeed, the picture would appear as a reference to the particular instance of the concept *Restaurant.* Note that if Alex had in his address book the address of the Jaguar restaurant, then the system should have reconciled the two references: that is, the address book entry and the picture of the restaurant.

Several data integration systems have been developed during the last decade. Most of them follow an approach called *global-as-view,* which consists in specifying the mappings so that the mediated schema is described in terms of the sources. More precisely, this is the case of TSIMMIS (Garcia-Molina, Papakonstantinou, Quass, et al. 1997), Garlic (Roth, Arya, Haas, et al. 1996), and many others. Conversely, other systems follow an approach, called *local-as-view,* in which data sources are described in terms of views over the mediated schema. We mention in particular Information Manifold (Levy, Rajaraman & Ordille 1996), which expresses the mediated schema in terms of a description logic. See Halevy, Ashish, Bitton, et al. (2005) for a recent snapshot of the current state of the art of the data integration industry.

The Digital Libraries Approach

Digital libraries (DL) are in some sense an extension and enhancement of information storage and retrieval systems that manipulate digital data in any medium (text, images, sounds, and static or dynamic images). A personal digital library effectively exists in everyone's personal computer. The content of digital libraries includes data, metadata that describe various aspects of the data (e.g., representation, creator, owner, reproduction rights), and metadata that consist of links or relationships to other data or metadata, whether internal or external to the digital library.

Some common points may be identified across several different definitions that can be found for DLs:

- DLs can comprise digital as well as nondigital entities;
- The realm of libraries is constituted not only of library objects but also of associated processes, actors, and communities;
- The content of a DL can be extremely heterogeneous; and
- DLs must deal with interoperability issues, given the fact that collections and services are provided by many different organizations and information comes from many sources.

It appears that the key DL issue in this matter is to provide a coherent view of the (possibly) large collection of available materials (Lynch & Garcia-Molina 1995). In a sense, we can view a DL as an information environment with information producers and consumers; producers may also be consumers at the same time and vice versa. In a personal DL the user definitely plays both roles and switches between them very often.

Among the many and diverse issues existing in DL research, ranging from intellectual rights management to user collaboration to architectural interoperability, the most relevant from a PIM point of view (and from the point of view of structuring the information) are issues related to the management of metadata (and more generally with the so-called semantic interoperability) and the various types of multimedia data. Metadata capture additional knowledge about a digital library, typically in the form of taxonomies, ontologies, thesauri, and other abstraction mechanisms.

In the context of a DL, creation and maintenance of data as well as metadata may be supported manually or (semi-) automatically. Metadata may be generated out of data or even existing metadata, and in order to provide integrated access over distributed DLs. One of the prominent approaches toward achieving semantic interoperability in DLs is based on standardization (see, e.g., the Dublin core approach [NISO 2003] that includes: the form and meaning of metadata, shared concept definitions, and the use of names and construction of identifiers for concepts and real-world items).

Standardization has many obvious advantages, such as immediate merging and communication of information without any transformation. But it also has several disadvantages, including the difficulty of obtaining verification that sources conform to standards, and the huge effort needed in producing the standard itself. Also, with standards typically set up for only one domain or even one application, they cannot work universally. Of course, one cannot pretend to standardize every PIM of every single user even if the use of some standard terms and definitions can be exploited.

An alternative to standardization in DLs is the notion of interpretation, which may comprise the mapping of metadata and content schemata, the correlation of concepts defined in different sources, the translation of names, and reformatting of identifiers for concepts and real-world items (Doerr 2001; Doerr, Hunter & Lagoze 2003). The interpretation-based approaches are definitely more flexible and not intrusive with respect to sources but require a great effort to produce the knowledge base for an interpreter (typically this has to be done largely manually and only partially automatically). If the number of formats in use increases, interpretation may need to go through a common switching language that is very close to another standard (see, e.g., the LIMBER (www.limber.rl.ac.uk) and SCHOLNET (www.ercim.org/scholnet/) projects).

Also, in the DL realm one of the most well-accepted mechanisms for achieving semantic interoperability is the utilization of ontologies. Several classes of ontologies exist that may be exploited in PIM, such as *foundational ontologies*, which are axiomatic ontologies that address very general domains; *upper ontologies*, where basic, domain-independent concepts as well as relationships among them are defined (e.g., WordNet); *core ontologies*, which are essentially upper ontologies for broad application domains (e.g., the audiovisual domain); and *domain ontologies*, where concepts and relationships used in specific application domains are defined. The idea here is that well-accepted upper ontologies should exist, where basic concepts and relationships are defined, and these can be extended by appropriate domain ontologies.

This approach has been successfully applied in the audiovisual domain— see, among others, Troncy (2003) and Tsinaraki, Polydoros, and Christodoulakis (2004), where the ontologies guide the annotation of the audiovisual content and the metadata produced are compliant with the MPEG-7 standard. Indeed, digital libraries, as well as PIM, typically contain multimedia collections that may involve digital representations of not only textual items but also graphical and spatially indexed items, acoustical items, and video items. An important issue relating to the items of such collections is that they may require significant levels of intermediate processing or interpretation, such as image or acoustical signal processing, that are not required for collections of traditional textual materials. A second important issue relates to integration of specific materials that are even more complex than in the case of alphanumerical and textual data.

Metadata management is crucial even in this case. In particular, it is useful to categorize metadata according to whether it is domain-dependent or domain-independent and whether, in the latter case, it is related to "low-level" content or to aspects of the origin and representational aspects of the item. Such distinctions are very important in the case of multimedia libraries. Items such as images and maps, for example, have huge numbers of interpretations concerning their content and require significant extensions of traditional cataloguing practices in order to characterize them in a manner that is useful for user access and browsing. An enhancement to traditional libraries that arises in relation to metadata involves the variety of "annotations" that may be stored in association with items. Thus, in our working scenario, by following a typical DL approach, Connie would access the municipality Web site and look for pictures of restaurants. Then she would search the pictures metadata for the type of cooking (Argentinean), and then browse all appropriate pictures until she would recognize a restaurant inside a hotel.

7.2.2 What Needs to Be Done

In this subsection we give an overview of the main issues related to structuring personal information, while adopting an ontology-based (data integration-like) approach. We will do so by exploiting a recent proposal, namely OntoPIM (Katifori, Poggi, Scannapieco, et al. 2005), for a PIM system architecture (see Figure 7.2.2). The main goal of OntoPIM is to allow the user to (1) store any object of interest according to its semantics, or in other words to relate it to the concepts of the personal ontology, where an object may be a mail, a document, a picture, or any other type of data; (2) effectively query such a personal ontology according to the user's needs and preferences. In what follows we describe the main modules of OntoPIM.

Note that all modules interact with three different data layers that, starting from the bottom, are: (a) the physical layer, storing files or relational tables or any other physical objects that can be stored on a PC; (b) the first wrapper layer (DI layer) representing domain independent (DI) objects from the physical layer, such as Alex's address book entries, emails, documents, photos, and so on;

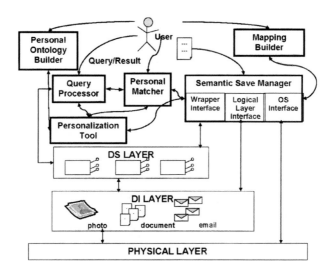

Figure 7.2.2 – OntoPIM architecture.

and (c) the second wrapper layer (DS layer) representing domain specific (DS) objects, such as family presentations or invitation cards, in the running scenario. Note that references in OntoPIM correspond to DS object attributes.

The user interacts with the **Personal Ontology Builder (POB)** in order to build her own personal ontology. Such a representation is intended to be completely independent of the physical representation of information. Note that this module is required in all PIM systems that aim to offer users a personal ontology for accessing their data. This is actually the module that Alex uses to specify that his laptop contains data about persons, friends, and the restaurants they like. **The Personalization Tool (PT)** interacts with the POB to automate the creation and the modification of the ontology on the basis of an appropriate user profile. Clearly, in order for the ontology to be useful, the user should be able to personalize, change, and expand it. Among the several issues related to this requirement an important one concerns the initial ontology available to the user. Two solutions are possible:

■ Create the ontology from scratch. One option is to start with an empty ontology and allow the user to build it. The advantage of this approach is the flexibility it offers, as the ontology created will reflect very accurately the user's needs. Its disadvantage is that such an approach applies only to technically savvy users.

■ Modify an existing ontology. A basic, common ontology could be created, one that can be used as a basis for extensions and modifications during the personalization process. Furthermore, the system could offer several ready-to-use templates of ontologies for the user to choose from that could be more suitable to her needs. The advantage of this option is that it minimizes the user's effort in creating her ontology. This option requires, on the other hand, a very elaborate user study in order to build the initial basic ontology and the templates and to develop the appropriate personalization mechanisms for the adjustments on the templates.

Both of these options may be available to the user, allowing various degrees of flexibility in creating a truly personalized ontology. Obviously the more demanding option from the research point of view is the second one.

The **Mapping Builder (MB)** allows the user to create and modify the types his DS objects. In our scenario, as soon as Alex starts preparing for the surprise party, he saves every new object he creates via the Semantic Save. In particular, he would like to save the presentation "This is your life" as a DS object of type "Family Presentation." Suppose that such a type was not introduced yet. Alex needs to create a new DS object type. For this purpose he uses the MB and defines the "Family Presentation" DS type having the suitable set of attributes, namely, "Why," "Where," and "When," describing the occasion, the location, and the dates for the projected presentation. Then he relates the new DS type to elements of the personal ontology. More precisely by means of the MB, he defines a mapping that for each object of type "Family Presentation" shows an instance of the concept "Event." He can also specify how to map the references that can be extracted from the "Family Presentation" object, such as the value of the attribute "Where," to concepts related to "Event,"—such as "Restaurant"—that participates to the relation "Takes_Place" between the concept "Event" and the concept "Restaurant." Note that the design of a user-friendly MB is a crucial and challenging issue that needs to be solved.

The **Semantic Save Manager (SSM)** takes as input a physical object "o" and uses the mapping created by the MB module to perform the Semantic Save which: (1) invokes the operating system in order to save "o" in the file system, (2) creates the appropriate DI abstraction of "o," and (3) links it to the corresponding wrapper. Coming back to the example above, after having defined the mappings for the DS type "Family Presentation," Alex is able to use the Semantic Save to actually store the presentation "This is your life" as a "Family Presentation" object. Doing this, he will have the opportunity to enter other details about the instance of the concept "Event" that is associated through the mapping with the presentation; for example, he will be able to specify that it is also an instance of the concept "Birthday," related to the instance of the concept "Person" denoting Edna. The SSM module is required to structure desktop data according to certain semantics. However, instead of requiring the user interaction, this may proceed by *learning* how to save automatically data that pertain to the personal ontology. This issue is actually far from having been solved.

The **Query Processor (QP)** is responsible for processing and answering the queries posed by the user over the personal ontology. More specifically, the QP exploits the abstraction created by the SSM, and the mapping created by the MB, in order to rewrite the query in terms of queries to wrappers that retrieve the actual data from the physical layer. This module is similar to the data-integration system query processor module and does not pose any issue that is particular to PIM.

The **Personal Matcher (PM)** performs reference reconciliation. It is therefore responsible for identifying attribute values of different DS objects that are references representing the same real-world object. This module may either produce an output that is the set of matching rules describing how to perform the reference reconciliation, or it may actually perform the reference reconciliation. While the former approach needs to be explored, the latter approach is the one that has been followed by the Semex system, which will be presented in the next section.

7.3   Diving In

7.3.1 *Why Reference Reconciliation Is Important*

In order to combine multiple sources and to support effective browsing and querying across different data sources, a PIM system needs to solve the reference reconciliation problem. The system needs to decide when two references represent the same object in the real world. As we already pointed out, this would allow finding the name and the address of Edna's favorite restaurant by inspecting a picture that would have been identified as a reference to the appropriate instance.

Reference reconciliation is one of the issues addressed in the Semex System (Dong, Halevy & Madhavan 2005), where the authors describe a general framework for propagating information from one reconciliation decision to another.

7.3.2 *What Is Being Done to Explore Reference Reconciliation*

In this section we present a PIM system that is based on the use of an ontology to structure personal data. Semex complements OntoPIM in that it focuses on automatically extracting entities and relationships on the desktop, and it combines structured and unstructured modes of querying data. Hence a user can start with entering a keyword search, but can also refine her query using a structured search paradigm, leveraging the relationships discovered by the system.

The Semex system (short for *Sem*antic *Ex*plorer) aims at offering users a flexible platform for personal information management. Semex has two main goals. The first is to enable browsing personal information by association. The challenge is to *automatically* create associations between data items on one's desktop. While it will never be possible to create all possible associations, the goal is to create enough of them so Semex becomes an indispensable tool.

Consider the way Derek manages his information. Suppose Derek has taken a class called Economic Law and at the end of the quarter he needs to prepare for the final. He wishes to find all information related to this course, including the Web site of the course, the notes he took during class, the homework, the discussion emails with the instructor and his classmates, and so on. Using a traditional system Derek needs to open different applications and conduct each search separately. Instead, Semex analyzes Derek's files, emails, and Web pages cached during the quarter, creating a *Course* object (for the course), several *Person* objects (for the instructor and classmates), *Note* objects, *Homework* objects, *Email* objects, *Webpage* objects, and so on. Now, when Derek searches for "Economic Law," Semex returns a set of objects, including the object representing the course. When Derek selects it, Semex presents all objects associated with the course, categorized into instructors, students, Web pages, notes, homework, emails, and so on. To see all emails with the instructor, Derek can click the corresponding Person object and Semex presents the emails sent to and from the instructor, shown in email traces.

Semex's second goal is to leverage the associations created, to increase users' productivity. In addition to the increased productivity a better search tool offers, we also show how Semex leverages the association database to enable lightweight information integration tasks that are discouragingly difficult to perform with today's tools. Continuing with the previous example, Derek can ask Semex to integrate with a departmental database on courses. In this way, Semex creates more objects (e.g., *Course* objects, *Person* objects, *Book* objects), and Derek can easily search through them and browse related information, such as course instructors and books.

We next consider each of these goals in detail.

Browsing by Association

The key impediment to browsing personal information by association is that data on the desktop is stored *by application* and in directory hierarchies, whereas browsing by association requires a *logical view* of the objects on the desktop and of the relations between them. In the above example, information about the Economic Law course is scattered across emails, the Web cache, and text and presentation files. Even answering a simple query, such as finding all information related to a course, requires significant work. Semex provides a logical view of one's personal information, based on *meaningful* objects and associations. We refer to the instantiation of the logical view as the *association database*. Importantly, since users are typically not willing to tolerate any overhead associated with creating additional structure in their personal data, Semex attempts to create the association database automatically.

It is impossible to anticipate in advance all the sources of associations between objects in one's personal information. Hence, it is important that Semex be extensible in the ways in which associations can be added. Semex obtains objects and associations from multiple types of sources. First, some associations are obtained by programs that are specific to particular file types. In the simple case, Semex extracts objects and associations from contacts and email clients (e.g., senders and recipients, phone numbers, and email addresses). In more complex cases, Semex extracts some associations (e.g., *AuthorOf*) by analyzing LaTeX files and PowerPoint presentations. Second, associations can be obtained from external lists or databases (e.g., a list of one's graduate students or departmental colleagues). Finally, complex associations are derived from simple ones (e.g., one's coauthors).

It is interesting to contrast the role of the ontology in Semex and in OntoPIM. In Semex, the ontology is built piecemeal, when interesting relationships can be discovered. For example, if we have a method of extracting the relationship *AuthorOf* between people and papers, then we add the relationship to the ontology. In this sense, Semex's ontology is very open. Whenever useful information can be obtained about instances, then new concepts and relationships are added to the ontology. In fact, the user may not be aware of the entire ontology underlying the system, but may still benefit from it during querying.

On-the-fly Data Integration

The second goal of Semex is to leverage the association database to increase users' productivity. On-the-fly data integration refers to lightweight data management tasks that require combining information from multiple online sources to achieve a task. Suppose, for example, a chair for a conference wishes to generate a list of candidates for the program committee. The chair is looking for people who have published at the conference but have not served on the program committee in previous years. There are disparate sources of data that can help the user in this task, such as a spreadsheet of recent program committee members and the Database and Logic Programming Bibliography (DBLP, http://www.informatik.uni-trier.de/~ley/db/), but integrating them with today's tools is tedious at best. With Semex, the user would import each one of them into the association database, and then be able to query across them and other personal data.

The field of data integration has made substantial progress in recent years, fueled by data-sharing opportunities on the Web, within enterprises, and in large scientific projects. Today, data integration projects proceed by identifying needs in an organization, typically focusing on *frequently recurring* queries throughout the organization. As a result many small-scale and more transient data integration tasks that we face on a daily basis are not supported. In particular, integration that involves personal data sources on one's desktop, or in one's laboratory, is not supported. The goal of on-the-fly data integration is to fundamentally change the cost-benefit ratio associated with integrating data sources. We want to assist nontechnical users to more easily integrate diverse sources, possibly for transient tasks. The intuition behind our approach is that the association database of Semex provides an *anchor* into which we can easily integrate external sources, as detailed in the following paragraph.

Semex enables users to easily incorporate new data sources into their association database in several steps. First, Semex helps the user *prepare* the data so it can be processed. For example, this may require scraping the data from a Web page, file, or spreadsheet. Second, Semex helps the user establish these Semantic relationships between the external data source and the Semex domain model. In some cases, this step may involve *extending* the user's personal information model by introducing new classes and associations. In the third step, Semex imports the data into the personal information space, and reconciles references to guarantee high-quality import at the instance level. Finally, Semex analyzes the imported data to find patterns that may be of interest to the user. The key insight that enables Semex to support these steps easily in comparison to other contexts is that Semex leverages the knowledge it has about the domain model and previous activities that the user has performed. In particular, Semex leverages previous preparation and mapping activities and the collection of objects and associations it already has in its database.

7.4 Looking Forward

We now mention several higher-level themes that we believe will pervade many of the challenges in PIM.

First, many of the challenges arise because personal information is long-lived and continually evolving. In contrast, most data management is used to model database states that capture snapshots of the world. The evolution occurs at the instance level as well as the schema level. So far, the evolution has manifested itself in challenges to querying, reference reconciliation, and schema mapping.

The second theme is finding the right granularity for modeling personal data. It is often possible to model the data at a very fine level. However, since PIM tools are geared toward users who are not necessarily technically savvy, it is important to keep the models as simple as possible. As we continue to investigate this trade-off, we may find an interesting middle point between the models traditionally used for structured data and those for unstructured data.

Third, when designing PIM systems it is important to think from the perspective of the user and her interactions with data in her daily routine, rather than from the perspective of the database. We need to build systems to support users in their own habitat, rather than trying to fit their activities into traditional data management. Thus, a very important issue would be to automate the process of saving documents to some extent. For example, the system may propose possible concepts of the ontology to be associated with the document, or to assist the user when posing queries over the personal ontology. In particular, the system may propose to the user appropriate query completion, on the basis of her preferences and actions (Koutrika & Ioannidis 2005). Personalization would help in those directions by automating things for the user, completing queries with things implied by the user, and so on. Also, reference reconciliation may take advantage of such a user's profiling mechanisms.

Fourth, consider again our scenario. Alex travels a lot for work. He is very meticulous and stores in his laptop all details about his travels, such as the dates, the meeting plans, and all the expenses for which he is supposed to get reimbursed. However, each time he comes back from a trip he wastes a lot of time filling out a reimbursement form, which makes him feel really frustrated. Suppose now that Alex starts using PIM to structure the data about his travels by means of a personal ontology, as described in the previous sections. One very promising research direction is to give the user a means for defining his activities in such a way that the system is able to carry them out almost automatically. In our scenario, given the dates of Alex's last travel, the PIM system would fill out the reimbursement form automatically by posing appropriate queries over the personal ontology. Note that this could be considered a high-level e-service to the user, because it interacts with the personal ontology in order to obtain input and possibly to store output.

Finally, there has been a lot of interest in systems that combine structured and unstructured data in a seamless fashion. We believe that PIM is an excellent application to drive the development of such systems, and in turn raises challenges concerning storing, modeling, and querying hybrid data.

8 Unify Everything: It's All the Same to Me

David R. Karger

8.1 Introduction

Information fragmentation is a pervasive problem in personal information management (PIM). Even a seemingly simple decision, such as whether to say "yes" to a dinner invitation, often depends upon information from several sources—a calendar, a paper flyer, Web sites, or a previous email conversation. This information is fragmented by the very tools that have been designed to help us manage it. Applications often store their data in their own particular locations and representations, inaccessible to other applications. Consider the information Alex maintains about Brooke. He must keep Brooke's address in his address book, her picture in a photo album, her home page in his Web bookmarks, a birthday invitation he is editing with her in his file system, and an appointment with her in his calendar.

This fragmentation causes numerous problems. There is no single "directory" Alex can use to find all the information about Brooke; nor any way to link pieces of information about Brooke to each other. Instead, Alex must launch multiple applications and perform numerous repetitive searches for relevant information, to say nothing of deciding which applications to look in. He may change data in one place (a new married name in the address book) and fail to change it elsewhere, leading to inconsistency that makes it even harder to find information (which name does Alex use to search the photo album?).

While the computer has fragmented information, it can also be used to put the pieces together again. This chapter surveys some of the ways in which our personal information might be better unified.

8.1.1 *Motivation*

Data unification offers many benefits to end users. The general motivation is that users often need to work simultaneously with several information objects in order to complete a given task. Here, we explore this motivation in greater detail.

One motivation for unification is that a user may need to observe several distinct information objects in order to draw conclusions about them. Looking at them one at a time can be slow and difficult, particularly if we must return to each several times—for example, when we must compare two information objects element by element. Even if direct comparison is unnecessary, shifting from one object to another to access different attributes can cause a user to lose their place and waste time finding it again when they return to an object. Given the value of seeing all the relevant information at the same time, it is unsurprising that almost all users have adopted window managers that let them display several application windows simultaneously.

A second motivation for unification is the desire to shift data easily from one application to another. At some point you have likely found yourself reading information out of one application and manually entering it into another, when the two applications could not agree on a common representation for that information that would allow it to be transferred by a simple cut-and-paste operation. As a fortunate exception, most applications nowadays offer uniform cut, copy, and paste interaction with whatever *text* information they hold.

Needing to copy data between applications is a sign that the same information (possibly in different aspects) is being managed by multiple applications. For example, a person might appear in a user's address book, and also as the creator of a photograph in the user's album. This creates several problems that can be fixed by (and therefore motivate) better unification. One arises when the user records the information in multiple places, and gets caught by inconsistent versioning when changes to one version of the data (a new married name, for example) do not propagate to other versions of the data.

Even when users record information in only one place, they may not remember which one. This can make it hard to find. For example, a user might record a person's birthday in their calendar, but then try and fail to look it up in his address book entry about that person. Conversely, if they first discovered that birthday in their calendar, and wanted to send a congratulatory email, they would have to look up the person's email in their address book. Arguably, this is a wasted search: if we are already looking at the person's name on the screen (in the calendar), why can't the application tell us their email address without further searching? We can understand this as a failure in two ways: first, there is no easy way to link from the information about the person in their address book to the information in the calendar (doing so would also help fight inconsistency). Alternatively, we can argue that the functionality of sending email should not be locked up in the address book, but should instead apply to any person we encounter in any application—calendar, photo album, and so on.

In a study of users' desktop environments (also discussed in chapter 2 of this book), Ravasio, Schär, and Krueger (2004) observed that users are themselves aware of this value of unification. They state that "the systematic separation of files, emails and bookmarks—was determined by three users to be inconvenient for their work. From their points of view, all their pieces of data formed one single body of information and the existing separation only complicated procedures like data backup, switching from old to new computers, and even searching for a specific piece of information. They also noted that this separation led to unwanted redundancy in the various storage locations" (p. 168).

Another motivation for unification is our need to manipulate multiple pieces of information in ways that cross application boundaries. Users like to gather information objects into groups that will be used together, and organize or annotate those groups in ways that will make it possible to retrieve them based on their intended usage. The artificial separations imposed by separate application data models can interfere with this organizational urge.

Besides grouping information objects, users often want to record or exploit information that directly *links* multiple objects. Much of the information about a given object lies in its relationship to other objects; thus, when viewing one object, a user may well want to see those relationships, and may want to learn more about those other related objects. For example, Brooke may want to identify the creator (a relationship) of a given song, and may then want to explore that creator in order to learn about where they lived. When data is not unified, there may be no way to record the relationship between objects stored in different applications (except by redundantly duplicating the related objects in both applications, which has the drawbacks discussed above). The World Wide Web offers perhaps the most massive example of the value of linking information objects to indicate relationships between them and to help users explore those relationships.

As another motivation for linking, recent work highlights users' preferences for finding information by *orienteering* (Teevan, Alvarado, Ackerman & Karger 2004, and chapter 2 of this book). Rather than jumping directly to needed information, users often try to locate it by starting with a known object and taking repeated navigation steps to related objects, aiming to home in on the desired information. We use this approach frequently when navigating the Web, or when seeking files in our directory hierarchies. To support such orienteering, it is necessary to connect information objects to other related ones. When data is fragmented, it may be impossible to record some of those linkages, meaning that they will be absent when the user needs them for orienteering. Again, Ravasio et al. (2004) indicate that users are aware of their desire for linking: "most interviewees expressed the need to have their information linked together (e.g., article author and respective address book entry, or citation and cited article, etc.) and in general, to have more content-based and context-based access to their information" (p. 169).

8.1.2 *Approaches to Unification*

The multitude of motivations for unification is matched by a multitude of different approaches to unification that have been developed in the past or are currently being investigated. We will survey and taxonomize this variety of approaches.

At its root, unification aims to bring information together for some useful purpose. To achieve this goal, any unification approach *must* choose some "least common denominator" into which it can shoehorn *all* the information it aims to encompass.

Although an application need not store its information in any particular standard form, it must offer hooks through which its data can be treated as instances of the common information representation. For if information is to be unified, there must be some implicit or explicit contract about how that information is modeled and manipulated. There are many possible common denominators, each imposing different constraints and offering different benefits. Modern window managers treat all applications as rectangular regions of pixels, so they can be placed next to each other and manipulated on the screen. File systems treat each data object as a collection of bytes, so it can be read and written (though perhaps not understood) by any application, or attached to an email without constraint on its type. The World Wide Web assumes that every object has a URL, which can therefore be easily referred to on any Web page.

Using such a common denominator is in tension with applications' needs for rich, specialized representations of their content. Rich representations let applications offer powerful, domain-specific operations. The tradeoff is that a simplified shared representation lets applications interact in a unified fashion with data from many applications and domains without needing to understand a multitude of rich representations.

In taxonomizing different approaches to unification, we ask the following questions about each unification paradigm:

■ What is its API? What is the commonality that it assumes about all the data that is to be unified? Into what common model/representation does all the data fit? What primitive operations does that common model support? What does an application have to offer if its data is to be part of the unification, and what can it assume about data offered by other applications?

▓ What can you do with it? What information that the user cares about can fit in the common model? What information management activities can be performed via invocation of the API primitives?

▓ Why is it useful? How do the supported information and activities enhance the user's ability to work with information?

▓ What are its limitations? Where does the unification fail to provide what the user needs? What information will still need to be stored in an application-specific fashion because it does not fit in the model?

Below, we will explore three major categories of unification, outlined in Table 8.1.2:

▓ **Visual unification** aims to place multiple data objects in view side by side, and is one benefit offered by modern window managers that support multiple applications. Visual unification lets users see and relate the multiple objects that are relevant to a given task, but offers no mechanism for directly indicating, or letting users manipulate, data relationships between objects that are managed by different tools.

▓ **Standard data types** such as text and files have relatively undemanding semantics (sequences of characters or bytes) and are pervasive, so they tend to be supported by almost all applications. Thus, one application can move another application's file, or paste text copied from another application. The undemanding semantics is both the strength of this approach (because every application is willing to support these types) and its weakness (because much of information's rich meaning is lost when it is squeezed into these semantics-poor representations).

▓ **Metadata** treats information objects as opaque, but offers a standard model for talking *about* those objects in assorted ways. Examples include grouping (as in file directories), annotating (as in ID3 tags for media and del.icio.us tags for Web pages) and linking (as in the World Wide Web). As we will argue below, much information management relies only on object metadata, so can be supported over data objects of all types. While current metadata standards (such as ID3) are limited to specific application data-types, new frameworks such as XML and RDF offer the possibility of unifying substantial portions of people's information spaces using only metadata.

Table 8.1.2 – Different Unification Techniques (offered by diferent software systems)

Technique	Offered by	Operations	Enable
Visual unification	window manager, wincuts, embedding	layout, tile, show, hide	simultaneous view of information
Standard datatypes	text, files	cut/copy/paste, read/write	unified searching, data transfer
Metadata		refer, describe	list below
Grouping	directories, TaskMaster, Presto	add/remove items from group	organize, browse, simultaneous view
Cross-reference	OLE, COM WWW	embed, traverse	simultaneous view, orienteer
Attribute/value	XML, Presto	annotate, query	annotate, search, organize, browse
Relations	RDF, Databases, Haystack		record relationships, unified search

NOTE: Each unification technique supports different types of operations and enables different data management activities by the end user.

8.2.3 Overview

Having motivated and taxonomized unification, we will now explore in detail a variety of unification approaches that have been developed, and discuss the tools that make use of them. Then we will turn to considering a number of research efforts that are exploring new ways to unify information. Among others we discuss WinCuts, an effort to improve visual unification of information; the World Wide Web, the greatest example of the power of linking; the Presto system for organizing files using arbitrary metadata annotations; the TaskMaster system, which tries to turn email into an environment for unified information management; and the Haystack system, which emphasizes the power of recording, displaying, and navigating arbitrary relationships between arbitrary information objects.

One type of unification that we raise just to set aside is *physical* unification of information. The information a user works on is often stored in several physically distinct locations. It is a significant burden for a user to move physically from location to location to get the information they need. Thus, in the absence of appropriate communication mechanisms, it may be effectively impossible for a user to access and unify some remote piece of data. For cases where communication *is* possible, protocols such as FTP (for data transfer) and X windows (for display transfer) have long existed to bring data from where it is to where a user needs it. More recently, tools such as network file systems (NFS) and the World Wide Web have tried to free the user from even having to think about the physical location of the desired data. A user can visit a directory on a networked file system in a way that is indistinguishable from a directory on the local machine, and a user can click on a Web link and navigate to the target without considering the machine that is delivering it.

While recognizing that it is a prerequisite for much of the unification we discuss, we will generally ignore the issue of physically remote information in order to avoid drifting into a consideration of networking and operating system protocols.

8.2 Visual Unification

The first strategy we consider, unification at the display, relies on the fact that most of today's applications run in desktop environments where the final step in the presentation of information to a user is rendering it into pixels on a graphical display. We can therefore choose, as the common denominator for all these applications, rectangular groups of pixels, and ask how such groups of pixels can be unified. The window manager is the current solution. Applications run inside one or several windows, and delegate to the window manager the control over those windows being stacked, tiled, moved, resized, opened, and closed. Thanks to the window manager, a user can simultaneously view and manipulate all the information objects they care about, in multiple application windows laid out side by side on the display.

On the downside, it often seems that each application wants the entire display to itself. To get at the data managed by an application, users typically need to launch the entire application, which lives in a large window with its attendant menus, toolbars, jumping-off points, and default presentations. Because the window manager treats the application opaquely as a rectangle full of pixels, it cannot select out the one piece of the display that the user actually cares about. A common consequence is *window clutter*—a desktop filled with tens of windows, all obscuring each other, each bearing a small fragment of information that a user cares about. To get at it, users must continuously locate and rearrange windows to find the fragments they need. One often sees significant effort invested in laying out windows just right, so that the desired information in one window obscures only unimportant information in another window. But this requires a significant investment of effort, is unlikely to remain the right layout as the user continues to manipulate the information, will be lost when the applications are exited, and is often simply impossible due to the topological constraints imposed by the location of the key information in each window. One coping mechanism, virtual desktops (Henderson & Card 1986), allows a user to maintain a distinct desktop for each "context" or task that they are currently involved with, holding only windows relevant to that context. Often, however, even the windows of a single context are too much for a single desktop. And frameworks for actually managing the contexts remain primitive.

As a further drawback, even if users can get the window layout exactly right, this only gives them a convenient view of the information. Since only the display, and not the underlying data model, is unified, each piece of information must still be managed by the application responsible for it. Since each window is managed by a different application, there is still no guarantee that the user will be able to effectively manipulate information across the application boundaries. A window manager does not offer expanded opportunities to pass data from one application to another, or to create machine-usable linkages between data from multiple applications. The fact that Alex can display Connie's address in an address book and, at the same time, display a photograph of Connie in a photo album offers no guarantee that he will be able to use either application to associate Connie with her photo.

8.2.1 *WinCuts*

One significant limitation of the window-manager approach is its all-or-nothing management of application displays. When an application window is open, one sees the whole window, even if only a small portion of it is relevant to the given task. Tan, Meyers, and Czerwinski (2004) have addressed this problem by developing *WinCut*. The idea of WinCuts is that a user can select a (rectangular) subregion of an application's window, "cut" it out of the application, and "paste" it into an entirely different region of the display. The user can then close the original application window while leaving the WinCut open, now displaying only the portion of the application that is of interest at the present time. The WinCut is alive: application updates of the display are propagated to the WinCut, and user-interface actions within the bounds of the WinCut region are mapped back (indistinguishably to the application) as if they were applied within the application window. Reducing the screen space occupied by one application means that more applications can be visually unified.

Perhaps the greatest appeal of the WinCuts approach to unification is its universality: essentially *all* current desktop applications work through the window manager, and are thus amenable to the WinCuts approach, without any application modification whatsoever. Conversely, WinCuts is very much aimed at graphical displays: it is not clear what analogous approach might work with speech interfaces, for example.

WinCuts suffer from some of the same limitations as traditional window managers. The information layouts persist only as long as their application is running. Thus it is difficult for users to permanently modify the way information is presented to them; instead, they must recustomize it each time they tackle a given task. Also as in window managers it is the views, not the data, that are unified, so cross-application manipulation, annotation, or linking of the data is not possible.

8.2.2 *Embedding*

Besides the window manager, we find that applications nowadays will often manage subwindows of their own, *embedding* another application in some subregion of their display to support visualization of data managed by that application. Historically, Microsoft has offered this capability in their Office products under the name OLE (object linking and embedding). Nowadays, many plug-ins are available for Web browsers as tools to handle, inline, a variety of data types that are encountered on the Web, including various video data types and flash. As with window managers, the containing application generally cedes all control of the embedded region to a different application; this means that the data can be displayed and manipulated but not linked to the data of the containing application. And such embedding is often not under the user's control: the content embedded in a Web page is determined by the creator of that Web page, not by the reader.

A particular example of an embedding-oriented application is the Web Montage system (Anderson & Horvitz 2002). Web Montage lets users assemble a single page containing embedded versions of numerous other Web pages, so that the user can see all of them simultaneously—it is effectively embedding HTML documents in HTML documents. Because many pages are squeezed into one, each is cropped so that all can fit; the details of crop-sizing can be controlled by the end user. Web Montage offers a capability that is already present in the desktop window manager—in theory, Web Montages could be created simply by launching, sizing, and tiling multiple Web-browser windows and navigating to each page of the montage in a separate window. Unlike the window manager, however, Web Montage is able to persist both the content and the layout of its aggregation after the application exits. This is a significant benefit for content that a user expects to interact with repeatedly. Such persistent aggregation of views is also offered by various "portal" Web sites such as Yahoo, which allow users to build complex pages by choosing from a menu of possible inclusions.

Web Montage and other Web portals achieve view persistence by limiting their content to Web pages, unlike window managers that unify the display of anything. In Web Montage, the data to be embedded can be named by a URL. Because there is no standard model by which applications expose "what they are currently looking at," it is not feasible for a window manager to offer Web Montage's persistent visualization over an arbitrary class of applications and data.

8.3 Unification by Standard Data Types

We have discussed the benefits of a unified display, but observed that they are only skin deep—that the simultaneous visualization of different information fragments need not offer any way to unify those fragments as data. To achieve this deeper level of unification, we need a *data* common denominator. Here we identify standard data representations that are so pervasive that any application developer feels compelled to support them in any application. Historically, several such standard data types including text and files have played an important role in data unification. Looking ahead, it appears that XML and possibly RDF will offer richer standard data types that offer better unification of a variety of information.

8.3.1 *Text*

A significant portion of the data managed by many applications is text. It may come formatted in many different ways: within HTML documents on the Web, in bulleted lists in Microsoft PowerPoint, formatted in a word processing document, or typeset in Adobe PDF. But strip away the formatting, and one is left with a sequence of characters.

When a data type is shared in this way by all applications, it becomes possible to easily transfer information from one application to another, achieving one of the unification goals stated above. Most applications are able to offer text to and accept text from other applications—typically with the assistance of a clipboard application with which they all communicate. The quotes offered earlier in this chapter could therefore be "cut" from Adobe Reader and "pasted" into an Emacs word processing buffer. The typical linear flow of text means that even interfaces for those operations are somewhat standardized—mouse drags from the beginning to the end select the text to be cut, and clicks within the text indicate the "insertion point" of text to be pasted.

Of course, this textual "lowest common denominator" is necessarily low.

One generally loses finer aspects of the information when it is represented this way—the specific nesting of a PowerPoint slide, or the serifs and precise intercharacter spacing in a PDF document. But this is likely the reason for the success of the standard: any more-complex representation would have been too demanding for many applications to support.

The common model of text also means that most applications can contribute some (stripped down) representation of their data to a *text search engine*. Such an approach gives the end user a well-understood framework for searching by content over all of their data, independent of which application owns any given piece. Significant enthusiasm has developed around the recent set of "desktop search engines" such as Google desktop and MSN desktop that offer this capability. These systems are discussed in detail in the following chapter.

This support is not universal—had the PDF source document instead been postscript, which does not provide a text model, it would have been necessary to manually retype the quotes instead of cutting and pasting them. Another unfortunate omission is error messages: it is often impossible, when a dialog box pops up with an error message, to cut and paste its text into an email to technical support.

8.3.2 *The File System*

The other obvious common data format is that of the file. All applications can make use of the notion of a sequence of bits that can be read from, copied, or written to. An email application can attach a file for delivery to another computer without any understanding of which application created the file or what its contents mean.

The file system also offers a unified interface for the end user. Using the now-standard model of hierarchical directories or folders, a user can organize files according to whatever principle they find useful. For example, a user may gather into a single directory all the files necessary for accomplishing a particular task, regardless of which applications manage those files. Working inside that directory gives the user immediate access to all of those files.[1] The file system lets users name individual files and list the names of files in a directory, an important aid to organizing and searching. Most applications let users specify files to open or save.

On the negative side, the semantics of files are so weak that, unlike text, they offer relatively little opportunity for data sharing. Except on a planned, case-by-case basis, one application is generally unable to construct meaning from the bits it reads out of a file written by another application. Significant effort goes into writing converters that translate a file written by one application into one that can be understood by another. The lack of standard file semantics also means that any significant manipulation of any file requires launching an appropriate application. This will take a user away from the directory view of all files relevant to a given task, and back to an application view that shows only some of the information they want to work with.

Additionally, files are typically large. An address book, for example, will usually be stored as a single file, rather than as one file per entry. This precludes using the file system for fine-grained organization. A user will not be able to put, into a directory aimed at writing a particular paper, the address-book entries of all his coauthors. He can certainly place a link to the address book, but from within that directory he would need to launch the address book and then go through an address-book-specific process to find the coauthors.

8.3.3 *XML*

Recently, enthusiasm has grown for XML as another potential standard data type for unification and sharing of data. XML offers the possibility of standardizing a richer structure than files' bit sequences. XML offers a standard syntax and model for representing arbitrary, hierarchically structured information. For example, XML can use its standard syntax and model to represent that a playlist is made of a collection of songs, that each song consists of a media file, a title, a genre, and a creator, and that a creator has of a name, an age, and a birthplace. This richer representation holds out the possibility of transferring data from one application to another and having the second application take advantage of some piece of the hierarchical structure that makes sense to it. For example, given a media file, an address book may be able to work with some address-oriented parts of the "author" object, even if it cannot work with the media file at all. XML's standard for representing attributes of information objects also offers useful benefits for unified organization and searching, as we will discuss below.

XML does not solve the entire unification problem, because any given XML fragment obeys some *schema* that characterizes its different parts, and any tool aiming to work with that fragment needs to understand the schema. Thus, a media application looking for a "creator" fragment in an XML document could be stymied if some other application instead recorded an "author" fragment— these two descriptive terms may mean the same thing, but there is no way to tell just by looking at the data. Someone must still take responsibility for unifying different schemas that talk about the same information. However, the fact that different pieces of the structure are clearly indicated means that an application only needs translation for the specific fragments it aims to use, so the translation problem becomes smaller and local. Furthermore, XML may lead to the emergence of standard schemata—for example, a consensus that one should always use the term "author" to talk about the creator of a document— that become dominant schemata the same way that text and files have become dominant data formats. Agreeing on names for particular fields seems less demanding than agreeing byte-for-byte on file formats for all applications' data. In particular, someone writing an application can use the standard schemas where they are relevant (e.g., for an author), and simultaneously use idiosyncratic schemas for representing the nonstandard parts of the data they work with (e.g., color of the ink). The standard XML syntax means that tools that understand the standard schemas will be able to work with the standard elements, while ignoring the idiosyncratic ones.

8.3.4 SQL Databases

In the corporate world, relational databases with SQL interfaces are the dominant paradigm for handling the massive amounts of data companies need to manage. As corporations merge or begin to cooperate, they invariably need to merge the incompatible databases they have maintained. The field of information integration is concerned with developing tools and procedures for making such mergers easy, and making queries to the merged data efficient. While somewhat connected to the data unification themes we are discussing here, information integration is focused more on dealing with the process of forcing together heterogeneous repositories, as opposed to developing frameworks within which an individual user's data can be kept from becoming heterogeneous in the first place.

The database community has argued for decades that we would all be better off storing all our personal information in (personal) databases. This clearly has not happened, most likely due to the apparent complexity of interacting with a database. No one has yet come forward with applications that hide the complexity of installing and maintaining a database, designing the schemas for the data to be stored, and creating the queries that will return the desired information. And people seem generally allergic to having all their information presented to them as lists of tuples. It is noteworthy, however, that both XML (discussed above) and RDF (discussed below) have representational power equal to that of databases; thus, the work on PIM tools that makes use of these formats may indicate that we are creeping up on the database community's perspective from a different direction.

8.4 Unification by Metadata

Perhaps the simplest general unification strategy is to ignore the complex structure of objects themselves and instead to record *metadata* that talks about the objects from the outside. In this section, we will discuss three powerful uses of metadata: *grouping* related information objects together (as in file directories), *annotating* objects with interesting attributes and values (e.g., recording the title and composer of a particular song in ID3 tags), and *linking* complex objects to each other (as we do with pages on the World Wide Web).

8.4.1 *What's in a Name*

While a metadata scheme can ignore the complex formats of the objects it is talking about, there must still be a common API for talking about those objects. In particular, any metadata scheme needs some standard way to indicate *which* object is being talked about. This may be a standard scheme for *naming* objects (e.g., file names or URLs) so that their names can be used to talk about them, or it might be accomplished by *embedding* the metadata with the object being annotated (as with ID3 tags in media files).

While embedded metadata is common, it tends to belong to a single application or data type: Microsoft Office manages embedded author and title information for its documents; MP3 software manages ID3 tags; email programs understand Sender and Date headers. In a sense, these embedded metadata become part of the complex data object, and are understood by the programs that understand those objects. Name-based metadata seems more often to span multiple applications; for example, many applications, including Web browsers, word processors, email clients, and music players, offer special handling of URLs. This is likely because naming requires only understanding of the names, while embedding requires understanding the file format of the object that contains the embedded metadata. Also, if embedded metadata talks about multiple objects, it may need to be embedded in multiple locations, and can therefore become inconsistent, as we discussed in the Introduction.

Technically, unification by naming objects is already often available, in that users can use various text fields in their applications to refer to other objects by names that make sense to them. For example, a user might set the filename of a photograph to include the name of the individual in the photograph, or the location where that photograph was taken. Or, they might use the "memo" field in an accounting application to name the individual who received a certain payment.

But this form of unification burdens the user with all the work of interpreting the name and then remembering exactly how to retrieve the named information. The user will have much less work to do if names are designed to be machine readable, and applications provide built-in support for working with named objects. For example, many applications today will make URLs or email addresses "live"—clicking on them will launch a Web browser or email client to view the given URL or compose a message to the given address.

Although we have mainly set the issue aside, it is also worth noting that a name-based scheme lets us talk about and organize information that is not actually accessible: for example, a Web page can link to and discuss another Web site that is temporarily down.

Besides referring to the objects, there needs to be some standard way to describe the metadata itself. We will discuss several standards below, including XML and RDF.

8.4.2 *Grouping*

Grouping is a powerful organizational technique that requires only naming the entities that make up the group. This technique is pervasive. For decades, the file system has exploited the idea of named opaque objects. Since every file has a unique file identifier, tools such as the directory manager (and graphical interfaces for it), with no need to interpret any file's contents, can let users manipulate their file organizations. The file system places no restriction on the types of files that can be in its directories. The same folder interface typically used to manage these directories, with its well-understood click-to-open and drag-to-move semantics, is also used by many applications to manage the groups that arise in those applications: mail messages by a mail program, bookmarks by a Web browser, songs in a media application, people in a contact manager, and so on. In each case, the applications manage only their own data. But the typical organization steps—inserting, deleting, and moving an object from one collection to another—require only a reference to the object, not any understanding of its internals. If all these objects were subject to a common naming scheme, it would be possible to group files and all these other information types without any change to the user interface. This would allow the data currently separated by application boundaries to be jointly organized. A user could create a "directory" containing some files, some email messages, a few relevant address-book entries, some payment records from an accounting program, and so on.

Recently, another interesting use of grouping has appeared in the "social tagging" Web services. Tools like del.icio.us (for Web pages) and Flickr (for photographs) let users tag objects with text terms germane to those objects. Users can then navigate to the group of objects that have received a particular tag, or perform queries to locate objects with all of a set of tags (thus intersecting groups). Tagging has begun to appear as an option on mainstream Web sites such as Amazon.

Although tagging offers a unified mechanism for grouping arbitrary Web pages, it also highlights a potential unification failure in grouping: failure to agree on the name of a group. A single tag might seem plausible for two distinct groups (e.g., "apple" for computers or fruit), or a single group might plausibly be named by several tags (e.g., "hci" or "chi" for human-computer interaction). When there is more than one possibility, a user may run into trouble if they make inconsistent choices during organization and retrieval. del.icio.us explicitly recommends tagging a page with all plausible tags, so that any one of them will locate the page later. This failure of unification in tagging has been noted (Guy & Tonkin 2006), and debate continues about whether it is a bug (because it impairs retrieval) or a feature (because it allows for serendipitous discovery of new information).

8.4.3 Annotation

Annotation is another organizational technique that, in principle, depends only on the ability to refer to the subject of the annotation. Everywhere we manage information, we find tools that let us associate certain *attributes* and certain *values* of those attributes with our information objects. Files have creators, creation times, modification times, and types. Email messages have senders and subjects. Music files have genres, composers, artists, and bit-rates. Photographs have subjects, resolutions, and shooting conditions.

Annotations are extremely useful for organization and search. Users will often identify an object by some of its metadata ("the email that Brooke sent me last week") and so will be able to find it easily when search over that metadata is supported. Metadata also provides an opportunity to make information coherent for browsing—media management tools will offer music organized by artist, and subdivided by album. As was the case with grouping, many applications offer almost identical frameworks for using their metadata: tabular lists with one column per data attribute, sorting on a given attribute by clicking on the attribute's column header, and search dialogue boxes that let users specify and filter by certain metadata attributes. All of these steps require access *only* to the metadata and not to the annotated object.

Ironically, given that metadata is generally extrinsic—it talks *about* the object without being part of the object—many metadata representations are embedded, in domain-specific ways, in the objects they manage. For example, ID3 tags are stored in a specialized format as part of the music file they are annotating.[2] A similar situation holds for images.

The emerging XML standard[3] may help to resolve this problem. XML offers a natural syntax for recording metadata about objects. To the extent that metadata representation becomes standardized, it may become possible to offer unified organizational tools across data types—such as tabular metadata presentations that explore music and photographs at the same time.

While there appears to be only one notion of "group," the set of possible attributes is potentially unlimited. As we discussed in Section 8.4.3, divergent choices of annotations can lead to a new kind of fragmentation—even if the representation of the annotations can be understood, the annotations themselves may not be. However, as we discussed there, the simple standards such as XML for representing annotations mean that an application can seek out and manipulate the annotations it understands even when they are mixed with other unknown annotations.

8.4.4 *Linking*

Often, discussions of metadata emphasize the attachment of some literal information—a date, a name, or a price—to some complex object. But there is also great value in linking pairs of complex objects. Links serve as a richer version of metadata—allowing one to connect a mail message not just to the email address of the sender (a string) but to an entire rich address-book entry. Besides simply providing the information about the connection, links provide a natural step for users to follow from one information object to another. This in turn supports the popular *orienteering* strategy we discussed in the Introduction: navigating from object to related object in order to home in on the desired information (Teevan et al. 2004, and chapter 2 of this book).

Ravasio et al. (2004) indicate that users explicitly desire linking: "most interviewees expressed the need to have their information linked together, e.g., article author and respective address book entry, or citation and cited article, etc." (p. 169).

Probably the most recent big success of this linking approach was the World Wide Web. One of the most important contributions of the WWW was to define a single, shared URL namespace that lets users craft names for arbitrary Web objects. By placing references to those objects in other Web pages, authors give users the ability to navigate smoothly from object to related object.

As with annotation, many tools support linking of complex objects within their own domain. A mail program may let you navigate to the address-book entry describing a sender by clicking on the mail header, or navigate to a Web page by clicking on a URL in an email message. But the absence of a single standard hampers cross-application linking. It is not currently possible to link from the composer of a music file to their address book entry, or from the location of a meeting in one's calendar to a map of that location, unless a specific application has decided to offer that specific functionality.

8.4.5 RDF

Resource description framework, or RDF, is a relatively new model being propounded by the World Wide Web Consortium,[4] and may help us take better global advantage of the linking paradigm. Central to RDF is the perspective that *anything*, not just Web pages, can receive a *URN* (essentially a URL, but not necessarily fetchable on the Web) so that it can be referred to elsewhere. Like XML, RDF can be used to record the values of arbitrary attributes of a given object. But while XML typically records attributes that are literal values, such as strings or numbers, RDF can record other URNs as values. While it would be typical, using XML, to record that the person in a given photo was named "Connie," RDF might instead be used to record that the person in the photo is the one identified by the URN "urn:a74fj83jfn." The URN offers two key advantages. First, it removes ambiguity: to seek an address associated with the name "Connie," Alex might need to do a search in his address book, look over the multiple individuals named "Connie," and decide which one he intended at this time. But the URN identifies a single individual. With an address book that supports URNs, Alex could get the right address with a single click and no cognitive effort. The second benefit is to separate the (machine-usable) URN identifier from a human being's preferred descriptive name. In the introduction, we discussed how the change to a new married name could create inconsistency that makes it harder to find information; using a URN to identify the person ensures that a (human) name change does not break the association between photo and individual.

8.5 Systems That Unify

Many researchers have realized the opportunities data unification can offer. Below we discuss a number of systems that explore this concept. We have already discussed WinCuts and Web Montage in the course of introducing various unification approaches; here we discuss several other systems and the way they apply the unification techniques we have discussed.

8.5.1 *The World Wide Web*

Much of the impact of the World Wide Web can be attributed to its success in unifying a tremendous range of information. The Web rides on the concept of the universal (we might say unified) resource locator, or URL: every Web page has one, and any Web page can use one to link to any other Web page. As the Web grew, many different entities—institutions, people, books, recipes, and so on—became represented as HTML documents on the Web, linked to each other with no restrictions as to type. The standard representation as HTML meant that a single tool, the Web browser, could present all the different information types. Also, the fact that much of the content was text meant that search engines could be built to search the entire Web, years before anything similar was attempted for the end-user desktop.

The names linked to in Web pages can refer to objects that a Web browser could not interpret; this failure becomes apparent only if the user chooses to actually navigate to the named object. This works quite well in an environment where some users have and others have not installed plug-ins and extensions to handle a variety of new object types. Users can see references to and discussions of the named objects even without the extensions, and can then make individual choices about whether it is worth the work of extending their own environment to handle the new object type.

With this appealing unification tool already present, we can ask why it has not been adopted as the primary environment for personal information management. Hypothetically, a user could create a separate Web page for each email message, each directory, each music file, each calendar appointment, each individual in their address book, and so on. Editing these pages, the user could indicate arbitrary relationships between their information objects. Feeding these Web pages to a tool like Google would give users powerful search capabilities, and combining them with the orienteering opportunities offered by the user-created links would surely enhance users' ability to locate information.

In response, we observe that HTML is quite an impoverished data representation, offering little more than a rich formatting of text and images. Users' rich, structured, personal information spaces can certainly be boiled down to HTML for presentation, just as they can be boiled down to pixels, but such a representation loses much of the semantics of the underlying data. While an application could hypothetically store its richly structured information in HTML, it would have to select canonical rules for representing it, and would not be able to cope with a user or another application making modifications to other valid HTML that does not obey the canonical rules. At the interface level, while the

Web browser is certainly a good tool for *browsing* data, it is often too limited a tool for *manipulating* data. Web forms are useful only for relatively primitive data entry, not the sophisticated manipulations offered by the applications' carefully specialized interfaces and operations. This demonstrates that while the Web may at first glance seem unified, there are fundamental ways in which the Web's data remains highly fragmented—there are few tools that let us bring together the pieces of it that we want.

8.5.2 *Presto*

Presto (Dourish, Edwards, LaMarca & Salisbury 1999) is one system that tries to give users a powerful unified data organization environment. Dourish et al. realized that, as discussed above, many of the operations that users want to apply when organizing information, such as grouping, annotating, and linking, are independent of specific document types, and can be offered by a system that treats the documents themselves as opaque objects. They also observed that the file system's typical model of a hierarchical directory structure, with each file occupying a single position in the directory structure, fails to let users organize documents in natural ways.

Presto operates over (references to) arbitrary files, and lets end users define arbitrary *attributes*, represented as attribute/value pairs such as "author/David R. Karger" that can annotate documents and that can then be used to group or search for them. Such attributes can be extracted by type-specific automated tools. Alternatively, a simple drag-and-drop interface lets users associate new attributes with any document. Presto operates in the same way over locally and remotely stored documents. This is because, when organizing based on extrinsic attribute/value pairs, the question of where a document is located is as unimportant as the precise details of the document's internal representation. As Dourish et al. (1999) state:

> The user is not presented with a distinction between one document type and another; they see a seamless document model in which all documents support the same operations: reading and writing, adding them to collections, setting properties on them, searching for them and so forth. . . . Documents can appear in the same collection despite the fact that they reside in completely different repositories, in different servers, or are retrieved via different protocols. Similarly, all documents can be managed using the same uniform attribute operations. (p. 149)

Presto gives substantial attention to the management of collections. Users can create collections by defining queries over certain attributes, and can also explicitly place documents in collections. These collections can be shown open (displaying the documents in them) or closed, where they are represented as "piles" whose size indicates the size of the collection. Because collections are often defined dynamically, documents can easily appear in multiple collections. Indeed, since all collections are considered somewhat fluid, there is no real main collection containing a document, and no distinction between the true containment (hard links) and aliases (soft links) that are distinguished in traditional file systems.

Presto also offers a task-focused "workspace" model similar to that in the Xerox Rooms system (Henderson & Card 1986) to help reduce clutter. Individuals can set up a different workspace for each task and populate the workspace with those documents (and attributes) that are relevant to the given task.

On the downside, Presto continues to focus on the document as the entity that should be annotated; it does not appear to consider working with finer-grained information objects such as individual address-book entries or appointments. Presto also does not support the linking of complex objects by relations: the value of an attributes is always a primitive value such as a number or string.

8.5.3 *TaskMaster*

Bellotti, Ducheneaut, Howard, and Smith (2003) performed field studies that demonstrated how end users have shoehorned a substantial portion of their data inside their email clients—a kind of ad hoc unification. Bellotti et al. then developed a new email client, TaskMaster, with this usage in mind, offering a more effective unified environment centered on email. TaskMaster is discussed in greater depth in chapter 10.

As the Presto group did in defining task-specific workspaces, TaskMaster takes a task-centric view of the world. TaskMaster lets end users define and manage "thrasks" (task threads) containing all the information items relevant to a given task: the email messages, their attachments, and any other files that become relevant at some later time. TaskMaster thus breaks through two levels of opacity that typically interfere with the organization of email: that the email clients offer their own data representation (so that the desktop environment cannot manage individual email messages) and that attachments stay locked up inside individual email messages (so that even if each email message were stored as a file, the desktop environment still could not manage the attachments as individual files to be organized). In TaskMaster, a user tackling a given task has direct access to any individual relevant item (through a folder holding all the task items). A user can move a particular attachment to a different thrask than its containing message, and have the attachment persist even after the containing message is deleted, and can add task-relevant items that did not originate as attachments.

In addition to grouping, TaskMaster allows the user to attach metadata such as "deadline" or "action" to each information object, regardless of type, and to use these attributes to organize and retrieve information in the system. Thrasks could contain not only files (email and attachments) but also links to objects on the Web. TaskMaster was therefore able to blend data that was typically managed separately by the file system and the bookmark manager—an explicit wish of some of the users in the study by Ravasio et al. (2004).

TaskMaster offers a "preview pane" that presents the currently selected information object (as displayed by its application) without launching a new window. As discussed above, this kind of embedding lets a user see information about neighboring objects without leaving the context that they are currently occupying.

8.5.4 *Haystack*

Haystack (Bakshi & Karger 2005; Huynh, Karger & Quan 2002; Sinha & Karger 2005) takes the notion of "opaque information objects with attributes and links" to a much finer grain than individual files or email messages. We observe that even inside individual applications much of the information management reflects the creation and usage of (binary) relationships connecting information objects. For example, people are a data type appearing in various applications that manage their relationships to email messages (as senders in an email application), to music (as composers in a jukebox program), and to appointments (as people to meet in a calendar program). For some users (as in the entertainment industry) those sets of people might overlap. It is therefore worth exposing the individual information objects, and the relationships between them, in a unified manner, and allowing those exposed objects to be annotated, organized, and linked independent of their "home" application.

As was discussed above, the only real prerequisites for such an approach are to give each information object a unique identifying name and to choose a representation for the metadata. Haystack uses RDF[5], an emerging World Wide Web standard model for naming information objects and for recording relationships about those objects. In RDF, any object can be given a Unique

Resource Name (with a syntax similar to URLs), and any two information objects can be linked by connecting their URIs with a *statement* naming (in a machine-readable fashion) the relationship between them. In the Haystack data model, a typical file will be shredded into many individual information objects of various types connected by application-specific relationships.

Haystack's user interface is responsible for taking these many small objects and assembling them into traditional-looking information displays. But since each information object visible in, say, an email management interface is itself a distinct entity in the data model, a Haystack user can operate directly on any object in view. Haystack gives the user a Web-like navigation paradigm. By clicking on (say) the author of the message, the user can navigate to a view of that author (which is constructed by looking up important objects related to that person, and laying them out in the style of an address book). Users can benefit from being able to orienteer from an email message to its authors, to a photograph of that person, to a representation of the location where that photograph was taken, to a map of that location, and so on. Similarly, traditional drag-and-drop operations can be applied by users to create collections of related objects, or to create annotations linking information objects together.

Haystack also offers Presto-like specification of collections of arbitrary objects (not just files) using queries over the metadata about those objects; Alex could assemble a "Birthday folder" containing all the people coming to Edna's party, all the bills not yet paid to the caterer, and the predicated weather, and have that folder stay up to date as RSVPs come in, payments go out, and the weathermen change their minds. This is a capability that Haystack shares with Semex, discussed in chapter 7. However, we believe that basic linking, viewing, and orienteering are likely to make up a more substantial part of most users' interactions than complex queries, so Haystack's user interface focuses on enabling those more elementary behaviors—Haystack aims to feel less like a database, and more like an application.

Tools like Presto and TaskMaster continue to work with a fixed set of information types (files in Presto, email, projects, and tasks in TaskMaster). Haystack focuses almost entirely on the metadata surrounding objects, and thus does not need to understand anything about the objects themselves. Thus, Haystack is able to smoothly support the inclusion of arbitrary new types of information by an end user. Anyone interested in knitting can easily introduce objects representing different types of yarn, different weaves, and different needles, and craft presentations of those objects that integrate smoothly with the rest of their information space. Thus, unification is not limited to preexisting data types, but can stretch to incorporate whatever a given user considers important.

8.6 Conclusion

We have described some of the benefits of offering users a unified data model, one in which information is not firmly partitioned into the domains of distinct applications but can instead be viewed, grouped, annotated, and linked flexibly according to the end-user's needs. We have argued that the key step for such unification is the choice of an appropriate common API—a representation of the data and interfaces to it that can be accessed by all applications. Such an API must be simple enough not to discourage application builders from supporting it. We have touched on a few such APIs: pixels, text, files, groups, annotations, and links. We have discussed the representations those APIs offer and the actions they enable.

We have discussed a number of unification-oriented research projects. One commonality we observe is a move toward *finer granularity*: grabbing small fragments of windows in WinCuts, breaking up objects into fine-grained hierarchical representations in XML, and referring to arbitrarily small objects in RDF and Haystack. Such approaches appear to recognize that it is not possible to predict and design a single monolithic data model or presentation that will be appropriate in all circumstances, so users should be able to work with the small pieces they actually need at a given time.

8.6.1 *Looking Forward*

Given that users would like to cross domains in their organizations, and that the interfaces are already often nearly identical in each domain, one can ask why we do not already see unified organizational tools. As one possible answer, note that to expose their data to be organized by such unified tools, applications need some standard naming scheme by which they can refer to their data items. One such scheme would be file identifiers. But this would require that each data item be stored as a file, which could be highly inefficient if the items are numerous, small, and frequently changing.

The two new related data representations, XML and RDF, hold out a possible solution to this problem. XML offers a standard syntax and model for defining a hierarchical nesting of information objects and their attributes and values, while RDF offers a model for representing arbitrary information objects connected by arbitrary relationships. Either of these models can represent heterogeneous grouping, and both implicitly assume that the individual information objects may be small and numerous, requiring support from tools more like databases than file systems. Most important, in each of these models, the individual information objects can be referred to individually by machine-readable names. Using XML or RDF, an email program can expose its individual emails, a calendar program its individual appointments and to-do items, an address book its individual addresses, and a document its individual authors and sentences, to be organized or annotated into heterogeneous task-specific collections.

Some, when faced with the idea of such a unified organizational framework, have objected that it could have a significant downside, as all information is suddenly squashed into a "one size fits all" (and therefore ill-fitting) organizational structure. It is important to distinguish, however, between a *unified* organizational system and a *single* organizational system. Even if it is possible to create heterogeneous collections, there is still likely to be value in seeing a homogeneous collection of, say, all of a user's email. Since references to an individual item can appear in multiple places, we can simultaneously maintain today's application-driven data partitions (to the extent that they are useful) and also offer task-specific, cross-application collections of the same information.

It is important to recognize that unification is not a complete solution, but an *enabler* of solutions. A unified data model does no good if it sits inert on disk; interfaces must be designed to exploit the unified model. Much research is ongoing to find the right metaphor or paradigm for letting people interact with their unified information. Lifestreams (Fertig, Freeman & Gelertner 1996b) offers a purely chronological metaphor, giving users access to all the information they used at a given past time. Presto sticks to our current files and folders metaphor of organization. ContactMap (Nardi, Whittaker, Isaacs, et al. 2002; Whittaker, Jones, Nardi, et al. 2004) centers information organization around the people with whom one is interacting to accomplish tasks. TaskMaster, discussed above and in chapter 10, aims to frame all its information management as a generalization of email interaction. The Universal Labeler (Jones, Munat & Bruce 2005) uses "projects" as the framing device, without wrapping them in email like TaskMaster—the authors argue that planning a project, and breaking it down into subprojects with annotations about planned actions provides an effective information organization. The UMEA system (Kaptelinin 2003) instead tries to identify projects implicitly, by observing the user and gathering together all the information they seem to be using consistently at one time. Haystack adopts the Web metaphor of individual information elements linked for orienteering.

All these metaphors are worth an entire additional chapter of discussion, and the question of which metaphor "works," and whether more than one is needed, is central to PIM research going forward. Common to all of them, however, is the recognition that the partition of information induced by diverse data formats and solitary applications is *not* the organizational metaphor consistent with people's uses of their information, and that a unified data model is a critical contribution toward organizing and presenting information to people the way they want it.

NOTES

1. While directory organization may seem inextricably entwined with the file system, we will see below that directories are more accurately characterized as a form of *metadata-based* unification.
2. This can cause some interesting problems in practice. The act of playing a music file, which seems like a read-only operation, can actually cause that file to change (as the "last played" metadata is modified). This in turn can cause backup or synchronization systems to make a new copy of the entire file, based on those few-byte changes.
3. http://www.w3.org/XML
4. http://www.w3.org/TR/rdf-primer
5. http://www.w3.org/TR/rdf-primer

⑨ Search Everything

Daniel M. Russell and Steve Lawrence

9.1 Introduction

Face it: people have terrible memories. Don't get me wrong, human memory is wonderful and subtle, able to remember a scent from decades earlier, recognize the handwriting of a loved one or the particular gait of a friend walking down the street. The memory of a first love, high school graduation, or a child's birth are all marvelously rich, sweet, multimodal, and detailed.

But when it comes down to login names and corresponding passwords, telephone numbers or mailing addresses, human memory is a leaking bucket that needs all the technology support it can get.

Personal information management tools can rescue human memory from the transient mistakes and failures that are commonplace, giving a remarkable ability to look up things quickly. An important basic capability for personal information management is *search*—that is, a method to find an item that has been saved somewhere on the computer's hard drive amid all the files, folders, and obscurely named junk that's accumulated over time. In a very real sense, the contents of a person's computer is personal information; it's the repository of letters, emails, images, calendar entries, and saved instant messages that forms the basis of personal information. Search is the key capability that makes personal information management into a useful tool. Saving and organizing all personal information is one thing, and browsing that stored information is nice, but being able to search and find it when it's needed is critically necessary for successful use whenever personal information storage becomes even slightly larger than what short-term human memory can handle (Cutrell, Dumais & Teevan 2006).

9.1.1 *Scenario*

Derek is supposed to be meeting up with Alex, Brooke, and Connie to talk about Edna's surprise birthday party. He's busy with classes at law school, and while he's responsible, he knows that he can't possibly remember all the details. The meeting is today, but is it at *Mario's* or *Maria's* pizza? Is it at 6:30 p.m. or 7:30 p.m.?

He turns to his desktop search tool (one hotkey away) and enters the search terms:

[Edna party planning meeting]

In less than a second, the desktop search tool shows that Derek's desktop has a document he made in a text-editor while talking to Alex last week. The desktop also has two email threads on the topics of "where to have the party" and "what about the scrapbook?" and a picture of a whiteboard he and Alex filled with notes during a late afternoon conversation at his office last week. The picture is labeled with "Edna's Party Whiteboard" and has a long list of the action items they agreed to work on . . . and a note about where today's meeting will be held. With one more click, he opens the notes files and sees that he's supposed to meet the others at Mario's on Fifth Street at 7:15 p.m. (not on the half-hour, as he'd thought). Another click brings up the map from a mapping Web site, and Derek heads out the door to his meeting in 45 minutes, armed with the time, place, and purpose of the upcoming meeting.

At that same moment in another part of the city, Connie is on the phone with Alex, trying to figure out who will drive to Mario's for the planning meeting. She's been scrolling message-by-message through her email trying to recognize the one describing what they'd be talking about at tonight's meeting. "If I could find the message," she says to Alex, "we'd know what to bring . . . " Alex is scrolling up and down on his handheld PDA visually searching through the past few days of emails, sequentially looking through his "Edna Party" folder for the right message. "I'm sure it's in here . . ." he replies.

After a few minutes, Connie comes up with the information—it was written on the outside of a file folder labeled "Party Info." Alex continues to look in his PDA for the right folder with the same information. Now it's starting to bug him. "Where did that information go?" he thinks.

Connie and Alex continue talking, planning to meet on the way to Mario's. "Aha! Found it!" Alex exclaims. "What?" Connie asks. "My notes file is in a folder marked 'Surprise Party' . . . no wonder I couldn't find it, I'd been looking for one labeled 'Birthday' on my PDA!"

9.1.2 Why Search Is Important

It's clear that search is a key operation—for this scenario and many personal information uses. In this scenario, Derek solves his problem quickly and easily because he has a wide-ranging, broad-scope search capability that's quick, effective, and easy to access.

While both Connie and Alex have different approaches to organizing information, both of their approaches are problematic, since search isn't neatly integrated into their tool use. Connie has multiple information resources that need to be searched (piles of paper, two email accounts) while Alex has his information filing structures well-organized. But as Alex's plight demonstrates, a single misfiled note can be difficult to re-find if there isn't a competent search mechanism robust enough to find the object in the face of small errors. As Malone and others have pointed out, a physical filing structure is a hierarchical category structure (Jones, Phuwanartnurak, Gill & Bruce 2005; Malone 1983). Putting an object into a tree structure is a process that is exquisitely sensitive to choices made while descending the hierarchy. An error made in choosing the category can result in an object being very far from its "correct" file location. And since filing structures frequently change in response to shifting tasks, organizations, and task requirements, the probability of perfect filing grows ever smaller with time and changes.

But hierarchical filing systems do have a point—they define plausible scopes for organizing content. That is, content objects that are superficially similar can be organized within a hierarchy, with the hierarchy defining metadata properties. With a competent search tool that can search for objects within the entire computer, the user can always search the entire space. But when even a little bit of metadata is known (especially if encoded within the structure of the hierarchy) search can often be scoped to a subportion of the hierarchy, and therefore to a particular set of metadata values.

Personal information systems have commonly included search tools as part of their base function set. Calendars without search are still useful, but calendars *with* a search capability are often used in very different ways. (Imagine trying to find a particular appointment that occurred sometime in the past five years of calendar data without search!)

Interestingly, Ducheneaut and Bellotti (2001) found that sorting email as a way to find a particular message was common, and perhaps dominant over standard search in Microsoft Outlook (see also Ducheneaut & Bellotti 2003). However, as Google has found with Gmail, when search is fast and simple, usage of the search function to locate an individual message skyrockets. The point remains: whenever a document store contains significant personal information—be it email, contact lists, a file store, or physical files—search is a critical function. Thus, the need for search is fundamental for managing and using a large personal store. And when the data become large or sophisticated, the need for search tools becomes ever more important (Dumais, Cutrell, Cadiz, Jancke, et al. 2003).

9.1.3 *Basic Issues, Problems, and Challenges*

Personal information comes in many forms. Personal information has often been thought of as an extension of past practices—the Rolodex equivalent for contact information, calendars for scheduling, the 3-by-5 card for notes, and so on.

But personal information comes in a variety of forms: email, documents, contact management, personal journals and day logs, meeting notes, outlines, task management (from formal to informal to-do lists), lists of books to buy and groceries to pick up, class and soccer schedules, calendars of events by organization, and family boundaries.

It becomes clear through scenarios in this book that "personal information" comes in many kinds and forms, from different sources, and in unexpected ways. Personal information can be thought of as the *entire* collection of information that someone has within their immediate sphere of awareness. That is, personal information is more than just the contents of specialized databases or particular applications, and is effectively everything and anything that's within a user's controlled content space. Roughly speaking, everything that's on their personal computer, be that laptop or workstation—at home, at school, at work . . . or more likely, some combination of all. And, increasingly, personal information resides on several devices—PDAs, cell phones, multiple desktops—at the same time.

Personal information is also created by a user's behavior patterns, both explicitly and implicitly. People often maintain bookmark lists of frequently visited Web sites (another kind of personal information), but the bookmark list is a sample of their browsing and search history. This too is a kind of personal information—the history and paths of behavior that are collected implicitly and stored locally (e.g., by search browser history).

A basic question for personal information system design is understanding not just what personal information is, but how people would like to use all kinds of personally created, derived, and observed information. What kind of information needs to be stored and how will it be used? What needs to be retrieved? In short, what are the information hopes, needs, and desires of users?

It is clear that people have a very difficult time anticipating future need or retrieval requirements for personal data. The Rolodex is a well-known system for storing phone numbers and addresses. Alas, it just doesn't scale well to many thousands of email addresses (plus IM handles, plus mailing lists, plus passwords, etc). Unfortunately, just as the Rolodex model doesn't scale well without augmentation, the increasing amount and varying kinds of personal information imply that future personal information will come in an increasing number of forms and ever-increasing quantities. Personal information users need a capability that is robust and fairly general to accommodate future needs.

All in all, the challenges for personal information continue to grow and are being driven by new means of communicating, new devices, and the shift in the definition of what constitutes personal information. As Lansdale (1988a) pointed out long ago, the variety of personal information uses seen in real behavior isn't well reflected by the tools we have. User behavior is far richer than the tools they typically use. This disparity between what's needed, what's possible, and what's available for use drives research in this area.

9.2 Research Overview

9.2.1 *What Is Being Done?*

Personal information management (PIM) has a long history of capturing and organizing information to make our personal and work lives simpler. Searching within personal information has an equally long history (e.g., Bush 1945; Hearst 1999; Kidd 1994; Malone 1983; Morville 2006; Savage-Knepshield & Belkin 1999; Whittaker & Sidner 1996) As various trade-offs between capturing, storing, cataloging, and indexing personal information have been explored, one thing stands out: there have always been a diversity of ways to store personal information. And it becomes clear that after a non-trivial amount of personal information has been created and stored, getting back to it—searching it— becomes the next great task.

Research on search interfaces has had a long history in the areas of information science and human-computer interaction. The development of Web search systems greatly facilitated research and development in this area, as more and more users, from a wide variety of backgrounds, began using such services.

People have built PIM tools to capture many special-purpose kinds of information—contact information, personal health records, telephone numbers, login accounts and passwords, bank information, to-do lists. The list is as long as every special-purpose information collection that people have created. Someone, somewhere, at some time has written a program to record and find that kind of information.

Interestingly, people also widely appropriate other mechanisms to capture and make personal information findable. Whittaker, Bellotti, and Gwizdka (2006) and Ducheneaut and Bellotti (2001) describe how people often use email as a mechanism to capture their personal information. Why do people use this apparently nonoptimal behavior? Because email is ubiquitous, easily available, and most email systems have a reasonable search facility that lets the user search, filter, and sort by different properties. In addition, email has often been a repository of content since email attachments permit the user to associate arbitrary text with a file (e.g., a picture or an otherwise unfindable blob). As we shift from a time when storage was expensive to an age of large amounts of inexpensive storage, the cost of storing an item is no longer the dominant factor in determining storage versus use; now the cost of finding something again is. Email, as the great common denominator, has become the personal information manager for many (Czerwinski et al. 2006).

Another focus of work has been to broaden the range of personal material that is captured and stored as part of the desktop space, making a very rich and robust personal content collection. Microsoft's Stuff I've Seen project (Dumais et al. 2003) aims to cast a broad net over the digital information space we inhabit and to provide rich new ways to capture even more information (such as automatically capturing images and integrating multiple personal data trails into a single personal data space).

Personal information management breaks down to capturing information and then finding it again. Unfortunately, essentially every personal information tool's search system is particular; search has been idiosyncratic and specialized. While carefully tuned and specialized search mechanisms can be very effective when operating over controlled and moderated content domain (think, for example, of a system like Lexis-Nexis, which is tuned for search in the domain of legal records), personal information by its nature often has unanticipated needs and unanticipated structure. Thus, search becomes a driver for personal information management. We find it difficult to accurately anticipate what kinds of information needs people will have. And with the rapid growth of new media forms, one of the primary problems of personal information management is that of search. How can search work in such a volatile environment?

9.2.2 The Giant Shift in Search Interfaces

Traditionally, search interfaces have been specialized to their particular information content and style, featuring special access functions for dates and calendar operations, or for sorting along different properties and a variety of display formats. That is, the tools of personal information management were tuned for the tasks identified and to be efficient implementations for access and use. What's more, the searchable databases were primarily in the hands of large mainframe owners with carefully controlled content and index creation. With an increase in personal computing power, the stage was set for a shift in the way people thought about and used search capabilities.

A few years ago, a major change in search interfaces began with the introduction of Web-based and desktop-based full-text indices and a fast, simpler way of making queries over a large unstructured corpus (Morville 2006). While keyword-based search had been around for many years (as embodied in systems such as DIALOG's pay-for-search system of newspaper and bibliographic data), less-structured text-based search quickly gained ground as the dominant model of search. This was never more true than when AltaVista, Excite, InfoSeek, Lycos, and Yahoo launched free Web-search services in 1994. Very quickly, an expanding set of people began to understand search not as the construction of Boolean expressions over a rigorously defined database schema, but as a question of choosing the right keywords that would give back links to documents of specific interest.

The new, easily available capability had a profound influence on research in search. Until that point, search front-ends focused primarily on getting the expression builders to more accurately reflect the semantics of what the user intended. The biggest problem is that the common English usage of AND and OR are not quite the same as their Boolean counterparts. (Anderson 1990b) With free text as the predominant query model, tools other than Web search also began to adopt the new style for its simplicity and breadth of understanding by users.

Equally important, we now understood that search of personal information stores has become commonplace—a user could start to see how personal, local search would become a reality. The big question became "How should one organize and index personal information?"

9.3 Diving In

9.3.1 *One Approach: Desktop Search as Part of Ordinary Web Search*

One approach is to just "search everything" to answer personal information management questions. In our case, we're bringing the basic Google search model into daily information-seeking behaviors. We know that for many users Web search has become a common practice; it's the way people find the local pizza parlor, the latest news items, or technical articles on arcane topics in computer science. And as personal information becomes increasingly integrated into the fabric of our personal data stores, searching everything becomes a popular information management strategy (Cutrell, Dumais & Teevan 2006; Czerwinski, Gage, Gemmel, Marshall, et al. 2006).

While many desktop search systems have been built in the past (Apple 2006; dtSearch 2006; Yahoo 2006), the Google Desktop System makes personal information search just an ordinary part of every Web search done on a browser (Google 2006).

Normally, Web search is just that—searches applied to the contents of the World Wide Web. But if Google Desktop Search (GDS) is activated (by downloading a local client indexing application and letting it run in the background), the results of any Google search can have "local desktop" results blended into the results. In Figure 9.3.1, the two best local desktop search results are shown as the first hits. To see the rest of the desktop results, the user would click on the "831 results" link. In this approach, GDS makes the working contents of a personal computer into one large, searchable content repository that is effectively merged with the external Web. Thus, when a user does an ordinary Web search they also simultaneously search their local desktop files. Since GDS indexes many types of files (email, chat histories, Web search history, Microsoft Office documents, PDFs, calendar appointments, etc.), the single action of searching (using your Web browser) effectively searches your entire personal information space as well.

In operation, GDS sends the user's query to two locations. One copy is sent to Google.com and performs a standard Google Web Search. A duplicate query goes to the GDS application running locally, which searches the local index. GDS then intercepts the results page before display, merging in local desktop results just above the Web search results so the user can see both at once.

Figure 9.3.1 – Google search of local personal information is invoked by doing a regular Google search. When desktop Search is active, the desktop is indexed and the high-quality matching results mixed into the regular, organic, search results. Here, the top two best desktop results are shown next to the multicolored GDS "swirl" icon, with all 831 results available, including emails, notes, calendar entries, and image texts.

The interface challenge is to give the user a sense of the locally stored information without displacing too many of the organic Web search results. GDS includes a brief summary of the possible desktop hits, showing the total number of local results, along with two of the highest-ranked local results. Each high-ranking result is displayed as a regular Web-style link (blue and underlined), along with a summary snippet to the right. Unlike a standard Web-result snippet, the GDS snippet is limited to a single line of text, stretching from the end of the title to the end of the display region. This is a remarkably small amount of space in which to summarize a potentially large number of local results, but the tradeoff is clear: the user's original intent (determined by their action) was to do a Web search—GDS is only giving an indication of possibly relevant local results that the user might not have recalled.

GDS works by full-text indexing the content of files on the local desktop. As is standard practice for such personal system crawler/indexers, GDS runs in the background, limiting its overall performance so as to not disrupt the user when doing his or her normal work. A full-text index is made of the file system contents (including transient objects such as Web searches and chats) taking up basically only a small fraction of the total file system objects being indexed.

Crawling and indexing are fairly off-the-shelf technologies, with open-source implementations widely available (Apache 2006). The key value of GDS for personal information management is its integration with common activities (ordinary Web search) and the various extensions that support a range of personal information tasks. In its current implementation (Version 3, April 2006), GDS is the key part of a larger package (named Google Desktop) that also provides a number of other capabilities to manage personal information. This can include multiple desktop indexing (a search run on one computer will automatically also search all linked computers with a shared index, making it possible to have a distributed working environment), a Web sidebar for streaming information from multiple sources to the desktop, a scratchpad mechanism for taking fast notes, and a set of accelerators to help share information with friends via IM or email.

9.3.2 Two Approaches to Personal Search: Scoping and Broadening

Scoping means limiting a search to a particular range of things you intend to search—all PDF files, all emails from Derek, or just the files within a subdirectory. While this sounds like a bad idea, it's actually a useful way of looking for things that are common. For instance, searching for [June 24] over your entire personal information store is a terrible idea in general, but within the scope of your 2006 personal calendar it can be a very effective way of getting to an item you know you've got. Not only would such a scoped search quickly navigate to that particular day, but it would also bring up other references to that day that are hidden elsewhere in the calendar (such as a note written on May 2: "final paper due on June 24, 2006").

Most personal search tools implicitly scope their searches to the kind of information they're operating over. The calendar search tool, a personal-contacts search, a search of to-do lists—each kind of search is scoped to the extent of their specialized data sets.

The trade-off is pretty clear: a scoped search can be easier to use because the search terms need not be as precise. That is, the user doesn't have to find *exactly* the right search terms that would unambiguously select out the target from the entire information store. The user can use terms that would be fairly common (and therefore low precision) in an unscoped search, but that would be uncommon (and precise) in a scoped search.

This is particularly true for personal information stores, where the user's meta-knowledge of the information store can allow for very effective use because the user knows about the relative frequency of terms. For instance, a search such as [Diane] that's scoped (limited) to just my personal store of emails will pull up all of my emails with "Diane." As a general query, [Diane] is too broad a question, but I happen to know that only two Diane's have ever sent me mail, so it is in fact a reasonable approach to finding a specific email.

By contrast, searching over a fairly heterogeneous information store (e.g., your personal desktop) *broadens* the search to encompass data objects over many different stores.

Traditionally, many personal information applications have created their own private, uninspectable data storage forms. Calendars and contact-managers have usually maintained information in their own databases for performance reasons. As a side effect, indexing these databases has generally been difficult to do from other applications, requiring special-purpose format converters to transcode the internal data into accessible content.

More recently, though, the trend has been toward increasing openness in data storage formats. The consequence of this has been to make more content available to general-purpose search engines that can crawl and index a large personal workspace. This lends itself to searches that cut across application boundaries.

Broadly operating search tools such as GDS, Yahoo Desktop Search (YDS) or Apple's Spotlight let the user pose queries that apply across multiple scopes, crossing many application types and storage formats.

There is a clear tradeoff. A specialized tool can more easily support complex queries that rely on a detailed knowledge of metadata and content structure, but broadly operating search tools provide exactly the breadth and coverage lacking in specialized applications.

These two approaches to the same problem point out that no single solution seems right for all personal information search tasks. Each approach has its benefits and costs: in many personal information management cases it seems as though multiple views of data approach might be best. For example, Yahoo's

Figure 9.3.2a – Google Desktop Search can also be invoked from an ordinary desktop icon. When started up this way, GDS is limited to searching just the desktop and does not reach out to the Web as a whole. Note that emails, files, Web history, and chat transcripts are all searched. The user interface of "just desktop" search differs from that shown in Fig. 9.3.1 to reflect this differently scoped search. The Google logo includes "Desktop," and Desktop" is incorporated just below the blue separator line. Scoped search (just emails, just files, etc.) can be selected by clicking on one of the links in the Desktop: line.

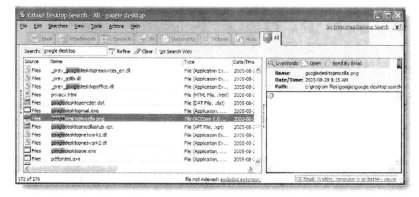

Figure 9.3.2b – The Yahoo Desktop Search application is invoked as a background application, typically via a hotkey. It indexes a wide variety of file types, providing previews of the documents (in the right-hand panel, here showing the Google Dekstop icon) and letting the user sort and refine the query.

display (Figure 9.3.2b) shows a high density of results with preview, while the Google display has text snippets with a thumbnail and views by document type (as in Figure 9.3.2a).

Such broad desktop search tools index email and a wide variety of file types. Yahoo also provides tabs for entries in the desktop contact list, and IM transcripts, while Google offers Web history search. It is clear that desktop search has become much more than just providing a full-text index of ordinary documents—it is a general mechanism for finding content, often personal content, that can be scattered over a variety of sources, places, and filing systems.

Apple also has a desktop search mechanism—Spotlight—that has a large number of sort-by and filtering capabilities (see Figure 9.3.2c). It too provides capabilities for scoping documents by file-type and sorting to get to the right information quickly.

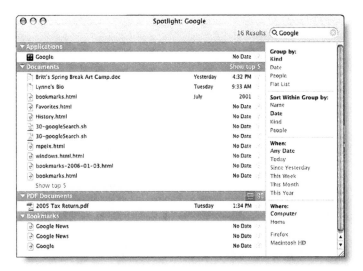

Figure 9.3.2c – Apple's Spotlight desktop search tool is easily invoked by clicking on an ever-present button on the desktop. The right-hand side panel allows grouping of search results and sorting within the group on different properties of the documents. Here personal information about kids' spring camps is intermixed with bookmarks, tax returns, and news.

As these three desktop search tools show, there is a wide variety in the way found objects can be displayed to the searcher. Yahoo and Apple desktop searches provide different sort orders by object metadata (date, file type, etc.), where Google has different file-type views (all, email, files, Web history). Google desktop search provides a short snippet summarizing the document with a thumbnail of the document, while Yahoo Desktop Search provides a document preview in the right-hand side pane.

9.3.3 *Access Everywhere: Toolbars and the Future of Integration*

Just as there has been a trend toward an opening up of content storage formats, allowing the growth of broad search tools, we believe there will also be a continuing trend toward allowing search to become a commonplace feature of all applications.

Not only will search be a basic capability (as common as, say, text editing in dialog boxes), but search will be both scoped and broadened simultaneously as search becomes available across a wide variety of places within the desktop environment. We expect search toolbars and desktop widgets (small applications embedded in the desktop) to proliferate, providing search access for specialized tasks (such as global search from within an application) and universally by providing rapid access to search from anywhere. Information that was previously difficult to find (because it was in a special data repository with awkward, unmemorable access methods), suddenly becomes easily available with a specialized desktop search widget that provides a single-purpose, scoped search.

And just as search continues to expand to provide key access methods for personal information, we see personal information as becoming increasingly scattered across multiple devices. Many knowledge workers have multiple desktops, and the ability to think of their personal information cloud as the aggregate of all their personal information (regardless of what devices currently carry it). Recently, Google Desktop announced the ability to merge search results over multiple indexed desktops (Google 2006).

9.4 Looking Forward

We will continue to see innovation in the user interface (UI) arena—but also in the opportunity for mashups (that is, unexpected combinations of data resources and visual presentations, often Web-based) of different content types and different kinds of contextual information.

Advances will continue to be made in text- and Web-document-indexing, with newer analytic capabilities providing new kinds of indices and retrieval capabilities. Currently there is relatively little higher-order recognition of objects in the document. While full-text *understanding* is still a ways off, the ability to recognize and identify proper nouns, dates, and place names seems feasible in the not-too-distant future. Such capabilities will enable smooth integration between different kinds of information streams within one's personal data space. Calendars and calendar entries will become indexable and useful across devices and data sets (Collins 2001).

Just as personal search tools allow integration across multiple personal computers, including other kinds of personal devices seems to be almost a given. Of all the information devices in your personal space, should all be searchable from any device? Coordination between multiple devices is still an open problem. But the future path is clear—a single user "data cloud" will be accessible and searchable from any personal device, with synchronization happening automatically in the background.

9.4.1 *Outstanding Challenges*

The goal of personal information management is to let users search all of their information assets—desktop content, personal notes, Web, information streams, to-do lists, calendar information—and the list continues to grow as new information types become commonplace.

Yet the growth of new media types is a trend that shows no signs of slowing down. From our vantage point in early 2006, we are impressed by the number of new media types over the past 18 months, such as video blogs, photo blogs, instant message transcripts, tags on files, mashed-up maps-and-data. The list is impressive, and future users will want to be able to search all the content they identify as personal, including types and media that we have not yet anticipated.

The shift from structured query tools to more free-text forms wasn't made without a loss. Performance is still an issue when crawling and indexing large, semistructured data for broad use. Users will continue to want increasingly efficient access to a larger number of content types, with some deeper kinds of computed analysis over the content. Increasingly, the ability to refer to dates, people, and places in subtle and sophisticated ways will become part of our expectations of information management.

And ultimately, the pursuit of ever more personal information could plausibly extend beyond computational desktops and obvious data devices (phones, PDAs, etc.) and into physical objects tagged with radio frequency identification (RFID) and spatial location systems. The extension of personal information management from phone numbers to tracking and locating objects in your personal space doesn't seem all that far away (Want & Russell 2000).

10 Everything through Email

Steve Whittaker, Victoria Bellotti, and Jacek Gwizdka

10.1 Introduction

Email is one of the most successful and frequently used computer applications. According to marketing surveys, over 4 billion corporate email messages were exchanged per day in 2001, increasing to a projected 35 billion in 2005. Moreover, 97 percent of workers report using email multiple times per week for a daily average of 49 minutes (Gartner 2001; Levitt 2000; Pitney Bowes 2000). For many people, work is interpersonal rather than solitary, and email is the main conduit through which their work and information are distributed. They tend to "live" in email, as evidenced by the sheer amount of time they spend using it (Bellotti, Ducheneaut, Howard, et al. 2005), and by their evaluation of its importance, with 71 percent of people stating that it is "essential" for their everyday work (Pitney Bowes 2000).

Email serves as an information conduit—acting as a delivery channel for different types of information, including documents, slides, contact information, and schedules. Its use as conduit naturally leads to its being used for key PIM functions. People use their inboxes as to-do lists to manage current tasks, their email folders as a repository for archival information, and their email address books to find contacts. They even use email to find and schedule calendar appointments.

Despite its success, there are significant problems with email. Users complain about feeling overwhelmed by the volume of messages they receive, and are concerned about processing incoming messages effectively (Bälter & Sidner 2002; Bellotti et al. 2005; Venolia, Gupta, Cadiz & Dabbish 2001; Whittaker & Sidner 1996). They have difficulties, too, in organizing and managing archives (Bälter & Sidner 2002; Boardman & Sasse 2004; Whittaker & Sidner 1996). They experience severe problems using email to manage tasks, leading them to forget tasks and obligations (Bellotti, Ducheneaut, Howard & Smith 2003, Bellotti et al. 2005; Whittaker 2005; Whittaker, Jones & Terveen 2002). Email's failure to address these PIM problems threatens to seriously reduce individual and corporate productivity.

Why is email so hard to process and manage and why does it generate such serious personal information management problems? And yet why is it still so popular and so essential in PIM? And what can be done to make it better able to support this essential role? This chapter will illustrate how many of email's PIM problems stem from its conduit function. Email is incessant, because it is often the primary delivery channel for work and information (Ducheneaut & Bellotti 2001; Venolia et al. 2001; Whittaker 2005). It is hard to process and organize because it is a mixture of different types of information (tasks, documents, FYIs, meeting scheduling), some of which are important (work tasks) and others unimportant (jokes). And most email is generated by others—making it harder to understand, evaluate, and organize than personally generated information (Boardman & Sasse 2004). These problems are exacerbated by the fact that most email systems have no inbuilt support for PIM aside from folders, so that users have to devise ad hoc ways to manage tasks, find contacts, and organize useful information (Bellotti et al. 2003, 2005; Whittaker 2005; Whittaker & Sidner 1996).

This chapter discusses how people use email to manage their personal information and describes the tools that can support such behavior. We look at important aspects of PIM through the lens of email: allocating attention, deciding actions, managing tasks, and organizing messages into folders.

10.2 Email Activities and Their Relation to Finding, Management, and Keeping Aspects of PIM

Figure 10.2 shows major email activities and the relations between them. We now describe these activities and identify the PIM problems that each creates. In each case we discuss the extent to which these problems overlap with problems occurring in other areas of PIM.

1. **Allocating attention.** Email messages differ in their importance, urgency, and interest (Dabbish, Kraut, Fussell & Kiesler 2005). They also take differing amounts of time and effort to process. As a result, users do not access email messages sequentially, instead deciding which messages they attend to first (Bälter & Sidner 2002; Bellotti et al. 2005; Venolia et al. 2001).

2. **Deciding actions.** Unlike other information items obtained from the Web or document repositories, email messages may communicate expectations from others of some kind of response. Users have to assess whether this is the case and decide what action to take for a given message. This is similar to, but more complex than, the classic PIM "keeping" decision (Bellotti et al. 2005; Dabbish et al. 2005; Venolia et al. 2001).

3. **Managing tasks.** Many email tasks are not one-shot and cannot be discharged in a single session (Bellotti et al. 2005; Gwizdka & Chignell 2004; Whittaker 2005). Often this is because they require input from others, or the complex collation of information from multiple sources. We refer to collaborative tasks that require inputs from others as interdependent. Task management relates to re-finding activities. Users need to structure personal information to guarantee it can be found easily and at the appropriate time.

4. **Organizing messages and folders.** As in other aspects of PIM, users have to decide how to organize information. This relates to keeping and management activities. If users decide to file, which folder should they put an item in? Again these decisions are complicated by the fact that much email information is generated by others, sometimes without the context of personal user goals or initiatives. This in turn means that folder organization is often unsuccessful (Bälter 1998; Whittaker & Sidner 1996).

Note that the above list does not imply a strict temporal sequence, with messages first being attended to, decisions made, tasks managed and then filed. As shown in Figure 10.2, email processing can take different forms depending on

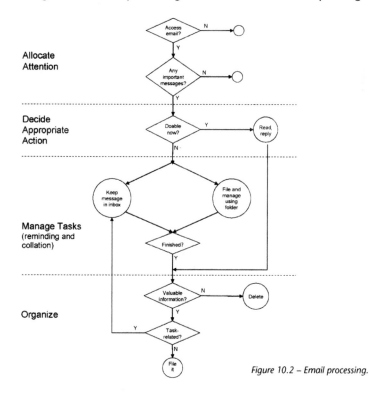

Figure 10.2 – Email processing.

the nature of the message, its relation to other tasks, and user workload. Simple irrelevant messages may be scanned and deleted immediately. Other messages may be left in the inbox, returned to several times as the user scans the inbox, later judged to be irrelevant and deleted. Yet other messages may be scanned and filed if they relate to ongoing projects or interests but do not demand a response. Messages related to interdependent tasks may be filed or left in the inbox as reminders; they may be repeatedly revisited as the task unfolds, or as the user encounters them in the context of accessing their inbox. And older archived messages may be re-accessed if they have relevance for current tasks.

10.3 Understanding Email Tasks

We now review research of special relevance to email's role in PIM. To understand the challenges of managing email, it is important first to document its general properties. We present some general statistics on email volume, and inbox and folder characteristics, followed by a taxonomy of the different types of email message, and how people spend their time processing email.

10.3.1 *Scoping the Problem: Some Basic Email Properties*

Table 10.3.1 – Summary of Basic Email Statistics.

Data	Number of Msgs Received/Day	Number of Msgs Sent/Day	Number of Inbox Msgs	Percentage of Total Msgs Kept in Inbox	Total Number of Email Msgs Retained	Number of Folders
No. of Participants	86	200	206	183	183	244
Weighted average	43.7	13.7	1424	49.3	2846	38.8

Sources: Bälter & Sidner 2002; Bellotti, Ducheneaut, Howard, et al. 2005; Boradman & Sasse 2004; Dabbish et al. 2005; Ducheneaut & Bellotti 2001; McKay 1988; Venolia et al. 2001; Whittaker & Sidner 1996.

Table 10.3.1 summarizes eight studies that have collected general data about email behaviors. One important proviso in interpreting the data is that each of the reported studies reported large individual differences between users, depending on their email processing strategies—and there are large standard deviations for the data presented. Individual differences in PIM are discussed in detail in chapter 12. Note also that these studies have focused on workplace rather than recreational usage, and that the specific context of the workplace probably influences both the volume of emails and the manner in which they are processed.

Somewhat surprisingly, these studies do not suggest a huge increase email loads over the last 18 years. This may be because these studies researched populations working in high technology or academia where email throughput has always been high, and is perhaps closer to a natural saturation point.

Nevertheless, certain general observations may explain users' complaints about processing and managing email. For example, people have to process a large number (between 38 and 52) of messages each day. They send 31 percent as many emails as they receive—suggesting many messages they receive do not demand a response. On the management side, they keep hundreds or even thousands of messages in their inbox, accounting for about half the total messages they keep. With the proviso that there are large individual differences in how people organize information, these statistics can be explained by the use of the inbox as a "to-do" list for working tasks. On the organizational side, users create on average 38.8 folders.

Message Types

Various attempts have been made to categorize different types of messages that people receive. For example Whittaker and Sidner (1996) describe messages as "to-dos," "to-reads," "messages of indeterminate status," and "ongoing corres-pondence," based on properties such as message age, length, and whether or not messages are filed or left in the inbox. They also present some prevalence statistics, with "to-reads" accounting for 21 percent of the inbox. Dabbish et al. (2005) present a more systematic analysis of message types. Messages could serve multiple functions, but the overall breakdown was Action requests (34 percent), Information requests (18 percent), Information attachments (36 percent), Status updates for projects/tasks (21 percent), Scheduling requests/responses to scheduling requests (14 percent), Reminders for meetings/actions (16 percent), Social messages (8 percent), and Other (12 percent).

These data clearly show that most messages require the user *to act in some way that has implications for others*—whether this is to carry out an action, respond to a request, or to schedule a meeting. Such interdependence has implications for how effectively others carry out their tasks. Section 10.3.4 details the problems email presents in managing tasks.

Finally, there have been video studies of how people allocate time processing email (Bellotti et al. 2005):

- 54 percent composing messages
- 23 percent reading messages, attachments, and links
- 10 percent filing messages
- 6 percent scanning inbox messages for things to read or deal with

- 2 percent deleting messages
- 2 percent looking for messages in folders
- 2 percent managing attachments

In addition to the obvious dominant activities of reading and writing messages, users dedicate proportionally large amounts of time filing messages. In Section 10.3.5 we examine why filing is such a demanding activity and evaluate its success in creating useful structures for future retrieval. Section 10.3.2 and 10.3.3 discuss how new emails are processed, and Section 10.3.4 explains how the inbox is used for task management. We now review research on these key email activities.

10.3.2 *Allocating Attention*

There are two parts to attention allocation. The first involves *when and why* people decide to attend to email, and the second *how* they decide which messages to attend to, and in what order. Allocation of attention is influenced by multiple factors including user workload, available time, nature of the message, identity of its sender, and so on. Deciding which emails to attend to is similar to typical PIM finding tasks (Barreau & Nardi 1995; Lansdale 1988a), as it involves judging items of varying importance to determine which are immediately relevant. It differs from typical PIM finding because items do not have to be actively generated by the user; as they are already in the inbox and do not have to be searched or actively browsed for.

Deciding when to attend to email. Despite email's importance for task delegation, there has been relatively little systematic study of what causes people to attend to their email. Mackay (1988) and Whittaker & Sidner (1996) note how email dominates people's work lives. Similar findings led Ducheneaut & Bellotti (2001) to make the observation that people "live" in email—leading them to characterize it as a "habitat." In Mackay's (1988) study, 13/27 informants stated that they read email "constantly." However, as Venolia et al. (2001) observe, people cannot spend their entire work time in email, raising questions about how often they access email, as well as the factors that lead them to switch to email from other activities. Dabbish et al. (2005) report that people check email 19 times per day, so what prompts this? For some, any incoming unread message serves as a trigger. Venolia et al. present survey data from 406 Microsoft employees suggesting that most of their respondents attend to incoming messages as soon as these arrive. Participants also usually access email as soon as they can after they have been away from it, that is, first thing in the morning, or upon returning to their desk after an absence. And because email serves as a task manager, archive, and contact manager, email access may be prompted by the need to retrieve to-dos, reminders, or archived information relevant to a current task (Ducheneaut & Bellotti 2001; Whittaker & Sidner 1996). Access frequency is directly influenced by task management demands; Gwizdka (2004b) reports that the more task-related messages users keep in the inbox the more likely they are to constantly read email, rather then at specific times only.

Deciding which messages to attend to. Users generally don't access messages sequentially in the order in which they arrive, and they often don't access all messages. Bälter & Sidner (2002) observed that their ten users scanned the inbox a mean of 2.3 times to decide which messages to focus on, and Venolia et al. (2001) report that 70 percent of their interviewees processed messages out of sequence. Bälter and Sidner also found that only half their informants accessed all the emails they received. But how do people decide which messages to access first and which to ignore? One possibility is that people focus on *important messages*, and Venolia et al. list a variety of factors that affect perceived importance, such as the identity of the sender, number of recipients, the nature of the message, and whether the message is a reply. Dabbish et al. (2005) found that important messages were those that demanded action, conveyed task status, discussed schedules, or were reminders. Important messages were also more likely to be sent by people with whom the recipient had a strong working relationship, and to be personally addressed rather than to a wide distribution list. They were also highly unlikely to be social messages.

10.3.3 *Deciding Actions*

Having decided *which* messages to attend to, users then have to decide *what* to do about them—for example, whether to respond, file, delete, or defer action until later. In other areas of PIM, users have to make decisions about the information that they encounter, such as whether to keep it or not (Jones 2004). In email, these decisions are more complex, and they may also have important implications for the work of others; that is, when the information concerns an interdependent task.

Dabbish et al. (2005) found that people only respond (or intend to respond, in cases where they defer action) to about 35 percent of the messages they receive. Contrary to their expectations, Dabbish and colleagues also discovered that perceived importance is only weakly correlated with responding; people are only 8 percent more likely to respond to important messages. In contrast, sender characteristics (15 percent), whether the message is personally addressed

(20 percent) and, most strikingly, whether the message is social (23 percent) are all stronger determinants than importance in predicting responding. Another notable strategy is that users *defer* responses to 37 percent of messages they intend to respond to. There are several possible reasons for this, including leaving time for reflection, or, with interdependent tasks, communicating with others to gather and collate the information needed for a collective response. Whether people respond to a message immediately or not, their most likely action for a message requiring a response is to leave it in the inbox. Even when they have already replied to the message, users leave it in the inbox 55 percent of the time, whereas if the message has not been responded to, they leave it in the inbox 79 percent of the time. This suggests that people are using the inbox as a reminder to respond—using the inbox for task management as described in the next section.

Dabbish et al. also examined whether incoming messages were filed, deleted, or retained in the inbox. Overall, people filed 27 percent of their messages, deleted 24 percent, and kept the remaining 49 percent in the inbox. People were more likely to keep important messages in the inbox, although message type and sender characteristics did not directly affect retention behaviors. Individual differences were important here—accounting for 48 percent of the variance in the probability of a message being left in the inbox.

Of the messages that don't demand a reply, users file 28 percent of (presumably useful) messages, delete a further 30 percent of (presumably irrelevant) messages, but then retain the remaining 42 percent in the inbox. Why do users retain so many of these informational messages that don't demand a reply? Some messages may be kept for later reading. Immediate time pressure may lead people to defer reading these until they have more time. Whittaker and Sidner (1996) found that 21 percent of inbox messages contained more than 5 screenfuls of text. These to-reads may not be filed because leaving them in the inbox is a way to remind users that they still have to be processed. Other messages are retained because users don't know what to do with them. Rather than investing valuable time in reading a new message at once, users register its arrival, but defer dealing with it until they are more certain of its importance. Rather than delete it immediately, they conservatively retain it, in case it turns out to be important.

Messages are often revisited multiple times, with different decisions taken about how they should be processed. For example, a message might be kept in the inbox or stored in a folder and accessed multiple times until a task is complete, when it might be filed in an archive (Bellotti et al. 2005).

One obvious conclusion is that deciding what to do with email messages is rather more complex than the typical PIM keeping decision. While users do end up keeping the majority of messages, their decisions are more complicated than making a binary choice to keep or delete a message. Having decided to keep a message, users also have to decide what action to carry out on it, such as whether and when to reply to it. There also seem to be two distinct and important types of keeping activity: (1) filing—which is the typical PIM task of categorizing information for future use, and (2) inbox retention—where information is not organized, but kept in a working buffer to remind people it may require some future action. The next section describes this complex management activity.

10.3.4 *Managing Tasks*

A classic PIM activity is that of managing information to meet the demands of specific tasks, and many PIM studies have described how users categorize information in order to facilitate its future retrieval (Jones 2004; Kidd 1994; Lansdale 1988a; Teevan, Alvarado, Ackerman & Karger 2004). Task management in email turns out to have rather different demands however.

Task management involves reminding oneself about current tasks and tracking task status, as well as collating and maintaining information relevant to those tasks. A direct consequence of email functioning as a conduit for work and information is that people use it as a de facto task manager. Many email tasks are too complex or lengthy be executed in one shot (Bellotti et al. 2005; Venolia et al. 2001; Whittaker 2005; Whittaker & Sidner 1996), leading to deferral for 37 percent of messages that require replies (Dabbish et al. 2005).

Deferral is often a direct consequence of *interdependent* tasks, such as those involving others (Bellotti et al. 2005). Two problematic aspects of managing interdependent tasks result from *iteration* and *delays* between messages relating to the task. Iteration arises because interdependent tasks often require multiple exchanges between participants before they can be resolved (Bellotti et al. 2005; Venolia & Neustaedter 2003; Venolia et al. 2001; Whittaker & Sidner 1996). People may need to negotiate exactly what a task involves, or multiple responses may need to be synthesized. Delays occur because collaborators lack the necessary information to respond immediately to address their part of the task. One way to estimate the prevalence of interdependent tasks is by determining how many emails are part of a *conversational thread*, as threads indicate relations and common underlying activities among messages. Threading estimates range from 30 to 62 percent of messages (Bellotti et al. 2003; Fisher & Moody 2001; Klimt & Yang 2004; Venolia et al. 2001).[1] The largest available public email corpus from Enron has 62 percent of messages appearing in threads, with a mean thread length of 4.1 messages, though the median length is only 2 (Klimt & Yang 2004).

Delays and iteration give rise to two critical activities in managing inter-dependent tasks. Users have to leave themselves reminders about outstanding tasks, and to collate different elements of the same collaborative task. We now look at how people address these problems in order to carry out core task-management activities.

People predominantly use email itself to manage tasks arriving in email, rather than relying on a dedicated task-management application, such as a to-do list on a PDA (Bellotti, Dalal, Good, et al. 2004; Venolia et al. 2001). New messages relating to a particular task arrive in email, which, as email is constantly processed, serve to remind users about that task, whereas copying information into a separate application requires additional effort and bookkeeping.

One *reminding* strategy involves setting up a dedicated to-do folder containing reminders about outstanding tasks (Bellotti et al. 2003, 2005; Whittaker & Sidner 1996; Whittaker et al. 2002). However, Whittaker & Sidner (1996) report that 95 percent of users abandoned this strategy because it requires an additional cognitive step. Instead of being reminded about tasks as they access new email in their inbox, people have to explicitly remember to open the to-do folder, and they often forgot to do this. Another strategy is to organize emails relating to current tasks into active folders, returning to these folders when they need to deal with those tasks (Bellotti et al. 2005; Gwizdka 2004b). This has the advantage of grouping messages, allowing them to be more efficiently worked on together. But this strategy only works if users develop the habit of routinely returning to inspect those folders, as most users do with the inbox.

But the most common strategy for managing interdependent tasks is to respond or forward the original message to relevant others, leaving the original message in the inbox as a reminder about the task (Dabbish et al. 2005; Mackay 1988; Venolia et al. 2001; Whittaker 2005; Whittaker & Sidner 1996). This serves to manipulate attention. Users know that they will return to the inbox to access new messages. In the course of doing so, they hope that they will see the reminder and recall the outstanding task. Users may even send themselves emails as reminders, or that contain important information (Jones, Dumais & Bruce 2002). This inbox reminding strategy is far more common than other techniques such as using message flags, classifying messages as to-do items, relying on external applications, or external reminders (Gwizdka 2004b; Venolia et al. 2001).

A second problem with interdependent tasks is *collating* information, or assimilating the disparate pieces of information relating to a common task. Collation is difficult because messages relating to the same activity may come from multiple individuals using different subject lines, and may even end up in different folders. As a result, some users feel that that keeping messages in their inbox makes them more *collatable*, in part because the multiple passes carried out when processing the inbox serve to remind them about its contents (Whittaker 2005).

However, many users experience severe problems with using the inbox for task management. Reminding and collating are highly dependent on *visual scanning*, which becomes less effective as the number of inbox items increases. Most email interfaces present a header list along with message body information for a selected message. Although users differ in how they configure their header list, they tend to operate with 10 to 20 message headers visible on the screen (Whittaker & Sidner 1996; Whittaker et al. 2002). This means, on average, that less than 2 percent of inbox messages are visible.

Because most inbox message headers are not constantly in view, users have to actively remember to scroll back to view older messages. And it is hard to identify specific, related messages scattered at intervals through the inbox among hundreds of other unrelated items. The alternatives of searching and sorting by metadata, such as sender or subject, are only effective when users can remember salient information about the message. For this reason, older inbox messages are often characterized as being "out of sight and out of mind" (Whittaker & Sidner 1996).

And relying on folders or messages threads is little better: Venolia et al. (2001) found that 23 percent of message threads occurred in more than one folder. Using threads is also unreliable, because they rely on a common message subject line—and this turns out to be an inconsistent indicator that messages relate to the same task (Ducheneaut & Bellotti 2003).

A related problem is *obligation management*, or keeping track of the tasks that you "owe" others or that are "owed" to you. Although the strategy of leaving messages in the inbox works reasonably well for reminding about tasks that one receives, it is much less effective when delegating tasks to others. Most email programs keep a copy of sent messages, but these are generally stored in a separate "Sent" folder. Having to remember to access the Sent folder suffers from the same weaknesses as using a to-do folder. Some users attempt to avoid this by copying themselves on every sent message to generate inbox reminders, but this overloads the inbox with duplicate messages for every task (Bellotti et al. 2005; Whittaker 2005; Whittaker et al. 2002).

In conclusion, task management is problematic in email. Although the default strategy is to use the inbox as a to-do list, there are numerous problems associated with doing this, including overlooking reminder messages and inability to collate information. These problems do not have clear analogues elsewhere in PIM.

10.3.5 *Organizing Messages into Folders*

People dedicate a great deal of time and effort to organizing their email. Many PIM studies have documented the problems of categorizing information in a way that facilitates later retrieval (Barreau & Nardi 1995; Boardman & Sasse 2004; Jones et al. 2002; Lansdale 1988a; Whittaker & Hirschberg 2001). Email presents similar organizational problems.

Creating email folders is a common activity, with users overall filing 27 percent of their messages, although there are large individual differences in the complexity of folder organization. Some users create organizations that include hundreds of folders with complex internal structure; others create few folders (Boardman & Sasse 2004; Venolia et al. 2001; Whittaker & Sidner 1996). One important reason for filing is that messages contain useful reference information such as documents, presentations, or Web links (Bellotti et al. 2005; Ducheneaut & Bellotti 2001; Venolia et al. 2001). For example, Dabbish et al. (2005) estimate that about 36 percent of incoming messages contain useful reference information. Indeed some people tend to use email as a document archive, sometimes using metadata such as sender and date to organize and version different document drafts (Bellotti & Smith 2000). And contrary to Barreau and Nardi's (1995) assertions, users do access old messages and value their archives (Boardman & Sasse 2004; Venolia et al. 2001).

Various studies have examined the *types* of folders that email users create. The most common types of folders relate to work projects, contacts, and mailing lists (Boardman & Sasse 2004). There have been fewer studies of the process of creating folders, however, although Whittaker and Sidner (1996) examined the problems users experienced with this, and we summarize their findings here.

Filing is a cognitively difficult task (Lansdale 1988a). Successful filing is highly dependent on being able to anticipate future retrieval requirements. It is hard to decide which existing folder is appropriate, or, if a new folder is needed, how to give it an appropriate and memorable name.

Users may not file messages because failing to remember where information has been filed could be disastrous. And we have already seen that another reason for not filing is to postpone judgments, in order to determine the value of information. Users want to avoid archiving information that later turns out to be useless or irrelevant.

Even when users do decide to file, folders may not turn out to be especially useful. Users may be unable to remember folder names, especially after a time has elapsed, or when they have large numbers of folders. They have to remember the definition of each when filing, and to be careful not to create new folders that duplicate or overlap with existing ones. Duplication detracts from their use in retrieval.

In addition, folders can be *too small* to be useful. A major aim of filing is to collate the huge number of undifferentiated inbox items into a relatively small set of folders containing multiple related messages. Filing is clearly not successful if each folder is small: a folder containing few items has not significantly reduced the complexity of the inbox, nor collated significant amounts of related material. However, Whittaker and Sidner (1996) show that filing often fails: 35 percent of users' folders contain only one or two items. Furthermore, the user has the dual overheads of (1) first creating these folders, and (2) remembering multiple definitions every time there is a new filing decision. Quantitative data illustrate the problems of trying to remember multiple folder definitions. The more folders a user has, the more likely they are to generate "failed folders" containing only one or two items.

Folders can also fail because they are *too big*. When there are too many messages in a folder, it becomes unwieldy. It is difficult to find relevant messages in a large folder, as the relationships between different messages in the folder become tenuous, and one of the main benefits of keeping them together is much reduced.

There has been less study of how users access their email archives. Some studies claim that users report few difficulties in locating information in their archives. Boardman and Sasse (2004) found otherwise: users experienced considerable problems when asked to find archived messages. The most common strategies for accessing archival information are to browse folders or to sort messages by sender or subject. Search is much less commonly used, although this may reflect the inefficiency of search in many email applications, and recent developments in desktop search should change this (Boardman & Sasse 2004; Dumais, Cutrell, Cadiz, et al. 2003; Venolia et al. 2001). Dumais et al. (2003) looked at common patterns of search over archives, finding that recency was a very strong predictor that a message would be accessed, and that access by sender or recipient name was another common search strategy.

In summary, various studies have shown that, in common with other areas of PIM, email users experience problems in organizing their information. They spend large amounts of time constructing structures for future retrieval that may not be greatly effective in supporting access.

10.4 Techniques to Support PIM in Email

Having characterized users' main email activities and PIM problems, we now discuss how current technologies address these issues. From our prior discussion it is clear that there are strong interrelations between different email activities. Thus, a particular technology such as automatic filing may help both with organization of email, and with task management; for example, by reducing inbox size it allows users to better focus on outstanding messages. And techniques that analyze message content and headers might help users to allocate attention to important messages as well as to decide what action to apply to a message. Table 10.4 shows a breakdown of different techniques and the PIM activities they support.

Table 10.4 – Techniques for Supporting Key Email Activities

Technique		Email Activities Addressed
Spam Filtering		Attention allocation
Personal filtering	sender specified	Attention allocation, deciding actions
	user created	Attention allocation, deciding actions
	machine learning	Attention allocation, deciding actions
	pre-defined rules	Attention allocation, deciding actions
AI message summarization		Deciding actions
Information structuring		Task management
Embedded task management support		Task management
Workflow systems		Task management
Assisted filing		Archive management, task management
Search		Archive management

10.4.1 *Allocating Attention*

Two main approaches have been taken to help users allocate attention more effectively. Both rely on filtering, but each has a different aim. *Spam filtering* aims to remove irrelevant information from the inbox. *Personal filtering* takes the opposite approach in attempting to identify, highlight, or prioritize important information in the inbox.

Spam filtering. Spam has become a major problem for most email users, with AOL estimating that it blocks 1.4M spam messages each day—an average of 22 per user per day (AOL 2003). Many organizations find it necessary to apply filters at the email server to remove suspect content. Spam detection has been relatively successful (if not yet completely accurate) because spam messages often have distinct properties such as large distribution lists, predictable headers, and somewhat predictable message content (Cranor & LaMacchia 1998). But the race between those who develop spam filters and the spammers evolving techniques to defeat them remains an ongoing contest, with recent spamming techniques involving the generation of more plausible message content.

Personal filtering. Personal filtering relies on various techniques, depending on how filtering rules are created. One technique relies on the sender to specify information that allows the user to better judge message utility. For example Information Lens (Malone, Grant & Turbak 1986) or the Co-ordinator (Flores, Graves, Harfield & Winograd 1988) allow the sender to specify the priority of the message or its projected action. Another technique used by many commercial email clients allows the user to define rules to prioritize incoming messages, using information about the sender, recipients, message content, subject line, and so on. Yet another (predominantly research) approach is to use machine learning to automatically induce prioritization rules. Horvitz, Jacobs, and Hovel (1999) and Metral (1993) built systems that track users' actions to learn the properties of messages the user attends to and in what order, using this information to identify new messages that are likely to be important. Finally, systems can provide predefined rules that users can tune to meet their needs. For example, Marx and Schmandt (1996) use information from calendar appointments, outgoing messages, phone calls, and the user's Rolodex to infer message importance. Bälter and Sidner (2002) propose a much simpler set of predefined rules that identify urgent messages, important senders, and personal messages.

Personal filtering has not been successful, however. It is not commonly used despite being prototyped almost 20 years ago, and being available for several years in commercial products (Bälter & Sidner 2002; Bellotti et al. 2003; Whittaker & Sidner 1996; Whittaker 2005). One problem is that writing filtering rules is a programming task—which most users find both hard and time-consuming. And often the users who are most in need of filters have the least time to dedicate to writing rules. Systems that provide predefined general rules simplify the programming task, but this approach has not been successful either. Although machine learning and bespoke filters do not require users to write rules, trust is a more serious concern with such approaches. Users are unconfident that rules will operate correctly (Pazzani 2000). In particular, they worry that misdefined rules will lead important messages to be overlooked (Whittaker & Sidner 1996). And whatever the approach to defining filtering rules, these must be modified frequently to reflect changes in people's work activities—making rule maintenance an important issue (Whittaker & Sidner 1996). In sum, while personal filtering may work for restricted message types with predictable characteristics (e.g., originating from specific newsgroups or users), this technique has limited utility for many messages that users receive.

10.4.2 *Deciding Appropriate Message Actions*

Recent research has developed techniques that suggest actions for new messages by analyzing past user actions on similar messages. As much of this work is at a preliminary stage, we postpone analysis to section 10.5, where we discuss future email trends.

10.4.3 *Managing Tasks*

People have proposed three approaches to task management: (1) *information structuring*, which seeks to impose organization on the inbox by clustering together messages related to the same task, (2) *embedded support for task management*—where techniques are used to recognize and organize task-related information-building in direct support for reminding and collation, and (3) *workflow*, which seeks to organize messages in terms of underlying task sequences and the roles of the people executing the task.

Information Structuring

Most *information structuring* work proposes novel visualizations for inbox message threads, imposing order on the undifferentiated inbox. Thread detection clusters related messages, allowing users to collate task information and work on related messages together.

Various approaches have been taken to visualizing inbox threads. These range from combining thread components linearly (Bellotti et al. 2003), to constructing complex tree structures with subthreads (Venolia & Neustaedter 2003). Most approaches are based on information derived from message subject lines (Rohall, Gruen, Moody & Kellerman 2001; Venolia et al. 2001; Venolia & Neustaedter 2003; Wattenberg, Rohall, Gruen & Kerr 2005). But topic drift and replying practices mean that the subject line is at best a weak indicator of relations between elements of a specific interdependent task (Whittaker 2005). One way to address this is to allow users to manually intervene, by combining different threads or redefining them according to their own view of what is related (Bellotti et al. 2003, 2005). But while these hybrid approaches are promising, most have not as yet been subjected to detailed evaluation, and to be effective they may have to be tuned to an individual user's email or to the user's workgroup.

Embedded Support for Task Management

Bellotti et al.'s (2003, 2005) prototype, TaskMaster, provides embedded support for tasks based around the notion of *thrasks*. TaskMaster is designed to present a task-centric view of email, addressing the problems of *collation* and *reminding*. The thrask model supports collation as follows: any related incoming messages (replies in a thread, along with associated files or links) are automatically grouped together, using message content and metadata. Each thrask is represented in the inbox by its first message's subject line, providing a compact representation that serves a reminding function. Clicking on the subject line reveals the relevant set of messages, allowing the user to work on the task. In a field trial involving nine users, the system performed well, with users finding many of the embedded task-management features compelling.

Whittaker, Swanson, Kucan, and Sidner (1997) also provided direct support for task management in the TeleNotes system. TeleNotes supported interdependent task management by mimicking people's current use of physical desktop piles and spatial location. Messages relating to a common task are organized into piles that appear on the users' computer desktop. This serves not only to remind users about outstanding tasks but also helps with collation, as related materials are clustered together. The system was positively evaluated by eight users in an extended field trial.

A slightly different approach to task management was taken in the ContactMap system (Nardi, Whittaker, Isaacs, et al. 2002; Whittaker, Jones, Nardi, et al. 2004). Instead of organizing the user interface (UI) in terms of messages involved in a task, it organizes in terms of the *people* involved in that task. The UI represents a social network of the important people in the user's work and social life, and messages (and tasks) can be accessed by clicking on individuals or groups involved in that task. It also supports reminders and alerting, and was positively evaluated in laboratory and field trials.

Workflow Systems

Workflow systems assume that organizational tasks have a predictable structure and that this is associated with different work roles (Prinz 1993; Winograd 1994). For example, a purchase order may have to be initiated by an employee, approved by a manager, and processed by the purchasing department before an item is ordered and delivered to the employee. In principle, workflow systems address *interdependent task management*; they support reminding as well as message collation. In practice, however, they have three major limitations: *additional work, coverage,* and *lack of integration.*

Workflow systems are hard to set up, as workflows are often hard to define, and they often introduce *additional work* for senders. One reason users rejected early systems such as Information Lens (Malone et al. 1986) and Co-ordinator (Winograd & Flores 1986) was that these required senders to add additional information to the initiating message (Mackay 1990). The *coverage* problem arises because many interdependent tasks lack the predictability needed for the workflow approach to succeed. Workflow is effective for tasks that have predictable structure—but, as we have seen, most interdependent tasks have an evolving structure and require iterative negotiation for their solution. This makes them inappropriate for workflow tools (Bowers, Button & Sharrock 1995; Dourish, Holmes, MacLean, et al. 1996; Suchman 1993, 1997). And even when tasks are amenable to workflow, there are *integration* issues. With a few notable exceptions (Borenstein 1992; Borenstein & Thyberg 1988), most workflow systems are not well integrated with email clients, so that users have to switch to a separate application—introducing extra cognitive overhead.

10.4.4 *Organizing Email Information*

Organization is a major problem for email users, and several agent-based systems attempt to provide *assisted filing* (Boone 1998; Cohen 1996; Mock 2001; Segal & Kephart 1999; Takkinnen & Shahmehri 1998). These systems use machine learning techniques to automatically elicit the defining characteristics of existing folders, based on message headers and content. These definitions can then be used to classify each inbox message, suggesting the folder it best matches. Some of these algorithms have been tested offline on message corpora, showing that they can categorize inbox documents with a reasonable degree of success—achieving 85 percent accuracy (Cohen 1996).

Although these results are promising, none of the systems has been tested in real-usage contexts, and it may be that (as with the filtering techniques described above) users are unwilling to trust systems that automatically file their messages. It has been noted that users feel uncomfortable about automated mail classification, since they may not agree with the system's decision (Pazzani 2000). And if a message is automatically filed they may be unable to relocate it. MailCat (Segal & Kephart 1999) improves classification performance and partially addresses the problem of users not knowing where content has gone by presenting its best three guesses about where to place the message. Users then actively select their best choice. Crawford's i-ems intelligent classification application also allows user intervention if the system suggests inappropriate folders (Crawford, Kay & McCreath 2002).

While these recent designs address issues of user trust, another serious problem is that *assisted filing* may not cover important aspects of filing. Assisted filing classifies inbox messages into *existing* folder categories, whereas a major user filing problem lies in defining *new* folders (Whittaker & Sidner 1996). A related problem concerns individual differences in email handling, where a subset of users either do not file messages at all, or make rudimentary use of folders (Bälter & Sidner 2002; Boardman & Sasse 2004; Whittaker & Sidner 1996). Assisted filing cannot work for them because they have few folders for the system to learn. A final problem concerns messages that are hard to classify in part because they belong in multiple folders. With some exceptions (e.g., NotesMail) most systems force users to classify messages into a single folder.

10.5 Looking Forward: The Future of Email and PIM

We now speculate about the future of email. There are some aspects of email that we do not expect to change in the next few years. These include (1) *list views*, because they are convenient for viewing, archiving, and sorting; (2) *folders and sorting*, because even if the system can help search, people will still need multiple ways to organize and find something; (3) *information overload*, because email continues to be an easy means to distribute one message to many people and ever more collaborative work processes are being moved online; and (4) *prevalence of attachments*, because messages often concern discussion of (and work around) other content. We do anticipate changes in email and PIM for our four activities, however.

10.5.1 *Allocating Attention*

One recent development that promises to affect email is the popularity of other communication and publishing applications, such as instant messaging (IM), blogs, Wikis, and the Web. A large proportion of email traffic consists of messages that do not necessarily demand a reply (Dabbish et al. 2005). So, instead of using email to distribute such information, it might be better to publish it in a blog, Wiki, or on a Web page, reducing overall email traffic and allowing users to focus their attention on personal emails that demand a response. Similarly, one might migrate urgent messages out of email into more interactive applications such as IM. TeleNotes (Whittaker et al. 1997) does this by integrating email with IM. It presents IM messages on the desktop with alerting, but the same messages can also be viewed from within email if the user chooses. IBM's Activity Explorer (Muller, Geyer, Brownholtz, et al. 2006) is another unified communication application, blurring the boundaries between email chats and shared workspaces, and offering integration of six types of objects: message, chat, file, folder, annotated screen shot, and to-do item. Although these developments are promising, there are significant research questions raised by such melded communications. For example, if information is published rather than emailed, how are people alerted about important new information? Clumsy implementations of alerts (e.g., sending these through email) replicate the original problem by increasing email volumes. And if we have information distributed in different communication applications this may contribute to fragmentation—making it harder for users to collate related information. On a different note, we expect that advances in machine learning and text processing will lead to the development of effective methods to prioritize emails, identifying those that are urgent, and allowing users to better focus on important messages.

10.5.2 Deciding Actions

Deciding appropriate message actions is a difficult challenge for automated support, requiring insight into the meaning and importance of email. Given the current state of the art, we hardly want our intelligent email systems deciding to sign us up for distribution lists or to follow sponsored links to purchase products. But recent attention has turned to content-based techniques that identify task-related aspects of messages, so that they can be more easily acted upon by people.

Some of this new work simply focuses on summarizing messages or threads so that it is easier to extract key information (Abu-Hakima, McFarland & Meech 2001; Muresan, Tzoukermann & Klavans 2001; Rambow, Shrestha, Chen & Laurdisen 2004; Tzoukermann, Muresan & Klavans 2001). Other work goes further and attempts to identify the relationship between messages and activities that the user is engaged in. One approach is to recognize messages that are part of a standard automated workflow (such as purchasing a book online) and what steps they represent in such processes (Kushmerik & Lau 2005). Another is to combine analysis of senders' and recipients' addresses and message bodies to identify messages that are related to a common task, making it easier for the user to monitor it (Dredze, Lau & Kushmerick 2006). Yet another is to identify the actions expressed in the text of the email body and extract these for the user's optional addition to a to-do list (Corston-Oliver, Ringger, Gamon & Campbell

2004). More advanced systems suggest possible actions on a message. Horvitz, Jacobs, and Hovel (1999) and Metral (1993) built systems that track the history of user actions to learn which messages the user reads, deletes, responds to, or files—suggesting appropriate actions for new messages based on these inferred rules. And Carvalho and Cohen (2005) use machine learning to identify messages requiring an action, such as requests or commitments.

With continued advances in machine-learning techniques, we expect to see more such systems that assist users in determining appropriate actions on messages. So far, however, this work is somewhat preliminary, and even where there is a functional email client, problems of trust mean that how they act upon the message content still remains at users' discretion. Even as these techniques improve, they will still require both careful integration with existing systems and transparency of operation in order to engender users' trust in their effectiveness. And one important limitation of all this new work is that little of it has been evaluated with real users.

10.5.3 *Task Management*

Task management is currently *the* critical unresolved email problem for users, although there are a number of promising trends here. We expect future research will continue to generate novel visualizations of email, to help provide greater structure to the inbox (Kerr 2003; Viegas, Boyd, Nguyen, et al. 2004; Whittaker et al. 2004). And various novel email clients already provide embedded support for task management, including collation and reminding (Bellotti et al. 2003, 2005; Wattenberg et al. 2005; Whittaker et al. 2004; Whittaker et al. 1997). While only one of these, ReMail (Wattenberg et al. 2005), has been fully integrated into a functioning product, in all cases user trials suggest that they have features that support critical email problems.

What may significantly improve the performance and acceptability of these systems is developments in text processing and machine learning, allowing systems to automatically infer users' tasks (Canny 2004; Dragunov, Dietterich, Johnsrude, et. al. 2005; Dredze et al. 2006). Other similar techniques will improve inbox organization, by collating related information (Khoussainov & Kushmerick 2005; Surendran, Platt & Renshaw 2005; Wan & McKeown 2004). These clustering techniques not only help with task management by collating messages relating to outstanding tasks, but they may also clear the inbox by suggesting new folders. While clustering has been applied elsewhere to document collections and Web pages (Voorhees 1986; Willett 1988; Zamir, Etzioni, Madani & Karp 1996), as yet it has not been fully evaluated on email.

And other research directed toward identifying different message functions should help task management, for example by recognizing messages containing obligations, or standard messages that can be dealt with via autoreply (Carvalho & Cohen 2005). Of course these developments give rise to important issues that need to be addressed by careful interaction design. They introduce automated processes into a critical application where the cost of algorithmic error without human oversight is high.

10.5.4 *Organizing Messages into Folders*

Another recent innovation that promises radical change in organizational practice is the emergence of *desktop search*. Dumais et al. (2003) developed Stuff I've Seen, a prototype system that addresses the PIM finding problem by providing search that operates across different applications. This has been emulated by commercial desktop search from both Google and Microsoft. Unlike prior desktop or email search, these systems are fast and operate across entire archives, retrieving emails, documents, presentations, spreadsheets, or other items that relate to the user's query. Desktop search tackles a number of important email problems. It supports *collation* for task management—allowing information items concerning the same task to be retrieved and worked on together. This addresses the significant problem of reuniting originating emails with their attached documents when the documents have been filed in a forgotten location. It should also reduce users' filing burdens by retrieving information regardless of where it has been filed.

While desktop search undoubtedly addresses some email problems, it nevertheless suffers from some important limitations. One significant question concerns its accuracy, and information retrieval researchers have suggested that new techniques will be needed to customize existing search tools so that they can work effectively on private as opposed to public collections (Dumais et al. 2003). Some have speculated that desktop search means that users will no longer file emails, finessing problems of defining and managing folders, but this is unlikely to be the case. First, browsing rather than searching remains many users' preferred way to access personal information, even when search is available—in part because of users' familiarity with the structure of their own file systems (Barreau & Nardi 1995; Boardman & Sasse 2004; Teevan et al. 2004). Folders may also be retained because they provide important semantic information that would be hard to replace by search. For example, folder structure may replicate the relations between different subtasks of the project (Jones, Munat & Bruce 2005; Teevan et al. 2004). Most important, while search addresses the *finding* problem it does not address other critical aspects of task management, such as reminding oneself that certain tasks remain outstanding. It also cannot help users determine which messages they need to allocate attention to or decide what actions need to be applied to a message.

10.5.5 *Other Long-Term Research Questions*

There are other long-term developments that promise to affect our four main email and PIM activities. For example, alternative attentional models could fundamentally change email usage by imposing payments on sending messages, or rewarding recipients for reading messages (Kraut, Morris, Telang, et al. 2004). Implementing this would surely reduce email volumes, by addressing attention allocation and, indirectly, helping task management. Other key developments may be at the system level, where people have proposed radical solutions to PIM and email problems that demand changes in application architectures, by integrating all PIM activities into email, or by migrating information out of email into dedicated applications (Whittaker, Bellotti & Gwizdka 2006). There are important trade-offs here. Centralized systems reduce information fragmentation, but may not provide direct support for key PIM functions. Less radical but still important issues concern the question of how we can provide more direct support for the individual differences that are pervasive in PIM and email (see chapter 12). Finally, despite the centrality of email in our working lives, we lack good theoretical models of asynchronous communication and computer-mediated communication (CMC) that might drive new designs, providing new alternatives to our mission-critical but still problematic systems. More work is needed here to address these critical problems.

NOTE

1. These threading figures generally underestimate interdependent tasks. They ignore new interdependent tasks delegated to users who have yet to deal with them, and they do not register tasks forwarded to others. Furthermore, people are often casual when replying: sometimes failing to reply using re. They may occasionally overestimate interdependence; e.g., when someone initiates a new task by replying to an old message from another user (Erickson & Kellogg 2000; Herring 1999).

11 Understanding What Works: Evaluating PIM Tools

Diane Kelly and Jaime Teevan

11.1 Introduction

The chapters in Part II of this book discuss different solutions to personal information management (PIM) problems, and present tools built to embody these solutions. In this chapter, we discuss how PIM tools can be evaluated. Evaluation is necessary to understand which tools are better than others, and more importantly, why. With the aid of various evaluation methods and metrics, researchers can create principled, objective, and balanced assessments of the tools they design, and understand in a systematic way what works and what doesn't. Without evaluation, researchers are forced to rely on their own personal experiences, intuitions, and anecdotal evidence. While PIM evaluation shares many commonalities with human-computer interaction evaluation and interactive information retrieval evaluation, we believe that there are many issues unique to the PIM context that warrant a closer look at this topic.

A number of issues are associated with designing and conducting evaluations of PIM tools. One key challenge is the incorporation of realistic personal information management situations. Personal information is unique to each individual; over time, users create their own information collections and execute a wide variety of information management tasks and behaviors within the context of such collections. Further, tool use often happens at unspecified and usually unpredictable times, and the context in which it occurs changes constantly. People's inboxes change every minute and sometimes every second. New folders and documents are created daily. Users' interactions with information objects are not discrete, and are very often dependent on their interactions with other objects and applications. It is difficult to structure evaluation activities to accommodate all such collections, tasks, and contexts so that they can be captured completely and compared reliably. Another challenge of evaluating PIM tools is that users are usually invested in whatever tools, strategies, and routines they employ to manage their personal information; introducing a new tool can be disruptive and intrusive.

The purposes of this chapter are to present the challenges of PIM tool evaluation, highlight ways that researchers have dealt with these challenges, and make suggestions for how future evaluations might proceed. Here we look at how researchers can develop specific evaluation methodologies that incorporate what individual users do in real life. An earlier chapter of this book presented naturalistic approaches for understanding PIM behaviors. In this chapter, we focus primarily on the evaluation of PIM tools that facilitate the organization, retrieval, and use of electronic forms of personal information. We first present several general frameworks for evaluation. This is followed by a discussion of evaluation components, including participants, collections, tasks, baselines, and measures. Next, we discuss sharable test collections in the context of PIM. Finally, we conclude and identify future research directions.

11.1.1 *Scenario*

The following scenario is used to illustrate our discussion of PIM tool evaluation:

Like many people, Brooke has a lot of personal digital information, and a better desktop search tool could help her find information more quickly and easily. But not all improvements to desktop search will make her life better. The people who build desktop search tools need to be able to evaluate the quality of the tools they build in order to understand whether the tools actually improve Brooke's and other's experiences or simply create new problems.

11.2 Research Overview: Evaluation Frameworks

In this section, we present four general approaches to evaluating PIM tools: *naturalistic, longitudinal, case study,* and *laboratory*. Naturalistic approaches allow researchers to observe users' real-world information activities in their natural environments with their own data. Longitudinal approaches allow researchers to capture data over an extended period of time and take measurements at fixed points in time. Case studies provide an in-depth picture of a few individuals' behaviors, and laboratory studies allow the researcher to create and control particular situations and scenarios in their studies. None of these approaches are mutually exclusive. It is our stance that combining these approaches is the best approach to PIM evaluation.

A combination of naturalistic and longitudinal approaches, for example, would allow researchers to understand if and how users integrate an experimental tool with their other tools and into their daily lives and work routines, and even how this tool fits into users' multitasking behaviors. In the case of Brooke and the new desktop search tool, a researcher might log all of the desktop searches issued by Brooke over the course of a month, and ask Brooke to judge the usefulness of various retrieved documents at weekly intervals. A study of a particular search tool in isolation, for example, may miss the fact that the functioning of the search tool influences how she organizes her information and thus affects her in broader ways than merely helping her search. Example studies using longitudinal, naturalistic approaches include Thomas's (1998) study of the way more than 4,000 individuals used a Unix-based text editor over the course of seven years, and Rodden and Wood's (2003) six-month study of the way 13 people managed their digital photo collections with an experimental photo management tool, Shoebox.

One of the biggest challenges of conducting naturalistic studies is the lack of control over the environment. For instance, in their evaluation of TaskMaster, an email management tool, Bellotti, Ducheneaut, Howard, and Smith (2003) found that despite extensive development work, when TaskMaster was deployed in natural environments there were some unpredictable interactions between the tool and other applications, including the operating system. Although naturalistic studies are impossible to control completely, the ecological validity afforded through naturalistic approaches can provide great insight into the use and effectiveness of PIM tools in real-world settings. Some researchers have even managed to conduct evaluations of two versions of the same experimental tool in a naturalistic environment. For instance, Dumais, Cutrell, Cadiz, et al. (2003) deployed Stuff I've Seen, a desktop search tool, in a large company where it was used by 234 people over the course of six weeks. The large number of participants made it possible for two different versions of the tool to be deployed to different segments of the user population, which allowed for some cross-tool comparison.

Two specific challenges of conducting longitudinal studies are the determination of appropriate measurement intervals and study duration. *When* one measures is just as important as *what* one measures; the occurrence of particular activities and behaviors can vary greatly according to what people are trying to accomplish at any given moment in time. Thus, a general understanding of users' behaviors is necessary to establish a study duration and appropriate measurement intervals. A person's activities and behaviors are also often governed by external events that can impact how a person uses a particular PIM tool. For instance, Brooke's activities and behaviors will likely change if she is working toward a deadline, busy planning her grandmother's birthday party, or in the middle of holiday. When behaviors are monitored out of context, they are likely to appear sporadic and random; it is thus important for researchers to capture information about temporal context in order to interpret behaviors validly.

The case-study approach, which focuses attention on one or a few users, is also a valuable approach to evaluating PIM tools. This approach is quite often combined with naturalistic, longitudinal approaches. For example, a researcher might study the value of a desktop search tool by looking in depth at how Brooke finds personal information on her computer over time, interviewing her and asking her to fill out surveys at fixed points in time, and observing her behavior with her desktop search tool and other related tools. Conversely, another researcher might study Brooke's entire family or the organization where Brooke works. Although such intensive approaches to data collection do not usually permit the study of large samples, data collected in this way are very representative of the behaviors of the individuals under study. Often, having a holistic picture of a few users' activities and behaviors is more valuable than having a slice from a larger group. An example study that combined elements of naturalistic, longitudinal, and case-study-based approaches is Kelly and Belkin (2004). In this study, Kelly and Belkin monitored laptop-based information behaviors of seven users over the course of 14 weeks. While this was a study of behavior rather than a tool evaluation, the method is one that could be used in an evaluation context.

Finally, there is much value in using laboratory studies to evaluate PIM tools. Laboratory studies allow researchers greater control over the situation, permitting, for example, a within-subject design and the use of baselines and controls (discussed further in subsection 11.3.4). However, as laboratory studies involve a great deal of reduction, it is important that what is studied is well defined and narrow in scope. For instance, while it may not make sense to study general PIM tool usage in a laboratory setting, evaluating a small subset of features of a PIM tool or targeting a specific behavior, activity, or task might be appropriate. In a laboratory study of desktop search, Brooke and others may go to a lab to perform specific tasks with a desktop search tool that either ranks results by relevance or by the date the document was last viewed to determine which ranking method is more useful.

11.3 Diving In: Evaluation Components

In this section we discuss the components of evaluation—participants, collections, tasks, baselines, and measures—in greater detail.

11.3.1 *Participants*

One of the biggest challenges to conducting PIM tool evaluation is recruiting participants. Usually, participants must be willing to grant at least partial access to their personal information collections, such as email, files, and photos. Granting someone access to personal information collections and behaviors requires a level of self-disclosure that can make people uncomfortable. Users may be self-conscious about how they have organized and grouped things or of the types of communications in which they've engaged. Users may also be unsure about the contents of their collections and want to avoid embarrassment.

The time commitment required for participation and the potential disruption to regular activities can also make participant recruitment difficult. If a new email tool is under evaluation, then users must be willing to give up their old tool, have all of their information transferred to the new tool, learn the tool, and integrate it into their normal routines. In their evaluation of TaskMaster, a system designed to support email management, Bellotti et al. (2003) described email as "a mission critical application with much legacy data and structure invested in it" (p. 349). Clearly, users must be willing to accept some disruptions and delays to participate in an evaluation of a new tool, especially one that supports an activity as central as email. Experimental "mission critical" tools must be more robust than typical research prototypes. Bellotti et al. noted that subjects experienced many problems that were related to the technical limitations of TaskMaster, rather than problems with the design of the tool. Because of this, participation can be costly to users, and it is common for users to discontinue their participation. In Bellotti et al.'s study, nine people initially started the study, but only four completed the study in its entirety.

Documenting characteristics of one's participants is important because many studies involve a small number of users, and thus the findings may have limited generalizability and only apply to a particular population or subpopulation. Understanding to whom results may potentially generalize is extremely important. Our examination of the literature suggests characterizing users along several dimensions: age, sex, ethnicity, experience (search and otherwise), education, and various cognitive abilities (e.g., spatial, intellectual, and motor abilities). Because there have been relatively few full-scale evaluations of PIM tools, continuing to identify best practice for profiling users is an important topic for future study. The next chapter on individual differences presents characteristics specific to PIM behaviors that are also useful ways of describing users.

An alternative to studying real users is to use simulated users, such as Cooper's (1999) personas. Personas are abstract representations of users that contain information such as user goals, tasks, and specific activity scenarios, which are employed to help researchers walk through tool use. Pruitt and Grudin (2003) describe the use of personas in the evaluation of MSN Explorer. Personas are most appropriate for early evaluations of PIM tools.

11.3.2 *Collections*

In naturalistic evaluations, participants interact with their own information collections. In laboratory evaluations, creating appropriate collections to simulate users' real-world use environments is critical. Laboratory studies have traditionally involved the use of fixed collections of information objects, but asking users to conduct PIM tasks with collections about which they know little (or nothing) can be problematic because of the artificiality of the situation. One alternative is to ask users to provide their own information collections. For instance, as part of a laboratory evaluation of a photo management tool, Harada, Naaman, Song, et al. (2004) recruited users with large collections of digital photos and used these collections in the evaluation. While this is a novel and useful approach to collection building, this approach is not without problems. This approach requires users to do more preparation work for the study. In addition, users may be overly selective about what they include, and create unrepresentative collections. Such collections are likely to differ in content and size for each user and this may affect the evaluation. In the Harada study, one user had 474 photos while other users had many thousands. Some users may have photos spanning many years and many events, while other users may have photos that span only a few years and events. Although there are some significant issues that one must address, personalizing laboratory evaluations by requiring users to provide their own collections can increase a study's ecological validity and the potential relevance of laboratory activities to users.

11.3.3 *Tasks*

Identifying appropriate tasks to use in laboratory or naturalistic studies also presents some significant challenges. The types of tasks that are relevant to PIM are very broad, user-centric, and situation-specific. Further, tasks are often identified at varying levels of specificity. For instance, *doing email* is a task, but one might subdivide this task into searching for a specific piece of email, managing and filing emails, and setting up an address book. In natural environments it is difficult to anticipate the number and kinds of tasks that users are interested in accomplishing. While there are many generic classes of tasks that users do, such as *finding information about x, reading the news,* and *planning travel,* many tasks are idiosyncratic. Tasks also differ according to the length of time they take to accomplish and the frequency with which users work on them, and multitasking is also common. Understanding how to capture, document, and simulate these activities presents even more challenges.

Researchers have dealt with the problem of defining tasks in a number of ways, including the use of natural tasks. For instance, researchers have allowed subjects to self-identify tasks and structure their activities in ways that make sense to them (Czerwinski, Horvitz & Wilhite 2004; Kelly & Belkin 2004). While this approach presents its own problems, it does allow for a more user-centered task focus. Some studies have deployed a tool, observed what users did with it, and inferred tasks from these observations (Dumais et al. 2003), while others (Harada et al. 2004) have started with generic tasks and personalized them to individual users based on the content of such collections. Studies where tasks are assigned to users most often occur in laboratory settings and it is a challenge to create task scenarios that are robust enough to allow for comprehensive, valid, and reliable evaluations in this setting. Creating tasks and task scenarios requires a significant time investment, and there is no guarantee that such tasks will maintain their relevancy over time.

11.3.4 *Baselines and Controls*

Baseline measures provide researchers with data about how people currently use tools to accomplish particular tasks before an experimental tool is introduced. Baseline measures are similar to pre-test measures in more traditional experimental designs (e.g., Solomon four group, depicted in Figure 11.3.4), where a pre-test, which assesses initial knowledge and/or behavior, is followed by the introduction of an experimental stimulus and then a post-test. Researchers compare pre-test and post-test measures to determine if the stimulus (i.e., the experimental tool) has any affect on knowledge and/or behavior. Controls are introduced by adding additional study groups. In Figure 11.3.4, there are four groups of subjects (subjects are assigned randomly to groups). Baseline measures are taken at Time_1 and are represented by the letter "O" (i.e., observation). Next, the experimental ("E") and control ("C") stimuli are introduced. In the context of PIM, the experimental stimulus might be a desktop search tool and the control might be the user's standard desktop search tool. If no current tool exists, then the control would be the absence of a tool. Alternatively, researchers might be interested in measuring the effects of a single feature of their application, in which case the control stimulus would be the tool without the feature and the experimental stimulus would be the tool with the feature. Finally, after the tool has been used for some time, observations of behavior are taken again. Comparisons are then made of behaviors at Time_1 and Time_2 to identify the effect of the tool. Four groups are used to allow researchers to control for extraneous variables that might potentially threaten the internal and external validity of the experiment.

Group	Time_1		Time_2
1	O	E	O
2	O	C	O
3		E	O
4		C	O

Figure 11.3.4 – The Solomon four-group experimental design.

Establishing a baseline with which to evaluate new tools poses significant challenges, since users' baselines can differ greatly. Baseline behaviors depend on baseline tools, and these too can differ across individuals. For instance, with respect to the evaluation of a tool for desktop search, Brooke may use Google's Desktop Search, while another person uses the Windows search functionality, and another none at all. Since users are not necessarily starting from the same point, comparing use and behavioral change across users is difficult. The problem becomes even more complex in situations where new tools replace activities that were previously performed with physical objects and tools.

A challenge of measuring a new tool against a preexisting tool is that the benchmarks with which users evaluate their new experiences are grounded in their past experiences with other tools. For instance, designers of desktop search systems must overcome users' biases with respect to their standard search tool. Not only does the tool have to be as good as the users' current tool, but it also has to respond at a level much higher than the baseline tool in order to overcome initial user biases, expectations, and change inertia. *Trained incapacity* (Merton 1957) refers to a state in which a person is able to function adequately despite learned inadequacies. With respect to PIM activities, trained incapacity describes situations where users create unique (and often idiosyncratic) ways of using tools that the original designers may not have intended. Over time, users habituate to these ways of doing things and in many cases what at first was a very inefficient way of accomplishing a task becomes very efficient. Documenting and measuring baseline performance and comparing it to experimental performance is difficult, and consequently baseline usage is more commonly used to inform the development and design of the new tool at an earlier stage in the research rather than as a way of demonstrating effect.

11.3.5 Measures

Devising appropriate measures involves the provision to two basic types of definitions: *nominal* and *operational*. Nominal definitions state the meaning of concepts; for example, Nielsen (2003) defines *usability* as "a quality attribute that assesses how easy user interfaces are to use." and divides the concept into five dimensions (learnability, efficiency, memorability, errors, and satisfaction). Operational definitions specify precisely how a concept (and its dimensions) will be measured. For instance, an operational definition of *learnability* might include three questions and a 5-point Likert scale for responding. Alternatively, one might operationalize learnability as the length of time it takes a user to learn to use an interface. Without both nominal and operational definitions it is impossible to know exactly what concepts researchers hope to capture with their measures, and it is impossible to evaluate the validity of measures and subsequent results.

The identification of appropriate measures for evaluating PIM tools should be understood within the context of PIM goals. Through our examination of the literature we identified several measures that have been (or might be) used to evaluate PIM tools, including those related to general usability, those related to subjective and affective aspects of PIM tool use, and those related to performance and behavioral change. Each measure only provides a small window into tool use. For example, while measuring whether a tool is or is not adopted can say a lot about the value of the tool, it does not reveal why people adopt it. In most cases, it is advantageous to use multiple measures and methods (including both quantitative and qualitative) to fully understand the tool. While the measures we review in this section bias our discussion toward quantitative methods, we recommend highly the use of both quantitative and qualitative methods in any evaluation of PIM tools.

Standard Usability Measures

The International Organization for Standards (ISO) identifies effectiveness, efficiency, and satisfaction as core concepts of usability (ISO document 9241). Standard usability measures are relevant to any discussion of PIM evaluation because it is generally accepted that a good PIM tool should be usable. Other common usability concepts are usefulness, ease of use, and ease of learning. We discuss each of these in greater detail below.

Effectiveness. A tool is effective if it helps users accomplish particular tasks. In the example scenario, did Brooke find the piece of information she was looking for using the desktop search tool? While the way in which effectiveness is operationalized varies according to study purpose, one common way to measure effectiveness is to count the number of tasks a user is able to accomplish successfully.

Efficiency. A tool is efficient if it helps users complete their tasks with minimum waste, expense, or effort. A common way to measure efficiency is to record the time it takes a user to complete a task. For example, how long did it take Brooke to find what she was looking for? Efficiency can also be measured by the number of actions or steps taken to complete a task.

Satisfaction. Satisfaction can be understood as the fulfillment of a specified desire or goal. It is often the case that when people discuss satisfaction they speak of the contentment or gratification that is experienced when fulfilling particular goals. Was Brooke content with the search process? Did Brooke feel her needs were met by the tool she used? Satisfaction is often operationalized as one or more statements that users assess with Likert-type scales.

Usefulness. A tool is useful if it meets particular user needs. For instance, if Brooke never has cause to retrieve files from her desktop, then a desktop search system may not be particularly useful to her. The tool may be effective (i.e., Brooke may be able to successfully use to the tool to complete some specified task), but if Brooke normally does not execute such tasks then the tool's usefulness to her would be questionable. As with satisfaction, usefulness is often operationalized as a series of statements that users assess with Likert-type scales. Having a good understanding of a particular work domain also helps researchers determine the usefulness of a particular tool or feature before development and deployment.

Ease of use. Ease of use is related to the amount of effort that users expend executing and/or accomplishing particular tasks. For instance, Brooke may be able to find the file for which she was searching using the experimental search tool (effectiveness), but that does not necessarily mean that it was easy for her to do. Ease of use is very tightly related to efficiency: if a tool isn't easy to use, then it is likely to result in inefficient use. As with previous measures, it is common for ease-of-use data to be gathered via Likert-type scales. One might also measure the number of errors users make while trying to accomplish particular tasks.

It has been demonstrated that users tend to rate ease-of-use measures high even when they are unable to successfully use software to complete specific tasks (Czerwinski, Horvitz & Cutrell 2001). Czerwinski et al. (2001) investigated subjective duration assessment as an implicit measure of ease of use. Subjective duration assessment asks users to estimate the length of time it took them to complete particular tasks. The theory is that users will overestimate time when the task was difficult for them to accomplish and underestimate time when the task was easy for them to accomplish. The value of this measure is that it allows researchers to obtain an implicit measure of ease of use, which can then be compared to explicit ease-of-use measures.

Ease of learning. Finally, ease of learning is related to the amount of effort that users expend learning to use a system. Ease of learning can also be assessed with Likert-type scales or by time-based measures. In some cases, users have been quizzed after a system tutorial to gauge their proficiencies.

Usability measures in the PIM context. Although usability concepts are commonly used to evaluate information management tools such as search interfaces, using them in the PIM context requires special considerations. For instance, measuring effectiveness is problematic because management activities are often separated in time from when their value is realized. For example, while it may be obvious if a user can successfully file a particular piece of information using a particular tool, it is less obvious whether the person can subsequently recover and use the information. Measuring efficiency is also problematic because a good PIM tool can allow a task to be performed better, or allow a person to spend more time on important tasks, rather than allowing for the completion of more tasks in the same amount of time. PIM efficiency measures should consider quantity and quality of output in addition to time. Quality in particular is difficult to assess. In group work settings one might look at productivity rates or ask people to rate the quality of each other's work (Sun & Kantor 2006).

Performance

Performance measures are closely related to the effectiveness measure described above, except that these measures are usually tailored to specific tasks and use contexts. Performance measures are also used to gauge computational complexity. Each of these types of measures is relevant to PIM evaluation. Two traditional measures of performance for search-tool evaluation are recall (the ratio of relevant documents saved by a user to the total number of relevant documents in the collection), and precision (the ratio of relevant documents saved by a user to the total number of documents retrieved and saved by the user). Common measures of computational complexity are related to the number of steps or iterations that are needed by the computer to perform a task and the amount of computing resources that are needed to perform a task. Clearly, if a desktop search tool retrieves a lot of irrelevant information, takes a long time to do this, or taxes computational resources, then the tool is unlikely to be helpful.

Adoption and Use

Tool use can indicate a great deal about the value of the tool. The behavior of adopting a tool and incorporating it into one's normal routine can be considered as one of the most decisive indicators of the value or success of a tool. Using a tool repeatedly and/or recommending it to others can also be considered as indicators of success. Understanding how many people refuse, ignore, or abandon a tool also makes for good metrics.

Flow

It is generally agreed that good PIM ought to allow people to be *in the flow* when they work. In his book describing the optimal experience and flow, Csikszentmihalyi (1997) identified five characteristics of the experience of flow: challenge and require skill; concentrate and avoid interruption; maintain control; speed, and feedback; and transformation of time. Bederson (2004) relates these characteristics to human-computer interaction and suggests how flow can be used to evaluate tools. When flow is achieved users are able to concentrate on important rather than mundane tasks. Flow might decrease when people spend unnecessary amounts of time filing objects during critical tasks. To support flow, PIM tools must be integrated seamlessly into day-to-day activities and not create additional distractions. One's ability to ignore external distractions, interruptions, and the tool itself while working are also good indicators of flow.

Quality of Life

Quality-of-life measures (Endicott, Nee, Harrison & Blumenthal 1993) have received little attention in most evaluations of PIM tools. Two implicit goals of PIM tools are to make people's lives easier and to allow people to enjoy a larger variety of life experiences. Historically, quality-of-life measures have been used in economics, political science, and more recently health care, and can potentially provide information about the broader impact that PIM has in daily life. For instance, does Brooke have more time for hobbies and travel? Is Brooke able to spend more time with family and friends? Is Brooke less stressed? Does Brooke feel like her life has more balance and that she has more control over how she spends her time?

Measures of happiness (Layard 2005) might also be used as indirect indicators of PIM tool success. We did not find any studies in our review of PIM tool evaluations that included happiness as an evaluation measure. Using happiness as a measure also suggests the possibility of using other affective measures as part of PIM tool evaluation, and perhaps even assessing emotional, mental, and physical well-being.

11.4 Looking Forward: Sharable Test Collections

All the evaluation approaches discussed above involve the direct involvement of people managing their personal information. This is a good way to understand PIM behaviors and tools, but also makes it difficult to compare findings across studies. To encourage research in personal information management, we believe that it is important to develop common evaluation frameworks. Common frameworks make it possible to compare results, replicate findings, and explore alternative hypotheses. However, as seen above, there are also many challenges to using common evaluation frameworks, since individual behavior and personal collections vary; it makes little sense to give someone another person's collection and ask them to execute generic tasks. Thus, the design of shared test collections for PIM evaluation requires some creative thinking, because such collections must differ from more traditional shared test collections.

While there are a number of existing sharable test collections that can provide direction for a common PIM test collection, they do not meet the evaluation needs of PIM tools being developed. Information management test beds, such as the Distributed Integration Testbed Project, the D-Lib Test Suite, and those created as part of the Text Retrieval Conference (TREC), are intended to represent large databases and generic users—not personal information and individual users. Search engine logs are another good source for studying aggregate information behavior, but do not provide information about the individual for privacy reasons, and, depending on the information included in the logs, do not necessarily lend themselves immediately to testing tools. These collections also do not provide a complete picture of users' behaviors.

A limited number of test beds and tools have been developed with an eye toward how individuals deal with the information at hand, such as the TREC HARD track (Allan 2006), the Curious Browser (Claypool, Le, Waseda & Brown 2001), and the collection developed by Zhang and Callan (2005). Such resources are certainly valuable for the study of PIM, but all deal with external information and not an individual's personal information. A large corpus of email messages is available, and could be useful, for example, in understanding individual's email classification (Klimt & Yang 2004).

A PIM test bed should contain rich user information and individualized evaluations for important information management tasks. For example, a collection along the lines of the one created by Teevan, Dumais, and Horvitz (2005) for studying personalized search could be a good start if made publicly available: it involves aggregate information about individuals collected via their personal computers (e.g., word occurrence frequencies, document level information such as time of last access), and example searches run by the user with a listing of which results are relevant to which searches. Kelly and Belkin's (2004) collection is also a good candidate for a shared collection. It contains thousands of documents that have associated with them user-defined tasks and topics, relevance assessments, and behaviors such as document display time and retention. Of course, there are numerous privacy concerns associated with sharing collections. Privacy issues are discussed further in the final two chapters of this book and are likely to take priority in years to come.

A challenge in developing a PIM test bed is that PIM research must be done with a holistic understanding of information use to avoid creating more problems than it solves. For example, improvements to an individual's ability to access information can create difficulties for group information access. It is now common to direct someone to a Web page by giving him or her keywords to search for; however, if results were personalized this would be impossible. Another problem is that researchers might focus on research questions that are addressable by test beds because it's easier to do this than to collect new data. There is a further danger that test beds geared toward specific tasks will discourage researchers from thinking about holistic information use.

We believe that a valuable place to begin a discussion of sharable test collections is with the identification of common tasks. Whittaker, Terveen, and Nardi (2000) discuss the value of *reference tasks* that allow researchers to share tasks, datasets, evaluation metrics, and user requirements. Instead of allowing tasks for evaluating PIM tools to evolve in an ad-hoc fashion, with each research group creating their own tasks, it might be more appropriate to work together to create a sharable collection of tasks. This would save researchers time and would be likely to lead to more comparable evaluations. Because multitasking is so common in PIM, it might also be worth developing sets of tasks that simulate multitasking behavior rather than focusing on discrete tasks.

11.5 Conclusion

In this chapter, we have presented what we believe are appropriate approaches to the evaluation of PIM tools, discussed key components of evaluation, and proposed sharable test collections as an alternative approach for investigating PIM behaviors and tools. In each section we presented various challenges unique to the PIM context and provided examples of how some researchers have experienced and dealt with these challenges. In our presentation of evaluation frameworks, we discussed naturalistic, longitudinal, case-study, and laboratory approaches to evaluation, as well as various combinations of each approach. In the section on evaluation components, we discussed issues associated with participants, including recruitment and retention, collections, tasks, baselines, and measures. We presented several major classes of measures for PIM evaluation, including those related to usability, performance, adoption and use, flow, and quality of life. Finally, we considered the creation of sharable test collections for PIM investigations. This included consideration of existing test collections, as well as proposals and efforts at new collections designed with PIM in mind.

PIM tool evaluation introduces numerous challenges not present in other types of evaluation. Over the years, evaluation of computer applications has moved from system-centered, to user-centered, and now to person-centered. We, as a community, face the difficult task of developing robust, valid, and reliable evaluation methods and metrics that can accommodate individual use, group use, and general use. The chapters in this book begin to identify the scope of PIM and suggest possible ways that we might move forward with this very challenging task.

11.6 Acknowledgments

This chapter is based on a discussion group report written by the first author for the NSF Workshop on Personal Information Management that took place at the University of Washington in January 2005. We would like to acknowledge the following people who contributed to the initial report: Ben Bederson, Mary Czerwinski, Jim Gemmell, and Wanda Pratt. We would also like to acknowledge Richard Boardman for his contributions to this chapter.

PART III

PIM and
the Individual

12 Individual Differences

Jacek Gwizdka and Mark Chignell

12.1 Introduction

In an increasingly complex world where people routinely handle large amounts of information, individuals are constantly challenged to manage and effectively use the information that they are responsible for. While email is the canonical example of an information overloading application, other well-known personal information management (PIM) applications and tasks cited in earlier chapters of this book include maintaining addresses and contacts, scheduling, and organizing the various documents and bookmarks that one is interested in. Not surprisingly, there are individual differences (ID) in how, and how well, people cope with the challenge of personal information management. This greatly complicates any scientific analysis of PIM behavior. Thus, in addition to the evaluation methods discussed in the previous chapter, researchers and designers need to consider when and how individual differences should be included within parsimonious interpretations and explanations of PIM behavior. In this chapter, we propose an approach where differences between individuals are considered last, after the influences of the environment and the task context have first been considered, and after group difference (e.g., between job classifications) have been investigated. We believe that this is a logical way to proceed—much as if we were observing an ant walking over sand-dunes (cf. Simon 1996)—since we should not ascribe complexities to an individual if they can instead be explained as due to properties of the environment.

The goal of this chapter will be to review and synthesize some of the key findings in how PIM behavior differs between individuals. Some of the reasons why these differences occur and what can be done about them will also be discussed.

12.1.1 *Scenario*

Alex is very well organized with respect to his work-related information and immediately files (or labels) all documents and correspondence, incoming and outgoing, including email. He also files relevant Web pages immediately as he encounters them. Every time he meets a new person he puts their contact information in his PDA. The costs of not having the information when needed are extremely high, and he is willing to invest the extra time and effort to keep his information organization up-to-date. His personal information is also quite organized—paper documents, like old tax returns are properly filed away, and his collection of family photos is stored away in neatly labeled boxes. Brooke, on the other hand, is a piler, both at work and at home. Her job is much more fluid and she does not rely on information as much as Alex does. She does not like to file anything, electronic or paper, and sees little value in keeping "old stuff." In her work office and at home, we find a relatively small number of piles. Connie, in turn, has an elaborate paper-based filing system. She prints out Web pages and even email messages that she wishes to keep and then files these away in her filing system, where she also keeps documents and correspondence that she receives on paper. She claims she can find any piece of information from the past ten years in a matter of a few minutes. She admits, however, that to keep up with the growing amount of collected information, each month she needs to add a set of additional drawers for her hanging folders. Also, the filing task sometimes gets away from her and she can catch herself with large piles of items waiting to be dealt with.

Clearly, the members of the family that we met earlier in this book represent different types, and at the same time may exhibit somewhat unique coping behaviors and strategies. Alex, Brooke, and Connie differ in terms of their PIM behavior. Alex, Brooke, and Connie have different job requirements; they also have different ages, and differ in gender and educational background. Connie, for instance, was influenced to change her behavior based on a friend's visit (which inspired some spring cleaning in an earlier chapter), while people similar to Brooke will tend to rely on people like Alex and Connie to help her remember information that is relevant to the family as a whole. Brooke will need to remember information differently if she is the only one that cares or knows about it and if she cannot rely on others to store and retrieve it for her.

The unique factors and situations of different people influence their PIM needs and practices, as well as which PIM tools might suit them best. But even people who have quite similar profiles with respect to job and demographics can exhibit huge observable differences in PIM-related behaviors, their choices of strategy, and their preferences in tools. These differences apply both with respect to paper-based information management and to the management of electronic information.

PIM behavior plays a central role in personal cognition and life performance and is affected by many factors, internal and external. For instance, the organization of personal information involves psychological processes (Lansdale

1988a) that are sensitive both to cognitive differences and to the amplifying effect of age on those differences (e.g., Salthouse 1991). Given the variety of factors involved, it is not surprising that individual differences are frequently observed in PIM performance and strategies.

Understanding the individual differences that underlie PIM behavior may be difficult, since PIM is a complex topic where observed behavior has a multiplicity of causes, both from inside and outside the person. So why should we be interested in individual differences in PIM? This question will be addressed in the next section, focusing both on the importance of PIM as an activity and on the necessity of considering and attending to the considerable individual differences that exist.

12.1.2 *Practical Relevance*

We increasingly rely on online information in conducting our everyday lives. From accessing movie listings and saving product comparisons, to communicating with grandmother Edna through email or accessing health information, it is becoming difficult to find any parts of our lives that do not involve PIM skills.

And as if dealing with personal information such as financial and legal records were not enough, people also need to deal with their personal views of collaborative information. Within large corporate networks, each worker must maintain a personal view of his or her area of responsibility through the various information clients that they interact with (whether it be a desktop computer, a PDA, or some other tool or device). Thus, individual differences in the desktop computing setup are critical in designing collaborative work systems, as noted by Bentley and Appelt (1997) with respect to their discussion of the development of the BSCW collaborative software system.

For many individuals, email is a canonical example of an information tool that spans both personal and organizational boundaries (see chapter 10 of this book). The same email account may hold private and personally meaningful messages, along with other messages and attachments that are "owned" by a workgroup or corporation. As noted in chapter 10, there are interesting biases in email handling, with people tending to receive more messages than they send, and tending to reply more quickly to social messages. This leads to an interesting strategy where social greetings and content are embedded within work-related messages to make them more "sticky" and selectable, but presumably this strategy will be more successful with some personality types (e.g., extraverts) then with others.

For many knowledge workers, making a clear distinction between PIM on the one hand and corporate or collaborative information management on the other may not be possible, even in principle. A single email message may contain a draft contract, salutations to the family, and an invitation to lunch. Sometimes even the participants in a mixed work and social interaction would be hard pressed to identify exactly which parts of the interaction are work-related and which are personal. Thus, a broad population of individuals is engaged in PIM activities, at home and at work, and the nature of those activities is constantly shifting as people move though the information space handling it with (sometimes) continuously varying perspectives and motivations. Personal inclinations and abilities, corporate tools, policies, and training all interact with each other in determining how PIM is actually carried out. For instance, some people will continue to use Microsoft Outlook for their personal email because it is mandated for use at the office, while others may use Outlook when they have to but use Gmail otherwise.

Individuals perform PIM activities using a variety of tools in both paper and electronic environments, including a variety of desktop applications and mobile devices; PIM activities are performed in a variety of contexts (situations): at work, at home, and on the run. The combination of the four factors—people, tasks, tools, and context—creates a huge diversity in PIM behavior, with con-siderable scope for individual differences to express themselves in how work gets performed in various circumstances. At the same time the sheer complexity of these interactions (with all the potential causal factors involved) makes the isolation of the individual differences extremely difficult. One approach to reducing some of this complexity in the case of email is to use reference tasks (as explained in chapter 10) that create a basis for comparing findings between different studies.

Competing explanations are not the only reason why individual differences may get underreported. In the laudable push for equal opportunity and recognition, individual differences in performance and ability tend not to be emphasized. Yet in cases where differences exist, people will not be well-served by tools and systems that fail to recognize their abilities and preferences. However, mismatches between individual needs and the tools provided are most likely underreported. Workers may often displace negative feelings about poorly fitting tools and interfaces onto their attitudes toward the content of the work, blaming the company, the workplace, and/or management for what may be a problem concerning poor human factors. Someone who may have relatively low working memory and who has difficulty using an email client may not be aware of why he dislikes using email so intensely, and may blame it on boring work content, or on excessive demands being made by management.

Consequently, individual differences have received little research attention.

Thus, while individual differences may be difficult to disentangle from other factors, and may even be ideologically unwelcome in some cases, they nevertheless exist. Yet the mere presence of individual differences does not mean that they can or should enter into consideration as factors in design, documentation, training, or personnel selection. As is always true in design, the role of individual differences needs to be established and the costs and benefits of explicating, considering, and designing for individual differences in particular situations need to be assessed. Currently, we are only beginning to understand the role of individual differences in PIM. However, a number of relevant research studies have been conducted, and in the next section we summarize what is known thus far about the nature of IDs in PIM behavior.

12.2 Research Overview

In this section we will review relevant research on PIM to illustrate the progress that has been made and the key issues that have been identified. This research will be interpreted in terms of the selection and use of PIM and information-handling strategies, either within or between individuals. We will begin this review with a discussion of what strategies have been discovered, and how they relate to other factors that govern PIM behavior.

Dillon and Watson (1996) reviewed the large body of literature on individual differences in psychology. They argued that a core number of basic abilities (such as cognitive speed, perceptual speed, short-term memory, spatial ability, visual ability, to name just a few[1]) have been reliably and validly identified, and that appropriate user analysis ought to lead to better systems design and more appropriate training. Egan (1988) reviewed differences in performance in human-computer interaction, focusing on common computing tasks, such as text editing, information search, and programming, and concluded that differences between individuals (whatever their cause) typically explain a high proportion of the variability in performance with ratios of 20 to 1 sometimes observed between best and worst performance.

The remainder of this section will be organized according to the strategy outlined earlier in this chapter, where internal differences between individuals are considered only after various external aspects of the context of PIM usage (environment and task), and then any group differences that may pertain, have first been considered. We begin by considering task management, which is a major contextual factor in many situations.

12.2.1 *Task Management*

Variations in PIM behavior are situated in the variations that occur within task environments, corporate policies, and the current situations that people find themselves in. New tasks may inherit structures from old tasks or may require new structures. For instance, there may be a fixed folder structure reflecting tasks associated with conference travel. Two instances of conference travel may have very similar structure (e.g., plane schedule, hotel reservations, rental car booking, conference registration), and thus folders can be reused from other projects (conferences). In contrast, a new project may require dynamic assignment of information categories, with more emphasis placed on categorization decisions. Similarly, information handling strategies will likely change in an environment where there is a history of hardware or disk failure, and where there is a need to backup information or to store it in multiple locations. Frequently there is no clean separation between PIM and task management, and users do not manage information simply to retrieve it later—they also store items as reminders of the tasks they have to perform. For instance, people frequently use email messages (Bellotti, Ducheneaut, Howard & Smith 2005; Ducheneaut & Bellotti 2001; Gwizdka 2004b; Whittaker & Sidner 1996) as task reminders, and may even send themselves email messages as additional reminders.

In general, we can expect that, in terms of information handling, people will respond rationally to the demands placed on them, within the constraints of their abilities and the characteristics of their task environments. Yet given the natural variability of human behavior, IDs can be expected to remain even when other factors such as the properties of the task and its environment have been accounted for. For instance, a waiter may have a highly structured task that involves activities such as taking orders, serving food, taking away used dishes, bringing the bill, and responding to various requests made during the meal. Yet casual observation of waiters quickly shows wide variations of strategy and style even at the same establishment. Some waiters may use mnemonics and trust to their memory, while others may take quick notes (if they are allowed) to jog their memories. Some waiters may simplify the PIM task by ordering only part of a meal at a time (e.g., appetizers) while others with better memories may be able to take orders for entire meals or even collect orders for multiple tables before passing them on to the kitchen. Task requirements and work constraints are important, but it is only when they are brought together with internal individual differences and with other external factors that they jointly determine PIM performance and behavior.

12.2.2 External Influences on Strategy Selection and Use

Job requirements, information tools, and work structure may each influence and constrain the way that information is handled and managed. For example, as shown in Table 12.2.2, Jones, Dumais, and Bruce (2002) found that job position was related to email use—managers used email much more than other workers. Other external factors, such as the type of PIM environment (e.g., paper vs. digital) and kind of PIM tool may also be important. External factors can have a combined effect; for example, many information technology (IT) departments enforce a company-wide information retention policy where all messages older than a certain cutoff point (e.g., 45 days) are deleted. In cases like this employees' PIM behavior will inevitably be affected by that choice, making it harder to observe how their PIM behavior and performance is driven by internal factors.

Individuals also differ with respect to their preference of information presentation. For example, Krishnan and Jones (2005) found that some people preferred to access files via folders shown in a spatial representation, while others preferred textual keyword-based search to access their files.

Table 12.2.2 – Selected Research on External Influences on PIM Strategies (interindividual differences)

Factors	Reference	PIM Tool / Environment	PIM Activity	Key Findings
Job requirements	Jones et al. 2002	email	all	job role affects email use: managers vs. others
Information-presentation	Krishnan & Jones 2005	files	finding & managing	preference for external information representation: (a) spatial layout (recognition) or (b) filename patterns (recall).

12.2.3 Differences in PIM Strategies between Groups of Users

With respect to grouping users, early studies tended to categorize individuals engaged in PIM at the extremes of a continuum. Malone (1983) classified individuals into filers and pilers. Filers' information organization is well-structured and neat. In contrast, pilers' information organization is unstructured and messy. Further examples include MacKay's (1988) email prioritizers versus archivers distinction, and Whittaker and Sidner's (1996) tripartite grouping of email users into frequent filers versus spring cleaners versus no-filers. Abrams, Baecker, and Chignell (1998) divided Web users into four groups with respect to their keeping behavior (bookmarking): creation-time filer, end-of-session filer, sporadic filer, no-filer. These empirically established strategies have retained many similarities despite being observed with respect to a range of different PIM tools.

Table 12.2.3 summarizes some of the key early findings that have been obtained on individual differences in PIM.

Table 12.2.3 – Selected Research on PIM Strategies between User Groups

Reference	PIM Tool / Environment	PIM activity	Key Findings
Malone 1983	office environment	keeping and managing	filers, pilers
MacKay 1988	email	managing	prioritizers, archivers
Whittaker & Sidner 1996	email	keeping and managing	frequent filer, spring cleaner, no filer
Abrams et al. 1998	Web	keeping	creation-time filer, end-of-session filer, sporadic filer, no filer

12.2.4 Differences in PIM Strategies Across PIM Activities

Personal information processing strategies are influenced by the type of PIM activity being carried out and by strategies that were used in other PIM activities (see Table 12.2.4). Information organization strategies appear to be related to the user's retrieval preferences and style (Boardman & Sasse 2004; Teevan, Alvarado, Ackerman & Karger 2004). Filers used keyword search about as frequently as pilers. However, they did it in different contexts. Filers were found to use keyword search in their file systems and on the global Web, while pilers used keyword search on particular Web sites. Strategies in one activity were found to affect how other activities were carried out. For instance, keeping strategy affected re-finding. Pilers, who did not use metadata, and did not impose information structures at the time of filing, tended to perform local steps (navigate or browse around) before performing keyword search. In contrast, filers who used metadata in their filing process tended to use this metadata at the time of retrieval.

Table 12.2.4 – Selected Research on PIM Strategies across PIM Activities

Reference	PIM Tool / Environment	PIM Activity	Key Findings
Teevan et al. 2004	cross-tool (bookmarks, email, files)	managing vs. finding	search behavior of filers vs. pilers key findings: (1) filers search more for files than pilers; (2) filers rely more on keyword search than pilers
Jones et al. 2002, 2003; Bruce et al. 2004	Web / bookmarks	keeping vs. re-finding methods	key findings: each participant used more than one method; re-finding affected by keeping methods; however, most re-finding methods did not rely on keeping

The relation between keeping and finding (in the context of the Web) was further explored by Jones et al. (2002), Jones, Bruce, and Dumais (2003), and Bruce, Jones, and Dumais (2004). Participants in their studies used more than one keeping method. Although the choice of the keeping method was influenced by the reasons for keeping (sharing, reminding) and by preferred re-finding methods, a high proportion of re-finding methods did not rely on keeping at all. Examples of re-finding methods independent from keeping included direct entry of a URL, search, and access via another Web site.

12.2.5 Differences in PIM Strategies within Users

We conclude this presentation of related work on differences in PIM behavior with a review of how PIM strategies differ within users (see Table 12.2.5). Relevant research on this topic is summarized in, for instance, Jones et al. (2002), who found differences in strategies within the same individual between paper and electronic information environments. Similarly, Boardman and Sasse (2004) found that people change strategies between different computer-based PIM tools. They found that files tended to be organized more extensively than emails or bookmarks. This may arise because files are more externally constrained documents than are messages. Thus, while files are often subject to audit, inspection, or use by others, messages are generally considered to be more private and only subject to audit or inspection in special cases.

These kinds of differences may be habitual; PIM users may have learned (acquired) contextually conditioned PIM behavior and formed different "PIM-personalities," which are then triggered by different PIM contexts. The primacy of hierarchical file systems in desktop computing and in handling of papers within businesses may predispose people to filing strategies more than they would if they were following their natural inclination. Individual differences, as suggested by Boardman and Sasse (2004), may also be influenced by a range of factors related to PIM tools. Higher perceived value and ownership of information, as well as higher likelihood of information reuse both encourage people to invest more effort in information organization.

PIM strategies may also change within users in the absence of marked external changes (e.g., in terms of PIM tool, information environment, or job position). Bälter (1997) found that users may switch between (and/or gradually change) different information organization strategies within one PIM tool. He suggested that there are two competing trends, one toward more organization, and the other an "anti-organization" set of transitions that may be precipitated by information overload (amount of email messages) and time pressure. Similarly, Whittaker and Hirschberg (2001) found that people employed a combination of different PIM strategies (filing and piling) within the same environment (paper archives).

Barreau and Nardi (1995) studied behavior related to three information types: ephemeral, working, and archived. They suggested that people prefer to access ephemeral and working information by location-based browsing, while they accessed archived information by keyword-based search. In practice, specific behavior is likely to be influenced by both specific dispositions of the individual and properties of the task environment within which PIM is carried out.

Gwizdka (2004a) and Boardman and Sasse (2004) found that specific behaviors depend on the perceived importance and value of information (in email messages). For instance, in Gwizdka's study participants were observed to re-email important messages to themselves.

Table 12.2.5 – Selected Research on PIM Strategies within Users (intraindividual differences)

Factors	Reference	PIM Tool / Environment	PIM Activity	Key Findings
Information-environment	Jones et al. (2002)	Web	all	differences in strategies in different environments; influencing factors: information environment; paper vs. digital
Multiple strategies	Whittaker & Hirshberg 2001	paper documents	keeping and managing	filers, pilers key finding: combination of strategies filing and piling within paper archives
	Boardman and Sasse 2004	cross-tool (files, emails, bookmarks)	keeping, finding, and managing	frequent filers, file some now and spring clean rest, no filers key findings: multiple PIM strategies within specific collections; PIM strategies vary between tools (files organized more extensively than emails or bookmarks) influencing factors: (1) (perceived) value and ownership of information; (2) likelihood of re-use ; (3) degree of control over information creation
	Gwizdka 2004a	email	keeping, finding, and managing	email inbox processing: (1) immediate processing; (2) limiting; (3) encoding additional information; and (4) accumulation.
Information type	Barreau & Nardi 1995	files (primarily)	keeping, finding, and managing	influencing factors: information type (ephemeral, working, archived) relationships: preferred access to (1) ephemeral and working info by location-based browsing; (2) archived info by search (keywords)
Adaptive strategy change	Bälter 1997	email	keeping and managing	frequent filer, spring cleaner, folderless cleaner, folderless spring cleaner influencing factors: (1) information overload and time pressure; (2) willingness to expend increased organization effort

12.2.6 *Internal Influences on Strategy Selection*

There have been empirically motivated attempts to link observed differences in behavior to internal differences (e.g., in cognitive ability) between individuals (Table 12.2.6). For instance, based on empirical evidence Gwizdka (2004a) suggested flexibility of closure[2] as a possible internal source of influence on personal information management behavior.

Table 12.2.6 – Selected Research that Links Cognitive and Affective Factors with PIM Strategies

Reference	PIM Tool / Environment	PIM Activity	Individual Differences and Influencing Factors
Gwizdka 2004a, 2004b	email	keeping & managing	keepers (pilers) and cleaners (filers) influencing factors: flexibility of closure, email experience
Gwizdka & Chignell 2004	email	finding	influencing factors: working memory
Modjeska & Chignell 2003	2.5D / 3D info-landscape	finding	influencing factors: spatial ability
Allen 2001	database	finding	influencing factors: spatial scanning
Kim & Allen 2002	Web	finding	influencing factors: field dependence/independence, experience
Ford et al. 2005	Web	finding	Preference for Boolean vs. best-match Web search influencing factors: verbalizer-/ wholist-imager cognitive style, cognitive complexity
Nahl 2005	Web	finding	influencing factors: affective

In a study of information finding in email inboxes, Gwizdka and Chignell (2004) linked differences in efficiency to cognitive abilities. Working memory (WM) was found to be related with performance time (users who scored higher on a WM test were faster), while visual memory was related to user interaction with the inbox (the amount of scrolling and sorting).

Modjeska and Chignell (2003) examined the effect of spatial ability on searching for information in a hierarchy that was visualized using the "information islands" metaphor (Waterworth & Singh 1994). They found that individuals with relatively low spatial ability were significantly less successful in finding information in the information hierarchy, finding only about half as many of the targets in the timed task that was used.

Researchers in related areas, such as information searching on the Web, have also discovered relationships between user behavior and cognitive abilities and styles. For example, Kim and Allen (2002) found that field dependence and experience affect information-searching behavior on Web search tasks. Allen (2001) found that users with high spatial scanning ability performed better on an information retrieval task using a novel Boolean browsing interface. However, the advantage was found only for certain information retrieval tasks (low-recall tasks).

Other internal factors are also implicated. For example, affect and emotions associated with information also influence how an individual handles personal information. For example, affective factors (e.g., optimism, self-efficacy) have been shown to influence Web search behavior (Nahl 2004). Thus some differences in PIM behavior may be transient and attributable to mood or emotions.

12.2.7 *Summary*

As can be inferred from the preceding discussion and literature review, IDs are contextually dependent, and they respond to changing situations and task demands dynamically. People may exhibit a different "PIM personality" in different environments, and when dealing with different information types (e.g., paper vs. electronic; email vs. files). PIM personality may be thought of as the style of PIM use that people exhibit. It will presumably be influenced by context and by a variety of internal and external influences, and yet may be recognizable to others as a consistent style of behavior.

People may be neat or organized within one context (using one PIM tool, or one environment such as paper) while being messy in others. For instance, a neat office at work may not necessarily mean that an employee has a correspondingly neat home office. Thus variations in PIM behavior are contextualized.

Figure 12.2.7 summarizes the various influences on PIM behavior described earlier. The main point of the figure is that strategies lie at the heart of the malleability of PIM behavior, since people respond to a wide range of internal and external factors in dealing with information.

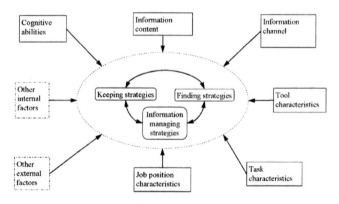

Figure 12.2.7 – Individual differences in PIM. PIM strategies are represented by rounded rectangles, and empirically established influencing factors are represented by solid-edge rectangles; while other factors, as yet unknown, are represented by dashed-edge rectangles.

In chapter 1, Jones proposed "keeping," "finding," and "information managing" (or more generally "meta-level" activities) as three main types of PIM activities. The detailed interaction of the characteristics and factors (shown in the outer part of Figure 1.6) with those types of strategies is not yet known. In the following section we suggest some research and design approaches that may help to elucidate the relationships shown in Figure 1.6, eventually leading to design guidance concerning more personalized and customized PIM tools and interfaces.

12.3 Looking Forward

Personal information management is a relatively young field. Given the youth of the discipline and the complexities of the phenomena to be studied, it is not surprising that research paradigms and methodologies are only beginning to emerge. This is especially true for research on IDs in PIM behavior, where previous findings have predominantly applied to differences in broadly defined strategies that differ between groups of people. In the following subsections we will examine a number of promising future directions, first in terms of research challenges, and then in terms of design challenges.

12.3.1 *Research Challenges*

Individual differences tend to be difficult to study because they interact with a variety of other factors in determining performance. Teasing out the precise effect of individual differences may not always be possible. Results of fieldwork investigation of PIM may be very specific to the participants under study and their current situation. Generalizations are risky for many types of research, but even more so given the richness and complexity of the real-word environments of PIM.

Yet personalized and customized solutions require an understanding of the mappings between the properties of the individual and the requirements of the application or tool. This in turn requires a more systematic approach to the study of individual differences. One of the major challenges for research in this area is to provide a consistent framework for ID studies and to elucidate the relationships between various internal and external factors on the one hand, and differences in PIM strategies and behavior on the other.

A systematic approach to studying ID could involve the development of a paradigm / methodology that includes formalized: (1) PIM tasks, (2) metrics, (3) sets (repertoires) of possible PIM behaviors (discrete), (4) ranges of possible behaviors (continuous), and (5) mappings between contexts (conditions) and PIM strategies / behaviors.

Given the complexity associated with disentangling internal factors and their impact on PIM behavior, we suggest an approach where factors influencing PIM behavior are considered in a sequence. The initial focus may be on observable differences in broad strategies. Questions are then asked concerning how environment, task contexts, and tools influence the strategies employed by PIM users. The effects of group differences are examined next. Human abilities and personality are considered after the influences of other factors have been investigated. Once some of the relevant individual differences are understood it should then be possible to link differences between people and their task environments to resulting differences in their PIM behavior.

12.3.2 *Design Challenges*

Designing for PIM is a most extreme case of user-centeredness because of the intense involvement that each person has with the rich amount of information that is relevant to them. Individual differences in PIM requirements call for thoughtful user-centric design in adapting tools and their interfaces to the needs, capabilities, and circumstances of each user. Caution, however, must be exercised in the design of PIM tools with respect to conclusions reached concerning their user evaluations. When people reject a tool it may not always be the fault of the tool's design per se, since other people may benefit from the tool. Instead the problem may be one of mismatch between tool and person.

In designing for PIM, there is a delicate balance between prescribing what to use PIM for and how, versus allowing people to express (and execute) their own PIM styles, habits, or preferences. In practice, designers will need to handle this trade-off carefully by judicious use of the following strategies:

■ Providing customization options or settings within a single tool;
■ Providing different tools for different types of user;
■ Employing an adaptive approach (e.g., Horvitz, Jacobs & Hovel 1999) where the behavior of PIM tools is contextually dependent and sensitive to the situation.

These approaches, or their combination, can be employed in the context of designing interactive systems to support PIM activities.

12.3.3 *Conclusion*

Much work remains to be done to define the boundaries of the discipline of PIM, particularly with respect to how it relates to other information disciplines, and which properties should be deemed relevant to determining or affecting individuals' PIM behaviors. Detailed findings are also needed concerning the effects of different combinations of situations and settings on PIM strategies and performance.

While millions of people are using PDAs of one form or another, billions of people are using mobile phones. In terms of technology diffusion, specialized personal information tools are used largely by early adopters, and not by the general population. Of all PIM-related tools, email is the most widely used, but in many cases this use is driven by job requirements. Even so, many people are turning to instant messaging as a frequent alternative to email, because of its much lower demands on working memory and its removal of the need to store and retrieve information. It is our belief that the current use of PIM tools is artificially constrained by inattention to the significant individual differences that drive the acceptability of PIM solutions and their adoption.

Individual differences in PIM are huge and there are a great many factors that influence the impact of IDs on PIM. The resulting behavior can be complex, idiosyncratic, and affected by context and changing situations. In spite of these problems, the research literature cited in this chapter demonstrates the existence of a healthy and growing group of pioneering researchers working on the topic of individual differences in PIM. It is possible that further progress in PIM design may require *individual-centered design* and that we are entering an era where PIM tools need to be highly customized, and customizable, in order to succeed. However, a considerable amount of work remains to be done on formalizing relevant frameworks and methodologies, and on obtaining detailed research results, before definitive guidance can be given to designers concerning when and how PIM functions and interfaces should be personalized and customized.

One of the factors not considered in this chapter is how an area of application may affect PIM behavior. While individual differences exist, PIM behavior can be quite malleable, as people respond to the situations they find themselves in, and deal with the various demands that are placed on them. Health care is a good example of an application where there may be special rules for PIM, arising from the criticality of the information as well as the enhanced requirements for privacy and confidentiality. This topic will be addressed in the following chapter.

NOTES

1. These factors are part of Carroll's (1993) three-stratum model of human cognitive abilities.
2. Flexibility of closure is the ability to hold a given visual percept or configuration in mind so as to disembed it from other well-defined perceptual material (Ekstrom, French, Harman, et al. 1976).

13 Personal Health Information Management

Anne Moen

13.1 Introduction

The payoffs for personal information management (PIM) may be especially large in targeted domains such as health care. The health care we can acquire and receive is increasingly sophisticated and complex. Treatments and care are offered at multiple sites, ranging from highly specialized hospitals, outpatient clinics, community hospitals, doctor's offices, physical therapy clinics, and nursing homes to the home dwelling. Therefore, health care has developed into a complex, and too often fragmented, set of episodes of care. More and more, health-care recipients and their families are invited, even expected, to engage in the complex activities of coordinating and integrating their health care and their health-care information.

Today's patients are saddled with common challenges of personal health information management. They have to manage complex regimens of longer-term outpatient care—combinations of chemotherapy, radiation therapy, hormonal therapy, and additional surgical procedures—while trying to maintain their normal lives at work and at home. For example, cancer patients commonly receive a primary intervention (e.g., surgery), that is followed by subsequent adjuvant therapy lasting additional weeks, months, or years. In addition, they are required to manage vast amounts of new and unfamiliar information given by health-care professionals from a range of different organizations and departments. To make the information management situations even more challenging, the information is often provided orally in conjunction with other procedures, and often in inconsistent forms. Moreover, patients may experience transient or permanent problems with focusing attention and remembering—if not related to the treatments and operations themselves, then related to emotional reactions (e.g., anxiety, depression) to their situations.

Assuming new roles, deciding which information to attend to, knowing which prevention recommendations to follow, choosing among available self-assessments, or deciding which health observations to perform and report to health-care practitioners adds to health information management responsibilities. Consequently, interest in and responsibility for personal health and the area of personal health information is growing in importance, and is already a fundamental, lifelong activity for many of us. Some of the activities in personal health information management (PHIM) relate to life processes, and other activities are initiated and become relevant when illness conditions are present in the household.

In this chapter, I will discuss PHIM in the context of the household the person belongs to, as the household provides one of the richest and most diverse contexts where PHIM activities occur. Activities in information management and health maintenance taking place in the home nevertheless remain largely invisible (Pratt, Reddy, McDonald, et al. 2004). Whether the focus of PHIM is prevention, self-care, surveillance, symptom management, seeking providers' advice, making treatment choices, or coordinate care, we seek and use a variety of information. These heterogeneous sets of information-intensive activities, such as acquiring, managing, and communicating information, seem aimed toward wellness, maintenance, and desired health outcomes. Consequently, what was formerly an individual's optional choice—whether to engage in or eschew personal health information management—has now become an essential responsibility.

13.1.1 *Scenario: Health Information at Home*

When Alex and Brooke still lived in the family home, Connie remembers how she used the shared family calendar to remember the kids' appointments for immunizations and the dates of their doctor visits, and coordinated them with the other activities the family was engaged in. She also recalls how she updated their baby books and filed health information along with the other pieces of information she considered important enough to keep.

Since she was diagnosed with breast cancer, Connie is much more active in her health information management. When she was diagnosed, she received some pamphlets to learn more about her diagnosis and available treatment options. She also collected some flyers in the pharmacy and printed off information from a cancer site she found and liked on the Web. She keeps the cancer-related information in a folder with her other health stuff. The folder was moved from the basement to her desk, where the computer and one of her telephones are, for ease of use and information retrieval. She also uses the Internet to search for information. Now that her chemotherapy is over, she is not so focused on symptom management but more interested in self-care and physical activity. She has bookmarked a few Web sites from institutions she trusted. She chooses to spend her time keeping up with work as well as family and friends and does not wish to participate in online support groups because she perceives support group participation as too time-consuming for her.

Connie keeps a diary and she writes down details from her health-care visits. This diary used to be on paper sheets kept together with her medical record information; summaries, lab results, and similar documents. Lately, her son Alex helped her move this information into a file on the computer. She also updates the synopsis of information about her health condition and key information like insurers, doctors' contact information, her pharmacy, allergies, and the medication she is currently on, in a little book she always carries in her purse. At home, Connie still writes scheduled appointments on the calendar on the refrigerator. When she had lunch with Edna a couple of days ago, they talked about how Edna developed a weekly, detailed itinerary when Connie's father was ill, because otherwise they could not have kept up with different appointments, treatments, and other activities. Edna suggested that Connie also write one for herself on the computer, and circulate "her list" to Alex and Brooke and other friends who would like to be informed.

This scenario illustrates some aspects of personal health information. People's contributions to and responsibilities for health goals or self-care activities are largely underarticulated, and can be considered invisible work (Strauss, Fagerhaugh, Suczek & Weiner 1985). Following current changes in the health-care arena, exemplified by isolated episodes of care and changing sites of care and treatment, health-related activities have migrated to the home environment. People are likely to face information fragmentation and overload that is similar to challenges in other aspects of personal information management. Therefore, considering personal health information management as a type of "work" carried out in the household rather than a personal health behavior provides a richer base from which we can identify strategies that complement and support complexities of contemporary health care.

In exploring aspects of personal health information management, I will focus on what people do with the health information they search for and retrieve, where they are when using these resources, and how they try to integrate health information and resources in their daily lives. I will draw on experiences from participation in the study "Advanced Technologies for Health@Home," hereafter Health@Home (Professor P. F. Brennan, University of Wisconsin-Madison, Principal Investigator; Sponsored by Intel Corporation). Other aspects of this study have been communicated in Moen and Brennan (2005) and Marquard, Moen, and Brennan (2006).

13.2 Overview: Support for Health Information Management and the Household

Contemporary health information management requires retrieval, integration, tracking, and sharing information across multiple care sites to get an overview of knowing what to attend to and when to share. The available information comes in different forms and formats, including books, leaflets, flyers, and word of mouth, as well as electronic formats. In addition, sources are distributed, making information retrieval fragmented by location, device, and forms (Pratt, Unruh, Civan & Skeels 2006). Therefore the burdens of selection and of understanding the relevance of the different available pieces most likely increase.

Information technology development inspires and enables new modes of interaction, and there are health-care institutions offering support to aspects of personal health information management. For example, "patient gateways" and "patient portals" allow secure, Web-based, controlled access to information kept in health-care facilities (Sands, Halamka & Pellaton 2001; Wang, Pizziferri, Volk, et al. 2004). These applications offer remote access to subsets of the health information about a person, and are open for online asynchronous interaction with the health-care institution and its affiliated health-care providers. These services are geared at activities related to health-care visits, pre-appointment self-care updates, medical record information, and information resources about a person's cure and treatment.

The development of personal health record (PHR) systems is another example of initiatives intended to develop repositories for a person's health-related information and to allow combinations of data, knowledge, and software to support active patient participation (Tang, Ash, Bates, et al. 2006). In contrast to the electronic health records that primarily support the information needs of health-care professionals, PHR systems offer access to personal health data and to credible health information and knowledge relevant to the individual's health or illness situation. Personally controlled health records would enable individuals to have an integrated record over time and across institutional settings (Simons, Mandl & Kohane 2005).

PHR as a tool for patients to record health histories and illness experiences depends on patients' participation, and on granting them autonomy to decide who may access and use their health information. PHR systems come in several forms, including stand-alone systems, patient gateways offering access to subsets of health information, and institutionally supported, integrated, and personally controlled applications. PHR systems, regardless of their form, can be seen as data repositories supporting interaction with the health-care system.

However, unresolved issues include interoperability between different systems, organizational and institutional concerns, as well as an understanding of what people do in PHIM, implications for a person's privacy and confidentiality, and jurisdiction for professional practice.

As illustrated in the scenario above, Connie has used and still uses different tools to organize, keep, and find information for different health-related activities. She also employs several health information management strategies. The information is scattered around the house, at locations familiar to her or other household members. Some pieces of information are also with her all the time. Her use of tools and organization of information may reflect her own organizing patterns, as well as the operating logic of other health-care users, but also how pieces of information are evaluated in terms of perceived importance and future use for health management purposes.

There are some studies reporting how people engage in health information management activities outside health-care institutions. Information services aimed at patients or family members for peer support, symptom monitoring, and self-care activities have been important to assure benefits of professionally provided care (Brennan, Moore, Bjornsdottir, et al. 2001; Gustafson, Hawkins, Boberg, et al. 2002; Safran 2003). Other researchers describe how patients fill in gaps and assume responsibilities to collect and manage information related to their health conditions for personal safety (Pratt et al. 2006; Unruh & Pratt 2004).

People participate in different aspects of their care, including (1) navigating the health-care system and coordinating distributed tasks across multiple providers and care settings; (2) engaging in health status monitoring and communicating with clinicians; and (3) choosing health-status monitoring and information about treatment that are within levels of available benefits (Unruh & Pratt 2004). In their PHIM activities people seek information to make choices related to treatment options, health outcomes, self-help and symptom management strategies, medications, available providers, and financial support. An important aspect concerns "what is normal" or what to expect (Hsieh & Brennan 2005). There may be variations with regard to the types of requested information and the timing of acquiring health-related information. Motivations for information seeking and integration of pieces of information in daily life are complex, and vary during the illness trajectory (Leydon, Boulton, Moynihan, et al. 2000). People access sources themselves, or acquire information from or through their care givers, in order to learn about health, welfare, leisure, and domestic concerns (Cooper & Urquhart 2005).

PHIM typically includes activities related to information exchange, use, retrieval, and storage for prevention of potential illness, to help in handling possible health hazards (e.g., poisoning), treatment, or to care for themselves or their family members. To more fully understand personal health information management, insight into what people do (i.e., their activities), and where they are performing their activities (i.e., the context), is important.

13.3 Diving In: A Study of Personal Health Information Management

Several health information management activities take place in organized health-care facilities. Exploring people's health information management activities in unique environments such as the household can provide important insight to fairly robust, operating strategies used for personal health information management. Hence an important aspect of the Health@Home study was to understand some of the health information management challenges in the context of the household and local health resources. To do so, we used a work-based approach with task analysis (Ford & Wood 1996) to study what people do in the context of their household.

A household is physically, psychologically, and socially constructed, with rooms, belongings, and artifacts with different meanings attached. A household is the coming together of its members, physical space, arrangement and uses of possessions, and cyclical routines that work together in ways that are predictable to the household members. People are in control of the home environment (Roush & Cox 2000) and their use of space could communicate important aspects of health information management activities. For example, studies indicate that activities are typically distributed throughout multiple spaces of varying significance to household members (Hindus, Mainwaring, Leduc, et al. 2001; O'Brien, Rodden, Rouncefield & Hughes 1999). The kitchen often serves as a primary space for awareness, coordination, internal communication, and shared information production and management in a household (Crabtree, Hemmings & Rodden 2002). There are also a multitude of meanings attached to a home. Routine activities act as a "glue" for everyday life (Tolmie, Pycock, Diggins, et al. 2002) and people seem to optimize physical and cognitive functions in these activities (Roush & Cox 2000). Lastly, most artifacts or devices found in a home carry multiple functions (Cummings & Kraut 2002).

The use of space and devices in the household can point to information uses, routines, rights, and responsibilities. Personal health information management is an important, but understudied, type of activity occurring in the home. To elaborate on PHIM, I attempt to integrate findings from household visits and findings from focus-group interviews from the Health@Home study. The

University of Wisconsin Health Science Institutional Review Board reviewed the study's protocol and gave Human Subjects' Approval. The empirical data used to learn about common information management situations comes from interactions with the household's self-identified information managers and from focus-group interviews. Data was collected during household visits to informants' main residence (n = 39), interaction at a location of the informant's choice (n = 10), and in two focus-group sessions held with participants not involved in earlier interviews. With the consent of participants involved in household visits, we took digital photographs to capture the context and location of artifacts without revealing specific personally identifiable content or people. The insights from analysis of the interviews and photographs were then discussed in focus-group interviews.

From the analysis of the collected data an interesting picture emerged. In the different "well" samples the majority of the self-identified health information managers are women. In the interviews, 47 of 49, or 95 percent, were women, and 5 of 6 participants in the focus group were women. Among our informants, one household member typically assumes the responsibility and takes care of most of the information. This person sifts through and chooses to keep information perceived relevant to household members. They also told how they tried different strategies to make health information management become shared and collective responsibility in the household.

Although concerns, sources, requirements, and needs varied, most health information management issues arose from health experiences by household members. Broadly speaking, the people managing health information at home engage in three different types of activities (Moen & Brennan 2005): (1) observing, assessing, and surveying their own and/or a household member's health conditions; (2) organizing, separating, and differentiating information according to importance or relevance; and (3) obtaining, retrieving, and keeping track of health information according to household needs, from sources such as family, friends, and own memory, providers, libraries, drugstores, and the Internet. Exploration of the types of information handled revealed three different types: (a) logistical information, such as health-care appointments, contact information, and coordination items; (b) personal health information, such as health record information, lab results, annual checkups, and insurance; and (c) reference material, such as pamphlets, topic-related books, and encyclopedias.

People acquire a variety of information and employ different artifacts to support for PHIM. Figure 13.3a is a collage of several examples of artifacts shown to us.

Figure 13.3a – Examples of artifacts to support personal health information management in the home.

Most commonly, we found that people use *paper* or some other durable medium for PHIM. In fact, in 95 percent of the 176 photographs acquired in the Health@Home study, the artifacts shown to us were low-tech or nonelectronic tools and technologies (Moen & Brennan 2005).

Some informants told about consistent and quite sophisticated practices to reenter information in a diary or into their personal computer, but stored the papers and printouts in folders or binders. Several study participants maintained a practice of updating special cards or notebooks that were most often kept with a household member. Information kept readily accessible with a household member included, for example, information concerning life-critical medications, blood types, and allergies. Participants also kept smaller information items, such as insurance cards or contact information for their family or family physician, in a purse or billfold for continual ready access in case of an unexpected event or emergency situation.

Among our informants very few told about or showed us use of Web-based services, such as PHR, patient gateways, or other personally controlled health information management repositories. When asked specifically about these initiatives, reluctance to use Web-based services was related to security issues, and potential threats of fraud or hackers were often cited. Other reasons for non-use related to time-consuming data reentry, which, as one participant said "would be like rewriting my recipes," and from the localization of the computer and choice of modes of interaction, as explained by another informant, who said "I don't want to be sitting in front of computer all the time. . . . I try to be away from the computer as much as possible."

The location and physical expression of artifacts served purposes of support for anticipated future use—for example, calendars, phone books, medical histories, or separate sheets of paper with information on procedures and medication side effects. In Figure 13.3b, different locations of calendars may reflect tradeoffs between accessibility, visibility, and anticipation of future need for the information.

Figure 13.3b – Different locations of calendars

The use and importance of calendars was frequently and repeatedly raised. The following quote—"my calendar is my bible; I keep them from year to year"— exemplifies this importance. In addition to calendars, informants showed how they stored relevant information in folders, and kept printouts of their medical record information, general books, printouts from Internet searches, or things they had heard on TV or radio. Providing information specific to a situation at hand and of perceived relevance to imminent experience or challenge is important to support PHIM.

In addition to health information management, individuals employed various devices to manage specific health conditions. For example, people integrate *support devices* such as walkers, crutches, knee-braces, or wheelchairs; *monitoring devices* such as a blood-pressure cuff and monitor, scale, glucose meter, and thermometer; and *treatment devices* such as a first-aid kit, insulin pump, asthma chambers, pill-box organizer, or medication containers, into their PHIM. These devices were kept in the kitchen area, in drawers, boxes, or cake pans, on bookshelves in living rooms or hallways, or kept in special files in their home office, bedroom cabinet, or basement.

Categorizing the photographs showed that 65 of the 176 photographs showed artifacts kept in the kitchen, while 27 of the collected photographs were of artifacts kept in the home office (Marquard, Moen & Brennan 2006). Our analysis of where PHIM artifacts were kept indicates that PHIM activities are likely to occur in the shared household spaces. As one of the informants told us,

"You are in the kitchen most of the time, and you just glance at the refrigerator and [are] reminded to do so and so; we had a magnet with it."

People acquire and use different types of health information. Exploring what people do and where they are when engaging in personal health information management demonstrated that the tools and technologies are kept in different places within the household, or with household members. People seem to evaluate the likelihood of needing different information in future situations and choose an appropriate storage strategy according to their perception of potential future uses. Frequently used items, or those perceived as important, are kept within sight or in designated areas, implying a reminder function, and are accessible and well known to the household members. For example, frequently used health information or artifacts were kept visible in shared spaces, and those less frequently used were kept in well-known places, usually out of sight, but familiar to the household members.

As a synthesis of the material from the Health@Home study, we have suggested a set of differentiated health information storage strategies for health information management in the household (Moen & Brennan 2005). They are:

- "Just-in-time," that is, a storage strategy where information and/or artifacts are with a household member at most times;
- "Just-at-hand," that is, a storage strategy where information and/or artifacts are visible or stored in readily accessible, highly familiar locations in the household;
- "Just-in-case," that is, a storage strategy where information and/or artifacts, either personal health files or general health information resources, are kept out of the way but readily accessible for any future situation;
- "Just-because," that is, a storage strategy where information and/or artifacts about a health concern are in the household because the information appeared significant, but lacked relevance beyond a specific point in time; no other storage strategy is assigned.

The variability in these storage strategies comes from the *location* of different types of information or artifacts, the *assigned importance* of information or an artifact, *visibility* for cues or reminders, and *anticipated urgency* or *available time* to locate the information or artifact when the need arises (Moen & Brennan 2005).

Similar to previous studies of the home environment, the Health@Home study gives examples of how storage of information and activities are distributed throughout multiple spaces (Tolmie et al. 2002), and trade-offs in how accessible health information or artifacts are (Crabtree, Hemmings & Rodden 2002). Visibility of the information contained in or on the artifacts contributes to coordination and awareness in the activities of health information management.

The present exploration in the Health@Home study points to several, important aspects of PHIM. One of them is that PHIM activities differ if a household's health concerns are wellness oriented or oriented to treatment. The empirical material indicates that the severity of the illness influences the intensity of information management, and that people organize information differently depending on the health and illness situation in the household. As one informant said, "when my husband was battling cancer, I took care of him [. . .] there was a lot of things to follow up, but I was able to keep him home until the last days." Other researchers have also pointed out that as health care dependencies increase or people deal with life-threatening illnesses such as cancer, their information needs increase, and activities relating to health information management intensify (Cooper & Urquhart 2005; Pratt et al. 2006; Unruh & Pratt 2004). There is also reported research about informal caregivers' efforts to compensate for distributed and often fragmented information in the medical record. For example, mothers of children with chronic conditions document more comprehensively, and also as an act of handing over responsibility in transition to adulthood (Østerlund, Dosa & Smith 2005).

Another aspect is that the Health@Home study showed extensive reliance on paper or other durable media. It also showed how health information is integrated with general PIM tools, such as calendars. Regardless of format, the plethora of important and incidental health information places management demands that require people to create and employ sophisticated strategies for evaluation, storage, and future use (Jones 2004). The rather sophisticated storage strategies discussed here embed cues about perceived importance and future use for information items. Differences in what people do and how they treat their personal information can be influenced by several factors (see chapter 12 of this book, Individual Differences). To complement the present exploration and the available literature, studies of the ways personal health information management changes, develops, or is made relevant and adaptive to health or illness needs in the household should be conducted.

13.4 Looking Forward

To date, most information technology innovations focus on improved access to and organization of health information in terms of identifying useful information available for look-up or re-retrieval. The health information management demands engendered by health-care practices complement current efforts to develop efficient tools and services. Consumer-oriented information and teaching material, patient portals, and PHR systems are examples of information tools and services that provide support in long-term or sustained treatments for chronic or acute health conditions, health promotion, illness prevention, or health maintenance. The Health@Home study provides examples of information and artifacts kept in the home for PHIM, use of the home environment to support a variety of important activities, and a set of storage strategies. This could complement development of PHR systems beyond the limitations of data repositories, supporting interactions with the health-care system and a variety of health-care providers.

People go to a doctor's office, clinic, or hospital to receive treatment. Activities occurring in the household before, after, or in between interactions with health-care facilities and providers are less studied but equally important to what happens and what is exchanged in clinical encounters. Consideration of the person(s) and their health goals, the context within which they reside, and collaborative aspects exemplified by informants' views of PIMH as a family responsibility add to the picture of PHIM. Currently, PHR systems largely focus on patients' interactions and collaboration with the health-care system and their health-care providers. Insights into PHIM can contribute to expand services, tools, and functionalities to empower patients and enable the population at large to manage and improve their health information. Understanding how people manage information related to their health care can be important for further development of the longitudinal PHR, as it provides insight to what people actually do with health information outside organized care settings. Identification of the different storage strategies adds important structural dimensions that demonstrate how people employ robust, complex strategies in their personal health information management. We found that tools are largely paper-based, and have a physical presence as visible tools to assist household members to maintain their health-related responsibilities. Therefore, it is reasonable to assume that PHIM strategies result from considerations of

- Importance—and as a result, people kept the information handy and in durable formats, most often paper-based;
- Timeliness and accessibility—and as a result, people employed different strategies to remember or recall, and embedded the strategies in their personal life or the life of the family;
- Privacy and visibility—and as a result, people's use of household space signaled trade-offs of visibility and privacy, while people were not partial to Web access.

Care must be taken not to infer behavioral patterns about the participants involved in the Health@Home study. Nonetheless, the study provides an example where exploration of a work practice can illuminate connections between user needs and future support tools. Equally important in exploring people's current health information management for self-care and health maintenance, is its ability to contribute to robust infrastructures that leverage operating strategies and integrate with other information management activities. Innovative models to support PHIM in the household should acknowledge emerging self-directedness in health information management, and support the division of labor among household members (as with collective family responsibility), as well as the transfer of ownership of information, in case of medical emergency, decline in condition, or—for children—coming of age.

13.5 Acknowledgments

The study "Advanced Technologies for Health@Home" was funded by a grant from the Intel Corporation to the University of Wisconsin-Madison (P. F. Brennan, PI), and carried out in collaboration with partners in Dodge and Jefferson counties, WI, USA. Dr. Anne Moen's participation in the study was made possible by a grant from the US-Norway Fulbright Foundation for Educational Exchange, and a postdoctoral fellowship from the Norwegian Research Council.

I acknowledge collaborations and support from the Health Systems Lab under the leadership of Professor Patricia Flatley Brennan, RN, PhD, University of Wisconsin-Madison, WI, USA, and in particular contributions by Mr. Christopher Brunette, MS, past project manager for the Health@Home study, research assistants Jared Wickus, MS, and Teresa Zayas-Cabán, PhD, who collected most of the data during the home visits, Kimberly Ann Ackerbauer, who coded the photographs, and Jenna L. Marquard, MS, PhD(c), in analysis of the photographs.

PART IV

PIM and
Other People

14 Group Information Management

Wayne G. Lutters, Mark S. Ackerman, and Xiaomu Zhou

14.1 Introduction

Activities of personal information management are often embedded in group or organizational contexts. To work effectively within a group an individual must manage information not only for his or her personal use but also to share with other members of the group. Obviously, one would like to leverage the activities of others around. Being able to obtain telephone numbers, schedule group meetings, determine the availability of one's peers, and obtain important collaborative information is invaluable. What are the issues, if any, in leveraging the work of others, in order to incorporate their calendar, contacts, and other information into one's own PIM system? And what would be involved in sharing one's own data for use by others?

This chapter reviews the host of issues involved in the collaborative use of personal information. Topics covered include motivation, adoption patterns, interaction styles, control over personal information, privacy, and trust. The goal is to facilitate sharing personal information by considering these issues; fully considered, they can enable the cooperative adoption and use of tools to support *group information management* (GIM). GIM refers to the practice and the study of the individual actions performed to support group activity. The support of this information management behavior includes the ability to acquire, organize, maintain, retrieve, and use artifacts such as documents (paper-based and digital), Web pages, and email messages. Groups can be small (such as a team of six or seven) or large (an organization with thousands of members). They can be ephemeral (chance encounters at a social event) or ongoing (a software project team). Groups can also be work-related (a business department) or not (a parent-teacher organization). They may be engineered social units (a training class) or emergent assemblages of individuals (an affinity group of hobbyists).

Collaboration and information sharing have been widely studied in many literatures. To explore the issues impacting GIM support, this chapter draws heavily on the computer-supported cooperative work (CSCW) literature. CSCW is part of the human-computer interaction field, and it broadly studies how people use computer systems and applications in group, organizational, or even Internet-scale contexts. (See Ackerman 2000b and Olson & Olson 1997 for brief surveys of this literature.) Where appropriate, however, we will also draw on a range of other literatures, including information science, organizational studies, and sociology. The list of issues is long, and we somewhat arbitrarily break that list into three sections. We will first consider a work context, examining the social issues in sharing, and then the more technical and cognitive issues in sharing information. We then note some of the issues in group information systems overall that may impinge on the successful adoption of GIM tools, again in a work setting. Next, we examine GIM in a different setting—the home and family. Finally, the chapter ends with a brief examination of interesting research possibilities for GIM.

14.2 Scenario

Brooke Monroe manages her own information for the many projects in her life and for her various roles and responsibilities. She shares a considerable amount of her time, her emotional energy—and her information—with her colleagues at a high-tech start-up. For example, coworkers are able to review and make meeting requests in each others' digital calendars—which has proven very useful when a meeting must be arranged quickly. People in the start-up discovered that they like to socialize with each other as well. They share a great love of new music and routinely exchange information about upcoming concerts and details about ones that they have recently attended. They like to stay aware of concerts they're planning to attend.

At his securities firm, Alex Monroe also shares information with his colleagues. However, in his situation people are much more circumspect about releasing calendar, task, or free-text information, as it can lead to security law violations. In addition, his coworkers jealously guard their Rolodexes, as their contents could provide a leg up in the competitive securities business.

Brooke and Alex, when they are at home, like to mesh their calendars. They also share their contact information. Brooke is a bit secretive, though, and likes to protect her private journal entries. While she's willing to share general calendar information (busy or free periods) with her mother, Connie, Brooke has been unwilling to provide detailed calendar, contact, or free-text information. Of course, since Connie needs help with her medical regime, Brooke and Alex both have to schedule items on their mother's paper calendar while synchronizing it with their own digital calendars.

This simple scenario illustrates some of the challenges of group information management at work and at home that will be unpacked in the following three sections.

14.3 Group Information Management at Work

As most CSCW research has focused on office environments, this review of the social issues impacting GIM will be presented within this setting and later contrasted with the home. First, we will describe the social and collaborative issues underlying the motivations for GIM, including reward structures, control, privacy, trust, and adoption patterns. Next, the situated nature of information exchange will be examined, highlighting the contextual elements of GIM and information sharing.

14.3.1 *Incentives and Social Issues in Groups*

As might be expected when people try to work together, there are a large range of personal and social issues. Before examining the specifics in the use of tools to support GIM, however, several basic social-theoretic findings need to be noted. These findings detail some important ways people operate within groups, and they frame any discussion of groups and their information use.

■ First, Goffman (1959) argued that people are very concerned about how they present themselves to others. People wish to govern how others view them, and so they tailor how they present themselves accordingly. For example, Alex may be a cutthroat security trader to one group of people and a caring son to another. Not all of the information passed on to others might be the same: Brooke may share ribald concert stories with her coworkers, but not with her mother. These identities, with their concomitant informational facets, were called "faces" by Goffman. He also argued that people want to control their impression management, or how they try to have others view them, and that losing this control can be very disconcerting.

■ As people control their information release, they often do it in a very flexible and nuanced manner (Goffman 1959). For example, Alex might tell one colleague about a new job possibility but not another. Brooke might give her home phone number to one coworker but not another. We often release information in a very highly contextualized manner as well. One doesn't consider only the people to whom the information will be given; the decision also weighs many aspects of the specific situation and circumstances.

238

People also control their information in a very flexible manner. One does not weigh or deliberate about his information within an overarching personal policy of control except under the most unusual circumstances. For example, Brooke could not uniformly say that she wants to share her social schedule with her mother; yet she will freely reveal information if a particular social event conflicts with Connie's need to be driven to a medical appointment. This is most often a fluid and natural exchange. People do not interrupt social interactions to make formal decisions about sharing. As well, one normally assumes an ambiguity in social interaction—one doesn't necessarily know why someone else shares or withholds information, and it is seldom considered socially appropriate to ask. Conflict and goal incompatibilities are often masked by this social ambiguity.

Finally, within groups—and especially within organizations—not everyone has the same goals and understandings (Orlikowski 1992a). Members may share some goals and not others. For example, Brooke might share the goals of working together and delivering a product. At the same time, she might have the goal to stay current technically so as to maximize her employability. These and other differences can lead to breakdowns between people, and these breakdowns must be repaired.

Accordingly any consideration of GIM support must include the often conflicting and always varying incentives and motivations in interpersonal use. The above social-theoretic considerations suggest that it is normal to have many incompatibilities in incentives and motivations among the people providing their information as well as the people receiving that information. This is an extremely important issue in group information management. As Grudin (1989) observed, there is often a mismatch between the incentives of various players in a group system. In a group calendar system, for example, it may be in the interests of the managers to have their employees keep their calendars so they can be seen. For the employees, it may be in their interests to keep their calendars private so they can control their time (and safeguard their face to the managers).

These differences in incentives vary among roles and among groups. Often within organizations, groups can have differing goals and reward systems. Orlikowski (1992a) studied Lotus Notes' adoption at a consulting firm. She found that varied groups and roles operated under differing organizational incentive structures, resulting in divergent motivations to share or not to share. The partners at the consulting firm wanted everyone to share their expertise and knowledge, and therefore became strong proponents of the system. The staff consultants needed billable hours and a recognized area of expertise in order to advance in the firm; thus, they had little incentive to contribute to the system. The computing people were highly motivated to learn and master Lotus Notes, since at the time it was the hot new technology. Simply, each group had a different incentive structure, which resulted in different patterns of adoption.

Later work has suggested that reward systems can be realigned within organizations and groups. Palen (1999) found that shared calendar systems are used, if employees' schedules are not abused. Similarly, work by Orlikowski (1992a, 2000) and others (Davenport & Prusak 1998) found that the rewards for sharing can be realigned appropriately, leading to more use and re-use. Moreover, even in Orlikowski's early study, agreement (e.g., in individuals' mental models about the world, organization, work, and technology) could be facilitated by common educational and professional backgrounds, work experience, training, and regular interaction.

In building tool support for GIM, it is important to preserve the control that individual members have over the exchange of their information with other members of the group. Without this control, group members may not make full use of GIM tools or, in the worst case, may actually work against initiatives to promote information exchange. Other work in this book addresses this issue directly (Karat & Karat, in chapter 15), but in general privacy has been found to be a central concern by those adding information to group information systems (Dourish, Bellotti, Mackay & Ma 1993). It is critical that users be given control over the dissemination of their personal data, including whether it is shared at all. Furthermore, this must be done in a noninvasive manner, as users expect their control to be nearly seamless.

It is important to note that privacy in tool support for GIM is more problematic than in tools directed toward PIM alone. Group information systems often serve a multiplicity of purposes. Not only may users share calendar, address book, and other PIM information, but the organization may also use the GIM data to provide group- and organizational-level data and reports. For example, GIM data could be used to generate time-on-task reports. As mentioned, management and staff may have different incentives and goals, and these may also vary among groups. Group information can have mixed governance and be owned by multiple groups or multiple levels of the organization (Ackerman & Halverson 2004). This can also reduce the motivation to share. In these situations privacy is critical, but one must also consider aggregated and even anonymized data and its uses. For many GIM activities it may not be necessary to share all aspects of personal information.

Privacy and mixed governance of data raise the issue of trust. Bannon and

Bødker (1997) argued that "trust or accountability is more in the role" (p. 88), which implies that the person who produces the information should have the responsibility for it. Yet not all information is personal; it may be produced or owned by several parties. To resolve these tensions one must consciously choose which source to rely on. Many criteria are typically used in establishing these different levels of trust, such as which source is more authoritative, which is up-to-date, or which is settled and definite (Ackerman & Halverson 2004; Dourish et al. 1993). Berlin, Jeffries, O'Day, et al. (1993) reported that even in the earliest evaluation of their GIM system issues of trust were already apparent. They quickly evolved a curator role to deal with this problem. For them, the curator's responsibility was to alert and fix classification problems. The resolution of trust remained a distributed responsibility. Given the importance of trust in successful GIM support, these notions of individual and collective curatorial activity warrant further research.

In examining these issues of user control, privacy, and trust in GIM, there is one particularly problematic aspect of support tools that must be addressed—user reliance on system defaults. Ascertaining the optimal preset configuration of what is to be shared and with whom is critical in GIM tools, because, simply, people do not customize their software. Mackay (1990) found that relatively few people varied from their default settings (about 10 percent) and even fewer actually programmed customizations (about 1 percent). This finding has held across a wide range of systems, and it is likely that it holds for GIM tools as well. Indeed, Palen (1999) found similar patterns for shared calendar systems, which led to very different patterns of use. In her study 81 percent of users maintained the defaults for their access settings, which implies that default settings are fundamental design decisions that can affect the model of collaboration. This is an often overlooked but important issue. Software developers must make it possible for companies to modify deployment of default settings to suit conditions. Further, Palen found that users with shared calendar systems that defaulted to open-access more often shared information (although they had workarounds to protect their private appointments). It is quite possible that, with the proper defaults, users could be protected from privacy issues at the same time they would use encouraged to share their information.

While the default settings of the initial tool installation are critical, recall from earlier in this chapter that all group information-sharing decisions are situated. The contextual nature of these exchanges may make establishing a general policy difficult.

In concluding this discussion of the motivations for using GIM support tools, it is useful to abstract to a higher level and examine common patterns of adoption. Our collective understanding of group adoption patterns is still nascent. While general principles have been outlined (e.g., Grudin 1989), most CSCW research provides conflicting and inconclusive evidence. For instance, Markus and Connolly (1990) claimed that mandated use (i.e., top-down managerial decision) is necessary to reach critical mass. Orlikowski (1992a) reported a mixed pattern of adoption and use of Lotus Notes at Alpha company; while the technical support staff successfully adopted Notes without managerial pressure, the staff consultants did experience top-down pressure. Palen and Grudin's (1999) study of electronic calendar use in two large organizations, Sun and Microsoft, found that no single adoption pattern could fit every group. However, their interview and survey results primarily supported a bottom-up adoption trajectory: respondents felt more pressure to use their electronic calendars from peers than from management.

Adding complexity to our understanding of groupware adoption patterns is the realization that the relationship between users and technology continues to evolve over time. Orlikowski's (1992b) duality of technology concept presented a structurational model of technology that posited artifacts as potentially modifiable throughout their existence in a technology's life cycle. Throughout interaction with certain technology, users have the potential to change it both physically and socially in a process of co-evolution (Orlikowski 1992b; O'Day, Bobrow & Shirley 1996). Palen (1999) labeled the same phenomenon as socio-technical evolution in her examination of group calendaring systems. Another helpful illustration of this effect is Star and Ruhleder's (1996) longitudinal study of the Worm Community System, which resulted in the emergence of locally tailored applications and repositories that combined with local knowledge and expertise. This evolution was facilitated by the features of infrastructure that supported the redefinition of local roles and the emergence of a community of practice.

Given the overall complexity of groupware adoption, the research community is split on successful strategies. Some prefer to consider how users can more fully participate in the design process (e.g., Greenbaum & Kyng 1991), while others reflect on how all participants come to slowly understand their needs and capabilities in a process of co-realization (e.g., Hartswood, Procter, Rouncefield, et al. 2007).

14.3.2 *Information Sharing in Groups*

The next set of issues involves information sharing as a technical and cognitive process. Again these issues are framed by a basic social-theoretic finding:

▓ People's emphases on what details to consider or to act upon differ according to the situation (Suchman 1987). This is as true in information sharing as any other activity, and it directly follows from Goffman's observations. That is, people's information sharing is heavily context-ualized and situated.

People are good at handling situated activity, and their activity is heavily contextualized around the particulars of the situation. People adding and retrieving information in a group information system must mesh their often idiosyncratic categories, indices, schema, and information routines. Moreover, even individuals change categories, indices, and routines, often losing valuable information in the process. This loss is magnified in group and especially organizational use. As an indication of the magnitude of the problem, Furnas, Landauer, Gomez, and Dumais (1987), found that when two people were asked to name commands there was less than a 0.20 probability of overlap in their terms. (While this study was performed in a command line environment, the scale of the problem in naming things most likely holds across domains.) This is especially true for unstructured data, such as free-form text. Unstructured items may not include enough description, which is needed for findability by someone other than the person who had submitted the item (Berlin, Jeffries, O'Day, et al. 1993).

In a particularly insightful study, Berlin, Jeffries, O'Day, et al. (1993) pointed to the different styles in group storage and retrieval. As they observed, "An inherent problem of a shared repository is that individual finding strategies do not work for a group" (p. 25). They go on to state:

Beneath our surface agreement on the categories lay crucial differences, exposed when we compared how we would classify a set of test messages based on project members' activities and recent e-mail. We differed along the following five dimensions:
1. purists and proliferators
2. semanticists and syntacticists
3. scruffies and neatniks
4. savers and deleters
5. the expected purpose for which the item is saved. (p. 25)

In their view, these are filing habits and preferences developed over a long period of time by individuals. People in their study differed over the number of categories (purists had one, proliferators many), whether people categorized by the event or the topic (semantics by event and syntacticists by topic), the number of categories (scruffies had but five top-level categories, neatniks had hundreds), how much was saved, and a user's expected future roles and tasks. Each user had his or her individual style, and in combination the differing styles made adoption difficult. In use, the differing styles meant that users found browsing more useful, since they had an imprecise sense of when an item was created, might not know how it was indexed or keyworded, and might not know the words in an item for full-text retrieval.

Berlin et al. also noted that group systems carry with them questions of private versus group storage. Users need to trust that the system will be there in the future, or they will store the information in their personal space instead. (This observation is further elaborated in Whittaker and Hirshberg 2001.) As well, Berlin et al. found that users questioned whether information belonged to the group or to the individual. This suggests that GIM tools may need to consist of federated PIM tools, or at least this would be advantageous. Users will weigh whether to store truly private data in a group information repository.

As well, many of these group-level issues, such as group categorizations, indexing, and information styles, are not one-time problems. Categories will shift over time as groups change their needs. As mentioned, Berlin et al. found this, and their group devised a curator role to alert the group to classification issues. As Suchman (1997) pointed out, these categorizations are political, in that they carry with them assumptions about the legitimacy of certain activities and work (see also Bowker & Star 2000; Star & Strauss 1999). This is especially true at the organization level. It may be difficult to find consensus around contested categorizations—or, alternatively, some users may resist sharing or using data (Markus 1983). As will be noted, an active area of research includes the tailorability of systems for both individual and group use.

Not only is categorization more difficult in group settings, more care must be given to prepare the information for later use by others (Lin, Lutters & Kim 2004; Markus 2001). The information must be decontextualized, stripped of its irrelevant or highly contextualized information, and abstracted for later use (Ackerman & Halverson 2004; Lutters & Ackerman 2002). Later, when the information is re-used by another person, the user must recontextualize the information, trying to understand the original context as well as the current context of use.

14.4 Group Information Management in the Home

Another domain for GIM is home life. The use of personal information in the home is predominantly collaborative and thus forms a type of GIM. While many of the dimensions of GIM already discussed in this chapter transfer appropriately from work life to home life, there are additional forces and considerations in this environment that warrant attention.

There is significant work required to maintain a well functioning household, some of it is explicit (e.g., housekeeping chores), but most of it invisible or articulation work (Strauss 1993). While the differences between home and office are pronounced (Crabtree & Rodden 2004), many of the underlying collaborative mechanisms that support work in each domain are similar (O'Brien, Rodden, Rouncefield & Hughes. 1999). Production in the home is of a significantly smaller scale, but of increased complexity from the office. With stronger individual interests, less defined organizational structure, and a web of intermeshed, often conflicting goals, collective action in the home is a continual compromise resulting from a dynamic, negotiated order (Strauss 1993). While home life necessitates its own activities, it is also the confluence of many external forces, such as work, school, community, and avocation (Brush, Palen, Swan & Taylor 2005).

As well, home life has its own work rhythms, in concert with the rhythms of the outside world (e.g., office, school) and the biological needs met in the home (e.g., meals, sleep). Time pressures drive much of the negotiation in the home. This trend is only increasing given the ongoing blurring of the boundaries between home and work (Frissen 2000).

All households develop their own means of managing these many conflicting goals. These often emerge from an artful appropriation of resources in the home to form organizing systems—"in which heterogeneous collections of artifacts are enrolled to capture, integrate and arrange, and convey information" (Taylor & Swan 2005, p. 647). Many of these appropriated resources become group information.

The most common forms of organizing systems in the home are paper-based household calendars (Crabtree, Hemmings & Mariani 2003) and lists (Taylor & Swan 2004). The joint calendar is the most obvious melding of personal information resources into a shared group resource (e.g., taping school activity flyers to relevant days on the calendar). Individual schedules are brought together in order to negotiate collaborative activity (e.g., who needs the car for what activity this week?). Publicly displayed lists also serve as points of negotiation, whether they are time-dependent task lists or communal shopping lists. As the fieldwork for the Casablanca project (Hindus, Mainwaring, Leduc, et al. 2001) revealed, managing the interpersonal relationships within and outside the home is a primary work task in home life.

Given the diversity of skills, interests, involvement, and ownership, the most successful group information technologies in the home are those that are infinitely reconfigurable. Self-organization in GIM support is critical to supporting the "full complexity of social organization in home life; allowing users to establish their own sets of usage practices" (O'Brien et al. 1999, p. 297).

In the negotiated space of the home, the kitchen reigns supreme. As the most public, highly trafficked, and multipurpose of all home spaces, it becomes the locus of collaborative action (Nagel, Hudson & Abowd 2004). Enthroned in this public space is the refrigerator (Swan & Taylor 2005). This highly configurable display space is often the focal point both for coordinating household activity (e.g., family calendar, chores rotation, shopping lists), and for displaying critical information. In many homes it is the primary activity center for coordinated action (Crabtree et al. 2003).

While most of the artifacts and information employed in the daily operation of the home are ephemeral, the home is also the primary center for capturing and preserving memories of the household members. The content varies from functional re-use (such as a list of items to pack when going on vacation) to sentimental value (a child's drawings). The means are equally diverse, from scrapbooks to bulletin boards to inaccessible corners on the side of refrigerators (Swan & Taylor 2005). This may be an additional role for domestic GIMs.

Traditionally the home has been technologically impoverished when compared to the workplace. This has fostered a reliance on nondigital GIM. However, this is shifting dramatically. Rapid diffusion of such technologies as cellular phones and broadband networking afford new possibilities for domestic GIM. As the distinctions between home life and work life continue to blur (Nippert-Eng 1996), their influence on the development of GIM support tools remains an open research question.

14.5 GIM Tools

At the time of this writing, software support for GIM is quickly improving. The tools supporting the opening GIM scenario are in a state of constant change and evolution. How Brooke and her colleagues, for example, organize themselves and their information exchange is clearly a product of their time, as are the constraints the tools impose on their sharing.

Of course, GIM tools have been in existence since computing began, but mainframe and time-sharing applications (e.g., PROFS calendar) were limited. They had prescribed interaction styles, limited information types and collaboration support, and it was difficult to create ad hoc networks of collaborating people, especially outside of organizational boundaries.

Since then several major changes have made GIM substantially easier.

Networks allowed greater sharing of information. The Internet brought email to society, evolving the possibilities for GIM. In the early 1990s, networking enabled the highly successful Lotus Notes system with its organization-wide calendaring, email, information sharing, and collaborative information applications. Notes also added the fluidity to define your own GIM interactions. Other notable GIM systems in the research literature include Answer Garden (Ackerman 1998) and BSCW (Bentley, Horstmann & Trevor 1997).

More recently, GIM tools have grown to include a large range of applications. These include Web-based applications such as group calendars (e.g., Google Calendar) and information sharing and presentation (e.g., MySpace, Flickr). Now in the age of the so-called Web 2.0, there are even more possibilities for collaborative use, including collaborative filtering and recommendations (e.g., Amazon), collaborative tagging (e.g., Flickr, CiteSeer), social networking (e.g., Friendster, LinkedIn, Fanpop), and blogs (e.g., Blogspot). It should also be noted that there are also a number of alternative architectures to the Web for GIM, including p2p (e.g., Napster, gnutella) and hybrid server/p2ps (e.g., Groove). With the large amount of interest as well as the number of new systems, one can expect that GIM applications will only increase in utility.

14.6 Looking Forward: Open Research Issue for GIMs

There are a number of open research topics in GIM. As mentioned, there are a variety of interesting opportunities for sharing personal data. For example, the Haystack project offers the opportunity to obtain recommendations for useful papers or monographs on a research topic. One Haystack system could ask another for a reference. Furthermore, since everything is clearly typed, it is relatively easy to ask for a specific phone number. The use of metadata and automated reasoning is key to these types of projects (Karger, chapter 8 of this volume; Berners-Lee, Hendler & Lassila 2001). This remains an active research area, and one of great promise.

Another open research topic is the provision of privacy and awareness. Awareness of what others are doing is an intriguing possibility through GIM tools. Any awareness of others seemingly necessitates the loss of privacy of those other individuals. As mentioned above, many GIM design possibilities suggest the loss of personal privacy. Hudson and Smith (1996) signaled one mechanism for controlling the loss of privacy while providing awareness. In their work, one can blur the multimedia streams, thus hiding the specific video image or audio words while letting the user know that someone is either present or talking. It may be possible to find similar mechanisms to ameliorate GIM privacy issues.

Another research frontier is that of collaborative visualizations and new representations. Begole, Tang, and Hill (2003) have used visualizations to see team patterns of activity and allow people to mesh more easily. (But see the comments on privacy.) As more and more data become digital, the opportunities for visualization and new representations will become even more important and interesting.

Finally, more needs to be determined about how GIM support will continue to evolve. It is likely that their use will coevolve: As users use a system, they begin to find new ways to use it. They push to add new features, which then adapt the system to their needs. However, little is known about this coevolution. Furthermore, as mentioned, it is likely over time that users will need and want to evolve indexing schemes, storage conventions, and retrieval styles. What is not known is how much users will want to use old material and how that material, if any, must be maintained over extended use.

14.7 Acknowledgments

This work was funded, in part, by the National Science Foundation, grant IIS-0325347. We would like to thank Jaime Teevan and William Jones for their patience and encouragement for this work.

15 Management of Personal Information Disclosure: The Interdependence of Privacy, Security, and Trust

Clare-Marie Karat, John Karat, and Carolyn Brodie

15.1 Introduction

The need for usable and trusted privacy and security is emerging as a critical area in the management of personal information. Media accounts of the occurrence of lost or fraudulently obtained personal information from data aggregators and banks are appearing with alarming frequency. Information is being improperly disclosed in ways that cause harm to people through identity theft. In the networked world in which we live, vast amounts of personal information are being collected, transferred, and stored by a variety of organizations ranging from health insurers to credit card companies, tax agencies, and local libraries. Making systems secure and enabling appropriate attention to privacy issues will require more than just a focus on the technology. The Computing Research Association (CRA) Conference on Grand Research Challenges in Information Security and Assurance has identified the ability to "give end-users security controls they can understand and privacy they can control for the dynamic, pervasive computing environments of the future" as a major research challenge (CRA 2003). This goal reinforces the findings of Whitten and Tygar (1999), who point out that "security mechanisms are only effective when used correctly" (p. 169), and that this is often not the case due to usability issues with security software.

If the security aspects of a system are so complex that technical users, business users, and end users cannot understand or trust them, then costly errors will occur and security is compromised. If a system is not secure, then it is impossible to protect the privacy of an individual's personal information on that system. And why should people care about the connection between the management of their personal information and organizational security and privacy? In today's industrialized world, it is efficient, productive, and nearly essential that an individual's personal information is shared for different purposes with organizations around the world. For social, familial, educational, health-care, legal, national security, and business reasons, among others, no man is an island. As citizens of the world today, it is our right and responsibility to be active participants in choices regarding policies governing the use of our personal information by our own pervasive devices and the systems within the organizations with which we interact in our daily lives. To make informed choices and manage the use of our personal information appropriately, the systems we interact with must have usable privacy and security that we trust.

People trust systems and applications when they can understand what the system is doing, achieve their goals, verify system actions, and feel that they are in control. Feeling in control includes understanding the default privacy and security settings and how to modify them if desired. Designing usable systems is a general goal of the field of human-computer interaction (HCI). Designing transparent, usable systems in support of personal privacy, security, and trust includes everything from understanding the intended users of system to the users' tasks and goals, as well as the contexts in which the users will employ the system or application.

Security systems employ technology to ensure that information is appropriately protected. These systems involve end users in that security features, such as passwords for access control or encryption to prevent unintended disclosure, often place requirements on users in order to function correctly. Password schemes must be hard to guess but should be easy to remember. Encryption mechanisms must prevent unintended decryption but be transparent (or nearly so) to the intended senders and recipients.

Privacy may be defined as "the ability of individuals to control the terms under which their personal information is acquired and used" (Culnan 2000, p. 21). Privacy solutions include mechanisms to support compliance with some basic principles (e.g., OECD 1980; U.S. Department of Health, Education, and Welfare 1973). Basically these principles suggest that organizations should collect the minimum amount of information needed and that people should be informed about information collection, told in advance what will be done with their information, and given a reasonable opportunity to approve of such use of information.

In this chapter, we examine the interdependency between personal information management (PIM), user trust, usability, and organizational privacy and security. A scenario illustrates key points in this interdependency, and special considerations regarding PIM and usability are raised. Key research results related to privacy and usability are discussed. We provide a "dive in" discussion of organizational privacy management, and a call to action for our peers who are professionals in the fields of human-computer interaction, computer architecture, security, and privacy to step up to the challenge of creating systems and interaction methods that reduce the complexity in defining, implementing, and managing privacy policies for the benefit of all parties.

15.2   Scenario and Research

15.2.1 *Scenario*

Alex, Brooke, Connie, and Derek are planning a surprise birthday party for Edna, who is turning 75. A number of the guests (friends and relatives) will be arriving from out-of-town and staying at a hotel that is part of a worldwide chain and offers a reward program to encourage customer loyalty to the hotel brand through repeat business. The planning team has worked with the local hotel on a group rate and perks. They will receive a discount rate and special offers for a brunch the morning after Edna's party. Many in the group are already members of the hotel's reward program. Based on Brooke and Connie's recommendations, others decide to join the reward program and opt-in to the personalization features when they arrive at registration in order to begin experiencing the benefits. The hotel staff has received some training on use of personal information but generally use their best judgment. The hotel clerks collect and use credit card numbers, driver's licenses, passport numbers, and contact information, including home and work addresses and phone numbers, and personal preferences about rooms. They also collect personal information about special dietary and health needs.

The hotel aggregates information across hotel stays to personalize the customer's experience and to determine the marketing offers to send to customers who have not opted out from receiving this information. Participants in the reward program can go online to update their personal preferences and explore options for using their loyalty points. The Web site and the corporate IT system have security in place to protect the data from inappropriate access on the Web site and in the backend databases and systems. The hotel has posted a privacy policy on their Web site. Their privacy policy enforcement in the hotels is handled by manual processes without audit trails. Hotel senior management would like to move toward automated enforcement of their privacy policy as soon as possible. They currently have no way of easily detecting misuse or verifying that personal data is being handled properly. Customer complaints are handled on an individual basis by investigators within the hotel's audit and compliance team. The organization has investigated and then fired employees who sold customer data such as credit card numbers.

Brooke and Connie are loyalty program members and have enjoyed the personalization that the hotel provides them based on the personal information they have disclosed as part of the program. They have not experienced any problems in misuse of information to date. Thus they decided on a special hotel package with this hotel chain. They were able to obtain the desired rooms with the special amenities for people with physical disabilities including limited mobility and sight and health issues such as asthma. The hotel's restaurant, which is one of Edna's favorites, tailored the buffet menu to the guests' dietary needs and requests and stayed within their negotiated budget. For example, they provided both vegetarian and meat dishes and eliminated any peanuts from the sauces for those with nut allergies. Based on the personalization data, the restaurant has a number of the guests' favorite drinks ready for them as the party begins. The celebration is a wonderful success!

15.2.2 Research Related to the Scenario

In field-interview research with target users of new privacy technology, our team identified connections between the concepts of privacy, security, trust, personalization, business processes, and education (Karat, Karat, Brodie & Feng 2005a). Good security enables and is a building block for privacy, and the users noted that as they focus on managing privacy in their organizations they have found ways to enhance their security as well (see Figure 15.2.2). The trust that internal and external users have in an organization is a paramount issue, and providing privacy protection is a critical means of ensuring that trust. Privacy education is important both for the internal users or employees in an organization and for their external users or customers. Many interviewees stated that education of their employees regarding privacy is an ongoing priority now

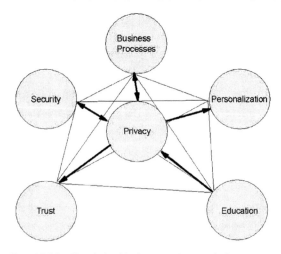

Figure 15.2.2 – The relationships between privacy and other concepts.

and that they believe that personal information cannot be effectively protected until employees, who use the data, believe privacy is important and follow through in their daily actions. The users stated that their customers would only provide personal data on the condition that it is protected and not misused, and this condition is a critical element in opting-in to personalization features. Users are finding redundancies in the collection of data and are realizing financial benefits from streamlining their privacy management processes. Customers are only asked for information once and a single source for the information tends to increase the accuracy of the information over time.

15.3 Privacy, Security, and Trust

15.3.1 *PIM Considerations in the Privacy, Security, and Trust Domains*

There are unique aspects of privacy and security that present challenges and opportunities when designing usable security and privacy functionality for PIM. First, a key issue to consider is that the use of security and privacy solutions is not the user's main goal. Users value and want security and privacy functionality and they are not likely to trust systems that do not provide them, but they regard them as only secondary to completing their primary tasks (e.g., completing online banking transactions, sending or answering email and messages, searching for information, ordering medications). It bears repeating that in the networked world in which we live, it is our right and responsibility to be active participants in choices regarding policies governing the use of our personal information by our own pervasive devices and the systems within the organizations with which we interact in our daily lives.

Second, as more of people's interactions in daily life involve the use of computing technology and sensitive information, disparate types of users must be accommodated. Security solutions in particular have historically been designed with a highly trained technical user in mind. The user community has broadened extensively as organizational business processes have come to include new types of roles and users in the security and privacy area.

Third, the risk of the negative impact of usability problems is higher for security and privacy applications than for many other types of systems. Although complexity is at the very heart of many security and privacy solutions, from the standpoint of usability and transparency that complexity is really the enemy of the success of security and privacy. In the case of security and privacy, badly designed functionality may put users at more risk than if they used less-sophisticated solutions.

Fourth, users will need to be able to easily update security and privacy solutions to accommodate frequent changes in the external world. Additionally, different domains within a person's life (e.g., health care, business, family) and geographies will have unique requirements. Systems must be designed to enable easy and effective updates to them.

15.3.2 *Research Overview*

This chapter primarily focuses on a view of privacy as the right of an individual to control personal information use rather than as the right to individual isolation (Kent & Millett 2003; OECD 1980; U.S. Fair and Accurate Credit Transaction Act 2003; Warren & Brandeis 1890). Organizations commonly provide a description of what kind of information they will collect and how they will use it in privacy policies. In some areas (e.g., the collection and use of health-care information in the U.S. or movement of personal information across national boundaries in Europe) such policies can be required, though the content of the policy is not generally specified in legislation. While there has been considerable consensus around a set of high-level privacy principles for information technology (OECD 1980), it is unlikely that a single privacy policy can be created to address all information privacy needs. For example, there will likely be considerable differences in privacy legislation in different regions of the world (Manny 2003).

Similarly, organizations in different fields (e.g., health care, banking, government) need to tailor policies to their specific domains and needs (Ball 2003; Baumer, Earp & Payton 2000). This chapter focuses on privacy policy, although privacy is not entirely about "setting rules and enforcing them" (Palen & Dourish 2002). To implement privacy within an organization, the coordination of people, business processes, and technology is required (Karat, Brodie & Karat 2005). Still we do believe that such policies are essential when interacting with technology and organizations, in that these policies enable people to better understand the boundaries between public and private information and technology (Altman 1975).

Central to our view of privacy is the notion that the parties involved in information exchanges have implicit or explicit policies with regard to the use of the information. This applies both to the person whom the information is about and to the person or organization collecting and using the information. In the privacy literature on organizations, while some attention has been given to the generally implicit policies of end users whose data is being collected and used (often called data subjects), the main focus is on the policies of the organization collecting the information. Smith (1993) described such organizational policies, and also noted the lack of technology in enforcing the policies. He described the rather unstructured ways in which organizations develop privacy policy—a characterization that has changed little in the period since his research was published, in spite of the increased legislation of the past few years. Future research must address both the needs of data subjects and of organizations by addressing the gap between policy and practice.

15.3.3 *Studies of Privacy and Usability*

While researchers have acknowledged the existence of privacy concerns in a wide variety of technological domains, including email (Bellotti 1996), e-commerce (e.g., Ackerman, Cranor & Reagle 1999), media spaces (e.g., Mantei, Baeker, Sellen, et al. 1991), data mining (e.g., Thuraisingham 2002), and homes of the future (e.g., Meyer & Rakotonirainy 2003), designing effective solutions to address these concerns is challenging. One of the reasons is that relatively few empirical studies have been conducted with the sole aim of studying privacy issues. In addition, empirical investigations of privacy pose numerous methodological challenges. To start with, privacy has proved hard to define due to its highly nuanced and context-dependent nature. Thus, individual differences in perceptions and interpretations of privacy could lead to researcher-introduced bias. Moreover, cultural differences in expectations and behaviors regarding these issues tend to be quite profound (Milberg, Burke, Smith & Kallman 1995) making it difficult to generalize findings across cultures, or to study settings that involve individuals from multiple cultures.

Differences in privacy laws in different countries could make it difficult to isolate actual intention from mere legal compliance. Further, methodologies for studying privacy may themselves be deemed too privacy-invasive, causing users to deviate from normal practice and/or to withhold revealing or sensitive aspects. As a result, relying on self-reported attitudes and behavior alone may not provide a valid view of normal practices (Spiekermann, Grossklags & Berendt 2001).

We examine a selection of key research topic areas to illustrate usability issues in the area of privacy. While this is not an exhaustive list, it will highlight issues in the area of privacy. These topic areas will include anonymity, personalization, end-user views of privacy, and privacy policies.

Anonymity

Anonymity and anonymization in information technology include the ability of users to maintain privacy while completing transactions on a network, as well as users' ability to keep the data they provide from identifying them personally. In researching anonymizing networks, Dingledine and Mathewson (2005) conclude that in order for users to be able to preserve their privacy on networks by completing transactions without revealing communication partners, it is critical that the system chosen is usable so that other users can successfully employ the system as well. Anonymizing networks are successful at hiding users among other users. An eavesdropper may be able to determine who is using the network, but cannot identify who completes a particular transaction. Moreover, the larger the group of users on the network, the more anonymous the participants become. The catchphrase in this area is "anonymity loves company" (Reiter & Rubin 1998).

Sweeney (2002) and Malin and Sweeney (2004) have demonstrated that minimal amounts of information believed to be anonymous can be used to personally identify an individual. Since data are aggregated from a myriad of databases in the networked world in which we live, users may falsely believe that they can remain anonymous by providing only minimal bits of information in transactions here and there over time. When the data are aggregated, though, the person can be identified fairly easily based on three minimal pieces of information. Users may not think about the types of data from different sources that might be combined and analyzed in order to identify them, and thus there is a false sense of privacy. This research also makes it clear that there is a gray area in terms of what data elements might be labeled as personal information versus personally identifying information, depending on the other data available in context.

Personalization

Karat, Karat, and Brodie (2004) state that the user experience will be different as the systems with which users interact become aware of the context of the interaction. Personalizing interaction involves the use of information about the user to alter the content presented to provide value to the user. In their empirical studies, Karat et al. (2004) found that the most critical element in the willingness of users to adopt and use personalization systems was user control of personal data. Users want to be in control of their privacy and appreciate the benefits of personalization when they have control over the use of their personal data.

Cranor (2004) complements this line of research with an analysis of privacy risks associated with personalization, and presents a set of design guidelines to reduce privacy risks in personalization systems. Teltzrow and Kobsa (2004) completed a meta-analysis of 30 consumer studies of user privacy preferences regarding personalization systems and found that consumer demands and current practice diverge significantly regarding control of personal information. The vast majority of businesses neither allow control over what information is stored nor provide the ability to access it for verification, correction, or updates.

End-User Views of Privacy

Researchers have conducted many studies on end-user preferences regarding privacy on the Web and the HCI factors that are necessary to satisfy the user's desire for privacy. Jensen and Potts (2004) found that while most surveys of user concerns about privacy show high rates of behaviors such as reading the privacy policy or taking concrete actions to protect their privacy, informal analysis of log-file data suggests that the actual rates of these user behaviors are much lower. Jensen, Potts, and Jensen (2005) found that users place inappropriate trust in the presence of trust indicators such as the TRUSTe mark or a privacy policy on the site, assuming quality in the presence of these trust indicators rather than understanding that the level of their trust should be dependent on the content of these policies. The users in their study were willing to divulge personal information when it was not warranted. Jensen et al. (2005) recommend that HCI professionals work to increase awareness of the relationship between privacy and policy issues associated with the trust indicators, since unscrupulous online vendors could use the trust indicators to mislead users to accept privacy policies and divulge private information that they would otherwise not willingly do. Buffett, Scott, Spencer, et al. (2004) have created a technique for enabling a user to compute the value of the consequences of exchanging personal information on the Web. The paper provides a demonstration of the effectiveness of the technique in improving a user's expected value in a simple privacy negotiation.

Privacy Policies

Cranor (2005) leads the W3C standardization work in the area of the Platform for Privacy Preferences (P3P) policies. P3P policies provide end users with information about the privacy policies of a Web site before they interact with it. Dr. Cranor and a team at ATandT Labs designed and developed the Privacy Bird (Cranor 2002), a browser help object, that provides summary information about the agreement or lack thereof between the end user's stated privacy preferences and the privacy policy of the Web site with which the person is considering interacting. Research continues to improve the usability of the Privacy Bird in communicating to users about Web-site privacy policies and in capturing user privacy preferences. At the present time, it is not possible to verify that organizations are operating according to their stated P3P policies. An important area for future research is the challenge of linking the P3P policy to the internal operational privacy policies and their implementation in organizations, and then enabling compliance audits of policy execution.

15.4   Protecting Privacy

15.4.1 *Diving In*

This section covers a more in-depth discussion of the views and requirements of
end users within organizations who are responsible for managing the personal
data collected, used, and stored by organizations. Here we cross the boundary
from management of personal information on pervasive devices to our rights
and responsibilities in determining how the personal information we have shared
with the organizations we interact with in our daily lives is used and protected.

15.4.2 *Organizational Requirements in Managing Privacy*

Research that is underway and focused on the organizational view of privacy
includes the Server Privacy ARchitecture and CapabiLity Enablement (SPARCLE)
Policy Workbench (Karat, Karat, Brodie & Feng 2005a). The researchers employed
user-centered design methods with 109 target users to identify organizational
privacy requirements, and then designed and tested a prototype system for
users to author privacy policies, implement the policies, and conduct compliance
audits of them. The initial prototype was a Wizard-of-Oz version of a system,
meaning that users were able to have an immersive and dynamic experience
with the system capability that seemed real, although the code behind the
screens was not fully functional. Empirical results showed that organizational
users highly valued a set of capabilities that enabled policy officers to use natural
language to author the policies, with the option of beginning with a template.
Users found a visualization of the policies very valuable for communication,
review, and also for identifying necessary modifications to rules and reaching
consensus on policies across the organization. The implementation capability
enabled the experts to approve the nominated mappings between rule elements
and database fields and applications in the organization's configuration. The
compliance audit capability enabled the users to run general audits to verify that
the policy was complying with regulations and was being enforced operationally
as stated in the policy, and to run specific inquiries based on individual requests
for information about use of personal information by the organization. The
organizational users who were the participants in the evaluation study rated the
prototyped functionality as being of very high value to them.

Karat, Karat, Brodie, and Feng (2006) conducted an empirical study to
determine whether the two methods of authoring rules that were prototyped
by Karat, Karat, Brodie, and Feng (2005b) (natural language with a guide, or
structured list) enabled users to create higher-quality rules than an unguided

natural language control method (using a word-processing window). Empirical results demonstrated that both prototyped authoring methods yielded higher-quality rules than the control condition. Users, with no training in use of the methods, were able to author privacy rules covering about 80 percent of the required rule elements described in scenarios when using either the natural language with a privacy rule guide tool or a structured list tool, as compared to covering about 40 percent of the required elements in scenarios using the unguided natural language control condition.

Research and development on the SPARCLE Policy Workbench is continuing. The general rule-authoring utility for the privacy domain is functional, working code that has been successfully tested with the privacy policies of banking/ finance, health care, and government organizations (Brodie, Karat & Karat 2006). Users can create new policies with SPARCLE, can import existing text versions of policies, or cut-and-paste sections of policies to form a new policy. Then SPARCLE employs natural language processing technology to parse and identify the rule elements. Users review and modify the rules, and when they are happy with the policy, the policy is transformed into XACML code (the OASIS international standard for the format of security access control rules with a privacy profile; see OASIS [2004]) for input to the enforcement engine. The team is continuing to design and create other components in the end-to-end solution for privacy, and believes that the Policy Workbench can be generalized to the security domain and possibly others.

15.5 Looking Forward: A Call to Action

The body of research that can inform the design of usable privacy mechanisms is growing (see Table 15.5). The central theme that emerges is informed user control over the disclosure of personal information. The study of PIM will be enriched by considering privacy more fully, and this research will cross-pollinate in several areas.

For example, cross-cultural studies of privacy can inform the growing interest in cross-cultural interfaces and coordination. Also, increased understanding of the diversity and complexity of user preferences and potential clustering of variables of interest are providing new impetus for research on individual differences. Further-more, considerations of visualizations and intelligent tutoring systems for privacy in a range of applications and tasks could germinate new emphases on usability.

Privacy in information technology ranges from the effective management of your personal information on your own pervasive devices to the use of your personal information by an organization's employees and business processes

Table 15.5 – Design Factors impacting usable privacy solutions

Networked World
• There is technology and data collection in most aspects of everyday life in the developed world.
Privacy Legislation
• Requirements for privacy vary by geography and across cultures. Organizations and end users must become knowledgeable.
Individual Differences
• People perceive and define privacy intrusions differently, and privacy solutions must be designed to support varying definitions and choices.
End User Desire for Anonymity
• End users must be informed of the risks of choices involved in different anonymity-enabling situations.
End User Desire for Personalization
• User control of data to be disclosed is critical for using personalization.
Platform for Privacy Preferences (P3P)
• Can inform user of any issues between their own policy and policy of a Website they are considering interacting with.
• No verification of adherence to policy possible at this time.
Organizational Management of Privacy: Requirements, Approaches, Perspective
• Authors of privacy policies, who have the knowledge of organizational practices, must be able to tie written policies to implementation through technology, with verification through compliance audits.

and storage of it in their systems. Privacy is likely to remain a critical issue for the foreseeable future.

We see privacy as a complex social issue concerned with individuals' rights to know what information is collected about them and how it might be used. Privacy of information held in information systems depends on security—the ability to protect a system's resources from harmful attack or unauthorized access, and the perception that privacy and security are provided is necessary for users to trust systems and make good decisions regarding the use and sharing of their personal information.

Usability has been identified as a major challenge to moving the results of security and privacy research into use in real systems (CRA 2003). Communication and collaboration is occurring between people who have expertise in one or more of these domain areas, and this emerging community is beginning to work together to incorporate usability in the design and development of effective privacy and security solutions. The emerging community needs many skilled professionals with varied experience and interests to join the cause of creating usable and trusted privacy and security solutions for end users and organizations worldwide. We invite participation in this effort by all who are interested in helping to design and build a world in which we would all like to live.

16 Privacy and Public Records

Michael Shamos

Much of the concern about data privacy centers on the surreptitious collection and sale of personal information outside the view or control of the data subject. Even if such dealings are prohibited by law, they are difficult or impossible to prevent because by its very nature the activity remains hidden. It is a transgression of an entirely different character when government itself at all levels voluntarily becomes complicit in the massive disclosure of data about its citizens. When public records are made available on a grand scale through free, publicly available Internet databases, we are forced to reconsider the very notion of what a public record is or ought to be.

To grasp the problem in a concrete way, please visit http://www2.county. allegheny.pa.us/RealEstate/Search.asp. This is a Web site maintained legally and officially by the government of Allegheny County, Pennsylvania, which paid more than $20 million to create it. Allegheny is the county in which I reside and own a house. Near the bottom of the Web page is a search box labeled "Owner's Name." Enter the name Shamos and click the "Search" button directly below the box. You will be presented with an array of information about me and my house. You'll learn my wife's name, how much we paid for the house, its assessed value, how many bathrooms it has, that we have central heating and air conditioning, how much we pay in real estate taxes, whether we were ever delinquent in paying, how much we were assessed in penalties, and a lot more data you didn't imagine the county even knew. You will also be treated to a photo of my house and its floor plan. Many people are horrified when they see how much is disclosed.

Here's the crux of the problem: there are very important and legitimate reasons for all of the above information about me to be publicly available. In general, records are designated as public to achieve some policy purpose. In this case, it has to do with the fairness of property assessments. Each homeowner needs to be able to verify that his assessment is equitable. The only way he can do that is to obtain data about nearby properties and learn their assessed values. For this reason, the decision has been made to allow the records to be viewed by the general public.

There's a rub, however. In the days before the Internet, the records were still public but difficult to access. They were stored in the county office building and a personal visit was required to see them. There was often a charge for copying, and the fact that physical files and binders had to be handled and the time needed to do that set a natural bound on the amount of effort, and the cost, that could be expended. When the very same records are digitized and made available with powerful search engines, the cost and pain of access dwindles to nearly nothing.

There are a multitude of unintended uses that can be made of the property database, ranging from the innocuous to the frightening. Of course the records have tremendous value for marketing purposes. Every home that has central heating or air conditioning is listed as such, and any company that provides services for such systems now has a free mailing list. It is the easiest chore to spider the entire property database and obtain your own copy of it. The set of people who have neither air conditioning nor heating has suddenly become a target for people selling those items, some legitimate, some not.

Are you interested in the complete set of properties your competitor owns so you can preview his expansion plans? The database will be happy to tell you. Planning a crime? The photos and floor plans will enable you to avoid casing the house, which might attract undue attention. Do you have some need for a complete list of the residents on a particular street, neatly sorted by house number? That's easy. Just type in the street name and you'll get more than you need. Might it be embarrassing which of your neighbors is delinquent in paying property taxes? The "tax information" tab will provide as much blackmail material as you could want.

When viewed in this light, the property database seems to be a huge intrusion into the private lives of land owners. There is no comparable resource that lists apartment renters, so the situation seems asymmetric. If you want to keep your data away from the public, don't buy any property. Yet it is difficult to argue that any single field of data ought to be kept from the citizen who has a legitimate question about the fairness of assessments. We will argue later that the source of the trouble is not the existence of the database, but the ability of anyone in the world to use for purposes *other* than checking the fairness of assessments.

The database has had unintended consequences, a common phenomenon that infects technological innovations. It has altered the social fabric of Pittsburgh to some degree. After meeting someone at a cocktail party, it is now commonplace to go to the Web, find out whether they are married, learn how valuable their house is, and view a picture of it. This is the sort of information that was not readily available previously. One may argue that it keeps people honest, knowing that if they lie about such things they will be found out in short order. But suppose they wish to keep mum? That is no longer a viable alternative.

The Allegheny County assessment database is just a small example of the sort of information published on the Internet. To see the magnitude of the issue, please visit www.searchsystems.net, a Web site that lists legal public records depositories available on the Web. As of the beginning of February 2006, it contained links to over 39,000 such databases. They range from the innocuous (such as lists of certified public accountants) to the highly controversial (sexual predator databases). They vary from the surprising (data on prisoners released from incarceration in Florida) to the simply macabre (last meals served to executed murderers in Texas). What is striking is the breadth and scope of information available, from which it is possible, through automated means, to develop whole dossiers on individuals, built purely by using data legitimately obtained.

Each individual fact about every person listed in any of these sources has been determined by a government authority to be a public record. Therefore, as a matter of policy the subject has by law lost the ability to conceal the data or control its dissemination and use. A thief who wants to steal guns in Florida can look up licensed gun owners in any part of the state and then, through a different database, find an aerial photograph of the owner's house and details of his property. Clearly this information is invaluable in planning crimes, a result surely not intended by the Florida officials who decided to build these databases and release them for public use.

How, then, can we ensure that databases are only used for their intended purposes and not others? Even if there were a way to do so, the problem would not be solved, though it might be alleviated to some degree. The reason is that all sorts of "public" information can be accumulated legally without ever accessing these official databases. Let us distinguish "public record" from "public information." A *public record* is data maintained by a government agency that, by policy, is made available to members of the public. *Public information* is information that may be obtained lawfully by all persons, with or without the help of the government. Whether a record is public or not is determined by duly authorized officials. The decision can be changed by executive or legislative action. Whether information is public is not so constrained.

Generally, all "public records" are "public information," but the latter class is much broader. It includes, for example, anything that a person sees on the street. Thus, if I see you walk into the Main Street Bank at 12:32 p.m. on Friday and walk out again at 12:54, that fact is public information. You have no legal right to prevent anyone from noticing the fact, writing it down, putting it in a database, or publishing it on a Web site. (We exclude from this discussion activities that could be considered threatening or stalking. I can't legitimately learn the fact that you were at Main Street Bank, for example, by following you around all day at a distance of three feet.) Suppose I am able to watch John Doe from a considerable distance, and only when I am in a public place and he is also. I can't follow him into his house, or go into the bathroom with him, or invade his office. But I can stay at a discrete distance and key into my PDA a brief description of where he is every five minutes throughout a 24-hour period. Logically, we must agree that each single individual fact about his whereabouts while he is observable from a public place must constitute public information. He has no capability to shield himself from view while in public.

Suppose now that my PDA is wireless and I create a publicly accessible John Doe Web site to which his location is uploaded every five minutes for the rest of his life. That is, at any time anyone in the world can tell not only where Doe is now but where he was at all times in the past. Most Americans would consider such a Web site to be a gross violation of Doe's "privacy." Indeed, when I conduct such a poll in my privacy lectures, almost all Americans indicate just that. The results are quite different for audiences in different countries. I have never seen a Chinese class in which even half of the people felt there would be anything at all wrong about such a Web site. Even the Americans, when pressed, are unable to articulate any ethical or legal reason that such a site could not be operated. And they all agree that Doe has no privacy interest in any of the individual facts listed on the Web site. Why should he be concerned if people know he visited the library at 2:32 p.m. on March 23?

He might not be worried about that, but by being observed constantly he has lost an important facet of privacy that he thought he had. When Doe engages in an act on the public street, he has the opportunity to inspect his surroundings to see whether anyone is watching. If not, he may do things that he would never consider doing while being observed. If he is spied upon surreptitiously, he has given up the ability to make this choice. He certainly expects to be able to tell whether anyone who knows him is watching, and he may make decisions based upon assumed anonymity. The Doe Web site forfeits his anonymity without his permission, yet under U.S. law he has no right to anonymity while in public.

There are two major problems with the Doe database. The first is in moving from the individual facts to a comprehensive collection (and then storing the collection for the subject's lifetime and beyond). The second is in making the collection freely available at essentially no cost to anyone and everyone, including anonymous and possibly malevolent users. There is a feeling, difficult to make precise, that at some point the database of Doe location data is just too intrusive to be acceptable. However, having just two lines of data would be innocuous. So where is the boundary beyond which the aggregation becomes objectionable?

To understand where the line might be drawn, consider how public records were accessed before the Internet. Generally they were maintained as paper files or bound volumes that could be examined by members of the public. To do that, they would have to go to the county hall of records, park, make a personal visit to the appropriate office, learn how to use the record indexes, locate the records they wanted, and pay to have copies made—if copying were even permissible. The time, effort and money expended acted as a natural limit on the volume of access by any individual.

At least it limited those who lacked resources. A single person could never accumulate a county-wide property database, for lack of both time and money. However, a corporation intent on selling the data could easily afford to station a representative at the county office building to make a copy of any new data that was recorded, and indeed companies did so and made the databases available online, but for a fee. Someone intent on building a dossier would still have to incur charges to do so and spend time searching through large numbers of databases. Nevertheless, hunting while sitting at one's own computer is vastly more efficient than making physical visits to government offices. The aggregation therefore permits not only the assembling of large amounts of data on one individual, but also allows invasion of many different lives all from the convenience of a desk chair.

What answer might there be? The European approach is to require registration and regulation of data gatherers, known as *data controllers* in EU parlance. Under a rather strict regimen, data controllers are highly constrained in taking data directly from subjects themselves. The controller must inform the subject of the purpose for which the information is being collected and will be used, must obtain the subject's permission, and cannot pass the information on to any party that has not also agreed to the same conditions. The penalty for violation of these provisions is to be stricken from the register of authorized data controllers, essentially making it impossible to remain in business. Thus, the privacy commissioner, who maintains the register, has substantial enforcement power.

Such a structure is unlikely to be adopted in the United States, where data is considered to be a commodity readily available for sale. Various state governments have enacted a variety of sunshine and freedom of information laws that require the governments to make data public. And neither the U.S. structure nor the European one prevents creation of the Doe database. Even in the EU, if data is to be collected on a subject from sources other than the subject himself, it is only necessary to inform the subject in advance that data is going to be gathered and to identify the gatherer. In the U.S., of course, no notice at all is required.

One approach that deserves further exploration is to arm the subject with a right to learn not only who is collecting data, but who is accessing it—the same sort of protection a person has in a public place, namely the ability to observe who is in the vicinity.

Suppose anyone collecting data on a subject were required not only to notify the subject and give him access to, and the ability to correct, the database, but also—and this is the key to symmetry—notify the user each time any data about him was accessed and identify the party who made the access. The "notification" can be nonintrusive; for example, the subject may be allowed to visit a Web site or perform a query to retrieve the promised information. It is not necessary to interrupt him constantly throughout the day every time he has been the target of an access.

A completely different approach is to restore the natural dampening role that cost played in traditional paper-based systems. If there were a mandatory cost to accessing personal information, its incidence would certainly decline. To avoid making public databases too expensive to examine, each citizen could be given a quota of free accesses each year at a level deemed sufficient to promote open-access policies but not to foster large-scale invasions of privacy. A similar proposal has been made to reduce the volume of spam emails. If a small charge akin to postage were made for every email, individual senders would suffer very little, but bulk spammers, who may send millions of messages at a time, would find the cost prohibitive. And so it would be for information access.

A third possibility is to restrict the use of public records to the purposes for which they are being maintained. If the reason for keeping a property ownership database is to allow verification of the fairness of assessments and confirmation of the chain of title to land, then using the database for those purposes ought to be free or so inexpensive that the rights of the public are not crippled. Other uses, such as marketing air-conditioning services to those unlucky enough to live in a county having an extensive home database, could be made expensive or even prohibited altogether. Whether a particular use is permissible or not can be determined by a simple administrative procedure with an associated appeals process of the usual kind.

The problem of tracking onward transfers of information remains, however. Suppose the data gatherer passes data about you to another party, and properly informs you of the transfer. If the transferee is outside the jurisdiction of the legal system, then you will not expect to see any further reports on the movement of your data. A way to diminish this possibility is to make it illegal to furnish data to a party that has not agreed to follow the same set of regulations, a policy similar to the EU approach. If there is a violation and you learn of it, presumably a remedy could be fashioned against the transferor.

The cost of Internet access and especially the cost of digital storage continues to decline precipitously. The retail cost of a gigabyte of disk in 2006 is under $0.50 in small quantities, and much cheaper in bulk. It is estimated that this cost will be under $0.02 in 2010. This means that $1,000 will be able to buy 50 terabytes of disk, enough to store 200K bytes of information on every person in the United States. It is obvious that, if the present trends continue unchecked, the desire and ability to accumulate vast amounts of personal information, once only the domain of large corporations, will drop easily into the hands of ordinary citizens. Long before that happens we need to face the potential consequences.

17 Conclusion

William Jones and Jaime Teevan

The chapters of this book tell a story of personal information management in both present and future tense. Chapters in Part I, "Understanding Personal Information Management," provide a composite view of the daily activities most of us must perform in order to manage, as best we can, in our information-saturated worlds.

People find information. In a typical day, people may seek information to meet many different kinds of needs, large and small. Sometimes the focus is on finding information to match a big need with fuzzy, undefined edges—perhaps through search on the Web, a visit to a local library, or access to some special-purpose database. In many other instances, finding is so routine, so mundane, as to occur almost without awareness. People find a phone number and call with the punch of a button or two on their mobile phones. People find and copy the display name from an email address and paste it into a greeting in order to be sure of its proper spelling. Often people re-find and re-access information they have already seen and used earlier. But even when people find new information they have never seen before, they do so prompted by and guided by the fabric of personal information they already have. For example, even as Alex seeks out directions he has never seen before to a restaurant he has never been to before, he does so as prompted by an email message from his sister or an appointment displayed in his calendar. Moreover, large parts of his path to these directions—such as the means of accessing an online mapping and directional service—may be well-trod and familiar.

People also keep information. In a typical day, information comes from many sources in many forms. An announcement of a bridge closure is heard from the radio on the way to work. Later, people stop by or talk around the proverbial water cooler about an impending reorganization. The phone rings. Email arrives in the inbox. A visit to the Web invariably leads to far more information than can be processed immediately. In all these cases and more, basic decisions must be made concerning the relationship of incoming information to personal need—both current and anticipated. What is this information anyway? Is it or might it be useful or important? Is immediate action required or can the information be considered again later? Are special actions required in order to insure that the information will be remembered and can be accessed again—re-found—later on? If so, what are these actions?

Finding and keeping, then, work in opposite and complementary directions. Finding activities take us from a current need to information; keeping activities take us from information at hand to a consideration of needs for which the information may relate. A good deal of a typical day is consumed in activities of finding and keeping—large and small. But frequency and immediacy do not equal importance. Other, *meta-level activities* of PIM, which focus more squarely on the overall mapping between information and need, can potentially have a far greater and longer-lasting impact on a person's practice of PIM.

Several senses of "meta" apply to a discussion of meta-level activities. Meta-level activities are "about" or apply "above" a collection of personal information as a whole. People may organize their email messages in an email account, for example, or the photographs taken during a summer vacation. Larger, collection-level questions must also be considered when deciding how best to maintain information over the long run. How should the information be kept? On what storage devices? In what formats?

Meta-level activities are important in the long run but are rarely urgent. Finding and keeping activities are constantly prompted by events in a typical day. We have a need and must find information to meet this need. We encounter information and must decide what do with it. Few events can similarly force us to consider the overall organization of a collection or its long-term maintenance. In this sense, meta-level activities are done "after" the events of a typical day—which is to say not at all or not frequently enough.

One problem looms across keeping, finding and meta-level activities and is often made worse by the very tools that are designed to help with these activities. This is the problem of *information fragmentation*. The information required to complete even a simple task, such as deciding whether to accept a dinner invitation for next Thursday, is often scattered in several forms, in several locations, on several devices, and in several different organizations. A Web page contains information concerning a conference that may conflict. Another commitment for Thursday may have been made in a previous email exchange. Calendars must be consulted—not just one digital calendar but perhaps several, and then also the shared paper calendar that hangs on the wall next to the refrigerator at home. Paper documents too—yet another form of information—must be consulted. A printed schedule of school events may indicate that a school play involving a daughter, son, or other loved one will also happen Thursday evening.

Information fragmentation creates different problems for different PIM activities:

- **Finding and re-finding.** Chapter 2 analyzes finding problems that can arise when information is scattered across devices, accounts, and applications. Where to look? On which device? Organized by which application? People may sometimes look in several places before finding a desired item of information. Worse, people may forget to look in the first place or forget about the information altogether until it's too late to be used. Problems of forgetting occur more frequently when information is fragmented for the simple reason that a person's attention may be similarly fragmented. Information that is literally out of sight may also be out of mind.

- **Keeping.** Chapter 3 analyzes the multifaceted nature of the decisions people face when deciding to keep information. Where does the information go? In what form? On what device? Or is it already "in here" somewhere?

- **Organizing and maintaining.** As analyzed in chapters 3 and 4, information fragmentation frequently forces the separate organization and maintenance of several distinct information collections. Email, e-documents, paper documents, and Web references each come with their own separate tools and techniques for organization and maintenance. Challenges of organization and maintenance are further multiplied if a person works on several computers, uses a PDA or full-featured cell phone, has several email accounts, or works in several different physical locations.

Information has long been fragmented by physical location. But just as online access to digital information begins to reduce a reliance on paper in physical locations, people must contend with a new, potentially even more vexing fragmentation of information by device, tool, and application.

17.1 Solutions for Personal Information Management

Just as information fragmentation is a dominant problem in activities of PIM, several seemingly divergent proposed solutions to PIM share in common an attempt to unify personal information—to bring the pieces back together again—in ways that make sense for people.

■ **Save everything.** Chapter 6 describes efforts to build a personal digital store that might record and interrelate the events in a person's life including sights and sounds, information items encountered, and even measures of a person's heart rate and body temperature. Such a recording has the potential to weave together not only external information items but also a person's memories where these might otherwise lie "scattered" and irretrievable for want of connecting associations.

■ **Search everything.** Once upon a time, there was no Web-wide searching and people navigated instead to information via hyperlinks and hotlists. While these methods are still used, keyword-based search has become an essential method for bringing together information relating to a topic that lies scattered across the vast reaches of the Web. Search technologies, as described in chapter 9, also have a potential to bring together topic- or task-related information that lies scattered across a personal space of information.

■ **Structure everything.** Not all information that might belong together (e.g., for the current task) can necessarily be brought together through keyword search alone. Chapter 7 describes efforts to complement search through the application of database management techniques that impose additional structure on collections of personal information. Some structure may be essential, for example, to insure that the corrected, current version of information is retrieved.

■ **Unify everything.** Chapter 8 reviews the many different levels at and ways in which information can be unified. Key kinds of unification happen already and can easily escape our notice. The file system, for example, or the ability to display multiple windows on a computer screen, each provides important kinds of unification. Chapter 8 concludes with a look at the potential advantages of a unification afforded by the uniform application of RDF for the representation of information.

■ **Everything through email.** Email is increasingly used by people as a means of unification. Chapter 10 notes the role that email serves as an "information conduit—acting as a delivery channel for different types of information, including documents, slides, contact information, and schedules." People use email in a variety of ways that go beyond simple communication with others to include the conveyance of information for personal use at different locations (e.g., home and work), the use of email to remind and to manage tasks, and even the use of email for the versioning and archival of documents. It's no surprise, then, that our email systems are seriously overloaded. Chapter 10 explores the challenges that must be met for people not to feel overwhelmed by their email in its many uses.

17.2 Looking Forward: Important Challenges for Personal Information

In our efforts to better understand and better support personal information management, we face many challenges:

▪ **Privacy protection.** We seek to manage not only the information we control directly (e.g., the information on our hard drives and email accounts), but also information about us that others can easily acquire or may have already. As explored in chapter 16, the ease and cheapness with which personal information can be recorded, saved, and transmitted in digital form creates new problems of privacy protection that did not exist, or were much less severe, when information was kept in paper form only. Chapter 15 notes that better privacy protection is not just a matter of better laws or improved technologies of security. Better privacy protection also depends upon user interfaces that more clearly communicate to people the implications of their privacy preferences and of the privacy policies advertised by organizations with which they interact.

▪ **Managing the transitions between personal and group information.** The study of PIM cannot succeed by considering a person in isolation from the various groups in which a person works and lives. Chapter 14 explores the interrelation and overlap between management of information by an individual and management of information within a group. Concerns of privacy in any group setting are matched by the mutual benefits that arise from the exchange and collaborative management of information.

▪ **Variations by group and circumstance.** Chapter 13 notes that "the payoffs for personal information management (PIM) may be especially large in targeted domains such as health care." Management of personal health information becomes especially important for people facing a serious, potentially life-threatening illness. Applications of PIM may also need to vary in substantial ways to reflect age and other demographics for targeted groups. How can PIM be applied, for example, in support of an aging workforce and population?

■ **Methodologies for the study of PIM and the evaluation of PIM tools.** The development of methodologies especially suited to PIM is still in its infancy. There is a need both for methodologies in *descriptive* studies aimed at better understanding how people currently practice personal information management, and for *prescriptive* evaluations to understand better the efficacy of proposed PIM solutions (usually involving a tool but sometimes focused, instead, on a technique or strategy). Methodologies to facilitate our understanding of how people do PIM and the problems they encounter are explored in chapter 5. Methodologies for the evaluation of PIM tools (and techniques) are discussed in chapter 11. Both chapters note the importance of studying people and their use of PIM tools in situ, in their everyday situations where they are interacting with their own information, over time and with minimal disruption. Can this be done within the limits set by the willingness of people to participate and the resources of a typical research project? Even as we meet these challenges, we need to consider the tremendous diversity in the way people do PIM as explored in chapter 12. Results obtained from the study of one person may diverge widely from those obtained from the study of another.

As we study and strive to improve PIM, we must never lose sight of the "personal" in personal information management. We, as individuals, don't manage information for its own sake. Information is a means to an end—whether the end is a completion of a well-defined task or something less well understood and harder to articulate ("just because I like looking at it" or "I like knowing it's there"). The special nature of the personal in our relation to information is nicely, albeit incompletely, expressed in the following quote:

> There's a fundamental difference between searching a universe of documents created by strangers and searching your own personal library. When you're freewheeling through ideas that you yourself have collated . . . there's something about the experience that seems uncannily like freewheeling through the corridors of your own memory. It feels like thinking. (Johnson 2005, p. 27)

Many of us probably share the experience described in this quote and understand that the ways of accessing and interacting with personal information are fundamentally different from the ways of accessing and interacting with information publicly available (through a library or the Web, for example). What is less common—much as we might yearn for it—is the experience that personal collections of email messages, Web references, files, paper documents, handwritten notes, and so on, are a natural extension to memory, or that working with these collections of personal information is like thinking. We have even less reason to be confident that information about us—as kept and distributed by others—is being used in ways that benefit or reflect well upon us. Personal information management owes its existence to a belief that we can—we must—do better.

Acknowledgments

We would like to acknowledge and thank a number of people for their help in putting this book together:

- Nick Belkin and two anonymous reviewers provided extremely helpful suggestions on the earlier drafts of the entire book.
- Andrea Lisabeth Civan, Alan Dix, Susan Dumais, Doug Gage, Diane Kelly, David Maier, Catherine Plaisant, and Daniel Solove gave us very helpful feedback on selected chapters in the book.
- Cheyenne Maria Roduin, Beth Fournier, and Glenda Claborne offered invaluable assistance in reviewing earlier drafts of the book for correctness and completeness.

Bibliography

Abrams, D., R. Baecker, and M. Chignell. 1998. Information archiving with bookmarks: Personal Web space construction and organization. In *Proceedings of the SIGCHI Conference on Human Factors in Computing Systems*, pp. 41–48. New York: ACM Press.

Abu-Hakima, S., C. McFarland, and J. F. Meech. 2001. An agent-based system for email highlighting. In *Proceedings of the Fifth International Conference on Autonomous Agents*, pp. 224–25. New York: ACM Press.

Ackerman, M. S. 1998. Augmenting organizational memory: A field study of Answer Garden. *ACM Transactions on Information Systems* 16(3):203–24.

Ackerman, M. S. 2000a. Developing for privacy: Civility frameworks and technical design. In *Proceedings of the Tenth Conference on Computers, Freedom, and Privacy: Challenging the assumptions*, pp. 19–23. New York: ACM Press.

Ackerman, M. S. 2000b. The intellectual challenge of CSCW: The gap between social requirements and technical feasibility. *Human-Computer Interaction* 15(2–3):179–204.

Ackerman, M. S., L. F. Cranor, and J. Reagle. 1999. Privacy in e-commerce: Examining user scenarios and privacy preferences. In *Proceedings of the 1st ACM Conference on Electronic Commerce*, pp. 1–8. New York: ACM Press.

Ackerman, M. S., and C. A. Halverson. 2004. Organizational memory as objects, processes, and trajectories: An examination of organizational memory in use. *Journal of Computer Supported Cooperative Work* 13(2):155–90.

Adar, E., D. Karger, and L. A. Stein. 1999. Haystack: Per-user information environments. In *Proceedings of the Eighth International Conference on Information and Knowledge Management*, pp. 413–22. New York: ACM Press.

Adler, P. A., and P. Adler, eds. 1994. *Observational techniques*. Thousand Oaks, CA: Sage.

Allan, J. 2006. HARD Track overview in TREC 2005 high accuracy retrieval from documents. In E. M. Voorhees and L. P. Buckland, eds., *The Fourteenth Text REtrieval Conference Proceedings (TREC 2005)*, pp. 1–17. National Institute of Standards and Technology.

Allen, B. L. 2001. Boolean browsing in an information system: An experimental test. *Information Technology and Libraries* 20(1):12–20.

Altman, I. 1975. *The environment and social behavior: Privacy, personal space, territory, and crowding.* Monterey, CA: Brooks/Cole Publishing.

Amento, B., L. Terveen, W. Hill, D. Hix, and R. Schulman. 2003. Experiments in social data mining: The TopicShop system. *ACM Transactions on Computer-Human Interaction (TOCHI)* 10(1):54–85.

Anderson, C. R., and E. Horvitz. 2002. Web montage: A dynamic personalized start page. In *Proceedings of the 11th International Conference on World Wide Web*, pp. 704–12. New York: ACM Press.

Anderson, J. R. 1990a. *The adaptive character of thought.* Hillsdale, NJ: Lawrence Erlbaum Associates.

Anderson, J. R. 1990b. *Cognitive psychology and its implications.* New York: W. H. Freeman.

AOL. 2003. Available from http://www.aol.com/

Apache Software Foundation. 2006. Nutch. Retrieved May 15, 2006, from http://lucene.apache.org/nutch/

Apple Computer Inc. 2006. Spotlight: Find anything, anywhere, fast. Retrieved April 15, 2006, from http://www.apple.com/macosx/features/spotlight/

Arms, C. 2000. Keeping memory alive: Practices for preserving digital content at the National Digital Library Program of the Library of Congress. *RLG DigiNews* 4(3). Available at http://www.rlg.org/preserv/diginews/diginews4-3.html#feature1

Arms, C., and C. Fleischhauer. 2005. Digital formats: Factors for sustainability, functionality, and quality. In *Proceedings of IS&T's Archiving 2005 Conference*, pp. 222–27. Springfield, VA: Society for Imaging Science and Technology.

Baker, N. 2001. *Double fold: Libraries and the assault on paper.* New York: Random House.

Bakshi, K., and D. Karger. 2005. End-user application development for the semantic Web. *Proceedings of the ISWC 2005 Workshop on the Semantic Desktop: Next Generation Information Management & Collaboration Infrastructure* 175. Available from http://sunsite.informatik.rwth-aachen.de/Publications/CEUR-WS/Vol-175/36_bakshi_endusersemdesk_final.pdf

Ball, E. 2003. Patient privacy in electronic prescription transfer. *IEEE Security and Privacy* 1(2):77–80.

Bälter, O. 1997. Strategies for organising email. In *Proceedings of the Twelfth Conference of the British Computer Society Human Computer Interaction Specialist Group—People and Computers XII*, ed. H. Thimbleby, B. O'Connail, and P. J. Thomas, vol. 12, pp. 21–38. Bristol, UK: Springer.

Bälter, O. 1998. *Electronic mail in a working context.* Doctoral dissertation (TRITA-NA-9820), Royal Institute of Technology, Stockholm, Sweden.

Bälter, O. 2000. Keystroke level analysis of email message organization. In *Proceedings of the SIGCHI Conference on Human Factors in Computing Systems*, pp. 105–12. New York: ACM Press.

Bälter, O., and C. L. Sidner. 2002. Bifrost inbox organizer: Giving users control over the inbox. In *Proceedings of the Second Nordic Conference on Human-Computer Interaction*, pp. 111–18. New York: ACM Press.

Bannon, L., and S. Bødker. 1997. Constructing common information spaces. In *Proceedings of the European Conference on Computer Supported Cooperative Work*, pp. 81–96. Dordrecht, The Netherlands: Kluwer Academic Publishers.

Barreau, D. K. 1995. Context as a factor in personal information management systems. *Journal of the American Society for Information Science* 46(5): 327–39.

Barreau, D. K., and B. Nardi. 1995. Finding and reminding: File organization from the desktop. *ACM SIGCHI Bulletin* 27(3):39–43.

Bates, M. J. 1989. The design of browsing and berrypicking techniques for the online search interface. *Online Review* 13(5):407–24.

Baumer, D., J. B. Earp, and F. C. Payton. 2000. Privacy in medical records: IT implications of HIPAA. *Computers and Society* 30(4):40–47.

Baumgartner, R., S. Flesca, and G. Gottlob. 2001. Supervised wrapper generation with Lixto. In *Proceedings of the 27th International Conference on Very Large Data Bases*, ed. P. M. Apers, P. Atzeni, S. Ceri, S. Paraboschi, K. Ramamohanarao, and R. T. Snodgrass, pp. 715–16. San Francisco, CA: Morgan Kaufmann.

Beagrie, N. 2003. *National digital preservation initiatives: An overview of developments in Australia, France, the Netherlands, and the United Kingdom and of related international activity.* Washington, DC: Council on Library and Information Resources.

Beagrie, N. 2005. Plenty of room at the bottom? Personal digital libraries and collections. *D-Lib Magazine* 11(6). Available at http://dx.doi.org/10.1045/june2005-beagrie

Bederson, B. 2004. Interfaces for staying in the flow. *Ubiquity* 5(27):1. Available from http://www.acm.org/ubiquity/views/v5i27_bederson.html

Bederson, B., and B. Shneiderman. 2003. *The craft of information visualization: Readings and reflections.* San Francisco, CA: Morgan Kaufmann.

Begole, J., J. C. Tang, and R. Hill. 2003. Rhythm modeling, visualizations and applications. In *Proceedings of the 16th Annual ACM Symposium on User Interface Software and Technology,* pp. 11–20. New York: ACM Press.

Belkin, N. J. 1980. Anomalous states of knowledge as a basis for information retrieval. *The Canadian Journal of Information Science* 5:133–43.

Belkin, N. J. 1993. Interaction with texts: Information retrieval as information-seeking behavior. In *Information retrieval '93. Von der Modellierung zur Anwendung,* ed. G. Knorz, J. Krause, and C. Womser-Hacker, pp. 55–66. Konstanz, Germany: Universitaetsverlag Konstanz.

Belkin, N. J., C. Cool, A. Stein, and U. Thiel. 1995. Cases, scripts and information-seeking strategies: On the design of interactive information retrieval systems. *Expert Systems with Applications* 9(3):379–95.

Belkin, N. J., P. G. Marchetti, and C. Cool. 1993. Braque: Design of an interface to support user interaction in information retrieval. *Information Processing and Management* 29(3):325–44.

Bell, G. 2001. A personal digital store. *Communications of the ACM* 44(1):86–91.

Bellotti, V. 1996. What you don't know can hurt you: Privacy in collaborative computing. In *Proceedings of HCI on People and Computers XI,* ed. M. A. Sasse, J. Cunningham, and R. L. Winder, pp. 241–61. London, UK: Springer-Verlag.

Bellotti, V., B. Dalal, N. Good, P. Flynn, D. G. Bobrow, and N. Ducheneaut. 2004. What a to-do: Studies of task management towards the design of a personal task list manager. In *Proceedings of the SIGCHI Conference on Human Factors in Computing Systems,* pp. 735–42. New York: ACM Press.

Bellotti, V., N. Ducheneaut, M. Howard, C. Neuwirth, and I. Smith. 2002. Innovation in extremis: Evolving an application for the critical work of email and information management. In *Proceedings of the Conference on Designing Interactive Systems: Processes, Practices, Methods, and Techniques,* pp. 181–92. New York: ACM Press.

Bellotti, V., N. Ducheneaut, M. Howard, and I. Smith. 2003. Taking email to task: The design and evaluation of a task management centered email tool. In *Proceedings of the SIGCHI Conference on Human Factors in Computing Systems,* pp. 345–52. New York: ACM Press.

Bellotti, V., N. Ducheneaut, M. Howard, I. Smith, and R. Grinter. 2005. Quality vs. quantity: Email-centric task-management and its relation with overload. *Human-Computer Interaction* 20(1–2):89–138.

Bellotti, V., and A. Sellen. 1993. Design for privacy in ubiquitous computing environments. In *Proceedings of the Third European Conference on Computer-Supported Cooperative Work, 13–17 September 1993, Milano, Italy*, ed. G. De Michelis, C. Simone, and K. Schmidt, pp. 77–92. Dordrecht, The Netherlands: Kluwer Academic Publishers.

Bentley, R., T. Horstmann, and J. Trevor. 1997. The World Wide Web as enabling technology for CSCW: The case of BSCW. *Computer Supported Cooperative Work* 6(2–3):111–34.

Berlin, L. M., R. Jeffries, V. L. O'Day, A. Paepcke, and C. Wharton. 1993. Where did you put it? Issues in the design and use of a group memory. In *Proceedings of the SIGCHI Conference on Human Factors in Computing Systems*, pp. 23–30. New York: ACM Press.

Berners-Lee, T., J. Hendler, and O. Lassila. 2001. The Semantic Web. *Scientific American* 284(5):35–43.

Bhavnani, S. K., and M. J. Bates. 2002. Separating the knowledge layers: Cognitive analysis of search knowledge through hierarchical goal decompositions. *Proceedings of the American Society for Information Science and Technology*, 39(1):204–13.

Boardman, R. 2002. Workspaces that work: Towards unified personal information management. In *Proceedings of the 16th British HCI Group Annual Conference, incorporating European Usability Professionals' Association Conference*. Vol. 2, pp. 216–17. London, UK: British HCI Group; see http://www.iis.ee.ic.ac.uk/~rick/research/pubs/wthatw-hci2002.pdf

Boardman, R. 2004. *Improving tool support for personal information management*. Doctoral dissertation, Imperial College, London.

Boardman, R., and M. A. Sasse. 2004. "Stuff goes into the computer and doesn't come out": A cross-tool study of personal information management. In *Proceedings of the SIGCHI Conference on Human Factors in Computing Systems*, pp. 583–90. New York: ACM Press.

Boone, G. 1998. Concept features in Re:Agent, an intelligent email agent. In *Proceedings of the Second International Conference on Autonomous Agents*, pp. 141–48. New York: ACM Press.

Borenstein, N. S. 1992. Computational mail as network infrastructure for computer-supported cooperative work. In *Proceedings of the 1992 ACM Conference on Computer-Supported Cooperative*, pp. 67–74. New York: ACM Press.

Borenstein, N. S., and C. A. Thyberg. 1988. Cooperative work in the Andrew message system. In *Proceedings of the 1988 ACM Conference on Computer-Supported Cooperative Work*, pp. 306–23. New York: ACM Press.

Borgman, C. L. 1989. All users of information retrieval systems are not created equal: An exploration into individual differences. *Information Processing & Management,* 25(3):237–51.

Borgman, C. L. 1999. What are digital libraries? Competing visions. *Information Processing and Management* 35(3):227–43.

Bouzeghoub, M., and M. Lenzerini. 2001. Introduction to the special issue on data extraction, cleaning, and reconciliation. *Information Systems* 26(8):535–36.

Bowker, G. C., and S. L. Star. 1999. *Sorting things out: Classification and its consequences.* Cambridge, MA: MIT Press.

Brennan, P. F., S. M. Moore, G. Bjornsdottir, J. Jones, C. Visovsky, and M. Rogers. 2001. HeartCare: An Internet-based information and support system for patient home recovery after coronary artery bypass graft (CABG) surgery. *Journal of Advanced Nursing* 35(5):699–708.

Brewer, W. F. 1986. What is autobiographical memory? In *Autobiographical Memory,* ed. D. Rubin, pp. 25–49. Cambridge, UK: Cambridge University Press.

Brewer, W. F. 1988. Qualitative analysis of the recalls of randomly sampled autobiographical events. In *Practical aspects of memory: Current research and issues,* ed. M. M. Gruneberg, P. E. Morris, and R. N. Sykes. Vol. 1, pp. 263–68. Chichester, NY: Wiley.

Brodie, C., C. Karat, and J. Karat. 2006. An empirical study of natural language parsing of privacy policy rules using the SPARCLE policy workbench. In *Proceedings of the Second Symposium on Usable Privacy and Security.* Vol. 149, pp. 8–19. New York: ACM Press.

Bruce, H. 2005. Personal, anticipated information need. *Information Research* 10(3). Available at http://informationr.net/ir/10-3/paper232.html

Bruce, H., W. Jones, and S. Dumais. 2004. Information behavior that keeps found things found. *Information Research* 10(1). Available at http://informationr.net/ir/10-1/paper207.html

Brush, A. J., L. Palen, L. Swan, and A. S. Taylor. 2005. Designs for home life. In *Proceedings of the SIGCHI Conference on Human Factors in Computing Systems, Extended Abstracts,* pp. 2035–36. New York: ACM Press.

Buckland, M. 2004. *Going places in the catalog: Enhancing scholarly and educational resources with geospatial information.* Paper presented at the WebWise 2004: Sharing Digital Resources, Chicago, Illinois, March 3–5.

Buffet, S., M. W. Fleming, M. M. Richter, N. Scott, and B. Spencer. 2004. Determining Internet users' values for privacy information. In *Proceedings of the Second Annual Conference on Privacy, Security, and Trust*, pp. 79–88. Available at http://dev.hil.unb.ca/Texts/PST/pdf/buffett.pdf

Bush, V. 1945. As we may think. *The Atlantic Monthly*, July(1): 101–08.

Canny, J. 2004. GaP: A factor model for discrete data. In *Proceedings of the 27th Annual International ACM SIGIR Conference on Research and Development in information Retrieval. SIGIR '04*, pp. 122–29. New York: ACM Press.

Capra, R. 2006. An investigation of finding and refinding information on the Web. Ph.D. diss., Virginia Polytechnic Institute and State University, Blacksburg, VA.

Capra, R., and M. A. Pérez-Quiñones. 2005a. *Mobile refinding of Web information using a voice interface: An exploratory study.* Paper presented at the 2nd Latin American Conference on Human-Computer Interaction (CLIHC 2005), Cuernavaca, Mexico, October.

Capra, R., and M. A. Pérez-Quiñones. 2005b. Using Web search engines to find and refind information. *IEEE Computer* 38(10):36–42.

Card, S., J. Mackinlay, and B. Shneiderman. 1999. *Readings in information visualization: Using vision to think.* San Francisco, CA: Morgan Kaufmann.

Carroll, J. B. 1993. *Human cognitive abilities: A survey of factor-analytic studies.* Cambridge, UK: Cambridge University Press.

Carroll, J. M., and M. B. Rosson. 1992. Getting around the task-artifact cycle: How to make claims and design by scenario. *ACM Transactions on Information Systems (TOIS)*, 10(2):181–212.

Carvalho, V. R., and W. W. Cohen. 2005. On the collective classification of email "speech acts." In *Proceedings of the 28th Annual International ACM SIGIR Conference on Research and Development in Information Retrieval*, pp. 345–52. New York: ACM Press.

Chan, L. M. 1994. *Cataloging and classification: An introduction.* 2nd ed. New York: McGraw-Hill.

Chatman, E. A. 1984. Field research: Methodological themes. *Library and Information Science Research* 6(4):425–38.

Chatman, E. A. 1992. *The information world of retired women.* Westport, CT: Greenwood.

Cheng, P. C. H. 2002. Electrifying diagrams for learning: Principles for complex representational systems. *Cognitive Science* 26(6):685–736.

Cheng, W., L. Golubchik, and D. Kay. 2004. Total recall: Are privacy changes inevitable? In *Proceedings of the First ACM Workshop on Continuous Archival and Retrieval of Personal Experiences*, pp. 86–92. New York: ACM Press.

Claypool, M., P. Le, M. Wased, and D. Brown. 2001. Implicit interest indicators. In *Proceedings of the 6th International Conference on Intelligent User Interfaces*, pp. 33–40. New York: ACM Press.

Cohen, W. 1996. Learning rules that classify email. In *AAAI Symposium on Machine Learning in Information Access*, pp. 18–25. Menlo Park, CA: AAAI Press.

Collins, M. 2001. Ranking algorithms for named-entity extraction: Boosting and the voted perceptron. In *Proceedings of the 40th Annual Meeting of the Association for Computational Linguistics*, pp. 489–96. Morristown, NJ: Association for Computational Linguistics.

Conway, M. A. 2005. Memory and the self. *Journal of Memory and Language* 53(4):594–628.

Cooper, A. 1999. *The inmates are running the asylum: Why high-tech products drive us crazy and how to restore the sanity.* Indianapolis, IN: Sams.

Cooper, B. F., and H. Garcia-Molina. 2002. Peer-to-peer data trading to preserve information. *ACM Transactions on Information Systems (TOIS)* 20(2):133–70.

Cooper, J., and C. Urquhart. 2005. The information needs and information-seeking behaviors of home-care workers and clients receiving home care. *Health Information and Libraries Journal* 22(2):107–16.

Corston-Oliver, S., E. Ringger, M. Gamon, and R. Campbell. 2004. Task-focused summarization of email. In *Proceedings of the 42nd Annual Meeting of the Association for Computational Linguistics (ACL 2004): Text Summarization Branches Out workshop.* East Stroudsburg, PA: Association for Computational Linguistics.

CRA. 2003. Conference on Grand Research Challenges in Information Security and Assurance (Warrenton, Virginia, November 16–19, 2003). Available from http://www.cra.org/Activities/grand.challenges/security/

Crabtree, A., T. Hemmings, and J. Mariani. 2003. Informing the development of calendar systems for domestic use. In *Proceedings of the European Conference on Computer Support for Cooperative Work*, pp. 119–38. Dordrecht, The Netherlands: Kluwer Academic Publishers.

Crabtree, A., T. Hemmings, and T. Rodden. 2002. Pattern-based support for interactive design in domestic settings. In *Proceedings of the Conference on Designing Interactive Systems: Processes, Practices, Methods, and Techniques*, pp. 265–76. New York: ACM Press.

Crabtree, A., and T. Rodden. 2004. Domestic routines and design for the home. *Computer Supported Cooperative Work: The Journal of Collaborative Computing* 13(2):191–220.

Cranor, L. 2002. *Web Privacy with P3P*. Sebastopol, CA: O'Reilly Media, Inc.

Cranor, L. 2004. 'I didn't buy it for myself': Privacy in ecommerce personalization. In *Designing Personalized User Experiences in eCommerce*, ed. C. Karat, J. Blom, and J. Karat, pp. 57–74. Dordrecht, The Netherlands: Kluwer Academic Publishers.

Cranor, L. 2005. Privacy policies and privacy preferences. In *Security and usability: Designing secure systems that people can use*, ed. L. Cranor and S. Garfinkel, pp. 447–72. Sebastopol, CA: O'Reilly.

Crawford, E., J. Kay, and E. McCreath. 2002. An intelligent interface for sorting electronic mail. In *Proceedings of the 7th International Conference on Intelligent User Interfaces*, pp. 182–83. New York: ACM Press.

Csikszentmihalyi, M. 1997. *Finding flow: The psychology of engagement with everyday life*. New York: Basic Books.

Culnan, M. 2000. Protecting privacy online: Is self-regulation working? *Journal of Public Policy and Marketing* 19(1):20–26.

Cummings, J. N., and R. Kraut. 2002. Domesticating computers and the Internet. *The Information Society* 18(3):221–31.

Cutrell, E., S. Dumais, and J. Teevan. 2006. Searching to eliminate personal information management. *Communications of the ACM* 49(1):58–64.

Cutrell, E., D. Robbins, S. Dumais, and R. Sarin. 2006. Fast, flexible filtering with Phlat. In *Proceedings of the SIGCHI Conference on Human Factors in Computing Systems*, ed. R. Grinter, T. Rodden, P. Aoki, E. Cutrell, R. Jeffries, and G. Olson, pp. 261–70. New York: ACM Press.

Czerwinski, M., D. Gage, J. Gemmel, C. C. Marshall, M. Pérez-Quiñones, M. M. Skeels, et al. 2006. Digital memories in an era of ubiquitous computing and abundant storage. *Communications of the ACM, Special Issue on Personal Information Management* 49(1):44–50.

Czerwinski, M., E. Horvitz, and E. Cutrell. 2001. Subjective duration assessment: An implicit probe for software usability. In *Proceedings of IHM-HCI 2001 Conference*, ed. J. Vanderdonckt, A. Blandford, and A. Derycke. Vol. 2, pp. 167–70.

Czerwinski, M., E. Horvitz, and S. Wilhite. 2004. A diary study of task switching and interruptions. In *Proceedings of the SIGCHI Conference on Human Factors in Computing Systems*, pp. 175–82. New York: ACM Press.

Dabbish, L. A., R. E. Kraut, S. Fussell, and S. Kiesler. 2005. Understanding email use: Predicting action on a message. In *Proceedings of the SIGCHI Conference on Human Factors in Computing Systems*, pp. 691–700. New York: ACM Press.

DARPA Information Processing Technology Office. n.d. LifeLog. Retrieved August 1, 2006, from www.darpa.mil/ipto/Programs/lifelog/index.htm

Davenport, T. H., and L. Prusak. 1998. *Working knowledge: How organizations manage what they know.* Boston, MA: Harvard Business School Press.

Death to folders! 2005. *The Economist Technology Quarterly* 376 (September 15):30–33.

Denzin, N. K., and Y. S. Lincoln. 2005. *The SAGE handbook of qualitative research.* 3rd ed. Thousand Oaks, CA: Sage.

Dervin, B. 1992. From the mind's eye of the user: The sense-making qualitative-quantitative methodology. In *Qualitative research in information management*, ed. J. Glazier and R. Powell, pp. 61–84. Englewood, CO: Libraries Unlimited.

Dervin, B., L. Foreman-Wernet, and E. Lauterbach, eds. 2003. *Sense-making methodology reader: Selected writings of Brenda Dervin.* Cresskill, NJ: Hampton Press.

Dervin, B., and M. Nilan. 1986. Information needs and uses. *Annual Review of Information Science and Technology (ARIST)* 21:3–33.

Dillon, A., and C. Watson. 1996. User analysis in HCI: The historical lessons from individual differences research. *International Journal of Human Computer Studies* 45(6):619–37.

Dingledine, R., and N. Mathewson. 2005. Anonymity loves company: Usability and the network effect. In *Security and usability: Designing secure systems that people can use*, ed. L. Cranor and S. Garfinkel, pp. 547–60. Sebastopol, CA: O'Reilly.

Doerr, M. 2001. Semantic problems of thesaurus mappings. *Journal of Digital Information* 1(8), Article No. 52, 2001-2003-2026 from http://jodi.tamu.edu/Articles/v01/i08/Doerr/

Doerr, M., J. Hunter, and C. Lagoze. 2003. Towards a core ontology for information integration. *Journal of Digital Information* 4(1), Article No. 169, 2003-2004-2009 from http://jodi.ecs.soton.ac.uk/Articles/v04/i01/Doerr/

Donadio, R. 2005. Literary letters, lost in cyberspace. *New York Times* September 4.

Donath, J. 2004. Visualizing email archives (Draft). Available from http://smg.media.mit.edu/papers/Donath/EmailArchives.draft.pdf

Dong, X., A. Halevy, and J. Madhavan. 2005. Reference reconciliation in complex information spaces. In *Proceedings of the 2005 ACM SIGMOD International Conference on Management of Data*, pp. 85–96. New York: ACM Press.

Dourish, P., V. Bellotti, W. Mackay, and C.-Y. Ma. 1993. Information and context: Lessons from the study of two shared information systems. In *Proceedings of the Conference on Organizational Computing Systems*, ed. S. Kaplan, pp. 42–51. New York: ACM Press.

Dourish, P., W. K. Edwards, A. LaMarca, J. Lamping, K. Petersen, M. Salisbury, et al. 1999. Extending document management systems with user-specific active properties. *ACM Transactions on Information Systems* 18(2):140–70.

Dourish, P., W. K. Edwards, A. LaMarca, and M. Salisbury. 1999. Presto: An experimental architecture for fluid interactive document spaces. *ACM Transactions on Computer-Human Interaction (TOCHI)* 6(2) June 1999, 133–61. DOI= http://doi.acm.org/10.1145/319091.319099

Dragunov, A. N., T. G. Dietterich, K. Johnsrude, M. McLaughlin, L. Li, and J. Herlocker. 2005. TaskTracer: A desktop environment to support multi-tasking knowledge workers. In *Proceedings of the 10th International Conference on Intelligent User Interfaces*, pp. 75–82. New York: ACM Press.

Dredze, M., T. Lau, and N. Kushmerick. 2006. Automatically classifying emails into activities. In *Proceedings of the 11th International Conference on Intelligent User Interfaces*, pp. 70–77. New York: ACM Press.

dtSearch Corp. 2006. dtSearch. Retrieved April 15, 2006 from http://www.dtsearch.com

Ducheneaut, N., and V. Bellotti. 2001. E-mail as habitat: An exploration of embedded personal information management. *Interactions* 8(5) 30–38.

Ducheneaut, N., and V. Bellotti. 2003. Ceci n'est pas un objet? Talking about objects in email. *Human-Computer Interaction* 18(1–2):85–110.

Dumais, S., E. Cutrell, J. Cadiz, G. Jancke, R. Sarin, and D. Robbins. 2003. Stuff I've Seen: A system for personal information retrieval and re-use. In *Proceedings of the 26th Annual International ACM SIGIR Conference on Research and Development in Information Retrieval*, pp. 72–79. New York: ACM Press.

Dumais, S. T., E. Cutrell, R. Sarin, and R. Horvitz. 2004. Implicit queries (IQ) for contextualized search. In *Proceedings of the 27th Annual International ACM SIGIR Conference on Research and Development In Information Retrieval*, pp. 594–594. New York: ACM Press.

Durso, F. T., and S. Gronlund. 1999. Situation awareness. In *The handbook of applied cognition,* ed. F. T. Durso, R. Nickerson, R. W. Schvaneveldt, S. T. Dumais, D. S. Lindsay, and M. T. H. Chi, pp. 284–314. Chichester, NY: John Wiley & Sons.

Egan, D. 1988. Individual differences in human-computer interaction. In *Handbook of human-computer interaction,* ed. M. Helander, pp. 543–68. Amsterdam: Elsevier Science Publishers.

Ekstrom, R. B., J. W. French, H. H. Harman, and D. Dermen. 1976. *Manual for kit of factor-referenced cognitive tests.* Princeton, NJ: Educational Testing Service.

Endicott, J., J. Nee, W. Harrison, and R. Blumenthal. 1993. Quality of life enjoyment and satisfaction questionnaire: A new measure. *Psychopharmacology Bulletin* 29(2):321–26.

Engelbart, D., R. Watson, and J. Norton. 1973. The augmented knowledge workshop. In *AFIPS Conference Proceedings (National Computer Conference, June 4–8, 1973).* Vol. 42, pp. 9–21. New York: American Federation of Information Processing Societies.

Erdelez, S., and K. Rioux. 2000. Sharing information encountered for others on the Web. *New Review of Information Behaviour Research* 1:219–33.

Erickson, T., and W. A. Kellogg. 2000. Social translucence: An approach to designing systems that support social processes. *ACM Transactions on Computer-Human Interaction (TOCHI)* 7(1):59–83.

Erlandson, D. A., E. L. Harris, B. L. Skipper, and S. D. Allen. 1993. *Doing naturalistic inquiry: A guide to methods.* Newbury Park, CA: Sage.

Feldman, S. 2004. The high cost of not finding information. *KM World.* Retrieved January 28, 2006, from http://www.kmworld.com/Articles/ReadArticle.aspx?ArticleID=9534

Fertig, S., E. Freeman, and D. Gelernter. 1996a. Finding and reminding reconsidered. *SIGCHI Bulletin* 28(1):66–69.

Fertig, S., E. Freeman, and D. Gelernter. 1996b. Lifestreams: An alternative to the desktop metaphor. In *Conference Companion on Human Factors in Computing Systems: Common Ground,* ed. M. J. Tauber, pp. 410–11. New York: ACM Press.

Fidel, R. 1993. Qualitative methods in information retrieval research. *Library and Information Science Research* 15(3):219–47.

Fidel, R., and A. M. Pejtersen. 2004. From information behaviour research to the design of information systems: The Cognitive Work Analysis framework. *Information Research* 10(1). Available from http://informationr.net/ir/10-1/paper210.html

Fisher, D., and P. Moody. 2001. *Studies of automated collection of email records (UCI-ISR-02-4)*. Irvine, CA: University of California.

Fisher, K. E., S. Erdelez, and E. F. McKechnie. 2005. *Theories of information behavior*. Medford, NJ: Information Today.

Fitzgibbon, A., and E. Reiter. 2003. "Memories for life": Managing information over a human lifetime. Retrieved August 1, 2006, from http://www.memoriesforlife.org/document.php?document=memories.pdf

Flores, F., M. Graves, B. Hartfield, and T. Winograd. 1988. Computer systems and the design of organizational interaction. *ACM Transactions on Information Systems (TOIS)* 6(2):153–72.

Foltz, P. W., and S. T. Dumais. 1992. Personalized information delivery: An analysis of information filtering methods. *Communications of the ACM* 35(12):51–60.

Ford, J. M., and L. E. Wood. 1996. An overview of ethnography and system design. In *Field methods casebook for software design*, ed. D. Wixon and J. Ramey, pp. 269–82. New York: Wiley.

Ford, N., D. Miller, and N. Moss. 2005. Web search strategies and human individual differences: A combined analysis. *Journal of the American Society for Information Science and Technology* 56(7):757–64.

Ford, N., T. D. Wilson, A. Foster, D. Ellis, and A. Spink. 2002. Information seeking and mediated searching. Part 4. Cognitive styles in information seeking. *Journal of the American Society for Information Science and Technology* 53(9):728–35.

Franklin, B. 1790. *The autobiography of Benjamin Franklin*. New York: Dover Publications, 1996.

Frissen, V. 2000. ICTs in the rush hour of life. *The Information Society* 16(1):65–75.

Furnas, G. W., T. K. Landauer, L. M. Gomez, and S. T. Dumais. 1987. The vocabulary problem in human-system communication. *Communications of the ACM* 30(11):964–71.

Garcia-Molina, H., Y. Papakonstantinou, D. Quass, A. Rajaraman, Y. Sagiv, J. Ullman, et al. 1997. The TSIMMIS approach to mediation: Data models and languages. *Journal of Intelligent Information Systems* 8(2):117–32.

Gartner Research. 2001. Trends in email usage. Available from http://www.gartner.com/

Gemmell, J., G. Bell, R. Lueder, S. Drucker, and C. Wong. 2002. MyLifeBits: Fulfilling the memex vision. In *Proceedings of ACM Multimedia'02*, pp. 235–38. New York: ACM Press.

Gemmell, J., L. Williams, K. Wood, G. Bell, and R. Lueder. 2004. Passive capture and ensuing issues for a personal lifetime store. In *Proceedings of the First ACM Workshop on Continuous Archival and Retrieval of Personal Experiences,* pp. 48–55. New York: ACM Press.

Gershon, N. 1995. *Human information interaction.* Paper presented at the Fourth International World Wide Web Conference, Boston, MA, December.

Glaser, B. G., and A. L. Strauss. 1967. *The discovery of grounded theory: Strategies for qualitative research.* New York: Aldine de Gruyter.

Goffman, E. 1959. *The presentation of self in everyday life.* New York: Anchor-Doubleday.

Google. 2006. Google Desktop. Retrieved March 16, 2006, from http://desktop.google.com/

Graham, A., H. Garcia-Molina, A. Paepcke, and T. Winograd. 2002. Time as essence for photo browsing through personal digital libraries. In *Proceedings of the Second ACM/IEEE-CS Joint Conference on Digital Libraries,* pp. 326–35. New York: ACM Press.

Gray, J., and P. Shenoy. 2000. Rules of thumb in data engineering. In *Proceedings of IEEE International Conference on Data Engineering,* pp. 3–12. Los Alamitos, CA: IEEE Press.

Greenbaum, J. M., and M. Kyng. 1991. *Design at work: Cooperative design of computer systems.* Hillsdale, NJ: Lawrence Erlbaum.

Greenberg, D. L., and D. C. Rubin. 2003. The neuropsychology of autobiographical memory. *Cortex* 39(4–5):687–728.

Grudin, J. 1989. Why groupware applications fail: Problems in design and evaluation. *Office: Technology and People* 4(3):245–64.

Grudin, J. 1990. The computer reaches out: The historical continuity of interface design. In *Proceedings of the SIGCHI Conference on Human Factors in Computing Systems: Empowering People,* ed. J. C. Chew and J. Whiteside, pp. 261–68. New York: ACM Press.

Guba, E. G. 1978. *Toward a methodology of naturalistic inquiry in educational evaluation.* Los Angeles, CA: UCLA Center for the Study of Education.

Gustafson, D. H., R. P. Hawkins, E. W. Boberg, F. McTravish, B. Owens, M. Wise, et al. 2002. CHESS: 10 years of research and development in consumer health informatics for broad populations, including the underserved. *International Journal of Medical Informatics* 65(3):169–77.

Guy, M., and E. Tonkin. 2006. Folksonomies: Tidying up tags? *D-Lib Magazine* 12(1). Available from http://dx.doi.org/10.1045/january2006-guy

Gwizdka, J. 2002. Reinventing the inbox: Supporting the management of pending tasks in email. In *Proceedings of the SIGCHI Conference on Human Factors in Computing Systems, Doctoral Consortium*, pp. 550–51. New York: ACM Press.

Gwizdka, J. 2004a. Email task management styles: The cleaners and the keepers. In *Proceedings of the SIGCHI Conference on Human Factors in Computing Systems, Extended Abstracts*, pp. 1235–38. New York: ACM Press.

Gwizdka, J. 2004b. *Cognitive abilities and email interaction: Impacts of interface and task.* Doctoral dissertation, University of Toronto, Toronto.

Gwizdka, J., and M. H. Chignell. 2004. Individual differences and task-based user interface evaluation: A case study of pending tasks in email. *Interacting with Computers* 16(4):769–97.

Hafner, K. 2004. Even digital memories can fade. *New York Times* November 10.

Halevy, A. Y. 2004. Structures, semantics and statistics. In *Proceedings of the Thirtieth International Conference on Very Large Data Bases*, ed. M. A. Nascimento, M. T. Ozsu, D. Kossmann, R. J. Mille, J. A. Blakeley, and K. B. Schiefer, pp. 4–6. San Francisco, CA: Morgan Kaufmann.

Halevy, A. Y., N. Ashish, D. Bitton, M. Carey, D. Draper, J. Pollock, et al. 2005. Enterprise information integration: Successes, challenges, and controversies. In *Proceedings of the 2005 ACM SIGMOD International Conference on Management of Data*, pp. 778–87. New York: ACM Press.

Harada, S., M. Naaman, Y. J. Song, Q. Wang, and A. Paepcke. 2004. Lost in memories: Interacting with photo collections on PDAs. In *Proceedings of the 4th ACM/IEEE-CS Joint Conference on Digital Libraries*, pp. 325–33. New York: ACM Press.

Harter, A., A. Hopper, P. Steggles, A. Ward, and P. Webster. 2002. The anatomy of a context-aware application. *Wireless Networks* 8(2/3):187–97.

Hartswood, M., R. Procter, M. Rouncefield, R. Slack, and A. Voss. In press. Co-realisation: Evolving IT artefacts by design. In *Resources, co-evolution, and artifacts: Theory in CSCW*, ed. M. Ackerman, T. Erickson, and C. Halverson. Amsterdam: Kluwer Academic Publishers.

Hearst, M. A. 1999. User interfaces and visualization. In *Modern information retrieval*, ed. R. Baeza-Yates and B. Ribeiro-Neto. Boston, MA: Addison-Wesley.

Heminger, A. R., and S. B. Robertson. 1998. Digital Rosetta Stone: A conceptual model for maintaining long-term access to digital documents. In *Proceedings of the Thirty-First Annual Hawaii International Conference on System Sciences*. Vol. 2, p. 158–67. Washington, DC: IEEE Computer Society.

Henderson, A., and S. Card. 1986. Rooms: The use of multiple virtual workspaces to reduce space contention in a window-based graphical user interface. *ACM Transactions on Graphics (TOG)* 5(3):211–43.

Herring, S. 1999. Interactional coherence in CMC. *Journal of Computer Mediated Communication* 4:23–38.

Hewins, E. T. 1990. Information need and use studies. *Annual Review of Information Science and Technology (ARIST)* 25:145–72.

Hindus, D., S. D. Mainwaring, N. Leduc, A. E. Hagström, and O. Bayley. 2001. Casablanca: Designing social communication devices for the home. In *Proceedings of the SIGCHI Conference on Human Factors in Computing Systems*, ed. J. Jacko and A. Sears, pp. 325–32. New York: ACM Press.

Hodge, G. M. 2000. Best practices for digital archiving: An information life cycle approach. D-Lib Magazine, 6(1). Available at http://dx.doi.org/10.1045/january2000-hodge

Hodges, S., L. Williams, E. Berry, I. Izadi, J. Srinivasan, A. Butler, et al. 2006. *SenseCam: A retrospective memory aid*. Paper presented at the Eighth International Conference on Ubiquitous Computing (Ubicomp 2006), pp. 177–93. Orange County, CA, September.

Hölscher, C., and G. Strube. 2000. Web search behavior of Internet experts and newbies. *Computer Networks* 33:337–46.

Hori, T., and K. Aizawa. 2003. Context-based video retrieval system for the life-log applications. In *Proceedings of the ACM SIGMM International Workshop on Multimedia Information Retrieval*, pp. 31–38. New York: ACM Press.

Horvitz, E., A. Jacobs, and D. Hovel. 1999. Attention-sensitive alerting. In *Proceedings of UAI '99, Conference on Uncertainty and Artificial Intelligence*, pp. 305–13. San Francisco, CA: Morgan Kaufmann Publishers.

Hsieh, Y., and P. F. Brennan. 2005. *What are pregnant women's information needs and information seeking behaviors prior to their prenatal genetic counseling?* Paper presented at the Biomedical and Health Informatics: From Foundations to Applications to Policy, AMIA annual symposium, Washington, DC.

Hudson, S. E., and I. Smith. 1996. Techniques for addressing fundamental privacy and disruption tradeoffs in awareness support systems. In *Proceedings of the 1996 ACM Conference on Computer Supported Cooperative Work*, ed. M. S. Ackerman, pp. 248–57. New York: ACM Press.

Hunter, J., and S. Choudhury. 2004. A semi-automated digital preservation system based on semantic Web services. In *Proceedings of the 4th ACM/IEEE-CS Joint Conference on Digital libraries*, pp. 269–78. New York: ACM Press.

Hutchins, E. 1995. *Cognition in the wild.* Cambridge, MA: MIT Press.

Huynh, D., D. Karger, and D. Quan. 2002. *Haystack: A platform for creating, organizing, and visualizing information using RDF.* Paper presented at the Semantic Web Workshop at the WWW 2002: The Eleventh International World Wide Web Conference, Honolulu, HI, May.

Jantz, R. 2005. Digital preservation: Enabling technologies for trusted digital repositories. *D-Lib Magazine* 11(6). Available at http://dx.doi.org/10.1045/june2005-jantz

Jantz, R., and M. J. Giarlo. 2005. Digital preservation: Architecture and technology for trusted digital repositories. *D-Lib Magazine* 11(6). Available at http://dx.doi.org/10.1045/june2005-jantz

Jensen, C., and C. Potts. 2004. Privacy policies as decision-making tools: An evaluation of online privacy notices. In *Proceedings of the SIGCHI Conference on Human Factors in Computing Systems,* pp. 471–78. New York: ACM Press.

Jensen, C., C. Potts, and C. Jensen. 2005. Privacy practices of Internet users: Self-reports versus observed behavior. *International Journal of Human-Computer Studies* 63(1–2):203–27.

Johnson, S. B. 2005. Tool for thought. *New York Times* January 30.

Jones, W. 2004. Finders, keepers? The present and future perfect in support of personal information management. *First Monday* 9(3). Available at http://www.firstmonday.dk/issues/issue9_3/jones/index.html

Jones, W. 2006. Personal information management. *Annual Review of Information Science and Technology (ARIST)* 41.

Jones, W. In press. *Keeping found things found: The study and practice of personal information management.* San Francisco, CA: Morgan Kaufmann.

Jones, W., H. Bruce, and S. Dumais. 2001. Keeping founds things found on the Web. In *Proceedings of the Tenth International Conference on Information and Knowledge Management,* pp. 119–26. New York: ACM Press.

Jones, W., H. Bruce, and S. Dumais. 2003. *How do people get back to information on the Web? How can they do it better?* Paper presented at the 9th IFIP TC13 International Conference on Human-Computer Interaction (INTERACT 2003), Zurich, Switzerland, September.

Jones, W., H. Bruce, and A. Foxley. 2006a. Project contexts to situate personal information. In *Proceedings of the 29th Annual International ACM SIGIR Conference on Research and Development in Information Retrieval,* p. 729. New York: ACM Press.

Jones, W., H. Bruce, A. Foxley, and C. Munat. 2006b. *Planning personal projects and organizing personal information.* Paper presented at the 69th Annual Meeting of the American Society for Information Science and Technology (ASIST 2006), Austin, TX, November.

Jones, W., and S. Dumais. 1986. The spatial metaphor for user interfaces: Experimental tests of reference by location versus name. *ACM Transactions on Office Information Systems* 4(1):42–63.

Jones, W., S. Dumais, and H. Bruce. 2002. Once found, what then?: A study of "keeping" behaviors in the personal use of Web information. In *Proceedings of the 65th Annual Meeting of the American Society for Information Science and Technology,* ed. E. G. Toms. Vol. 39, pp. 391–402. Medford, NJ: Information Today.

Jones, W., C. Munat, and H. Bruce. 2005. The Universal Labeler: Plan the project and let your information follow. In *Proceedings of the 68th Annual Meeting of the American Society for Information Science and Technology,* ed. A. Grove. Vol. 42 (online). Medford, NJ: Information Today.

Jones, W., A. J. Phuwanartnurak, R. Gill, and H. Bruce. 2005. Don't take my folders away! Organizing personal information to get things done. In *Proceedings of the SIGCHI Conference on Human Factors in Computing Systems,* pp. 1505–08. New York: ACM Press.

Jones, W., P. Pirolli, S. K. Card, R. Fidel, N. Gershon, P. Morville, et al. 2006. "It's about the information stupid!": Why we need a separate field of human-information interaction. In *Proceedings of the SIGCHI Conference on Human Factors in Computing Systems, Extended Abstracts,* pp. 65–68. New York: ACM Press.

Jones, W., and B. Ross. 2006. Human cognition and personal information management. In *Handbook of applied cognition,* ed. F. T. Durso, R. S. Nickerson, R. W. Schvaneveldt, S. T. Dumais, D. S. Lindsay, and M. T. H. Chi. Chichester, NY: John Wiley.

Kaptelinin, V. 1996. Creating computer-based work environments: An empirical study of Macintosh users. In *Proceedings of the 1996 ACM SIGCPR/SIGMIS Conference on Computer Personnel Research,* pp. 360–66. New York: ACM Press.

Kaptelinin, V. 2003. UMEA: Translating interaction histories into project contexts. In *Proceedings of the SIGCHI Conference on Human Factors in Computing Systems* (Ft. Lauderdale, Florida, USA, April 5–10, 2003). CHI '03. New York: ACM Press, pp. 353–360. DOI = http://doi.acm.org/10.11 45/642611.642673

Kapur, N., E. L. Glisky, and B. A. Wilson. 2002. External memory aids and computers in memory rehabilitation. In *The handbook of memory disorders,* ed. A. D. Baddeley, M. D. Kopelman, and B. A. Wilson. 2nd ed., pp. 757 –84. Chichester, NY: John Wiley.

Karat, C., C. Brodie, and J. Karat. 2005. Usability design and evaluation for privacy and security solutions. In *Security and usability: Designing secure systems that people can use,* ed. L. Cranor and S. Garfinkel, pp. 47–74. Sebastopol, CA: O'Reilly.

Karat, J., C. Karat, and C. Brodie. 2004. Personalizing interaction. In *Designing personalized user experiences in eCommerce,* ed. C. Karat, J. Blom, and J. Karat, pp. 7–18. Dordrecht, The Netherlands: Kluwer Academic Publishers.

Karat, J., C. Karat, C. Brodie, and J. Feng. 2005a. Privacy in information technology: Designing to enable privacy policy management in organizations. *International Journal of Human Computer Studies* 63(1–2): 153–74.

Karat, J., C. Karat, C. Brodie, and J. Feng. 2005b. Designing natural language and structured entry methods for privacy policy authoring. In *Proceedings for the Tenth IFIP TC13 International Conference of Human-Computer Interaction,* pp. 671–84.

Karat, C., J. Karat, J., C. Brodie, and J. Feng. 2006. Evaluating interfaces for privacy policy rule authoring. In *Proceedings of the SIGCHI Conference on Human Factors in Computing Systems,* ed. R. Grinter, T. Rodden, P. Aoki, E. Cutrell, R. Jeffries, and G. Olson, pp. 83–92. New York: ACM Press.

Katifori, V., A. Poggi, M. Scannapieco, T. Catarci, and Y. Ioannidis. 2005. *OntoPIM: How to rely on a personal ontology for personal information management.* Paper presented at the 1st Workshop on The Semantic Desktop at the International Semantic Web Conference, Galway, Ireland, November.

Kaye, J., J. Vertesi, S. Avery, A. Dafoe, S. David, L. Onaga, et al. 2006. To have and to hold: Exploring the personal archive. In *Proceedings of the SIGCHI Conference on Human Factors in Computing Systems,* ed. R. Grinter, T. Rodden, P. Aoki, E. Cutrell, R. Jeffries, and G. Olson, pp. 275–84. New York: ACM Press.

Kelly, D. 2006. Evaluating personal information management behaviors and tools. *Communications of the ACM* 49(1):84–86.

Kelly, D., and N. J. Belkin. 2004. Display time as implicit feedback: Understanding task effects. In *Proceedings of the 27th Annual International ACM SIGIR Conference on Research and Development in Information Retrieval,* pp. 377–84. New York: ACM Press.

Kelly, D., and C. Cool. 2002. The effects of topic familiarity on information search behavior. In *Proceedings of the 2nd ACM/IEEE-CS Joint Conference on Digital Libraries*, pp. 74–5. New York: ACM Press.

Kent, S. T., and L. I. Millett, eds. 2003. *Who goes there? Authentication through the lens of privacy*. Washington, DC: National Academies Press.

Kerr, B. 2003. Thread Arcs: An email thread visualization. In *Proceedings of the IEEE Symposium on Information Visualization (InfoVis2003)*, ed. T. Munzner and S. North, p. 27. Washington, DC: IEEE.

Khoussainov, R., and N. Kushmerick. 2005. *Email task management: An iterative relational learning approach*. Paper presented at the 2nd International Conference on Email and Anti-Spam (CEAS 2005), Stanford University, Palo Alto, CA, July. Available at http://www.ceas.cc/papers-2005/142.pdf

Kidd, A. 1994. The marks are on the knowledge worker. In *Proceedings of the SIGCHI Conference on Human Factors in Computing Systems: Celebrating Interdependence*, ed. B. Adelson, S. Dumais, and J. Olson, pp. 186–91. New York: ACM Press.

Kim, K. S., and B. L. Allen. 2002. Cognitive and task influences on Web searching behavior. *Journal of the American Society for Information Science and Technology* 53(2):109–19.

Kirsh, D. 2000. A few thoughts in cognitive overload. *Intellectica* 30(1):19–54.

Klimt, B., and Y. Yang. 2004. *Introducing the Enron corpus*. Paper presented at the First Conference on Email and Anti-Spam (CEAS 2004), Mountain View, CA, July. Available at http://www.ceas.cc/papers-2004/168.pdf

Kotovsky, K., J. R. Hayes, and H. A. Simon. 1985. Why are some problems hard? Evidence from Tower of Hanoi. *Cognitive Psychology* 17(2):248–94.

Koutrika, G., and Y. Ioannidis. 2005. A unified user-profile framework for query disambiguation and personalization. In *Proceedings of the Workshop on New Technologies for Personalized Information Access, in Conjunction with the 10th International Conference on User Modeling*, ed. P. Brusilovsky, C. Callaway, and A. Nurnberger, pp. 44–53. Available at http://irgroup. cs.uni-magdeburg.de/pia2005/Proceedings.htm

Kraut, R. E., J. Morris, R. Telang, D. Filer, M. Cronin, and S. Sunder. 2002. Markets for attention: Will postage for email help? In *Proceedings of the 2002 ACM Conference on Computer Supported Cooperative Work*, pp. 206–15. New York: ACM Press.

Krippendorff, K. 1980. *Content analysis: An introduction to its methodology*. Newbury Park, CA: Sage.

Krishnan, A., and S. Jones. 2005. TimeSpace: Activity-based temporal visualisation of personal information spaces. *Personal and Ubiquitous Computing* 9(1):46–65.

Kuhlthau, C. 1991. Inside the search process: Information seeking from the user's perspective. *Journal of the American Society for Information Science* 42(5):361–71.

Kuny, T. 1998. The digital dark ages? Challenges in the preservation of electronic information. *International Preservation News* 17(5).

Kushmerick, N., and T. Lau. 2005. Automated email activity management: An unsupervised learning approach. In *Proceedings of the 10th International Conference on intelligent User interfaces*, pp. 67–74. New York: ACM Press.

Kwasnik, B. 1989. How a personal document's intended use or purpose affects its classification in an office. In *Proceedings of the 12th Annual International ACM SIGIR Conference on Research and Development in information*, ed. N. J. Belkin and C. J. van Rijsbergen, pp. 207–10. New York: ACM Press.

Kwasnik, B. H. 1991. The importance of factors that are not document attributes in the organization of personal documents. *Journal of Documentation* 47(4):389–98.

Lamming, M. G., and W. M. Newman. 1992. Activity-based information retrieval: Technology in support of personal memory. In *Information processing 92, personal computers and intelligent systems*, ed. F. H. Vogt. Vol. 3, pp. 68–81. Madrid: Elsevier.

Lansdale, M. 1988a. The psychology of personal information management. *Applied Ergonomics* 19(1):55–66.

Lansdale, M. 1988b. On the memorability of icons in an information retrieval task. *Behaviour & Information Technology* 7(2):131–51.

Lansdale, M. 1991. Remembering about documents: Memory for appearance, format, and location. *Ergonomics* 34(8):1161–78.

Lansdale, M., and E. Edmonds. 1992. Using memory for events in the design of personal filing systems. *International Journal of Man-Machine Studies* 36(1):97–126.

Larkin, J. H., and H. A. Simon. 1987. Why a diagram is (sometimes) worth ten thousand words. *Cognitive Science* 11:65–99.

Lavoie, B., and L. Dempsey. 2004. Thirteen ways of looking at . . . digital preservation. *D-Lib Magazine* 10(7/8). Available at http://dx.doiorg/10.1045/july2004-lavoie

Layard, R. 2005. *Happiness: Lessons from a new science.* London: Penguin Press.

LeFurgy, W. G. 2003. PDF/A: Developing a file format for long-term preservation. *RLG DigiNews* 7(6).

Lenzerini, M. 2002. Data integration: A theoretical perspective. In *Proceedings of the Twenty-first ACM SIGACT-SIGMOD-SIGART Symposium on Principles of Database Systems*, ed. L. Popa, pp. 233–46. New York: ACM Press.

Levitt, M. 2000. *Email usage forecast and analysis, 2000–2005 (IDC Report W23011)*. Framingham, MA: IDC.

Levy, A. Y. 2000. Logic-based techniques in data integration. In *Logic Based Artificial Intelligence*, ed. J. Minker. Vol. 597, pp. 575–95. Norwell, MA: Kluwer Academic Publishers.

Levy, A. Y., A. Rajaraman, and J. J. Ordille. 1996. Querying heterogeneous information sources using source descriptions. In *Proceedings of the 22th International Conference on Very Large Data Bases*, ed. T. M. Vijayaraman, A. P. Buchmann, C. Mohan, and N. L. Sarda, pp. 251–62. San Francisco, CA: Morgan Kaufmann.

Levy, D. M. 1998. Heroic measures: Reflections on the possibility and purpose of digital preservation. In *Proceedings of Digital Libraries '98*, pp. 152–61. New York, NY: ACM Press.

Lewins, A., C. Silver, C. Lee, M. Macintyre, A. King, N. Fielding, et al. 2006. Computer assisted qualitative data analysis networking project. Retrieved August 1, 2006, from http://caqdas.soc.surrey.ac.uk

Leydon, G. M., M. Boulton, C. Moynihan, A. Jones, J. Mossman, M. Boudioni, et al. 2000. Cancer patients' information needs and information seeking behaviour: In-depth interview study. *BMJ* 320(7239):909–13.

Lieberman, H., B. Nardi, and D. Wright. 2001. Training agents to recognize text by example. *Autonomous Agents and Multi-Agent Systems* 4(1–2):79–92.

Lin, M., W. G. Lutters, and T. S. Kim. 2004. Understanding the micronote lifecycle: Improving mobile support for informal note taking. In *Proceedings of the SIGCHI Conference on Human Factors in Computing Systems*, pp. 687–94. New York: ACM Press.

Lincoln, Y. S., and E. G. Guba. 1985. *Naturalistic inquiry*. Newbury Park, CA: Sage.

Lofland, J., and L. H. Lofland. 1995. *Analyzing social settings: A guide to qualitative observation and analysis*. Belmont, CA: Wadsworth.

Lorie, R. 2002. A methodology and system for preserving digital data. In *Proceedings of the 2nd ACM/IEEE-CS Joint Conference on Digital Libraries*, pp. 312–19. New York: ACM Press.

Lucas, P. 2000. Pervasive information access and the rise of human-information interaction. In *Proceedings of the SIGCHI Conference on Human Factors in Computing Systems, Extended Abstracts*, p. 202. New York: ACM Press.

Lutters, W. G., and M. S. Ackerman. 2002. Achieving safety: A field study of boundary objects in aircraft technical support. In *Proceedings of the 2002 ACM Conference on Computer Supported Cooperative Work*, pp. 266–75. New York: ACM Press.

Lyman, P. 2002. Archiving the World Wide Web. In *Building a National Strategy for Digital Preservation: Issues in Digital Media Archiving*, pp. 38–51. Washington, DC: Council on Library and Information Resources and the Library of Congress.

Lyman, P., and B. Kahle. 1998. Archiving digital cultural artifacts: Organizing an agenda for action. *D-Lib Magazine* 4(7). Available from http://www.dlib.org/dlib/july98/07lyman.html

Lynch, C. 1999. Canonicalization: A fundamental tool to facilitate preservation and management of digital information. *D-Lib Magazine* 5(9). Available from http://dx.doi.org/10.1045/september99-lynch

Lynch, C., and H. Garcia-Molina. 1995. Interoperability, scaling, and the digital libraries research agenda: A report on the May 18–19, 1995, IITA Digital Libraries Workshop. Available from http://dbpubs.stanford.edu:8091/diglib/pub/reports/iita-dlw/main.html

Mackay, W. E. 1988. Diversity in the use of electronic mail: A preliminary inquiry. *ACM Transactions on Office Information Systems*, 6(4):380–97.

Mackay, W. E. 1988. More than just a communication system: Diversity in the use of electronic mail. In *Proceedings of the 1988 ACM Conference on Computer-Supported Cooperative Work*, pp. 344–53. New York: ACM Press.

Mackay, W. E. 1990. Patterns of sharing customizable software. In *Proceedings of the 1990 ACM Conference on Computer-Supported Cooperative Work*, pp. 209–21. New York: ACM Press.

Malin, B., and L. Sweeney. 2004. How (not) to protect genomic data privacy in a distributed network: Using trail re-identification to evaluate and design anonymity protection systems. *Journal of Biomedical Informatics* 37(3):179–92.

Malone, T. W. 1983. How do people organize their desks: Implications for the design of office information systems. *ACM Transactions on Office Information Systems* 1(1):99–112.

Malone, T. W., K. R. Grant, and F. A. Turbak. 1986. The Information Lens: An intelligent system for information sharing in organizations. In *Proceedings of the SIGCHI Conference on Human Factors in Computing Systems*, ed. M. Mantei and P. Orbeton, pp. 1–8. New York: ACM Press.

Mander, R., G. Salomon, and Y. Y. Wong. 1992. A 'pile' metaphor for supporting casual organization of information. In *Proceedings of the SIGCHI Conference on Human Factors in Computing Systems*, pp. 627–34. New York: ACM Press.

Mann, S., and H. Niedzviecki. 2001. *Cyborg: Digital destiny and human possibility in the age of the wearable computer.* Toronto, ON: Doubleday Canada.

Manny, C. H. 2003. European and American privacy: Commerce, rights, and justice–part 1. *Computer Law and Security Report* 19(1):4–10.

Mantei, M. M., R. M. Baecker, A. J. Sellen, W. A. Buxton, T. Milligan, and B. Wellman. 1991. Experiences in the use of a media space. In *Proceedings of the SIGCHI Conference on Human Factors in Computing Systems: Reaching Through Technology*, ed. S. P. Robertson, G. M. Olson, and J. S. Olson, pp. 203–08. New York: ACM Press.

Marchionini, G. 1995. *Information seeking in electronic environments.* Cambridge, UK: Cambridge University Press.

Markus, M. L. 1983. Power, politics, and MIS implementation. *Communications of the ACM* 26(6):430–44.

Markus, M. L. 2001. Toward a theory of knowledge reuse: Types of knowledge reuse situations and factors in reuse success. *Journal of Management Information Systems* 18(1):57–93.

Markus, M. L., and T. Connolly. 1990. Why CSCW applications fail: Problems in the adoption of interdependent work tools. In *Proceedings of the 1990 ACM Conference on Computer-Supported Cooperative Work*, pp. 371–80. New York: ACM Press.

Marquard, J. L., A. Moen, and P. F. Brennan. 2006. *Photographic data: An untapped resource to explore complex phenomena such as Health Information Management in the Household (HIMH).* Paper presented at the 9th International Congress on Nursing Informatics, Seoul, Korea, June.

Marshall, C. C. 2006. *Why a corpus-topics-relevance judgments framework isn't enough: Two simple retrieval challenges from the field.* Paper presented at the SIGIR 2006 Workshop on Evaluating Exploratory Search Systems, Seattle, Washington, August 10.

Marshall, C. C., and S. Bly. 2005. Saving and using encountered information: Implications for electronic periodicals. In *Proceedings of the ACM SIGCHI Conference on Human Factors in Computing Systems*, pp. 111–20. New York: ACM Press.

Marshall, C. C., S. Bly, and F. Brun-Cottan. 2006. The long-term fate of our personal digital belongings: Toward a service model for personal archives. In *Proceedings of the IS&T's Archiving 2006 Conference*, pp. 25–30. Springfield, VA: Society for Imaging Science and Technology.

Marshall, C. C., and G. Golovchinsky. 2004. Saving private hypertext: Requirements and pragmatic dimensions for preservation. In *Proceedings of the Fifteenth ACM Conference on Hypertext and Hypermedia*, pp. 130–38. New York: ACM Press.

Marshall, C. C., and W. Jones. 2006. Keeping encountered information. *Communications of the ACM* 49(1):66–67.

Marx, M., and C. Schmandt. 1996. CLUES: Dynamic personalized message filtering. In *Proceedings of the 1996 ACM Conference on Computer Supported Cooperative Work*, ed. M. S. Ackerman, pp. 113–21. New York: ACM Press.

McDonald, S., and R. J. Stevenson. 1998. Effects of text structure and prior knowledge of the learner on navigation in hypertext. *Human Factors* 40(1):18–27.

Mecella, M., M. Scannapieco, A. Virgillito, R. Baldoni, T. Catarci, and C. Batini. 2002. Managing data quality in cooperative information systems. In *On the move to meaningful Internet systems, 2002—DOA/CoopIS/ODBASE 2002 Confederated International Conferences Doa, CoopIS and ODBASE 2002*, ed. R. Meersman and Z. Tari, pp. 486–502. London: Springer-Verlag.

Mellon, C. 1990. *Naturalistic inquiry for library science: Methods and applications for research, evaluation, and teaching.* New York: Greenwood Press.

Merton, R. K. 1957. *Social theory and social structure.* Glencoe, IL: Free Press.

Metral, M. 1993. "Design of a generic learning interface agent." Bachelor of Science thesis, Massachusetts Institute of Technology, Cambridge MA.

Meyer, S., and A. Rakotonirainy. 2003. A survey of research on context-aware homes. In *Proceedings of the Australasian Information Security Workshop Conference on ACSW Frontiers*, ed. C. Johnson, P. Montague, and C. Steketee. Vol. 21, pp. 159–68. Darlinghurst, Australia: Australian Computer Society.

Milberg, S. J., S. J. Burke, H. J. Smith, and E. A. Kallman. 1995. Values, personal information privacy, and regulatory approaches. *Communications of the ACM* 38(12):65–74.

Miles, M. B., and A. M. Huberman. 1994. *Qualitative analysis: An expanded sourcebook.* Thousand Oaks, CA: Sage.

Miller, M. J. 2005. Google, Yahoo!, and MSN: The search continues. *PC Magazine* 5 (March 22).

Mitchell, J., and B. Shneiderman, B. 1989. Dynamic versus static menus: An exploratory comparison. *ACM SIGCHI Bulletin* 20(4):33–37.

Mock, K. 2001. An experimental framework for email categorization and management. In *Proceedings of the 24th Annual International ACM SIGIR Conference on Research and Development in Information Retrieval,* pp. 392–93. New York: ACM Press.

Modjeska, D., and M. Chignell. 2003. Individual differences in exploration using desktop VR. *Journal of the American Society for Information Science and Technology* 54(3):216–28.

Moen, A., and P. F. Brennan. 2005. Health@Home: The work of Health Information Management in the Household (HIMH)—Implications for Consumer Health Informatics (CHI) innovations. *Journal of the American Medical Informatics Association* 12(6):648–56.

Morrison, J., P. Pirolli, and S. Card. 2001. A taxonomic analysis of what World Wide Web activities significantly impact people's decisions and actions. In *Proceedings of the SIGCHI Conference on Human Factors in Computing Systems, Extended Abstracts,* pp. 163–64. New York: ACM Press.

Morville, P. 2006. *Ambient findability.* Sebastopol, CA: O'Reilly Media.

Muller, M., W. Geyer, B. Brownholtz, E. Wilcox, and D. Millen. 2004. One hundred days in an activity-centric collaboration environment based on shared objects. In *Proceedings of the ACM CHI 2004, Vienna, Austria,* April, pp. 375–382. New York: ACM Press.

Muresan, S., E. Tzoukermann, and J. L. Klavans. 2001. Combining linguistic and machine learning techniques for email summarization. In *Proceedings of the 2001 Workshop on Computational Natural Language Learning,* ed. W. Daelemans and R. Zajac. Vol. 7, pp. 152–59. Morristown, NJ: Association for Computational Linguistics.

Nagel, K. S., J. M. Hudson, and G. D. Abowd. 2004. Predictors of availability in home life context-mediated communication. In *Proceedings of the 2004 ACM Conference on Computer Supported Cooperative Work,* pp. 497–506. New York: ACM Press.

Nahl, D. 2004. Measuring the affective information environment of Web searchers. In *Proceedings of the 67th Annual Meeting of the American Society for Information Science and Technology.* Vol. 41, pp. 191–97. Medford, NJ: Information Today.

Nardi, B., S. Whittaker, E. Isaacs, M. Creech, J. Johnson, and J. Hainsworth. 2002. Integrating communication and information through ContactMap. *Communications of the Association for Computing Machinery* 45(4):89–95.

Nelson, T. H. 1999. Xanalogical structure, needed now more than ever: Parallel documents, deep links to content, deep versioning, and deep re-use. *ACM Computing Surveys (CSUR)* 31(4es). Available from http://portal.acm.org/ citation.cfm?id=345966.346033&dl=portal&dl=ACM&idx=J204&part=pe riodical&WantType=periodical&title=ACM%20Computing%20Surveys%2 0(CSUR)&CFID=11111111&CFTOKEN=2222222

Nielsen, J. 2003. Usability 101: Introduction to usability. *Jakob Nielsen's Alertbox.* Retrieved March 28, 2006, from http://www.useit.com/ alertbox/20030825.html

Nippert-Eng, C. 1996. *Home and work: Negotiating boundaries through everyday life.* Chicago: University of Chicago Press.

NISO. 2003. Information and documentation—The Dublin Core metadata element set (ISO 15836). Available from http://www.niso.org/ international/SC4/n515.pdf

Novick, L. R. 1990. Representational transfer in problem solving. *Psychological Science* 1(2):128–32.

Novick, L. R., S. M. Hurley, and M. Francis. 1999. Evidence for abstract, schematic knowledge of three spatial diagram representations. *Memory & Cognition* 27(2):288–308.

OASIS Open. 2004. OASIS, Privacy Policy Profile of XACML, Committee draft 01. Available from http://docs.oasis-open.org/xacml/access_control-xacml-2_0-privacy_profile-spec-cd-01.pdf

O'Brien, J., T. Rodden, M. Rouncefield, and J. Hughes. 1999. At home with the technology: An ethnographic study of a set-top-box trial. *ACM Transactions on Computer-Human Interaction* 6(3):282–308.

O'Day, V., and R. Jeffries. 1993. Orienteering in an information landscape: How information seekers get from here to there. In *Proceedings of the SIGCHI Conference on Human Factors in Computing Systems (Amsterdam, The Netherlands, April 24–29). CHI '93,* pp. 438–45. New York: ACM Press.

O'Day, V. L., D. G. Bobrow, and M. Shirley. 1996. The social-technical design circle. In *Proceedings of the 1996 ACM Conference on Computer Supported Cooperative Work,* ed. M. S. Ackerman, pp. 160–69. New York: ACM Press.

OECD. 1980. OECD guidelines on the protection of privacy and transborder flows of personal data. Available from http://www.oecd.org/document/ 18/0,2340,en_2649_201185_1815186_1_1_1_1,00.html

Oliver, N., and F. Flores-Mangas. 2006. HealthGear: A real-time wearable system for monitoring and analyzing physiological signals. In *Proceedings of the International Workshop on Wearable and Implantable Body Sensor Networks (BSN'06),* pp. 61–64. Piscataway, NJ: IEEE Press.

Olson, G. M., and J. S. Olson. 1997. Research on computer supported cooperative work. In *Handbook of human computer interaction*, ed. M. Helander, pp. 1433–56. Amsterdam: Elsevier.

Orlikowski, W. 2000. Using technology and constituting structures: A practice lens for studying technology in organizations. *Organization Science* 11(4):404–28.

Orlikowski, W. J. 1992a. Learning from Notes: Organizational issues in groupware implementation. In *Proceedings of the 1992 ACM Conference on Computer-Supported Cooperative Work*, pp. 362–69. New York: ACM Press.

Orlikowski, W. J. 1992b. The duality of technology: Rethinking the concept of technology in organizations. *Organization Science* 3(3):398–427.

Østerlund, C. S., N. P. Dosa, and C. A. Smith. 2005. *Mother knows best: Medical record management for patients with spina bifida during transition from pediatric to adult care.* Paper presented at the Biomedical and Health Informatics: From Foundations to Applications to Policy, AMIA annual symposium, Washington, DC.

Palen, L. 1999. Social, individual and technological issues for groupware calendar systems. In *Proceedings of the SIGCHI Conference on Human Factors in Computing Systems: The CHI Is the Limit*, pp. 17–24. New York: ACM Press.

Palen, L., and P. Dourish. 2003. Unpacking "privacy" for a networked world. In *Proceedings of the SIGCHI Conference on Human Factors in Computing Systems*, pp. 129–36. New York: ACM Press.

Palen, L., and J. Grudin. 1999. Discretionary adoption of group support software. In *Organizational implementation of collaboration technology*, ed. B. E. Munkvold. New York: Springer.

Patton, M. Q. 2002. *Qualitative research and evaluation methods*. 3rd ed. Thousand Oaks, CA: Sage.

Pazzani, M. J. 2000. Representation of electronic mail filtering profiles: A user study. In *Proceedings of the 5th International Conference on Intelligent Use Interfaces*, pp. 202–06. New York: ACM Press.

Perer, A., B. Shneiderman, and D. W. Oard. 2005. *Using rhythms of relationships to understand email archives.* Paper presented at the 22nd Annual Symposium of the Human-Computer Interaction Laboratory, University of Maryland, College Park, MD, June.

Pettigrew, K. E., R. Fidel, and H. Bruce. 2001. Conceptual frameworks in information behavior. *Annual Review of Information Science and Technology (ARIST)* 35:43–78.

Pirolli, P. 2006. Cognitive models of human-information interaction. In *Handbook of applied cognition*, ed. F. T. Durso, R. S. Nickerson, R. W. Schvaneveldt, S. T. Dumais, D. S. Lindsay, and M. T. H. Chi. 2nd ed. West Sussex, England: John Wiley & Sons.

Pitney Bowes. 2000. Increased use of electronic communications tools among North American and European workers. Available from http://www. pitneybowes.co.uk.frames4you.co.uk/dir/Pitnet-Bowes-UK.html

Pratt, W., M. C. Reddy, D. W. McDonald, P. Tarczy-Hornoch, and J. H. Gennari. 2004. Incorporating ideas from computer-supported cooperative work. *Journal of Biomedical Informatics* 37(2):128–37.

Pratt, W., K. T. Unruh, A. Civan, and M. Skeels. 2006. Personal health information management. *Communications of the ACM* 49(1):51–55.

Prinz, W. 1993. TOSCA: Providing organisational information to CSCW applications. In *Proceedings of ECSC '93*, pp. 139–54. Dordrecht, The Netherlands: Kluwer Academic Publishers.

Pruitt, J., and J. Grudin. 2003. Personas: Practice and theory. In *Proceedings of the 2003 Conference on Designing for User Experiences*, pp. 1–15. New York: ACM Press.

Rahm, E., and P. A. Bernstein. 2001. A survey of approaches to automatic schema matching. *VLDB Journal* 10(4):334–50.

Rainie, L., and J. Shermak. 2005. Pew Internet and American Life Project: Data memo on search engine use. Retrieved January 29, 2006 from http://www.pewinternet.org/pdfs/PIP_SearchData_1105.pdf

Ramakrishnan, N. 2005. The traits of the personable. In *LNCS/LNAI State-of-the-Art Survey on Intelligent Techniques in Web Personalization*, ed. B. Mobasher and S. S. Anand, pp. 53–68. Berlin: Springer-Verlag.

Rambow, O., L. Shrestha, J. Chen, and C. Laurdisen. 2004. *Summarizing email threads*. Paper presented at the Human Language Technology Conference of the North American Chapter of the Association for Computational Linguistics: HLT-NAACL 2004, Boston, MA, May 2–7.

Ravasio, P., S. G. Schär, and H. Krueger. 2004. In pursuit of desktop evolution: User problems and practices with modern desktop systems. *ACM Transactions on Computer-Human Interaction* 11(2):156–80.

Reichherzer, T., and G. Brown. 2006. Quantifying software requirements for supporting archived office documents using emulation. In *Proceedings of the 6th ACM/IEEE-CS Joint Conference on Digital Libraries*, pp. 86–94. New York: ACM Press.

Reiter, M., and A. Rubin. 1998. Crowds: Anonymity for Web transactions. *ACM Transactions on Information and System Security* 1(1):66–92.

Rhodes, B. 2003. Using physical context for just-in-time information retrieval. *IEEE Transactions on Computers* 52(8):1011–14.

Ringel, M., E. Cutrell, S. T. Dumais, and E. Horvitz. 2003. Milestones in time: The value of landmarks in retrieving information from personal stores. In *INTERACT'03*, ed. G. W. M. Rauterberg, M. Menozzi, and J. Wesson, pp. 184–91. Amsterdam: IOS Press.

Robertson, G., M. Czerwinski, K. Larson, D. C. Robbins, D. Thiel, and M. V. Dantzich. 1998. Data mountain: Using spatial memory for document management. In *Proceedings of the 11th Annual ACM Symposium on User Interface Software and Technology*, pp. 153–62. New York: ACM Press.

Rodden, K., and K. Wood. 2003. How do people manage their digital photographs? In *Proceedings of the SIGCHI Conference on Human Factors in Computing Systems*, pp. 409–16. New York: ACM Press.

Rohall, S. L., D. Gruen, P. Moody, and S. Kellerman. 2001. *Email visualizations to aid communications.* Paper presented at the IEEE Symposium on Information Visualization (InfoVis), San Diego, CA, October.

Rosch, E. 1978. Principles of categorization. In *Cognition and categorization*, ed. E. Rosch and B. B. Lloyd, pp. 27–48. Hillsdale, NJ: Lawrence Erlbaum.

Rosch, E., C. B. Mervis, W. Gray, D. Johnson, and P. Boyes-Braem. 1976. Basic objects in natural categories. *Cognitive Psychology* 8:382–439.

Roth, M. T., M. Arya, L. Haas, M. Carey, W. Cody, R. Fagin, et al. 1996. The Garlic project. In *Proceedings of the 1996 ACM SIGMOD International Conference on Management of Data*, ed. J. Widom, p. 557. New York: ACM Press.

Rothenberg, J. 1998. *Avoiding technological quicksand: Finding a viable technical foundation for digital preservation.* Washington, DC: Council on Library and Information Resources.

Roush, C. V., and J. E. Cox. 2000. The meaning of home. How it shapes the practice of home and hospice care. *Home Healthcare Nurse* 18(6):388–94.

Russell, D. M., M. Slaney, Y. Qu, and M. Houston. 2006. Being literate with large document collections: Observational studies and cost structure tradeoffs. In *Proceedings of the 39th Annual Hawaii International Conference on System Sciences (HICSS'06) Track 3*, p. 55. Los Alamitos, CA: IEEE.

Russell, D. M., M. J. Stefik, P. Pirolli, and S. K. Card. 1993. The cost structure of sensemaking. In *Proceedings of the ACM SIGCHI Conference on Human Factors in Computing Systems*, pp. 269–76. New York: ACM Press.

Safran, C. 2003. The collaborative edge: Patient empowerment for vulnerable populations. *International Journal of Medical Informatics* 69(2/3):185–90.

Salthouse, T. A. 1991. *Theoretical perspectives on cognitive aging.* Hillsdale, NJ: Lawrence Erlbaum.

Sands, D. Z., J. D. Halamka, and D. Pellaton. 2001. *PatientSite: A Web-based clinical communication and health education tool.* Paper presented at the HIMSS 2001: Raising the Educational Bar, New Orleans, LA.

Sandstrom, A. R., and P. E. Sandstrom. 1995. The use and misuse of anthropological methods in library and information science research. *Library Quarterly* 65(2):161–99.

Savage-Knepshield, P. A., and N. J. Belkin. 1999. Interaction in information retrieval: Trends over time. *Journal of the American Society for Information Science* 50(12):1067–82.

Schwandt, T. A. 2001. *Dictionary of qualitative inquiry.* Thousand Oaks, CA: Sage.

Segal, R. B., and J. O. Kephart. 1999. MailCat: An intelligent assistant for organizing e-mail. In *Proceedings of the Third Annual Conference on Autonomous Agents,* ed. O. Etzioni, J. P. Müller, and J. M. Bradshaw, pp. 276–82. New York: ACM Press.

Seifert, C. M., and A. L. Patalano. 2001. Opportunism in memory: Preparing for chance encounters. *Current Directions in Psychological Science* 10(6):198–201.

Sellen, A. J., and R. H. R. Harper. 2002. *The myth of the paperless office.* Cambridge, MA: MIT Press.

Shipman, F. M., and C. C. Marshall. 1999. Formality considered harmful: Experiences, emerging themes, and directions on the use of formal representations in interactive systems. *Computer Supported Cooperative Work (CSCW)* 8(4):333–52.

Shiri, A. A., and C. Revie. 2003. The effects of topic complexity and familiarity on cognitive and physical moves in a thesaurus-enhanced search environment. *Journal of Information Science* 29(6):517–26.

Simon, H. A. 1996. *Sciences of the artificial.* 3rd ed. Cambridge, MA: MIT Press.

Simons, W. W., K. D. Mandl, and I. S. Kohane. 2005. The PING personally controlled electronic medical record system: Technical architecture. *Journal of the American Medical Informatics Association* 12(1):47–54.

Singleton, R., M. M. Straits, and B. C. Straits. 1988. *Approaches to social research.* New York: Oxford University Press.

Sinha, V., and D. R. Karger. 2005. Magnet: Supporting Navigation in Semistructured Data Environments. In *Proceedings of the ACM SIGMOD International Conference on Management of Data,* pp. 97–106.

Smith, H. J. 1993. Privacy policies and practices: Inside the organizational maze. *Communications of the ACM* 36(12):104–22.

Smith, J. A., F. McCown, and M. L. Nelson. 2006. Observed Web robot behavior on decaying Web subsites. *D-Lib Magazine* 12(2). Available at http://dx.doi.org/10.1045/february2006-smith

Smith, M. 2005. Eternal bits: How can we preserve digital files and save our collective memory? *IEEE Spectrum* 42(7):22–27.

Spiekermann, S., J. Grossklags, and B. Berendt. 2001. E-privacy in 2nd generation E-commerce: Privacy preferences versus actual behavior. In *Proceedings of the 3rd ACM Conference on Electronic Commerce*, pp. 38–47. New York: ACM Press.

Star, S. L., and K. Ruhleder. 1996. Steps towards an ecology of infrastructure: Design and access for large information space. *Information Systems Research* 7(1):111–34.

Star, S. L., and A. Strauss. 1999. Layers of silence, arenas of voice: The ecology of visible and invisible work. *Computer Supported Cooperative Work (CSCW)* 8:(1–2), 9–30.

Stefik, M. 1999. *The Internet edge: Social, technical, and legal challenges for a networked world.* Cambridge, MA: MIT Press.

Strauss, A. L. 1987. *Qualitative analysis for social scientists.* Cambridge, UK: Cambridge University Press.

Strauss, A. L. 1993. *Continual permutations of action.* New York: Aldine de Gruyter.

Strauss, A. L., and J. M. Corbin. 1990. *Basics of qualitative research: Grounded theory procedures and techniques.* Newbury Park, CA: Sage.

Strauss, A. L., S. Fagerhaugh, B. Suczek, and C. Weiner. 1985. *Social organization of medical work.* Chicago: University of Chicago Press.

Streitz, N., and P. Nixon. 2005. Special issue: The disappearing computer. *Communications of the ACM* 48(3):32–35.

Suchman, L. 1987. *Plans and situated actions: The problem of human-machine communication.* Cambridge, UK: Cambridge University Press.

Suchman, L. 1997. Do categories have politics? The language/action perspective reconsidered. In *Human values and the design of computer technology*, ed. B. Friedman, pp. 91–106. Cambridge, UK: Cambridge University Press.

Sumi, Y., S. Ito, T. Matsuguchi, S. Fels, and K. Mase. 2004. Collaborative capturing and interpretation of interactions. In *Proceedings of Pervasive 2004 Workshop on Memory and Sharing of Experiences*, pp. 12–8. Available at http://www.ii.ist.i.kyoto-u.ac.jp/~sumi/pervasive04/proceedings.pdf

Sun, Y., and P. Kantor. 2006. Cross-evaluation: A new model for information system evaluation. *Journal of American Society for Information Science and Technology* 57(5):614–28.

Surendran, A. C., J. C. Platt, and E. Renshaw. 2005. *Automatic discovery of personal topics to organize email.* Paper presented at the Second Conference on Email and Anti-Spam (CEAS 2005), Stanford University, Palo Alto, CA, July.

Sutton, B. 1993. The rationale for qualitative research: A review of principles and theoretical foundations. *Library Quarterly* 63(4):411–30.

Swan, L., and A. S. Taylor. 2005. Notes on fridge surfaces. In *Proceedings of the SIGCHI Conference on Human Factors in Computing Systems, Extended Abstracts,* pp. 1813–816. New York: ACM Press.

Sweeney, L. 2002. k-Anonymity: A model for protecting privacy. *International Journal on Uncertainty, Fuzziness and Knowledge-based Systems* 10(5):557–70.

Takkinnen, J., and N. Shahmehri. 1998. CAFÉ: A conceptual model for managing information in electronic mail. In *Proceedings of the Thirty-First Annual Hawaii International Conference on System Sciences,* 5:44–53. New York: IEEE Press.

Tan, D. S., B. Meyers, and M. Czerwinski. 2004. WinCuts: Manipulating arbitrary window regions for more effective use of screen space. In *Proceedings of the SIGCHI Conference on Human Factors in Computing Systems, Extended Abstracts,* pp. 1525–528. New York: ACM Press.

Tang, P. C., J. Ash, D. W. Bates, J. M. Overhage, and D. Z. Sands. 2006. Personal health records: Definitions, benefits, and strategies for overcoming barriers to adoption. *Journal of the American Medical Informatics Association* 13(2):121–26.

Tansley, R., M. Bass, D. Stuve, M. Branchofsky, D. Chudnov, G. McClellan, et al. 2003. The DSpace institutional digital repository system: Current functionality. In *Proceedings of the 3rd ACM/IEEE-CS Joint Conference on Digital Libraries,* pp. 87–97. New York, NY: ACM Press.

Taylor, A. G. 2004. *Wynar's introduction to cataloging and classification.* Rev. 9th ed. Englewood, CO: Libraries Unlimited.

Taylor, A. S., and L. Swan. 2004. List making in the home. In *Proceedings of the 2004 ACM Conference on Computer Supported Cooperative Work,* pp. 542–45. New York: ACM Press.

Taylor, A. S., and L. Swan. 2005. Artful systems in the home. In *Proceedings of the SIGCHI Conference on Human Factors in Computing Systems,* pp. 641–50. New York: ACM Press.

Taylor, C., G. Gibbs, N. Fielding, and A. Lewins. 2006. Online QDA. Retrieved August 1, 2006, from http://onlineqda.hud.ac.uk

Taylor, S. J., and R. Bogdan. 1984. *Introduction to qualitative research methods: The search for meanings.* New York: Wiley.

Teevan, J. 2007a. The Re:Search Engine: Simulaneous support for finding and re-finding. In *Proceedings of the 20th Annual ACM Symposium on User Interface Software and Technology* (UIST '07). New York: ACM Press.

Teevan, J. 2007b. "Where'd it go?": How people ask after lost Web information. In *Proceedings of the Annual Meeting of the American Society for Information Science and Technology* (ASIST '07). Milwaukee, WI. October

Teevan, J., C. Alvarado, M. S. Ackerman, and D. R. Karger. 2004. The perfect search engine is not enough: A study of orienteering behavior in directed search. In *Proceedings of the SIGCHI Conference on Human Factors in Computing Systems*, pp. 415–22. New York: ACM Press.

Teevan, J., S. T. Dumais, and E. Horvitz. 2005. Personalizing search via automated analysis of interests and activities. In *Proceedings of the 28th Annual International ACM SIGIR Conference on Research and Development in Information Retrieval*, pp. 449–56. New York: ACM Press.

Teevan, J., R. Jones, E. Adar, and M. Potts. 2007. Information re-retrieval: Repeat queries in Yahoo's logs. In *Proceedings of the 30th Annual ACM SIGIR Conference on Research and Development in Information Retrieval.* New York: ACM Press.

Teltzrow, M., and A. Kobsa. 2004. Impacts of user privacy preferences on personalized systems. In *Designing Personalized User Experiences in eCommerce*, ed. C. Karat, J. Blom, and J. Karat, pp. 315–32. Dordrecht, The Netherlands: Kluwer Academic Publishers.

Thomas, R. C. 1998. *Long term human-computer interaction: An exploratory perspective.* New York: Springer-Verlag.

Thuraisingham, B. 2002. Data mining, national security, privacy and civil liberties. *ACM SIGKDD Explorations Newsletter* 4(2):1–5.

Tolmie, P., J. Pycock, T. Diggins, A. MacLean, and A. Karsenty. 2002. Unremarkable computing. In *Proceedings of the SIGCHI Conference on Human Factors in Computing Systems: Changing Our World, Changing Ourselves*, pp. 399–406. New York: ACM Press.

Troncy, R. 2003. Integrating structure and semantics into audio-visual documents. In *The SemanticWeb—ISWC 2003*, pp. 566–81. Berlin: Springer-Verlag.

Tsinaraki, C., P. Polydoros, and S. Christodoulakis. 2004. Interoperability support for ontology-based video retrieval applications. In *Image and Video Retrieval: Third International Conference, CIVR 2004, Dublin, Ireland, July 21–23, 2004. Proceedings.* Vol. 3115, pp. 582–91. Berlin: Springer-Verlag.

Tzoukermann, E., S. Muresan, and J. L. Klavans. 2001. GIST-IT: Summarizing email using linguistic knowledge and machine learning. In *Proceedings of the Workshop on Human Language Technology and Knowledge Management, (Toulouse, France, July 06–07, 2001), Annual Meeting of the ACL*, pp. 1–8. Morristown, NJ: Association for Computational Linguistics.

U.S. Congress. 2003. *U.S. Fair and Accurate Credit Transaction Act. H.R. 2622.* Retrieved from http://thomas.loc.gov/cgi-bin/bdquery/z?d108: HR02622:@@@L&summ2=m&|TOM:/bss/d108query.html|

U.S. Dept of Health, Education, and Welfare. 1973. Records, computers, and the rights of citizens: Report of the Secretary's Advisory Committee on Automated Personal Data Systems. Available from http://aspe.os.dhhs.gov/datacncl/1973privacy/tocprefacemembers.htm

Unruh, K. T., and W. Pratt. 2004. *Patients as actors: The patient's role in detecting and preventing medical errors.* Paper presented at the IT in Health Care 2004: Socio-technical Approaches—To Err is system, Portland, Oregon.

Vakkari, P. 1999. Task complexity, problem structure and information actions: Integrating studies on information seeking and retrieval. *Information Processing and Management* 35(6):819–37.

Venolia, G., A. Gupta, J. J. Cadiz, and L. Dabbish. 2001. *Supporting email workflow (MSR-TR-2001-88).* Redmond, WA: Microsoft Research.

Venolia, G., and C. Neustaedter. 2003. Understanding sequence and reply relationships within email conversations: A mixed-model visualization. In *Proceedings of the SIGCHI Conference on Human Factors in Computing Systems*, pp. 361–68. New York: ACM Press.

Viegas, F., D. Boyd, D. Nguyen, J. Potter, and J. Donath. 2004. Digital artifacts for remembering and storytelling: PostHistory and social network fragments. In *Proceedings of the 37th Hawaii International Conference on System Sciences (HICSS'04)—Track 4*, p. 40109a. Washington, DC: IEEE.

Voorhees, E. 1986. Implementing agglomerative hierarchic clustering algorithms for use in document retrieval. *Information Processing and Management* 22:465–476.

Wan, S., and K. McKeown. 2004. *Generating overview summaries of ongoing email thread discussions*. Paper presented at the COLING 2004: The 20th International Conference on Computational Linguistics, Geneva, Switzerland. August.

Wang, T., L. Pizziferri, L. A. Volk, D. A, Mikels, K. G. Grant, J. S. Wald, et al. 2004. Implementing patient access to electronic health records under HIPAA: Lessons learned. *Perspectives in Health Information Management* 1(11).

Want, R., and D. M. Russell. 2000. Ubiquitous electronic tagging. *IEEE Distributed Systems Online*, 1(2). Available from http://dsonline.computer. org/portal/site/dsonline/menuitem.9ed3d9924aeb0dcd82ccc6716 bbe36ec/index.jsp?&pName=dso_level1&path=dsonline/archives/ ds200&file=ds2wan.xml&xsl=article.xsl&

Wardrip-Fruin, N. 1999. Hypermedia, eternal life, and the impermanence agent. In *ACM SIGGRAPH 99 Electronic Art and Animation Catalog*, p. 90. New York: ACM Press.

Warren, S. A., and L. D. Brandeis. 1890. The right to privacy. *Harvard Law Review* 4:195.

Waterworth, J. A., and G. Singh. 1994. Information islands: Private views of public places. In *Proceedings of MHVR'94, East-West Conference on Multimedia, Hypermedia and Virtual Reality. Moscow, September 14–16, 1994*, ed. P. Brusilovsky, pp. 201–206.

Wattenberg, M., S. Rohall, D. Gruen, and B. Kerr. 2005. Email research: Targeting the enterprise. *Human Computer Interaction* 20(1–2):139–62.

Wen, J. 2003. Post-valued recall Web pages: User disorientation hits the big time. *IT & Society* 1(3):184–194.

Westbrook, L. 1994. Qualitative research methods: A review of major stages, data analysis techniques, and quality controls. *Library and Information Science Research* 16(3):241–54.

White, R., I. Ruthven, and J. M. Jose. 2002. Finding relevant documents using top ranking sentences: An evaluation of two alternative schemes. In *Proceedings of the 25th Annual International ACM SIGIR Conference on Research and Development in Information Retrieval*, pp. 57–64. New York: ACM Press.

Whittaker, S. 2005. Supporting collaborative task management in email. *Human-Computer Interaction* 20(1–2):49–88.

Whittaker, S., V. Bellotti, and J. Gwizdka. 2006. Email in personal information management. *Communications of the ACM* 49(1):68–73.

Whittaker, S., and J. Hirschberg. 2001. The character, value and management of personal paper archives. *ACM Transactions on Computer-Human Interaction* 8(2):150–70.

Whittaker, S., Q. Jones, B. Nardi, M. Creech, L. Terveen, E. Isaacs, et al. 2004. Contactmap: Organizing communication in a social desktop. *ACM Transactions on Computer-Human Interaction (TOCHI)* 11(4):445–71.

Whittaker, S., Q. Jones, and L. Terveen. 2002. Persistence and conversation stream management: Conversation and contact management. In *Proceedings of HICCS'02*. New York: IEEE Press.

Whittaker, S., and C. Sidner. 1996. Email overload: Exploring personal information management of email. In *Proceedings of the SIGCHI Conference on Human Factors in Computing Systems: Common Ground*, ed. M. J. Tauber, pp. 276–83. New York: ACM Press.

Whittaker, S., J. Swanson, J. Kucan, and C. Sidner. 1997. TeleNotes: Managing lightweight interactions in the desktop. *ACM Transactions on Computer-Human Interaction (TOCHI)* 4(2):137–68.

Whittaker, S., L. Terveen, and B. A. Nardi. 2000. Let's stop pushing the envelope and start addressing it: A reference task agenda for HCI. *Human Computer Interaction* 15(2–3):75–106.

Whitten, A., and J. D. Tygar. 1999. Why Johnny can't encrypt: A usability evaluation of PGP 5.0. In *Proceedings of the 8th USENIX Security Symposium*, pp. 169–84. Berkeley, CA: USENIX.

Wikimedia Foundation Inc. 2006. Wikipedia, the free encyclopedia. Available from http://en.wikipedia.org/wiki/Main_Page

Wildemuth, B. M. 2003. The effects of domain knowledge on search tactic formulation. *Journal of the American Society for Information Science and Technology* 55(3):246–58.

Willett, P. 1988. Recent trends in hierarchic document clustering: A critical review. *Information Processing and Management* 24(5):577–97.

Wilson, M. B., J. J. Evans, H. Emslie, and V. Malinek. 1997. Evaluation of NeuroPage: A new memory aid. *Journal of Neurology, Neurosurgery and Psychiatry* 63(1):113–15.

Wilson, T. 2000. Human information behavior. *Informing Science* 3(2):49–55.

Wilson, T. D. 1999. Models in information behaviour research. *Journal of Documentation* 55(3):249–70.

Winograd, T. 1994. Categories, discipline and social coordination. *Computer-Supported Cooperative Work* 2(3):191–97.

Wittgenstein, L. 1953. *Philosophical investigations*. New York: Macmillan.

Wood, D. N. 1984. The collection, bibliographic control and accessibility of grey literature. *IFLA Journal* 10(3):278–82.

Woodruff, A., R. Rosenholtz, J. Morrison, A. Faulring, and P. Pirolli. 2002. A comparison of the use of text summaries, plain thumbnails, and enhanced thumbnails for Web search tasks. *Journal of the American Society for Information Science and Technology* 53(2):172–85.

Yahoo! Inc. 2006. Yahoo! Desktop Search. Retrieved May 15, 2006, from http://desktop.yahoo.com/

Zadeh, L. A. 1965. Fuzzy sets. *Information and Control* 8(3):338–53.

Zamir, O., O. Etzioni, O. Madani, and R. Karp. 1997. Fast and intuitive clustering of Web documents. In *Proceedings of the 3rd International Conference on Knowledge Discovery and Data Mining*, ed. D. Heckerman, H. Mannila, D. Pregibon, and R. Uthurusamy, pp. 287–90. Menlo Park, CA: AAAI Press.

Zhang, Y., and J. Callan. 2005. Combining multiple forms of evidence while filtering. *Proceedings of Human Language Technology Conference and Conference on Empirical Methods in Natural Language Processing*. Available from http://www.cs.utexas.edu/~ml/HLT-EMNLP05

Contributors

Mark S. Ackerman, School of Information and Dept. of EECS, University of
  Michigan
Gordon Bell, Microsoft Research
Victoria Bellotti, Palo Alto Research Center
Emma Berry, Addenbrooke's Hospital and Microsoft Research
Carolyn Brodie, IBM TJ Watson Research Center
Robert G. Capra, School of Information and Library Science, University of
  North Carolina at Chapel Hill
Tiziana Catarci, Dipartimento di Informatica e Sistemistica "Antonio Ruberti,"
  Università di Roma "La Sapienza"
Mark Chignell, Interactive Media Lab, Department of Mechanical and
  Industrial Engineering, University of Toronto
Mary Czerwinski, Microsoft Research
Xin L. Dong, Computer Science & Engineering, University of Washington
Karen E. Fisher, The Information School, University of Washington
Jim Gemmell, Microsoft Research
Jacek Gwizdka, School of Communication, Information and Library Studies,
  Rutgers University
Alon Y. Halevy, Google
Steve Hodges, Microsoft Research
William Jones, The Information School, University of Washington
Narinder Kapur, Addenbrooke's Hospital
Clare-Marie Karat, IBM TJ Watson Research Center
John Karat, IBM TJ Watson Research Center
David R. Karger, Massachusetts Institute of Technology
Diane Kelly, School of Information and Library Science, The University of
  North Carolina at Chapel Hill
Steve Lawrence, Google
Wayne G. Lutters, Department of Information Systems, University of Maryland,
  Baltimore County
Catherine C. Marshall, Microsoft
Brian Meyers, Microsoft Research

Anne Moen, InterMedia, University of Oslo and School of Nursing, University
of Wisconsin-Madison
Charles M. Naumer, The Information School, University of Washington
Nuria Oliver, Microsoft Research
Manuel A. Pérez-Quiñones, Department of Computer Science, Virginia Tech
Antonella Poggi, Dipartimento di Informatica e Sistemistica "Antonio Ruberti,"
Università di Roma "La Sapienza"
George Robertson, Microsoft Research
Daniel M. Russell, Google
Michael Ian Shamos, Carnegie Mellon University
Desney Tan, Microsoft Research
Jaime Teevan, Microsoft Research
Steve Whittaker, Information Studies Department, University Of Sheffield
Ken Wood, Microsoft Research
Xiaomu Zhou, School of Information, University of Michigan

Index

control of information: by the individual vs. by others, 9–11, 238–39; personal digital store, 104–5; user demands vs. current practice, 256; at work sharing and, 238–41. See also privacy

Cool, C., 25

Cooper, A., 194

Co-ordinator, 184

costs, decreasing for information storage, 62–63, 101, 267

Cranor, L. F., 256, 257

Crawford, E., 185

CSCW (computer-supported collaborative work), 79

CSCW (computer-supported cooperative work), 236–37, 242

Csikszentmihalyi, M., 201

Curious Browser, 202

cut and paste, 128, 137

Cutrell, E., 192

CyberAll project, 92

Czerwinski, M., 62, 90–107, 117–18, 121–24, 134

Dabbish, L. A., 171, 172, 173–74, 178

dark age, digital, 75

database management systems, 121–24

data cleaning, 114

data controllers, 265

data extraction, 113

data integration, 110–15, 123–26

data representations, standard, 128, 131, 136–39

data structuring: automaticity in, 122–23; for browsing by association, 123; introduction, 108–11; looking forward, 125–26; mapping builder, 120; on-the-fly integration, 123–26; personalization in, 119, 121; query processor, 121; reference reconciliation, 121–24; research overview; what is being done, 112–18; what needs to be done, 118–21; semantic save manager, 120–21; terminology, 109–11

del.icio.us, 141, 142

Denzin, N. K., 78

Dervin, B., 78–79

desktops, virtual, 134

desktop search: looking forward, 165, 188; as part of Web search, 159–61, 160f; scenario, 108–9; scoping and broadening in, 161–65. See also search

desktop search tools, 121–24. See also specific tools, e.g. Semex

diagramming, 85

email management: access frequency, 172–73; deferring actions, 175; deleting, 174; embedded support for, 183; individual differences in, 211, 212; information structuring, 182–83; interdependence in, 175–78, 183–84; looking forward, 187–88; obligation management, 177; prioritizing, 186; re-finding relation to, 168; replying, 174; retaining, 174, 177; scanning, 177, 182; techniques to support PIM, 180f, 182–84; time, allocating to, 171–72; workflow systems, 183–84

embedding, 135–36, 140, 143, 148

emotion: finding/re-finding activities and, 57–58; influence on strategy selection, 216; keep everything approach, 62–63

encryption, 250

Englebart, D., 91

ER (external representation) of information, 47–49

Erdelez, S., 81

ethnomethodology, 79

evaluating, 16, 200. See also PIM tools, evaluting

FacetMap, 94

Feng, J., 258

Fidel, R., 80

file systems, 137–38, 155

filing: email, 28, 43, 168, 172, 174, 178–80, 184–85; habits and preferences, 243–44; individual differences in strategy, 212, 213; piling vs., 28, 31, 42–43, 207, 212–13, 215; trigger for, 43

finding: conclusion, 269–70; defined, 13, 24; examples of, 7, 22–23; fragmentation and, 271; keeping relation to, 213–14, 270; looking forward, 33–34, 188; process, influences on the, 25–28; re-finding vs., 24–25, 29; research overview, 25–33; task, importance to, 28. See also re-finding; search

Fisher, K. E., 76–88

Fitzgibbon, A., 90

Flickr, 63, 73, 141–42

flow, characteristics of, 201

focus groups in naturalistic inquiry, 82f, 83f

folder hierarchy, 49, 51, 51f

folders: email, 168, 178–80, 188–89; file manager limitations, 49; KFTF project, 48–49, 55, 55f; labeling, 43; MyLifeBits foldering scheme, 102–3; physical, obsolescence of, 47; reflecting mental representations, 53–54; reuse behaviors, 52–53; smart, 32; in support of project planning, 48–49 fragmentation: conclusion, 270–71; data integration approaches to, 112; distributed storage and, 63, 66–67; elements contributing to, 186; examples, 127, 223; by information form, 31–32, 34, 38, 46; looking forward, 34; orienteering, effect on, 129; in personal health information, 189, 231; restrictions resulting from, 93. See also unification

Franklin, Benjamin, 3

Furnas, G. W., 243

Gage, D., 62

Garcia-Molina, H., 71

GDS (Google Desktop Search), 159–61, 160f, 162–64, 163f, 188

Gemmell, J., 62, 90–107

GIM (group information management): control, privacy, and trust concerns, 238–41, 273; defined, 236; home and family use, 244–46; introduction, 236–37; looking forward, 247–48; scenario, 237–38; tools, 241, 246–47; at work sharing, 238–44, 273

Glaser, B. G., 84, 85

Goffman, E., 238, 243

Gomez, L. M., 243

Google, 159

Google Desktop, 34, 108, 165

Google Desktop Search, 159–64, 160f, 163f, 188

Google Gmail, 33–34, 155, 209

Graham, A., 71

grouping, 128–29, 141–42, 147–48

Grudin, J., 79, 194, 239, 242

Guba, E. G., 77, 80, 86

Gwizdka, J., 157, 167–89, 206–20

Halevy, A., 108–26

happiness, measures of, 201

Harada, S., 195

Haystack, 148–49, 151

HCI (human-computer interaction), 17–18, 79, 210, 250

Health@Home study, 223, 226–31

health care. See PHIM (personal health information management)

Hewins, E. T., 78

HII (human-information interaction), 18

Hill, R., 248

Hirschberg, J., 215

Hodges, S., 90–107

the home: as context in studying PHIM, 226–31, 228f; group information
management in, 244–46

Horvitz, E., 181, 187, 202

Hovel, D., 181, 187

Howard, M., 147, 192

HTML, 145

Huberman, A. M., 84, 85

Hudson, J. M., 247

IBM, 186

ID (individual differences): conclusion, 219–20; introduction, 206; looking
forward, 218–20; practical relevance, 208–10; research and design
challenges, 210, 218–19; scenario, 206–8; strategies; between groups,
212, 213f; influences on selection and use, 212, 212f, 215–17, 216f, 217f;
within users, 215f; summary, 217, 217f; task management, 211

i-ems, 185

image collections. See photographs

IM (instant messaging), 185

impression management, 238

incapacity, trained, 197f

index, federated, 72

indexing, full text, 34

the individual: impression management, 238; the personal in PIM, 274–75

information, generally: access patterns, 30; digital lifecycle of, 62; integration
of, 139; internal and external representations of, 47–49; old, results of
maintaining, 53; predicting future value, 30, 31–32, 57–59, 62–66, 71,
100. See also physical information

information, personal: capturing, 29, 92, 94–101, 95f, 98f, 157–58, 188,
192; defined, 9–10, 156; disclosure of, 249–54, 259–60; the personal in,
274–75; personal space of, 10–12; sharing, 16, 237–44, 247, 273. See
also personal information, long-term storage and maintenance of digital;
PIM (personal information management)

information behavior, defined, 78

information form: challenges with proliferation in types of, 44; defined,
7; fragmentation with, 31–32, 34, 38, 46; introduction, 7–9; PICs
relationship to, 12; transformation, 42, 44, 56, 117, 201

information item, 7–9, 12, 53

Information Lens, 181, 184

Information Manifold, 115

information seeking. See seeking

information target, 27–28

Kuhlthau, C., 28, 79
Kuny, T., 75
Kwasnik, B., 40

Landauer, T. K., 243
Lansdale, M., 13, 29, 31, 45, 157
Lawrence, S., 153–66
learnability, 198
legacy content. See personal information, a digital lifetime store
legal issues of long-term storage, 105–6, 236–48
libraries, 55, 112, 116–18
life experiences, recording, 94–101, 95f, 98f. See also personal information, a
    digital lifetime store
LifeLog program, 90
Lifestreams, 151
Lincoln, Y. S., 78, 80, 86
linking, 129, 135, 143–44
Lofland, J., 84
Lofland, L. H., 84
Lotus Notes, 239–40, 242, 247
Lutters, W. G., 236–48

machine-learning techniques, 187
Mackay, W. E., 172, 212, 241
MailCat, 184
maintaining, 15, 40, 271
Malin, B., 256
Malone, T. W., 27, 43–45, 53, 155, 212
Mann, S., 91
mapping builder (MB), 120
mapping needs to information, 14–17, 14f
mappings in data integration, 113, 115
Marchetti, P. G., 25
Marchionini, G., 25
Markus, M. L., 242
Marquard, J. L., 223
Marshall, C. C., 57–75
Marx, M., 181
Mathewson, N., 255
McKechnie, E. F., 81
measuring, overview, 16

Mellon, C., 80

Memex, 91, 100, 102

memex, defined, 3

memoing, 85

Memories for Life Grand Challenge, 90

memory: alleviating/rehabilitating loss of, 91–92, 94–99; autobiographical, 94–99; fallibility of, 153–54; individual differences in waiters, 211; and long-term access to personal archives, 64–65; organizing and, 45–46

menus, dynamic, 32

meta-, common vs. contemporary usage, 17

metadata: multimedia collections, 117–18; unification by, 131, 140–44

meta-level activities, 13, 15, 17, 270

Metral, M., 181, 187

Meyers, B., 90–107, 134

Microsoft, 135, 172, 188, 242

Microsoft Desktop Search, 34

Microsoft Outlook, 50, 68–70, 94, 106, 155, 209

Miles, M. B., 84, 85

Modjeska, D., 216

Moen, A., 221–33

Monroe, Alex: about, 4; finding/re-finding strategy, 7, 22–23, 26, 108; keeping strategy, 7, 36, 41; organizing strategy, 4, 206–7; search strategy, 154; storage and recovery strategies, 58

Monroe, Brooke: about, 5; finding/re-finding strategy, 7, 57–58; keeping strategy, 36–37, 57–58; organizational strategies, 5; organization strategies, 206–7; sharing, 237–38

Monroe, Connie: about, 5; health information management, 222–23, 225; keeping strategy, 36, 207; naturalistic inquiry approach to, 77–78; organizing strategy, 5, 7, 47, 207; search strategy, 154

MSN Explorer, 194

multimedia collections: creation and maintenance of data and metadata, 117–18; naturalistic inquiry methodology, 78

MyLifeBits, 92–94, 96, 100, 102–3, 105–6, 109

Naaman, M., 195

naming, standard model for, 148–49

Nardi, B., 28, 178, 203, 215

naturalistic inquiry: characteristics, 80–81; data collection techniques, 77–78, 81–85, 82f, 83f; introduction, 76–77; looking forward, 87–88; methodology, 77–78, 82–83; qualitative data analysis, 84–87; research overview, 78–80; scenario illustrating, 77–78; trustworthiness of, 86–87, 87f

Naumer, C. M., 76–88
Nelson, T. H., 91
Nielsen, J., 198
Nilan, M., 78

object linking and embedding (OLE), 135–36
observation in naturalistic inquiry, 77, 82–83, 82f, 83f
observer effect, 87f
O'Day, V. L., 25, 241, 243
Oliver, N., 90–107
ontology, defined, 110
ontology builder, personal (POB), 119
OntoPIM, 118–19, 119f, 121, 123
order, the virtue of, 3
organizing: challenges in, 37–38, 54–56; defined, 36, 39; fragmentation and,
    271; importance of, 38–39, 47; keeping relation to, 37, 45–46, 90; key
    points about, 37–38; looking forward, 52–56; overview, 15; research
    overview, 45–47; sense-making and search for structure, 47–52, 55;
    trigger for, 39; virtue of order, 3
organizing strategies: examples, 7, 35–36, 47, 206–7, 213; neet vs. messy, 45;
    research findings, 46–47; reusing structures, 52–53
organizing structures: in libraries, 55; reflecting mental representations, 53–54;
    reusing, 52–53; sense-making and search for, 47–52, 55; UL (universal
    labeler) prototype, 50–52, 51f; unified vs. single systems, 151
orienteering, 26, 30–31, 33, 129, 143, 149
Orlikowski, W. J., 239, 240, 242
ownership of personal information, 9

P3P (Platform for Privacy Preferences) policies, 257
packrat behavior, 41
Paepcke, A., 71
Palen, L., 240, 241, 242
paper: calendars, 222–23, 228–30, 236, 245–56; storing, 93; using for PHR,
    228–29, 229f, 231
passwords, 68–69, 250
Patton, M. Q., 77, 80
Pérez-Quiñones, M., 22–34
performance measure of evaluation, 200

PIM (personal information management): activities essential to, 13–17, 14f, 270; background, 3–4; challenges, 125–26; conclusion, 269–75, 274; defined, 3, 13; email for, 157–58; goal of, 166; HCI in relation to, 17–18; HII in relation to, 18; long-term, importance of, 59–60; looking forward, 273–74; the personal in, 274–75; PKM in relation to, 18; research recommendations, 20n1; solutions, 272; study methodologies, 274. See also information, personal

PIM personality, 215, 217

PIM tools, evaluating: challenges, 203; components of; baseline measures and controls, 196–97; collections, 195; measures, 197–201; participants, 193–94; tasks, 195–96; conclusion, 203, 274; frameworks for, 191–93, 195; introduction, 190; looking forward, 201–3; measures of, 197–201; scenario, 191; study methodologies, 274

Pirolli, P., 47

PKM (personal knowledge management), 18

PM (personal matcher), 121

POB (personal ontology builder), 119

Poggi, A., 108–26

Polydoros, P., 117

Potts, M., 32, 257

Presto, 146–47, 149, 151

previewing, 147–48

privacy: defined, 250, 255; end-user responsibilities, 250, 253–54, 257; false beliefs regarding, 256; in long-term storage of personal information, 59, 64, 68–69, 104–5; protecting, 16, 258–59, 273; public records and, 261–67; research on, 255–58; trust and security as interdependent with, 249–53, 252f; at work sharing and, 238–41, 247. See also control of information

Privacy Bird, 257

privacy management, organizational, 238–44, 251–54, 258–59

privacy policies, end-user authoring, 258–59

privacy solutions, 250, 260f

project planning, 48–52, 51f

Pruitt, J., 194

PSI (personal space of information), 10–11, 20n1

PT (personalization tool), 119

public information, defined, 263–64

public records and privacy, 261–67

quality-driven query processing, defined, 111

quality in data integration, 114

quality-of-life measures, 201
query, in data integration, 115
query processor (QP), 111, 121

Rank Xerox, 91
Ravasio, P., 128, 129, 143
RDF (resource description framework), 144, 148–51
reactive measurement, 88n4
recall, post-valued, 31
redundancy in email, 67
reference, defined, 110
reference reconciliation, 110–11
re-finding: defined, 13, 24–25; in dynamic environments, 32–33; email,
    178–79; factors affecting, 29–30; finding vs., 24–25, 29; focus of, 25; in
    Internet searches, 30–32; keeping relation to, 24–25, 30–32, 38; looking
    forward, 33–34; organizing relation to, 30–32; physical location in,
    27–28; task, importance to, 28; time, importance to, 29. See also finding;
    search
Reiter, E., 90
ReMail, 187
Rembrance Agent, 91
Robertson, G., 90–107
Rodden, K., 192
Rolodex, 156
Ross, B., 45
Ruhleder, 242
Russell, D. M., 47, 153–66
Ruthven, I., 32

Salazar, Edna, 5–6, 37
Sandstrom, A. R., 80
Sandstrom, P. E., 80
Sasse, M. A., 32, 46, 53, 76, 179, 214, 215
satisfaction measure of standard usability, 199
save everything strategy, 272
Schär, S. G., 128
schema, database, 109
schema cleaning, 111
schema matching, 114
Schmandt, C., 181
Schwandt, T. A., 80

TRUSTe, 257
trustworthiness in naturalistic inquiry, 86–87, 87f
TSIMMIS, 115
Tsinaraki, C., 117
Tygar, J. D., 249

UI (user interface), 183
UL (universal labeler), 50–52, 51f, 151
UMEA, 151
unification: approaches to, 132; calendars (paper) for, 222–23, 228–30, 236,
    245–56; categories of, 132f; conclusion, 150; email and, 147–48, 272–73;
    email for, 272–73; goal of, 130; looking forward, 150–52; by metadata,
    131, 140–44; motivation for, 127–30; name-based, 140–41; physical,
    132–33; by standard data types, 131, 136–39; by systems, 144–49;
    taxonomy of approaches to, 130–31; visual, window managers for, 131,
    133–36. See also fragmentation
unify everything strategy, 272
universal labeler (UL), 50–52, 51f, 151
University of Tokyo, 91
University of Washington, Information School's Web site, 48
URI (uniform resource identifiers), 149
URLs (uniform resource locators), 67–68
URN (unique resource name), 144, 148–49
usability, 198, 253, 255–58
usefulness measure of standard usability, 199

Venolia, G., 172, 173
video. See A/V capture systems, wearable
virtues, the thirteen, 3

Watson, C., 210
Web information, keeping, 41
Web Montage, 135–36
Web pages: allocating attention and, 185; days active, on average, 68; as email
    attachments, long-term access to, 67–68; embedding in, 135–36; social
    tagging services, 141–42
Web portals, 135–36
Web search: affective factors influence on, 216; desktop search as part of,
    159–61; re-finding and, 30–32
Web sites, tagging services, 141–42
Web users, individual differences in, 212

CPSIA information can be obtained at www.ICGtesting.com
Printed in the USA
LVOW06s0035050814

397472LV00001B/33/P